Love Hina

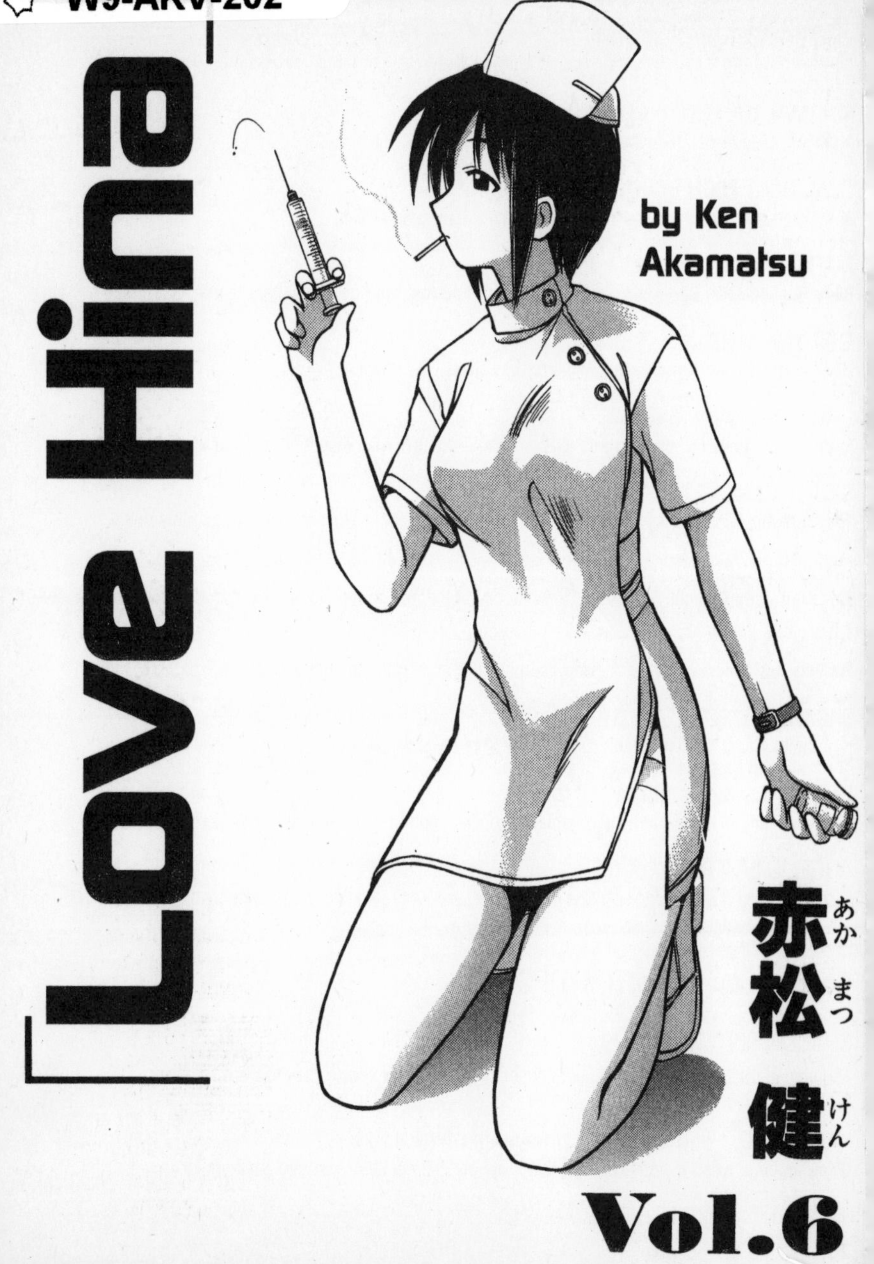

by Ken Akamatsu

赤松健（あかまつけん）

Vol.6

Love Hina

By
Ken Akamatsu

Volume 6

Los Angeles • Tokyo

Translator – Nan Rymer
English Adaptation – Adam Arnold
Retouch and Lettering – Jeremy Canceko
Graphic Designer – Anna Kernbaum

Editor – Luis Reyes
Production Managers – Mario Rodriguez and Jennifer Wagner
Art Director – Matthew Alford
Brand Manager – Kenneth Lee
VP Production – Ron Klamert
Publisher – Stuart Levy

Email: editor@TOKYOPOP.com
Come visit us online at www.TOKYOPOP.com

A  TOKYOPOP® Manga

TOKYOPOP® is an imprint of Mixx Entertainment, Inc.
5900 Wilshire Blvd. Ste 2000, Los Angeles, CA 90036

ISBN: 1-59182-017-0

First TOKYOPOP® printing: October 2002

10 9 8 7 6 5 4 3 2 1

Printed in the USA.

Love Hina

The Story Thus Far ...

Fifteen years ago, Keitaro Urashima made a promise to a girl that they would go to Tokyo University together. Now at the age of twenty, he's finding it more and more difficult to keep that promise, much less find that girl again.

He has already failed the entrance exam for Tokyo University three times, and has recently decided to stick it out, to go for it another time, to spend yet another crimson-R'ed year as a ronin.

He's inherited from his globetrotting grandmother the Hinata House, a quiet residential dorm where he can work as the landlord and prepare for his upcoming exams in peace... if it wasn't for that fact that Hinata House is actually a girls' dormitory with a clientele none too pleased that their new, live-in landlord is a man – or as close to a man as poor Keitaro can be. The lanky loser incessantly (and accidentally) crashes their sessions in the hot springs, walks in on them changing... and pokes his nose pretty much everywhere it can get broken, if not by the hot-headed Naru, then by one of the other Hinata inmates – Kitsune, a mid-twenties alcoholic with a diesel libido; Motoko, a swordswoman who struggles with feminine issues; Shinobu, a pre-teen princess with a colossal crush on Keitaro; and Su, a foreign girl with a big appetite. Also, Seta, a long time friend to Hinata and a past crush of Naru's, has recently left his ward, Sarah, to live at Hinata House while he galavants across the globe on archeological digs, bumping the Hinata harem to seven. And, on a trip around Japan to blow off some steam, Naru and Keitaro befriended the accident prone Mutsumi, who gave them as a gift Tama-chan, a unique turtle, and who returns in this volume.

Having spent some time at the beach where he and the crew helped Haruka, his aunt and Hinata's defaccto matriarch, run an oceanside cafe, performed in a children's play, attended a carnival, and searched for ship-wrecked treasures, Keitaro is buckling down to his studies once again, if he can only keep his thoughts (and hands) off Naru...

CONTENTS

LOVE♡HINA

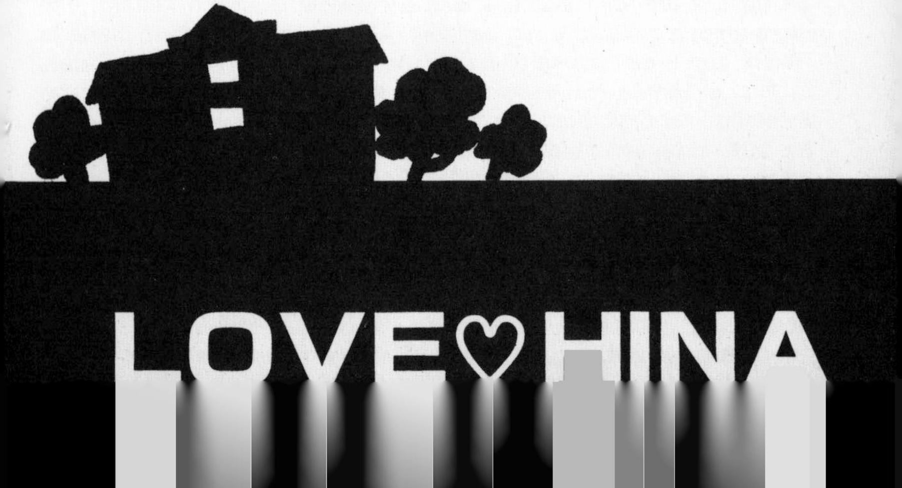

LOVE♡HINA

Love Hina

HINATA.43 Invite, Me Keitaro!

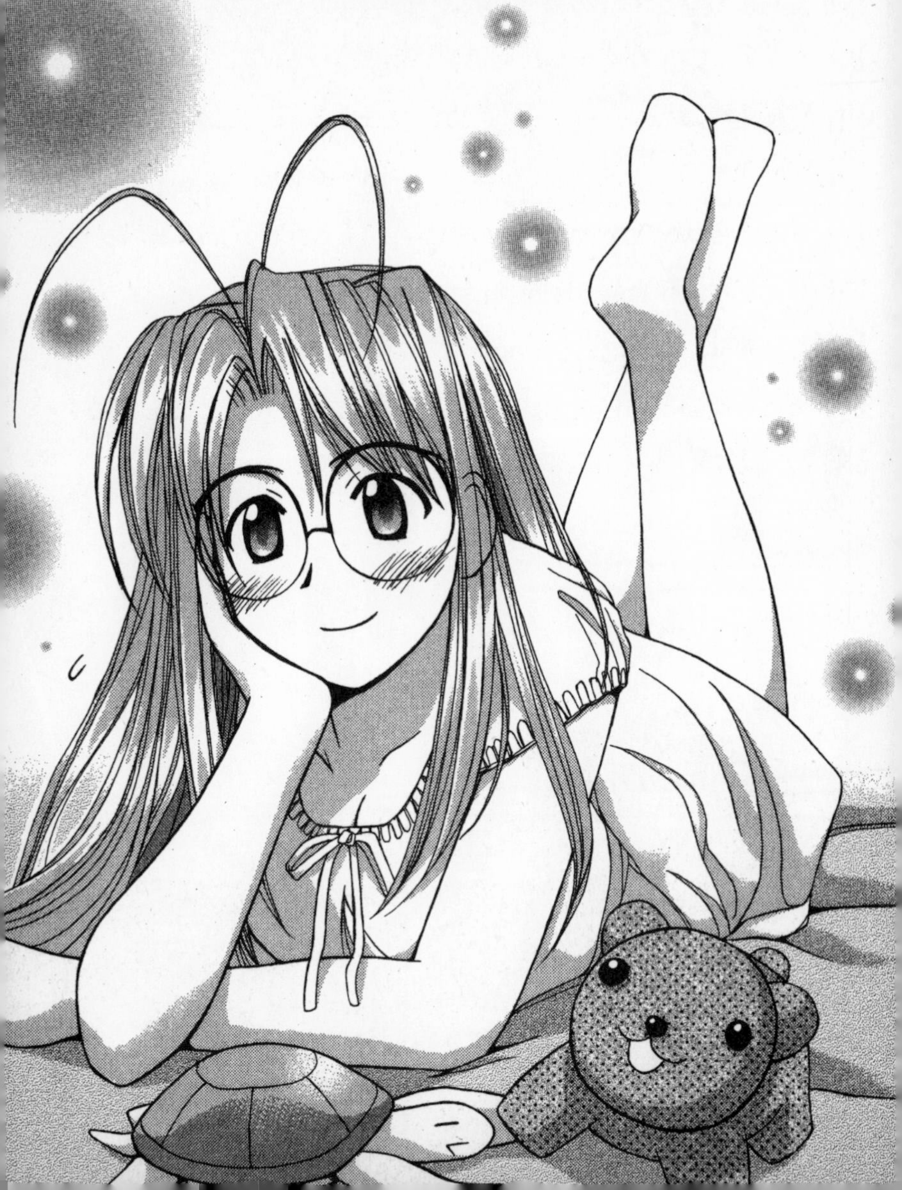

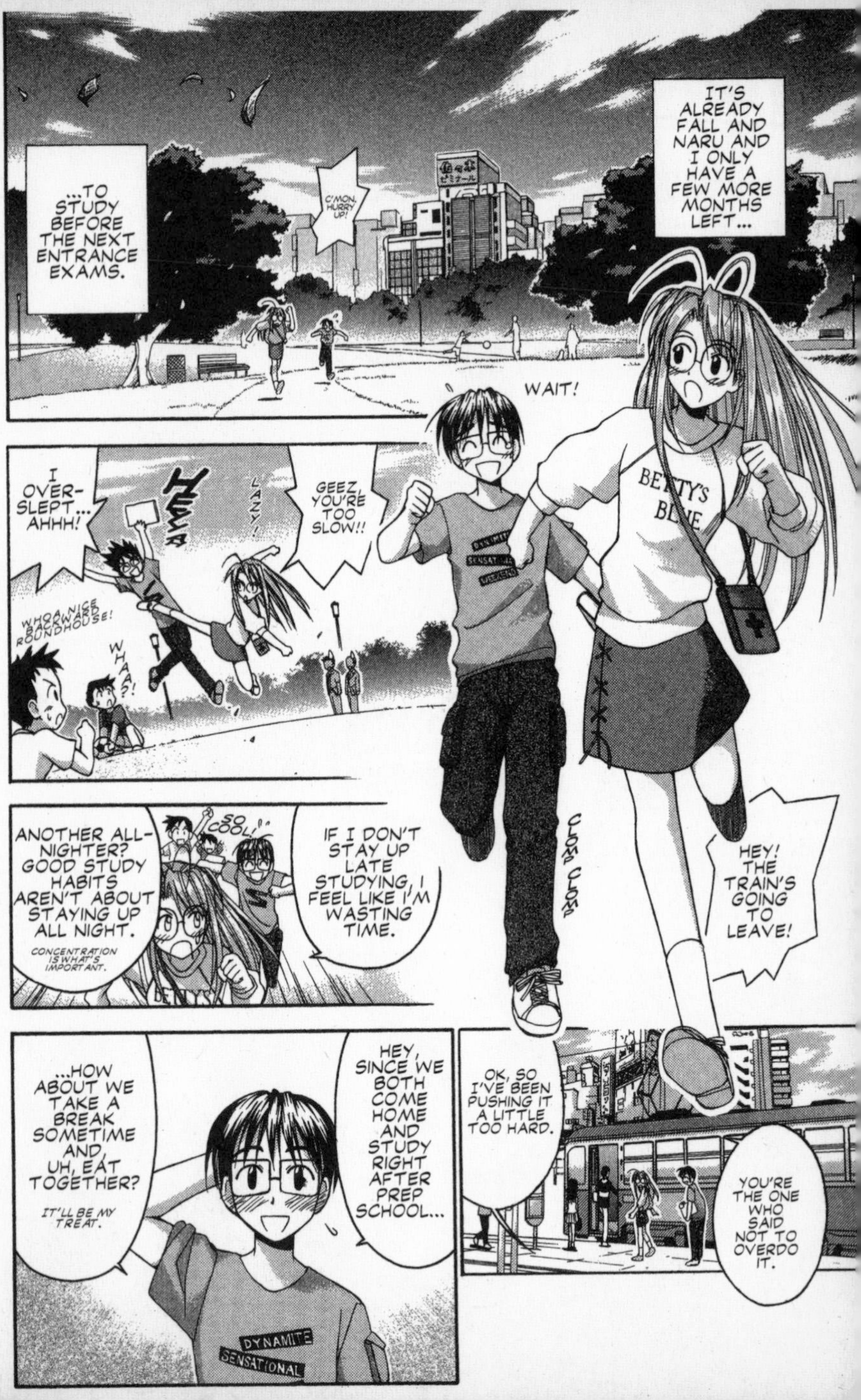
IT'S ALREADY FALL AND NARU AND I ONLY HAVE A FEW MORE MONTHS LEFT...
C'MON, HURRY UP!
...TO STUDY BEFORE THE NEXT ENTRANCE EXAMS.
WAIT!
GEEZ, YOU'RE TOO SLOW!!
LAZY!
I OVER-SLEPT... AHHH!
WHOA NICE BACKWARD ROUNDHOUSE!
WHAA?!
IF I DON'T STAY UP LATE STUDYING, I FEEL LIKE I'M WASTING TIME.
SO COOL!
ANOTHER ALL-NIGHTER? GOOD STUDY HABITS AREN'T ABOUT STAYING UP ALL NIGHT.
CONCENTRATION IS WHAT'S IMPORTANT.
CLOMP CLOMP
HEY! THE TRAIN'S GOING TO LEAVE!
YOU'RE THE ONE WHO SAID NOT TO OVERDO IT.
OK, SO I'VE BEEN PUSHING IT A LITTLE TOO HARD.
HEY, SINCE WE BOTH COME HOME AND STUDY RIGHT AFTER PREP SCHOOL...
...HOW ABOUT WE TAKE A BREAK SOMETIME AND, UH, EAT TOGETHER?
IT'LL BE MY TREAT.
DYNAMITE
SENSATIONAL

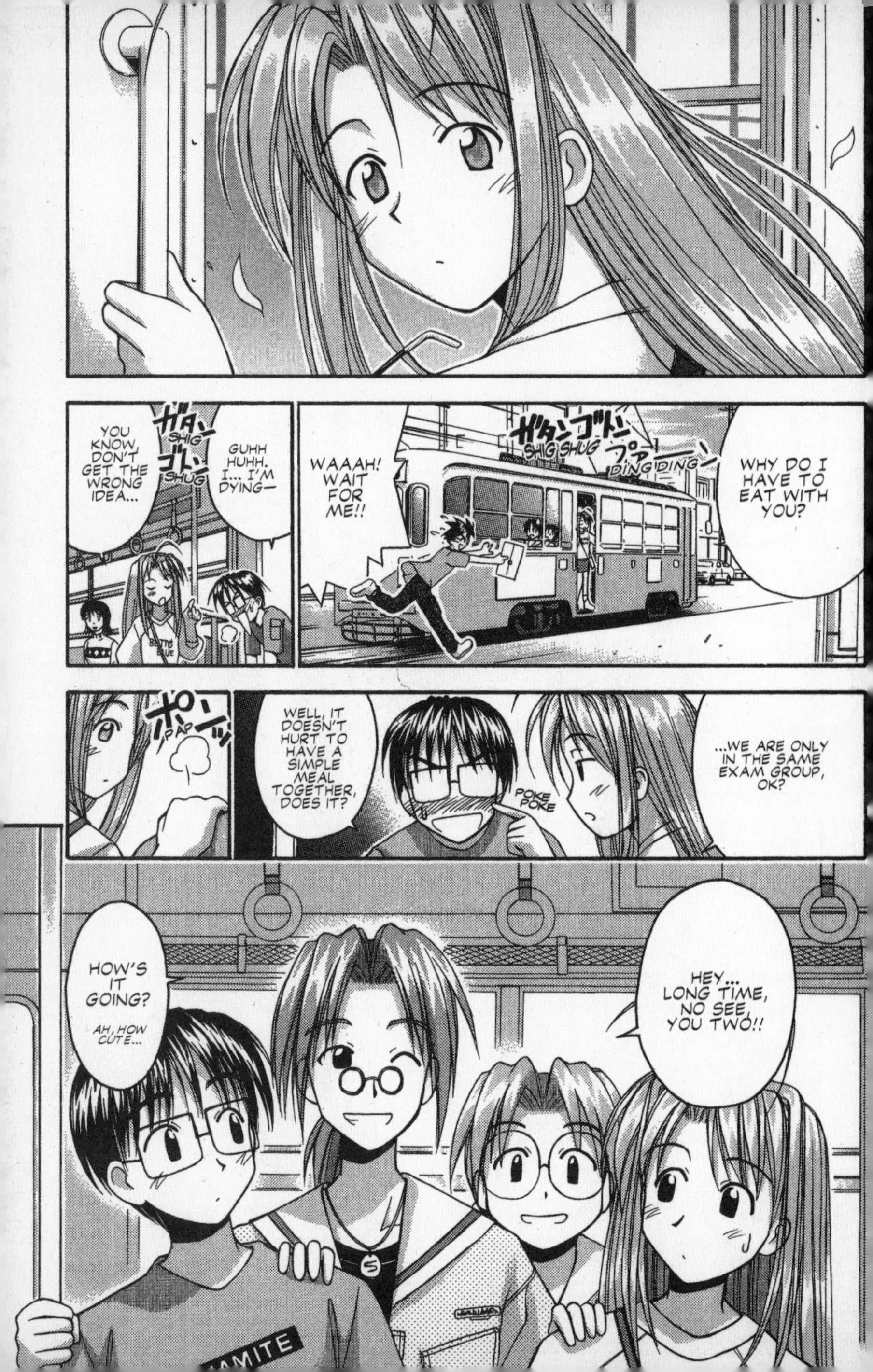
WHY DO I HAVE TO EAT WITH YOU?
SHIG SHUG
DING DING
WAAAH! WAIT FOR ME!!
GUHH HUHH. I... I'M DYING—
SHIG
SHUG
YOU KNOW, DON'T GET THE WRONG IDEA...
...WE ARE ONLY IN THE SAME EXAM GROUP, OK?
POKE POKE
WELL, IT DOESN'T HURT TO HAVE A SIMPLE MEAL TOGETHER, DOES IT?
PAP
HEY... LONG TIME, NO SEE, YOU TWO!!
HOW'S IT GOING?
AH, HOW CUTE...

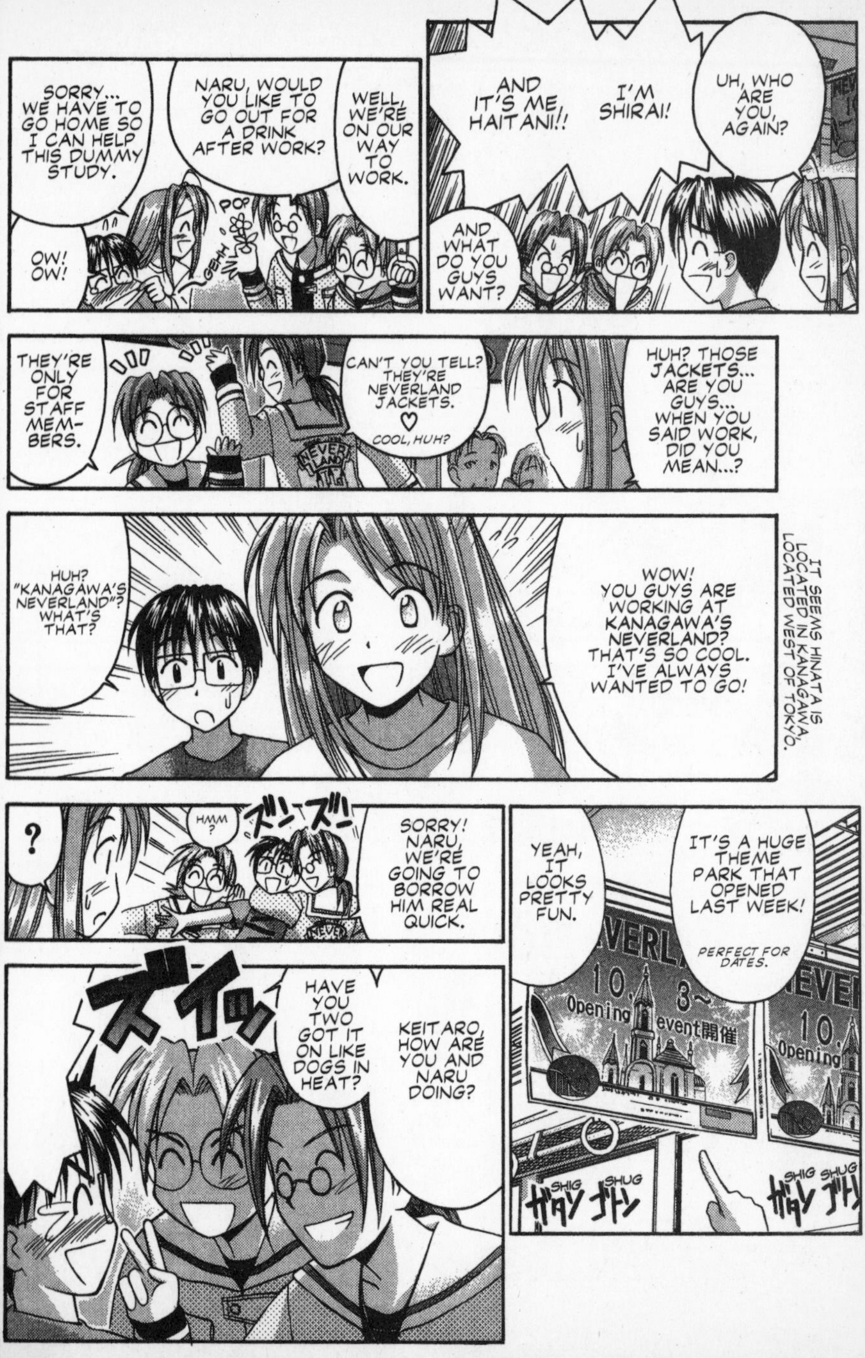
UH, WHO ARE YOU, AGAIN?
I'M SHIRAI!
AND IT'S ME, HAITANI!!
AND WHAT DO YOU GUYS WANT?
WELL, WE'RE ON OUR WAY TO WORK.
NARU, WOULD YOU LIKE TO GO OUT FOR A DRINK AFTER WORK?
POP
GEHH
SORRY... WE HAVE TO GO HOME SO I CAN HELP THIS DUMMY STUDY.
OW! OW!
HUH? THOSE JACKETS... ARE YOU GUYS... WHEN YOU SAID WORK, DID YOU MEAN...?
CAN'T YOU TELL? THEY'RE NEVERLAND JACKETS. ♡
COOL, HUH?
NEVERLAND
THEY'RE ONLY FOR STAFF MEM-BERS.
WOW! YOU GUYS ARE WORKING AT KANAGAWA'S NEVERLAND? THAT'S SO COOL. I'VE ALWAYS WANTED TO GO!
HUH? "KANAGAWA'S NEVERLAND"? WHAT'S THAT?
IT'S A HUGE THEME PARK THAT OPENED LAST WEEK!
PERFECT FOR DATES.
YEAH, IT LOOKS PRETTY FUN.
10. 3~
Opening event開催
NEVER
10.
Opening
ガタン SHIG ゴトン SHUG
ガタン SHIG ゴトン SHUG
SORRY! NARU, WE'RE GOING TO BORROW HIM REAL QUICK.
ズーズー
HMM?
?
NEVER
KEITARO, HOW ARE YOU AND NARU DOING?
HAVE YOU TWO GOT IT ON LIKE DOGS IN HEAT?
ズイッ

IT SEEMS HINATA IS LOCATED IN KANAGAWA, LOCATED WEST OF TOKYO.

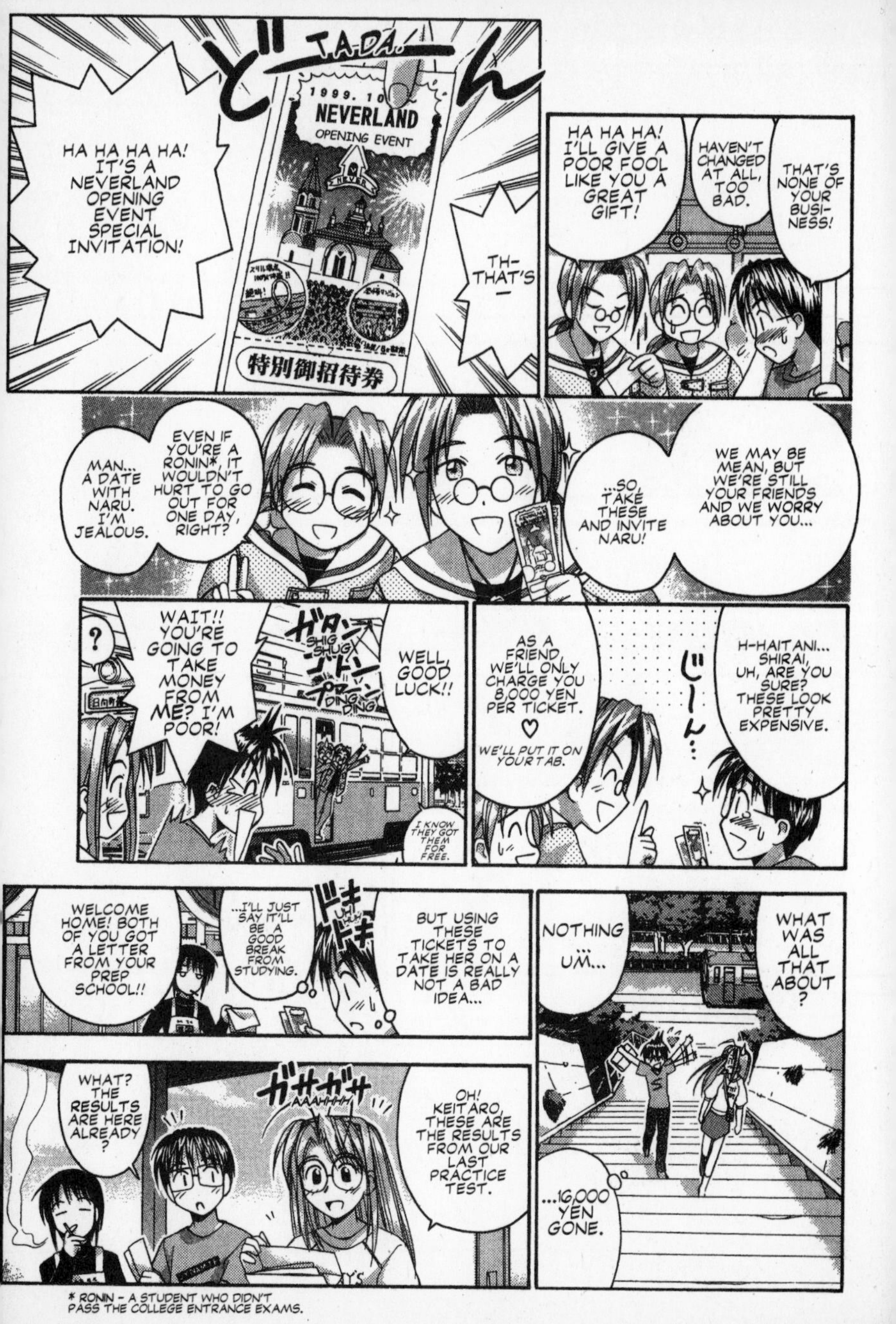
THAT'S NONE OF YOUR BUSINESS!
HAVEN'T CHANGED AT ALL, TOO BAD.
HA HA HA! I'LL GIVE A POOR FOOL LIKE YOU A GREAT GIFT!
どーん
TA-DA!
1999. 10
NEVERLAND
OPENING EVENT
特別御招待券
TH-THAT'S—
HA HA HA HA! IT'S A NEVERLAND OPENING EVENT SPECIAL INVITATION!
WE MAY BE MEAN, BUT WE'RE STILL YOUR FRIENDS AND WE WORRY ABOUT YOU...
...SO, TAKE THESE AND INVITE NARU!
EVEN IF YOU'RE A RONIN*, IT WOULDN'T HURT TO GO OUT FOR ONE DAY, RIGHT?
MAN... A DATE WITH NARU. I'M JEALOUS.
H-HAITANI... SHIRAI, UH, ARE YOU SURE? THESE LOOK PRETTY EXPENSIVE.
じーん...
AS A FRIEND, WE'LL ONLY CHARGE YOU 8,000 YEN PER TICKET. ♡
WE'LL PUT IT ON YOUR TAB.
WELL, GOOD LUCK!!
ガタンゴトン
SHIG SHUG
プァーン
DING DING
WAIT!! YOU'RE GOING TO TAKE MONEY FROM ME? I'M POOR!
?
I KNOW THEY GOT THEM FOR FREE.
WHAT WAS ALL THAT ABOUT?
NOTHING... UM...
...16,000 YEN GONE.
BUT USING THESE TICKETS TO TAKE HER ON A DATE IS REALLY NOT A BAD IDEA...
ドキドキ
UH UH
...I'LL JUST SAY IT'LL BE A GOOD BREAK FROM STUDYING.
WELCOME HOME! BOTH OF YOU GOT A LETTER FROM YOUR PREP SCHOOL!!
OH! KEITARO, THESE ARE THE RESULTS FROM OUR LAST PRACTICE TEST.
ガサガサ
WHAT? THE RESULTS ARE HERE ALREADY?

* RONIN – A STUDENT WHO DIDN'T PASS THE COLLEGE ENTRANCE EXAMS.

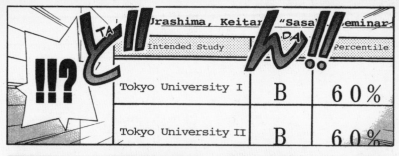

Urashima, Keitaro "Sasa" Seminar		
Intended Study		Percentile
Tokyo University I	B	60%
Tokyo University II	B	60%

IT'S BETTER THAN GOOD! I'VE GOT A 60% CHANCE OF GETTING INTO TOKYO UNIVERSITY AND FINALLY BEING A STUDENT! AT THIS RATE, GETTING IN WON'T BE JUST AN IMPOSSIBLE DREAM!!

IS THAT SUPPOSED TO BE GOOD?

ALRIGHT! I GOT A B!

WELL, ISN'T THAT NICE.

NOOO!! NOT BLOOD TYPE B! THE GRADE'S A B!!

WOW! KEITARO, I DIDN'T KNOW YOUR BLOOD TYPE WAS B.

I NEVER WOULD HAVE GUESSED.

HEY! HEY! WILL YOU JUST ACCEPT IT?!

COULD IT BE A COMPUTER GLITCH? THE Y2K BUG? A HALLUCINATION?

MINE IS TYPE AB!

I'M TYPE A.

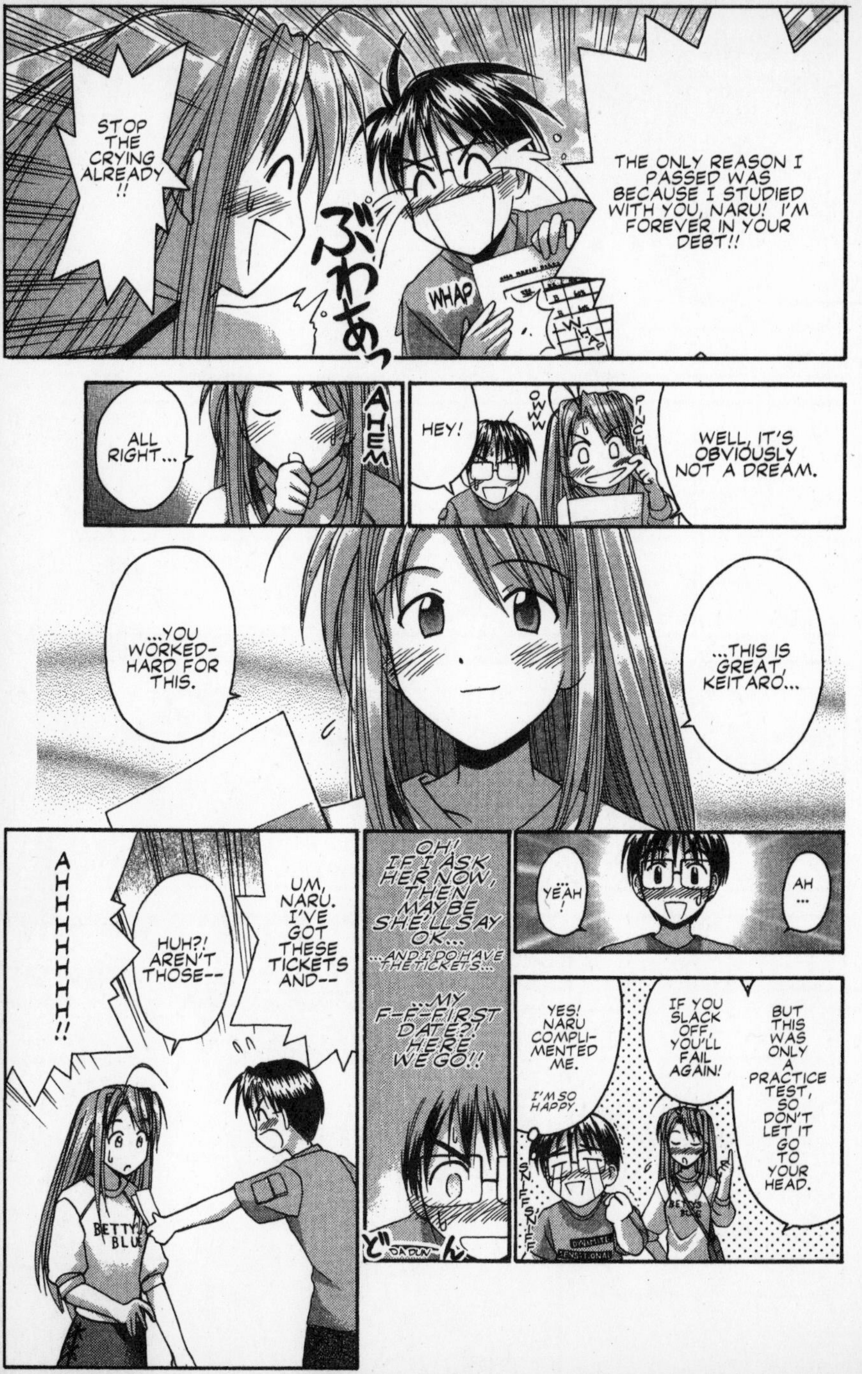
THE ONLY REASON I PASSED WAS BECAUSE I STUDIED WITH YOU, NARU! I'M FOREVER IN YOUR DEBT!!
ぶわあっ
WHAP
STOP THE CRYING ALREADY!!
WELL, IT'S OBVIOUSLY NOT A DREAM.
PINCH
OWWW
HEY!
AHEM
ALL RIGHT...
...THIS IS GREAT, KEITARO...
...YOU WORKED-HARD FOR THIS.
AH...
...YEAH!
BUT THIS WAS ONLY A PRACTICE TEST, SO DON'T LET IT GO TO YOUR HEAD.
IF YOU SLACK OFF, YOU'LL FAIL AGAIN!
YES! NARU COMPLI-MENTED ME.
I'M SO HAPPY.
SNIFF SNIFF
OH! IF I ASK HER NOW, THEN MAYBE SHE'LL SAY OK...
...AND I DO HAVE THE TICKETS...
...MY F-F-FIRST DATE?! HERE WE GO!!
どーん
DA DUN
UM, NARU. I'VE GOT THESE TICKETS AND--
HUH?! AREN'T THOSE--
AHHHHHHH!!

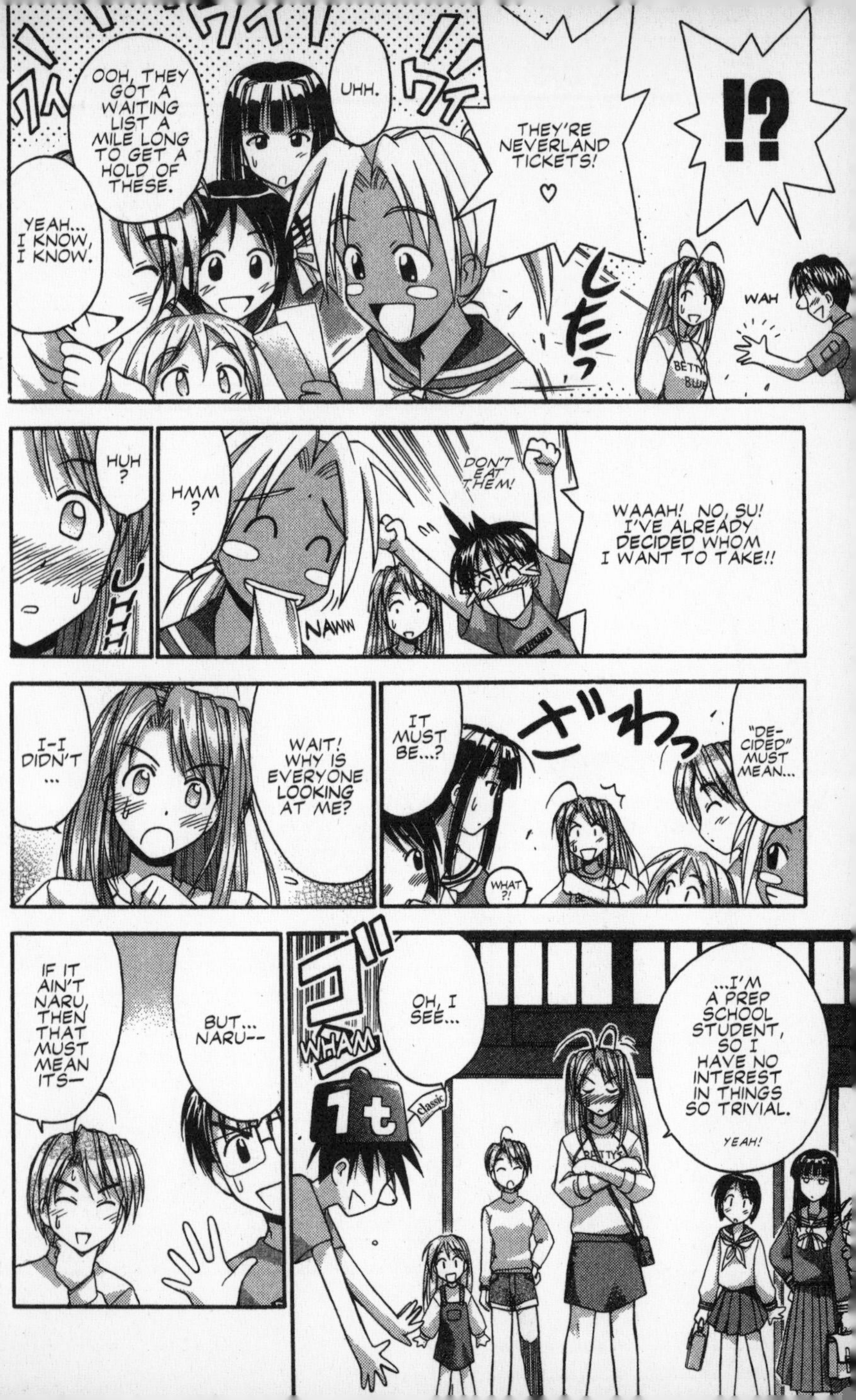
!?
THEY'RE NEVERLAND TICKETS! ♡
WAH
UHH.
OOH, THEY GOT A WAITING LIST A MILE LONG TO GET A HOLD OF THESE.
YEAH... I KNOW, I KNOW.
WAAAH! NO, SU! I'VE ALREADY DECIDED WHOM I WANT TO TAKE!!
DON'T EAT THEM!
HMM ?
NAWW
HUH ?
"DE-CIDED" MUST MEAN...
IT MUST BE...?
WHAT ?!
WAIT! WHY IS EVERYONE LOOKING AT ME?
I-I DIDN'T ...
...I'M A PREP SCHOOL STUDENT, SO I HAVE NO INTEREST IN THINGS SO TRIVIAL.
YEAH!
OH, I SEE...
WHAM
1t
classic
BUT... NARU--
IF IT AIN'T NARU, THEN THAT MUST MEAN ITS—

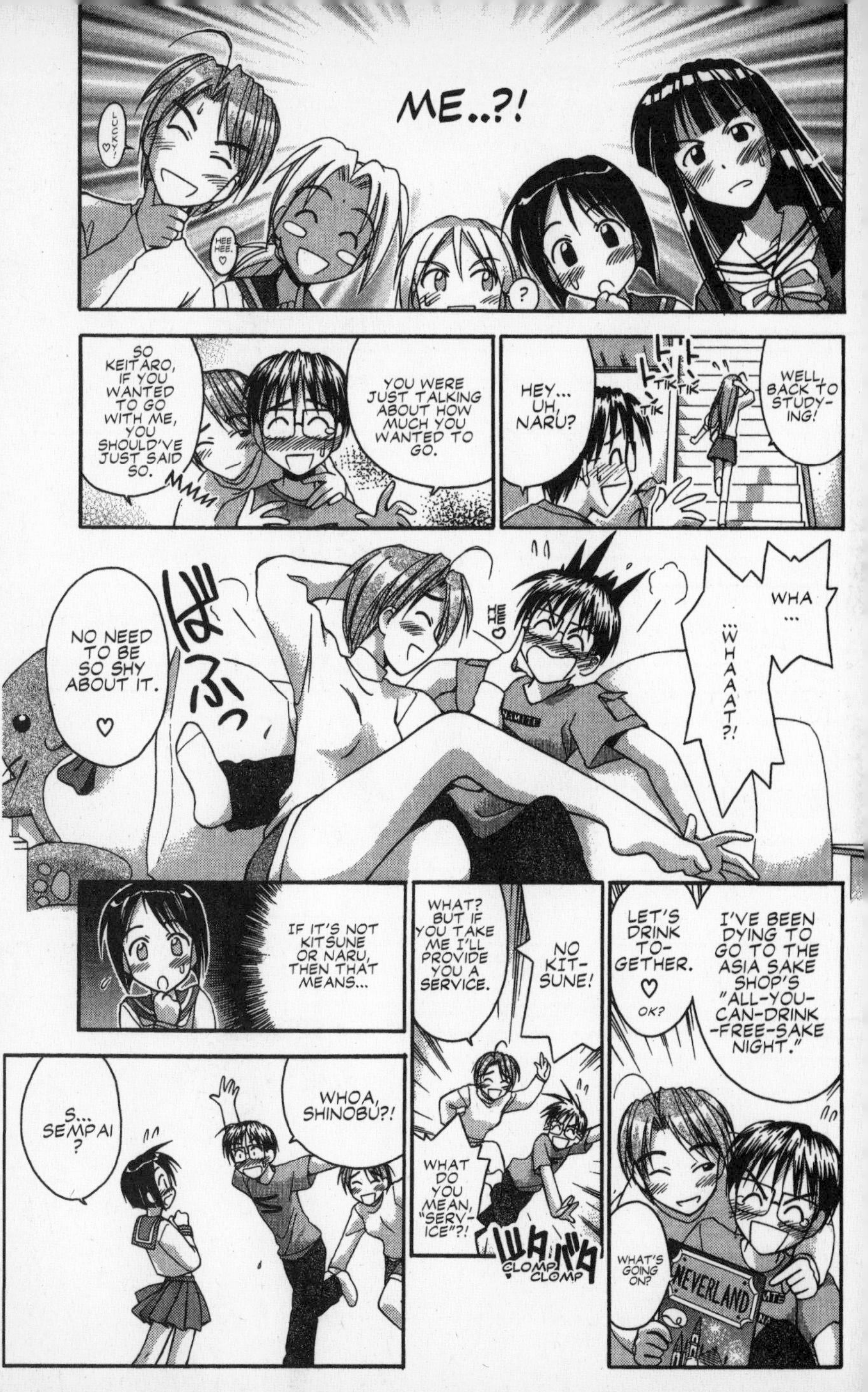
ME..?!
LUCKY! ♥
HEE HEE. ♥
?
WELL, BACK TO STUDYING!
TIK TIK TIK
HEY... UH, NARU?
YOU WERE JUST TALKING ABOUT HOW MUCH YOU WANTED TO GO.
SO KEITARO, IF YOU WANTED TO GO WITH ME, YOU SHOULD'VE JUST SAID SO.
MMM
WHA ...
...WHAAAAT?!
HEHE ♥
ぼふっ
NO NEED TO BE SO SHY ABOUT IT. ♥
I'VE BEEN DYING TO GO TO THE ASIA SAKE SHOP'S "ALL-YOU-CAN-DRINK-FREE-SAKE NIGHT."
LET'S DRINK TOGETHER. ♥ OK?
WHAT'S GOING ON?
NEVERLAND
NO KITSUNE!
WHAT? BUT IF YOU TAKE ME I'LL PROVIDE YOU A SERVICE.
WHAT DO YOU MEAN, "SERVICE"?!
ドタバタ
CLOMP CLOMP
IF IT'S NOT KITSUNE OR NARU, THEN THAT MEANS...
WHOA, SHINOBU?!
S... SEMPAI?

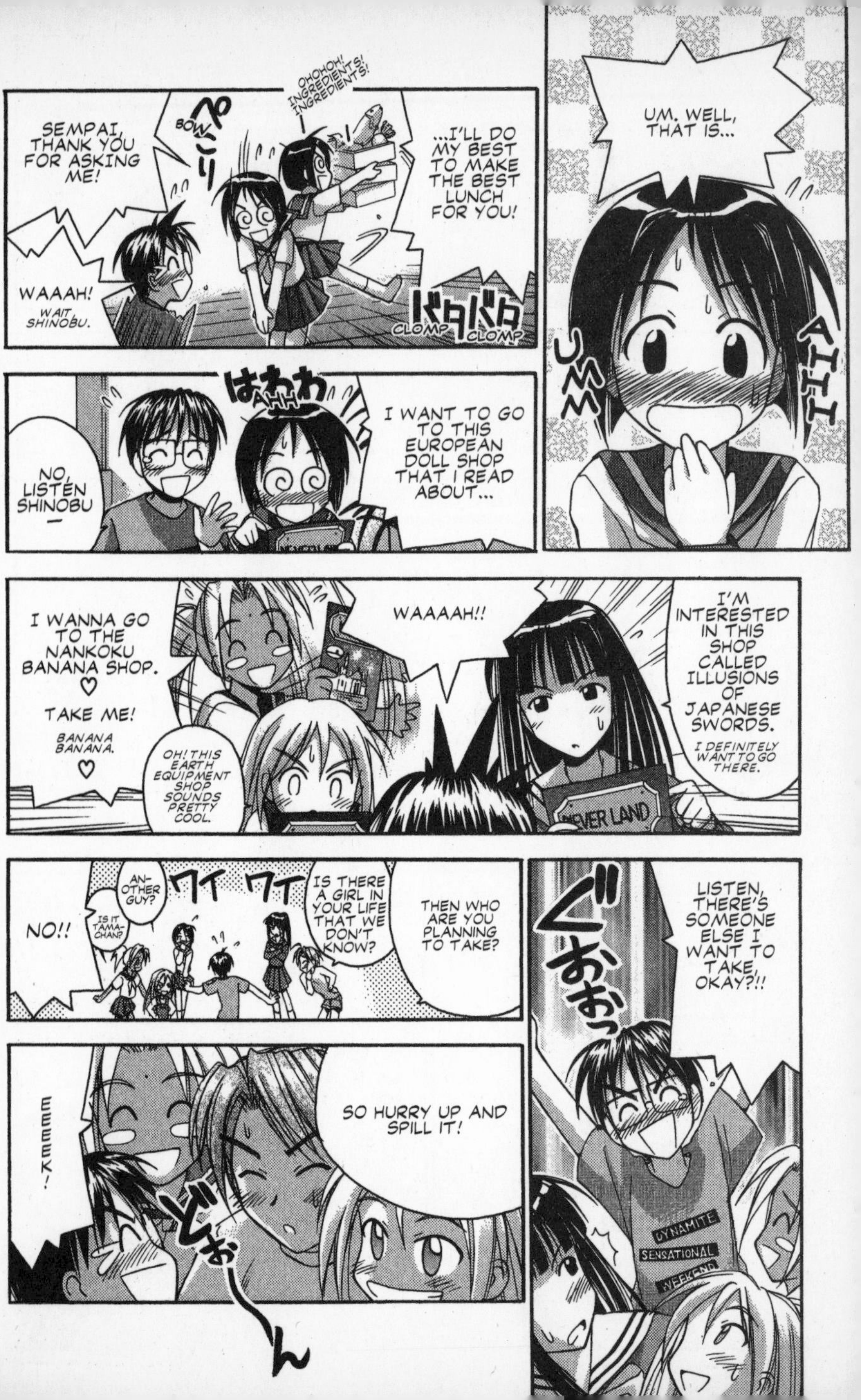
UM. WELL, THAT IS...
AHH
UMM
...I'LL DO MY BEST TO MAKE THE BEST LUNCH FOR YOU!
OHOHOH! INGREDIENTS! INGREDIENTS!
ぺこり
BOW
SEMPAI, THANK YOU FOR ASKING ME!
WAAAH!
WAIT, SHINOBU.
バタバタ
CLOMP CLOMP
I WANT TO GO TO THIS EUROPEAN DOLL SHOP THAT I READ ABOUT...
はわわ
AHH
NO, LISTEN SHINOBU—
I'M INTERESTED IN THIS SHOP CALLED ILLUSIONS OF JAPANESE SWORDS.
I DEFINITELY WANT TO GO THERE.
WAAAAH!!
NEVER LAND
I WANNA GO TO THE NANKOKU BANANA SHOP. ♡
TAKE ME!
BANANA BANANA. ♡
OH! THIS EARTH EQUIPMENT SHOP SOUNDS PRETTY COOL.
LISTEN, THERE'S SOMEONE ELSE I WANT TO TAKE, OKAY?!!
ぐおおっ
DYNAMITE SENSATIONAL WEEKEND
THEN WHO ARE YOU PLANNING TO TAKE?
IS THERE A GIRL IN YOUR LIFE THAT WE DON'T KNOW?
ワイ ワイ
AN-OTHER GUY?
IS IT TAMA-CHAN?
NO!!
SO HURRY UP AND SPILL IT!
どぉ〜ん
EEEEK!

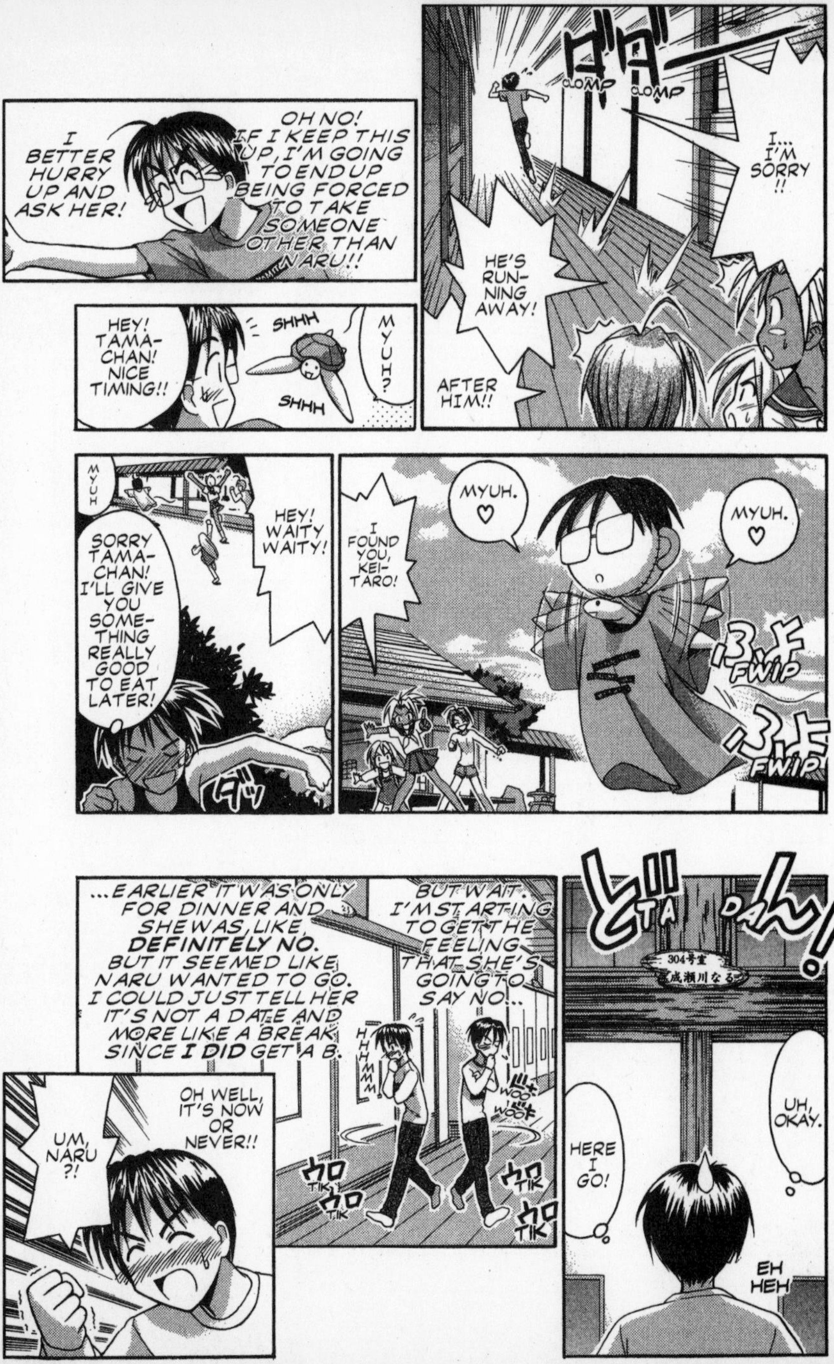
ダダー
CLOMP CLOMP
I... I'M SORRY!!
HE'S RUN-NING AWAY!
AFTER HIM!!
OH NO! IF I KEEP THIS UP, I'M GOING TO END UP BEING FORCED TO TAKE SOMEONE OTHER THAN NARU!!
I BETTER HURRY UP AND ASK HER!
MYUH?
SHHH
SHHH
HEY! TAMA-CHAN! NICE TIMING!!
MYUH. ♡
MYUH. ♡
ふよ FWIP
ふよ FWIP
I FOUND YOU, KEI-TARO!
HEY! WAITY WAITY!
MYUH
SORRY TAMA-CHAN! I'LL GIVE YOU SOME-THING REALLY GOOD TO EAT LATER!
TA DAH!
304号室
成瀬川なる
UH, OKAY.
HERE I GO!
EH HEH
BUT WAIT. I'M START-ING TO GET THE FEELING THAT SHE'S GOING TO SAY NO...
...EARLIER IT WAS ONLY FOR DINNER AND SHE WAS, LIKE, **DEFINITELY NO.** BUT IT SEEMED LIKE NARU WANTED TO GO. I COULD JUST TELL HER IT'S NOT A DATE AND MORE LIKE A BREAK SINCE **I DID** GET A B.
HHHMMM
WOOF WOOF
ウロ TIK
ウロ TIK
ウロ TIK
ウロ TIK
OH WELL, IT'S NOW OR NEVER!!
UM, NARU?!

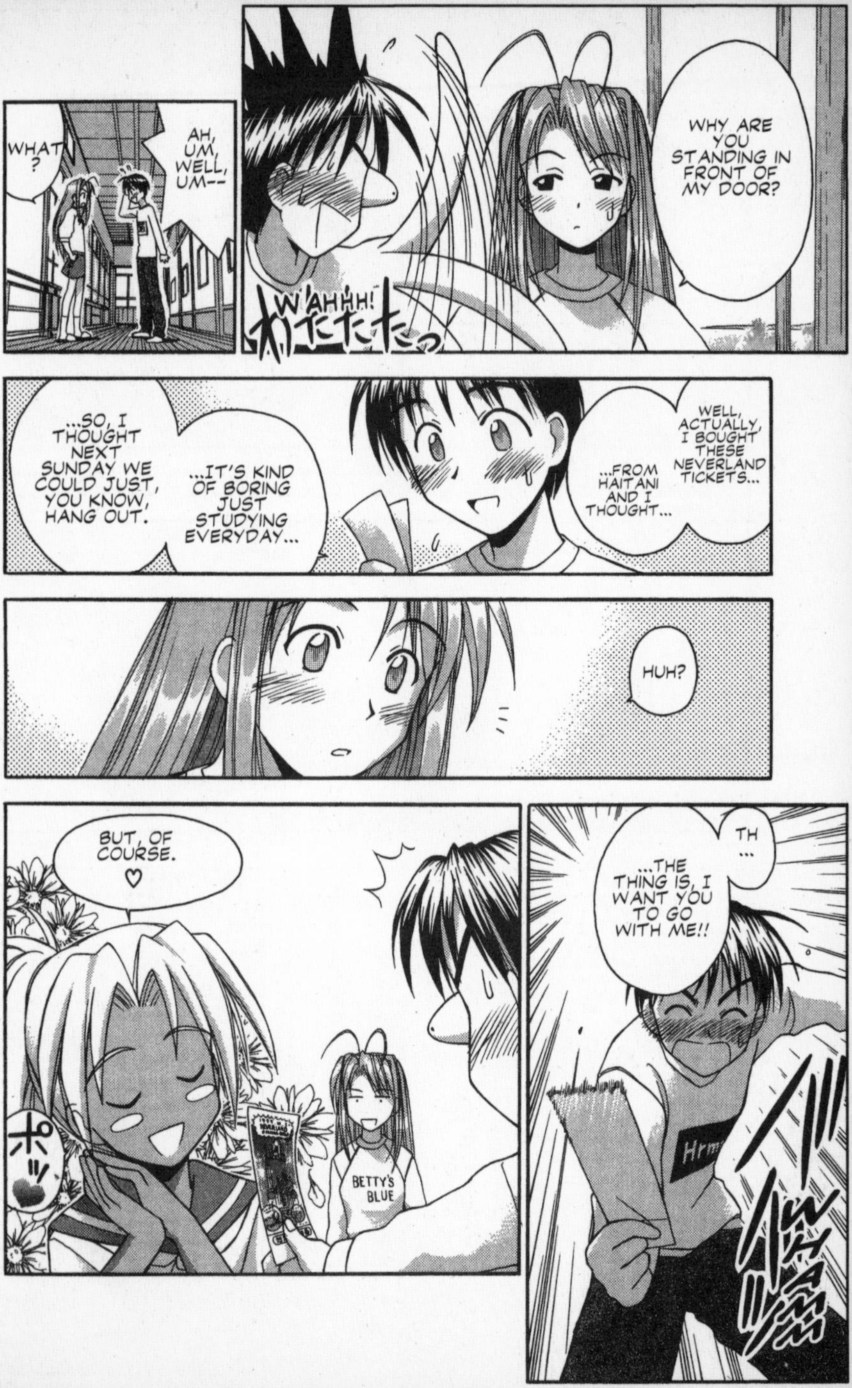
WHY ARE YOU STANDING IN FRONT OF MY DOOR?
W'AHHH!
AH, UM, WELL, UM--
WHAT?
WELL, ACTUALLY, I BOUGHT THESE NEVERLAND TICKETS...
...FROM HAITANI AND I THOUGHT...
...IT'S KIND OF BORING JUST STUDYING EVERYDAY...
...SO, I THOUGHT NEXT SUNDAY WE COULD JUST, YOU KNOW, HANG OUT.
HUH?
TH ...
...THE THING IS, I WANT YOU TO GO WITH ME!!
BUT, OF COURSE. ♡
BETTY'S BLUE

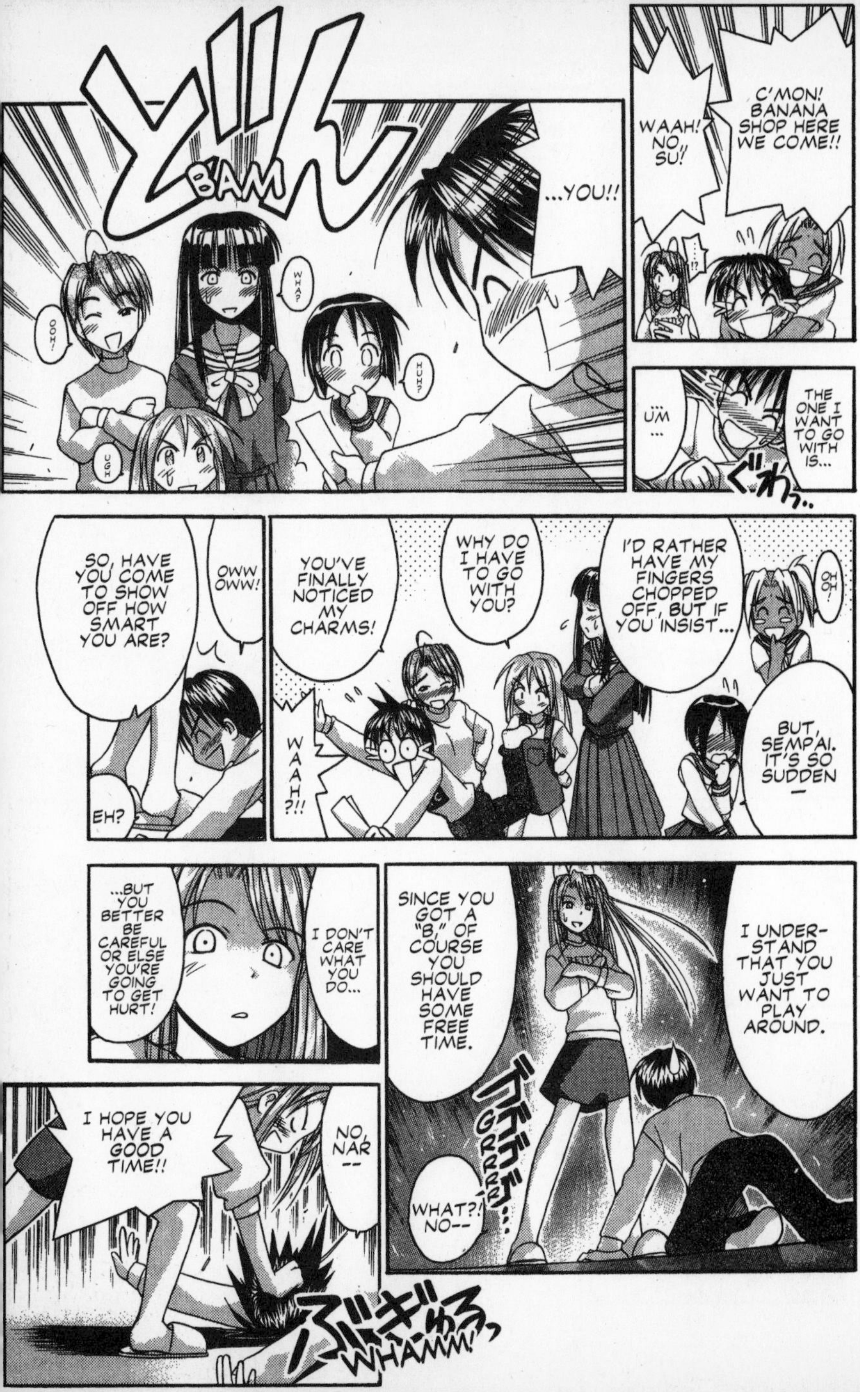
C'MON! BANANA SHOP HERE WE COME!!
WAAH! NO, SU!
!?
THE ONE I WANT TO GO WITH IS...
...UM...
...YOU!!
BAM
WHA?
HUH?
OOH!
UGH
OH OH!
I'D RATHER HAVE MY FINGERS CHOPPED OFF, BUT IF YOU INSIST...
BUT, SEMP'AI. IT'S SO SUDDEN—
WHY DO I HAVE TO GO WITH YOU?
YOU'VE FINALLY NOTICED MY CHARMS!
WAAAH?!!
OWW OWW!
SO, HAVE YOU COME TO SHOW OFF HOW SMART YOU ARE?
EH?
I UNDER-STAND THAT YOU JUST WANT TO PLAY AROUND.
SINCE YOU GOT A "B," OF COURSE YOU SHOULD HAVE SOME FREE TIME.
GRRR...
WHAT?! NO--
I DON'T CARE WHAT YOU DO...
...BUT YOU BETTER BE CAREFUL OR ELSE YOU'RE GOING TO GET HURT!
NO, NAR--
I HOPE YOU HAVE A GOOD TIME!!
WHAMM!

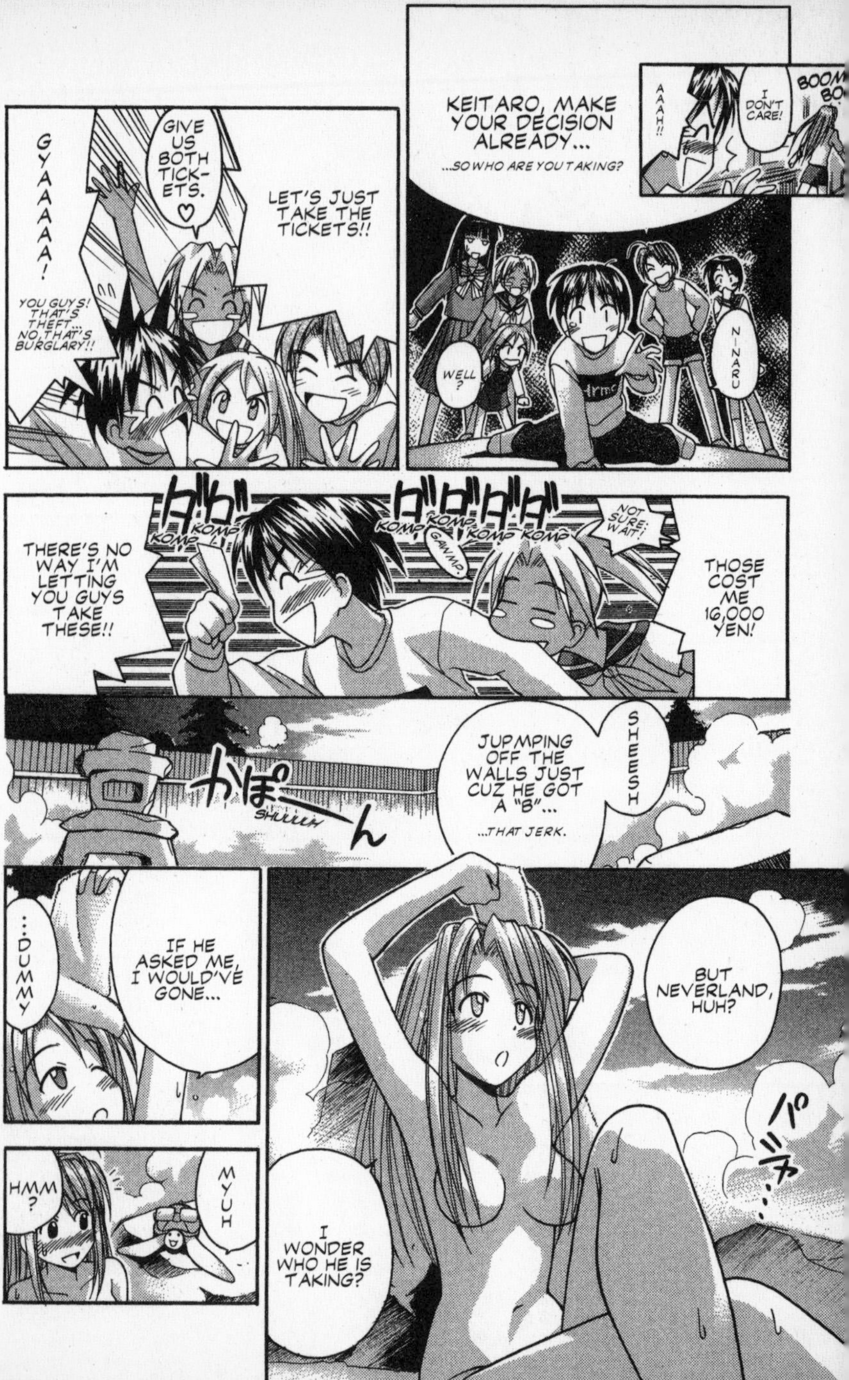
AAAAH!!
I DON'T CARE!
BOOM BO
KEITARO, MAKE YOUR DECISION ALREADY...
...SO WHO ARE YOU TAKING?
NINARU
WELL?
GIVE US BOTH TICK-ETS. ♡
LET'S JUST TAKE THE TICKETS!!
GYAAAAAA!
YOU GUYS! THAT'S THEFT... NO, THAT'S BURGLARY!!
THOSE COST ME 16,000 YEN!
NOT SURE: WAIT!
KOMP KOMP KOMP KOMP
GAWMP
KOMP KOMP
THERE'S NO WAY I'M LETTING YOU GUYS TAKE THESE!!
SHEESH
JUPMPING OFF THE WALLS JUST CUZ HE GOT A "B"...
...THAT JERK.
かぽーん
BUT NEVERLAND, HUH?
I WONDER WHO HE IS TAKING?
IF HE ASKED ME, I WOULD'VE GONE...
...DUMMY
MYUH
HMM?

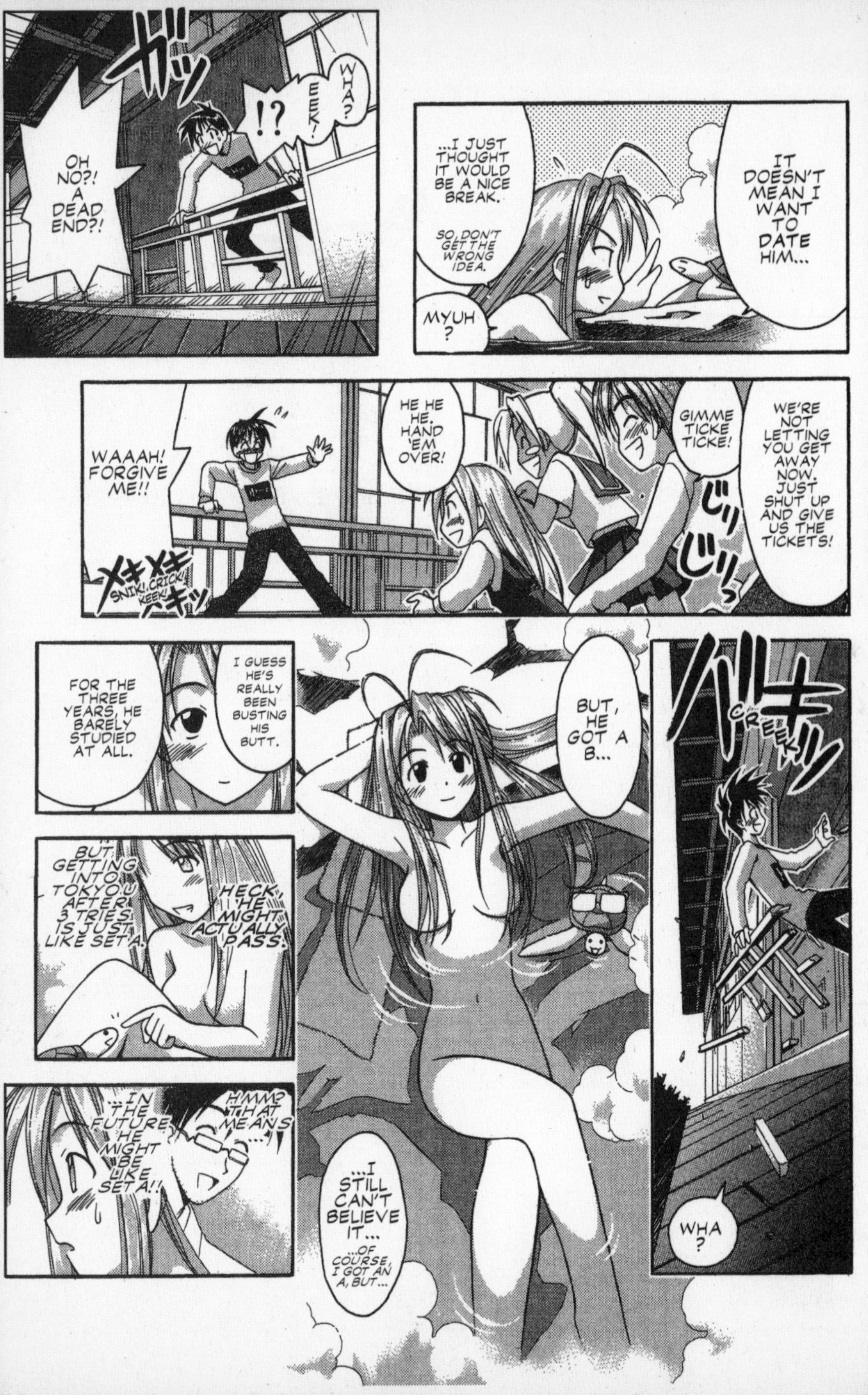
IT DOESN'T MEAN I WANT TO DATE HIM...
...I JUST THOUGHT IT WOULD BE A NICE BREAK.
SO, DON'T GET THE WRONG IDEA.
MYUH?
WHA?
EEK!
!?
OH NO?! A DEAD END?!
WE'RE NOT LETTING YOU GET AWAY NOW. JUST SHUT UP AND GIVE US THE TICKETS!
GIMME TICKE TICKE!
HE HE HE. HAND 'EM OVER!
WAAAH! FORGIVE ME!!
SNIK! CRICK! KEEK!
CREEEK
WHA?
BUT, HE GOT A B...
...I STILL CAN'T BELIEVE IT...
...OF COURSE, I GOT AN A, BUT...
I GUESS HE'S REALLY BEEN BUSTING HIS BUTT.
FOR THE THREE YEARS, HE BARELY STUDIED AT ALL.
HECK, HE MIGHT ACTUALLY PASS.
...BUT GETTING INTO TOKYO U AFTER 3 TRIES IS JUST LIKE SETA.
HMM? THAT MEANS...
...IN THE FUTURE HE MIGHT BE LIKE SETA!!

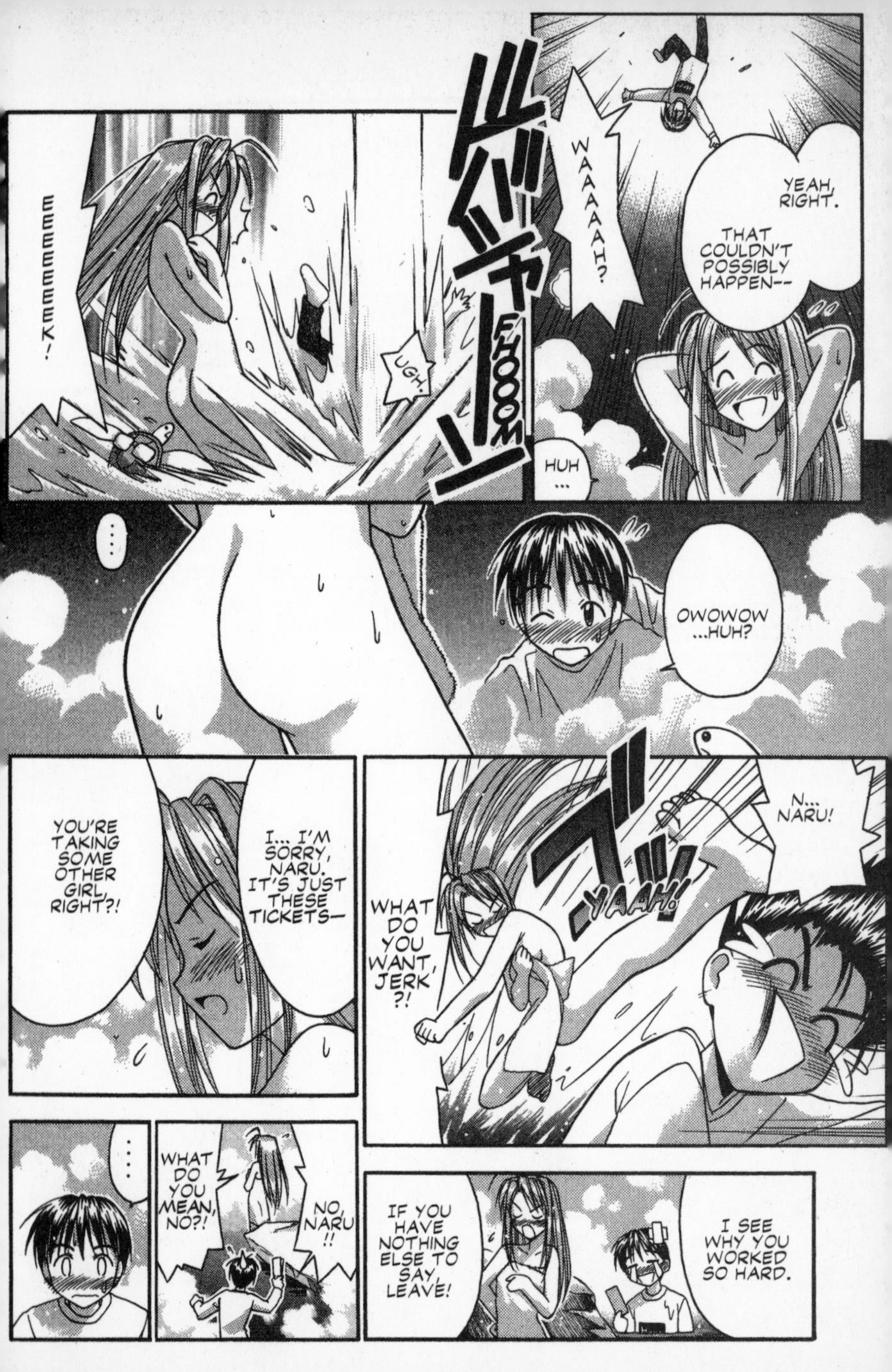
YEAH, RIGHT.
THAT COULDN'T POSSIBLY HAPPEN--
WAAAAAAH?
HUH ...
FHOOOM
UGH.
EEEEEEEEK!
OWOWOW ...HUH?
....
N... NARU!
YAAAH!
WHAT DO YOU WANT, JERK?!
I... I'M SORRY, NARU. IT'S JUST THESE TICKETS—
YOU'RE TAKING SOME OTHER GIRL, RIGHT?!
I SEE WHY YOU WORKED SO HARD.
IF YOU HAVE NOTHING ELSE TO SAY, LEAVE!
NO, NARU!!
WHAT DO YOU MEAN, NO?!
....

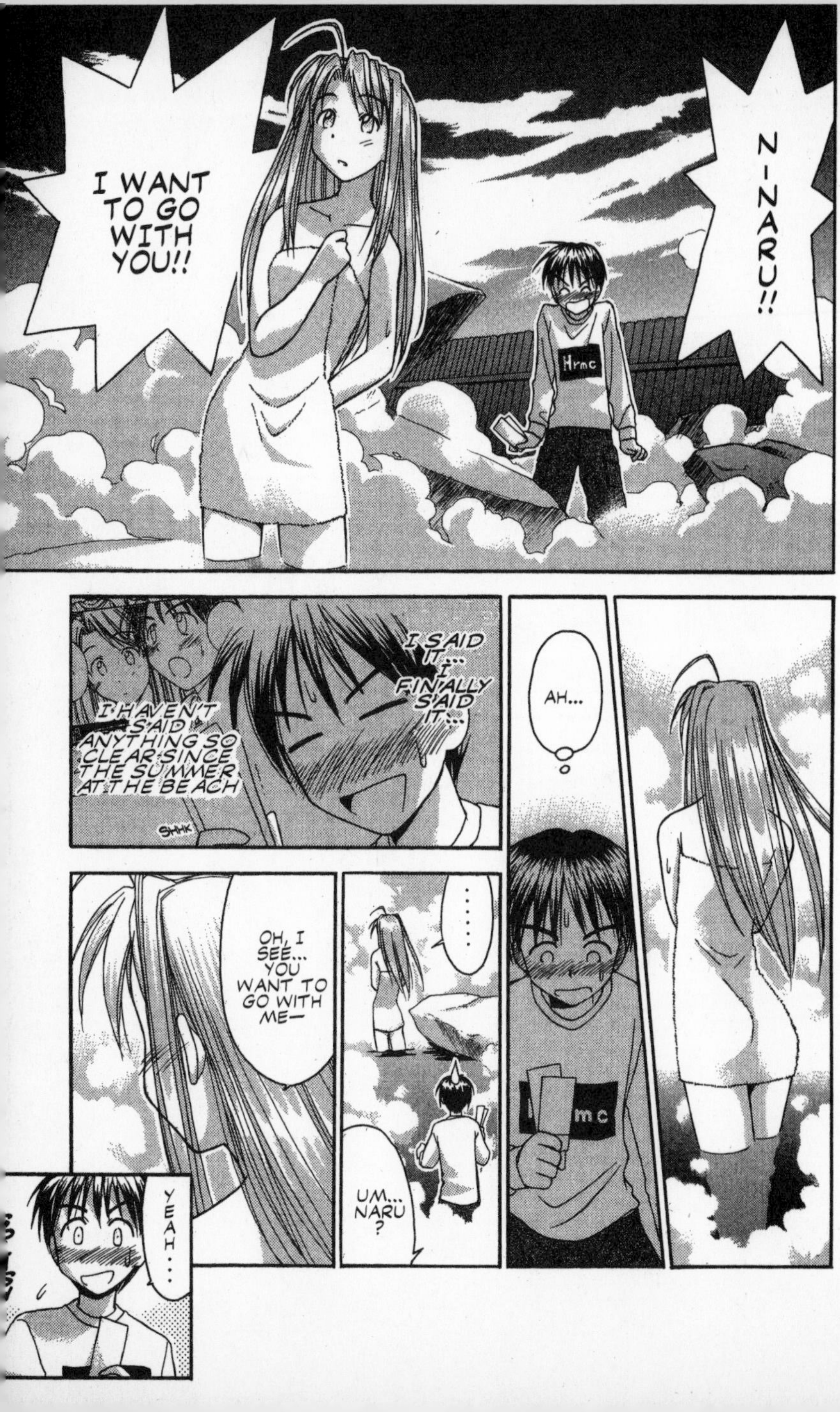
N-NARU!!
I WANT TO GO WITH YOU!!
AH...
I SAID IT... I FINALLY SAID IT...
I HAVEN'T SAID ANYTHING SO CLEAR SINCE THE SUMMER AT THE BEACH
SHHK
......
UM... NARU?
OH, I SEE... YOU WANT TO GO WITH ME—
YEAH...

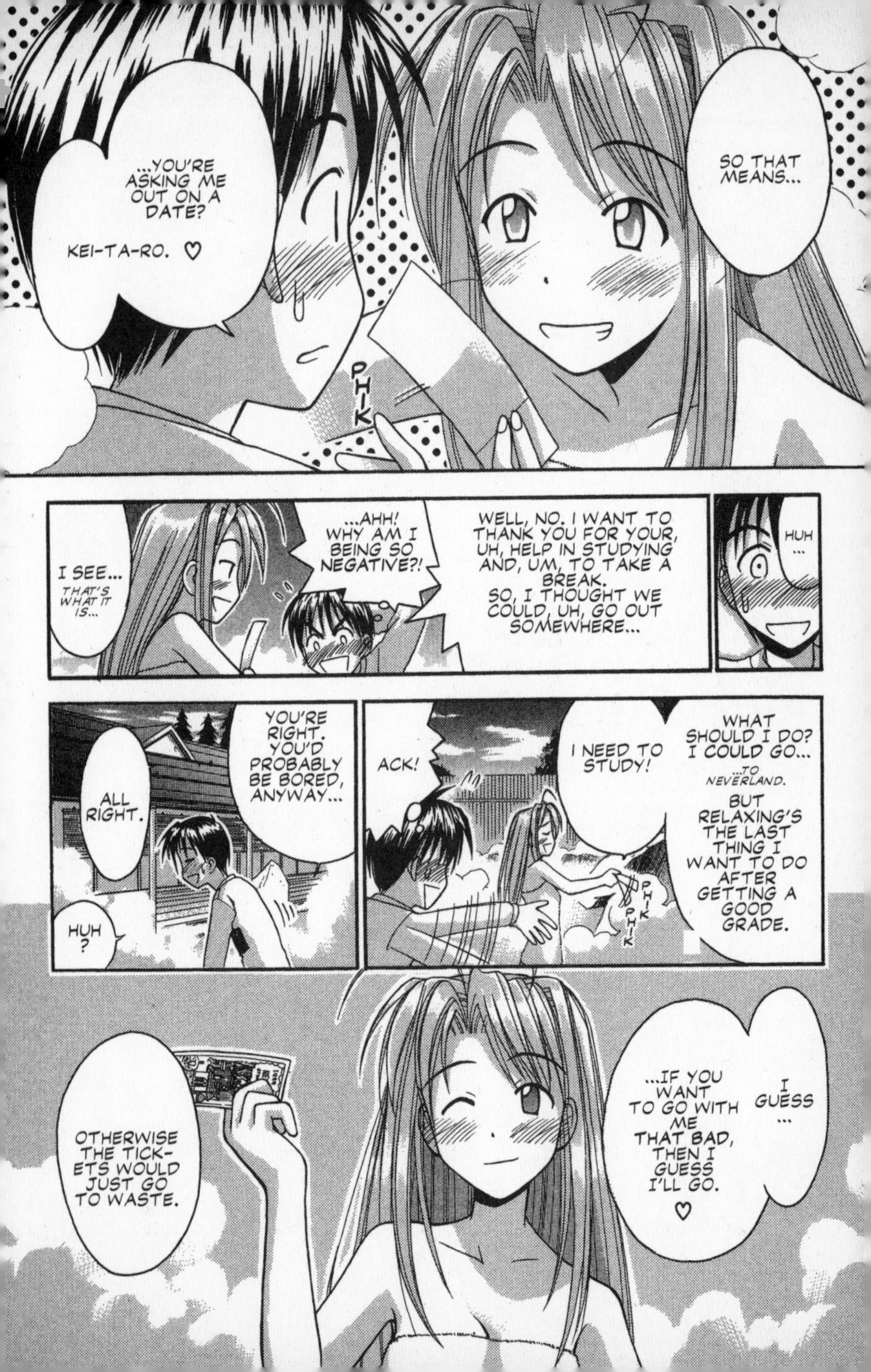
SO THAT MEANS...
...YOU'RE ASKING ME OUT ON A DATE?
KEI-TA-RO. ♡
PHIK
HUH...
WELL, NO. I WANT TO THANK YOU FOR YOUR, UH, HELP IN STUDYING AND, UM, TO TAKE A BREAK. SO, I THOUGHT WE COULD, UH, GO OUT SOMEWHERE...
...AHH! WHY AM I BEING SO NEGATIVE?!
I SEE... THAT'S WHAT IT IS...
WHAT SHOULD I DO? I COULD GO... ...TO NEVERLAND. BUT RELAXING'S THE LAST THING I WANT TO DO AFTER GETTING A GOOD GRADE.
I NEED TO STUDY!
ACK!
PHIK PHIK
YOU'RE RIGHT. YOU'D PROBABLY BE BORED, ANYWAY...
ALL RIGHT.
HUH?
I GUESS...
...IF YOU WANT TO GO WITH ME THAT BAD, THEN I GUESS I'LL GO. ♡
OTHERWISE THE TICK-ETS WOULD JUST GO TO WASTE.

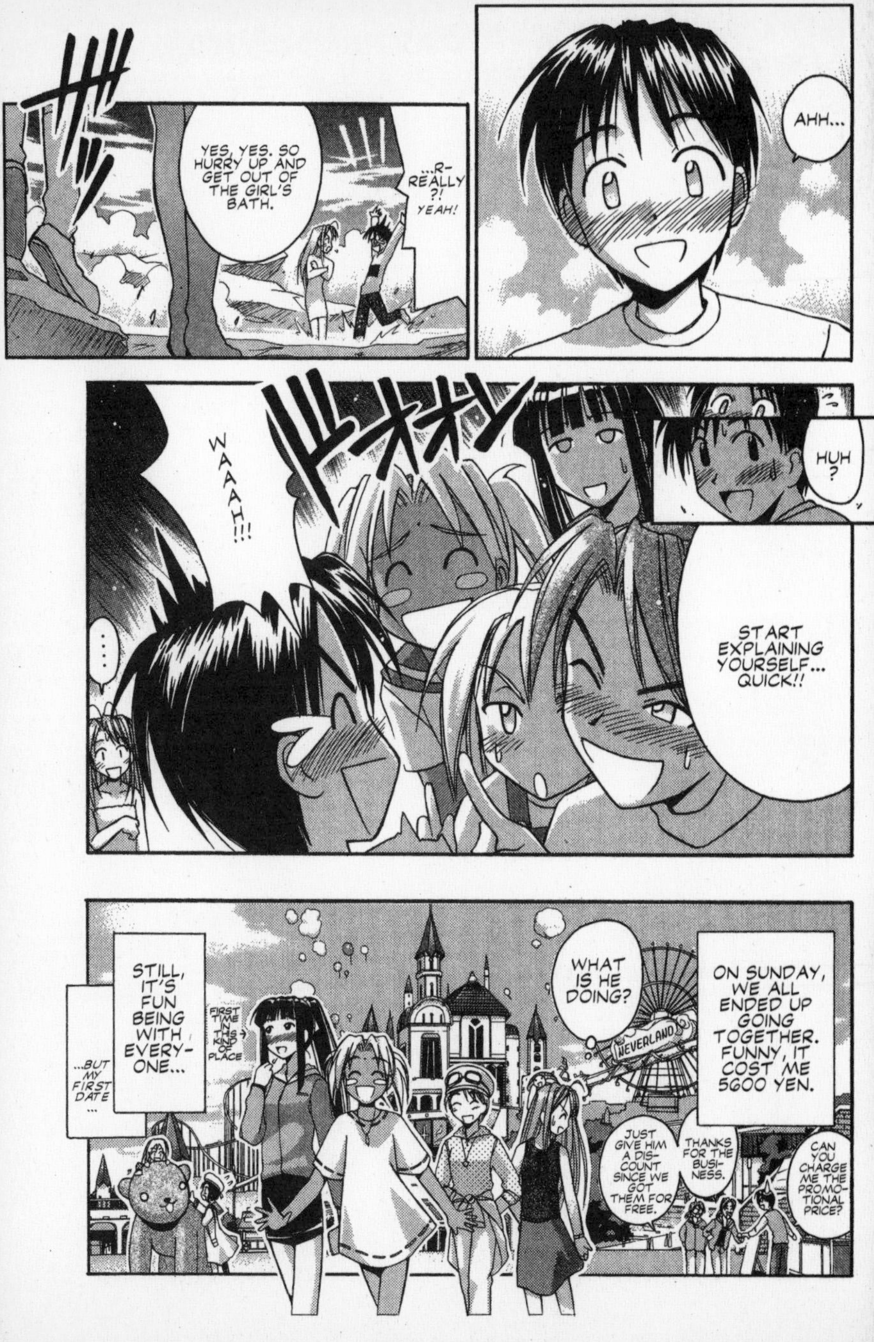
AHH...
...R-REALLY?! YEAH!
YES, YES. SO HURRY UP AND GET OUT OF THE GIRL'S BATH.
HUH?
START EXPLAINING YOURSELF... QUICK!!
ドオオン
WAAAAH!!!
...
ON SUNDAY, WE ALL ENDED UP GOING TOGETHER. FUNNY, IT COST ME 5600 YEN.
WHAT IS HE DOING?
NEVERLAND
CAN YOU CHARGE ME THE PROMOTIONAL PRICE?
THANKS FOR THE BUSINESS.
JUST GIVE HIM A DISCOUNT SINCE WE GOT THEM FOR FREE.
FIRST TIME IN THIS KIND OF PLACE
STILL, IT'S FUN BEING WITH EVERYONE...
...BUT MY FIRST DATE ...

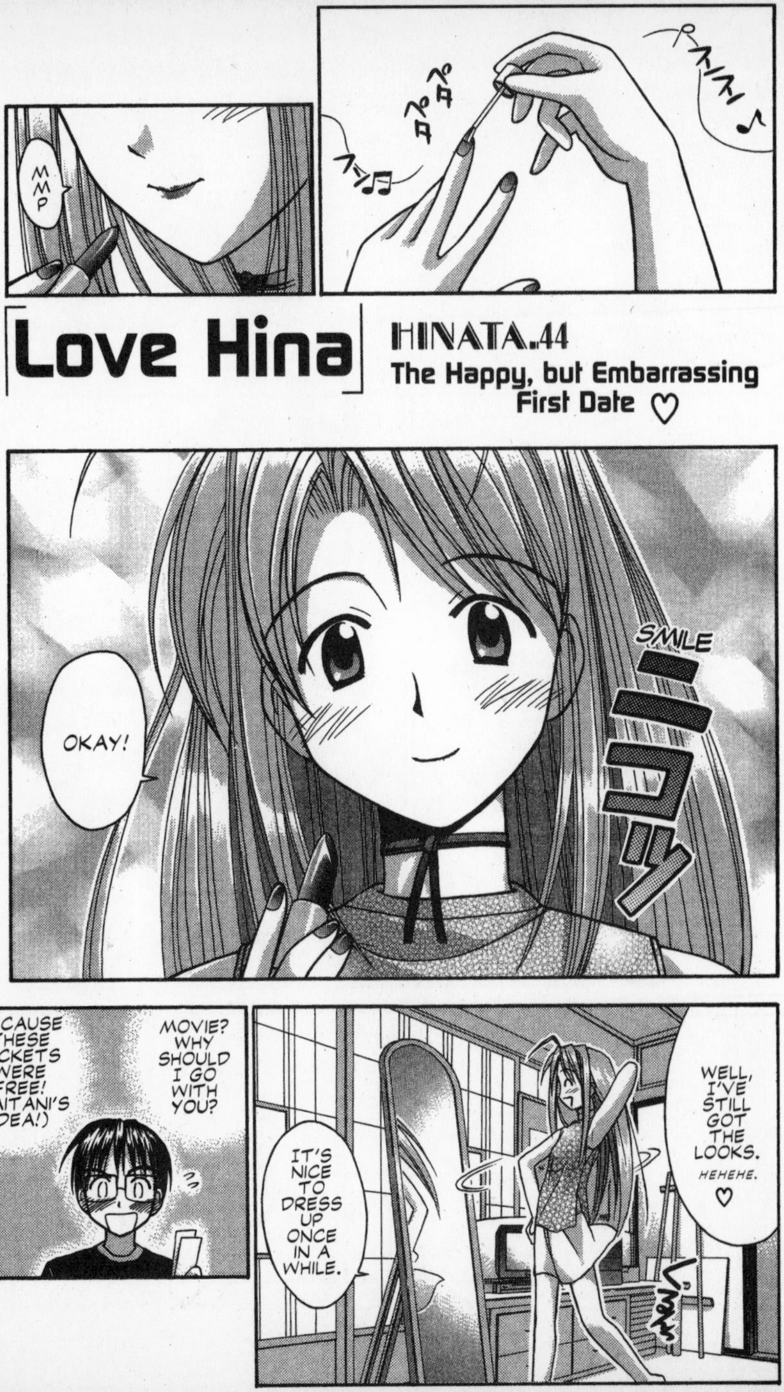
MMP
Love Hina
HINATA.44
The Happy, but Embarrassing First Date ♡
SMILE
OKAY!
WELL, I'VE STILL GOT THE LOOKS. HEHEHE. ♡
IT'S NICE TO DRESS UP ONCE IN A WHILE.
MOVIE? WHY SHOULD I GO WITH YOU?
BECAUSE THESE TICKETS WERE FREE! (HAITANI'S IDEA!)

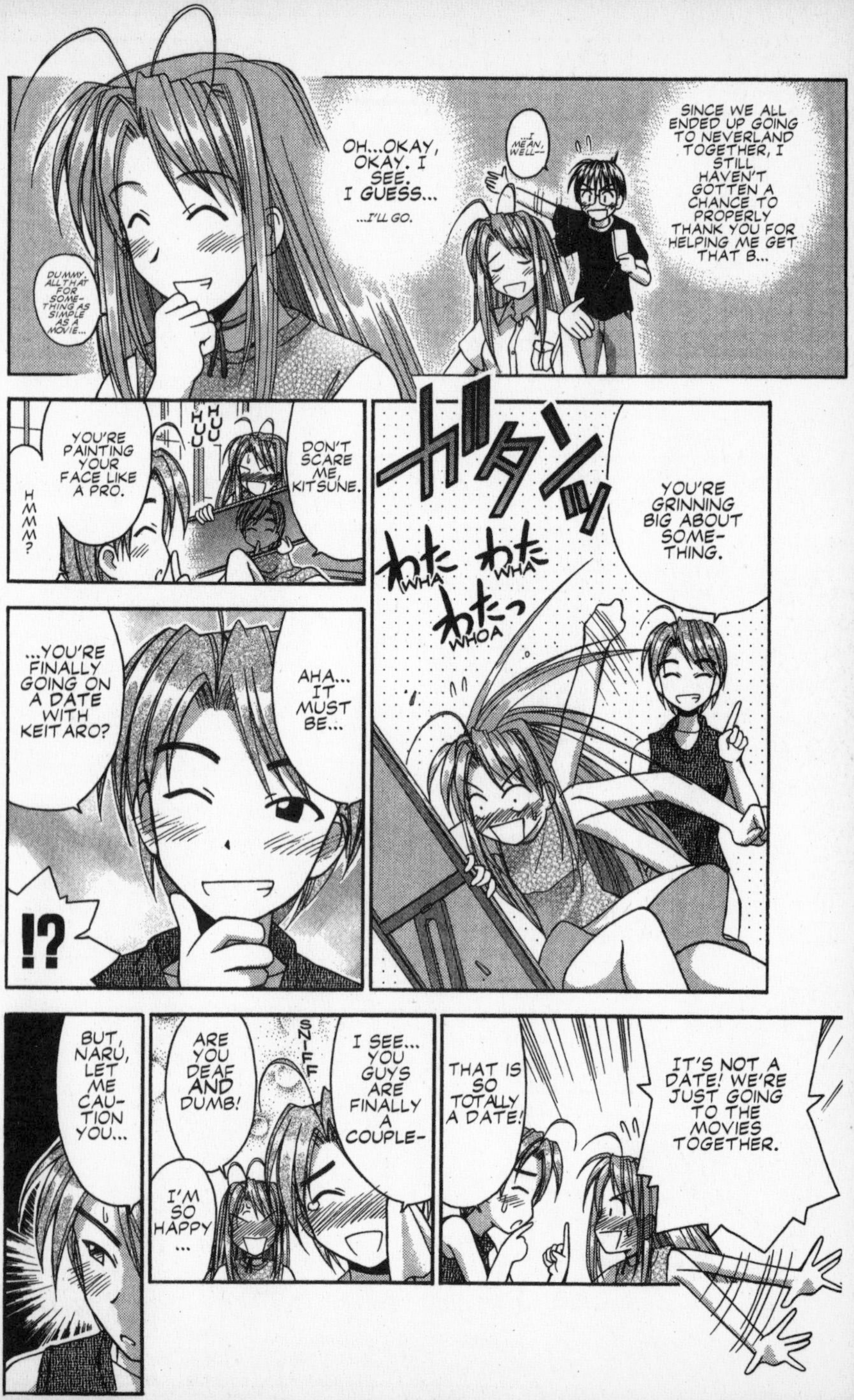
SINCE WE ALL ENDED UP GOING TO NEVERLAND TOGETHER, I STILL HAVEN'T GOTTEN A CHANCE TO PROPERLY THANK YOU FOR HELPING ME GET THAT B...
...I MEAN, WELL--
OH...OKAY, OKAY. I SEE. I GUESS...
...I'LL GO.
DUMMY. ALL THAT FOR SOMETHING AS SIMPLE AS A MOVIE...
ガタンッ
わた WHA
わた WHA
わたっ WHOA
YOU'RE GRINNING BIG ABOUT SOMETHING.
DON'T SCARE ME, KITSUNE.
HUU HUU
YOU'RE PAINTING YOUR FACE LIKE A PRO.
HMMM?
AHA... IT MUST BE...
...YOU'RE FINALLY GOING ON A DATE WITH KEITARO?
!?
IT'S NOT A DATE! WE'RE JUST GOING TO THE MOVIES TOGETHER.
THAT IS SO TOTALLY A DATE!
I SEE... YOU GUYS ARE FINALLY A COUPLE-
SNIFF
ARE YOU DEAF AND DUMB!
I'M SO HAPPY...
BUT, NARU, LET ME CAUTION YOU...

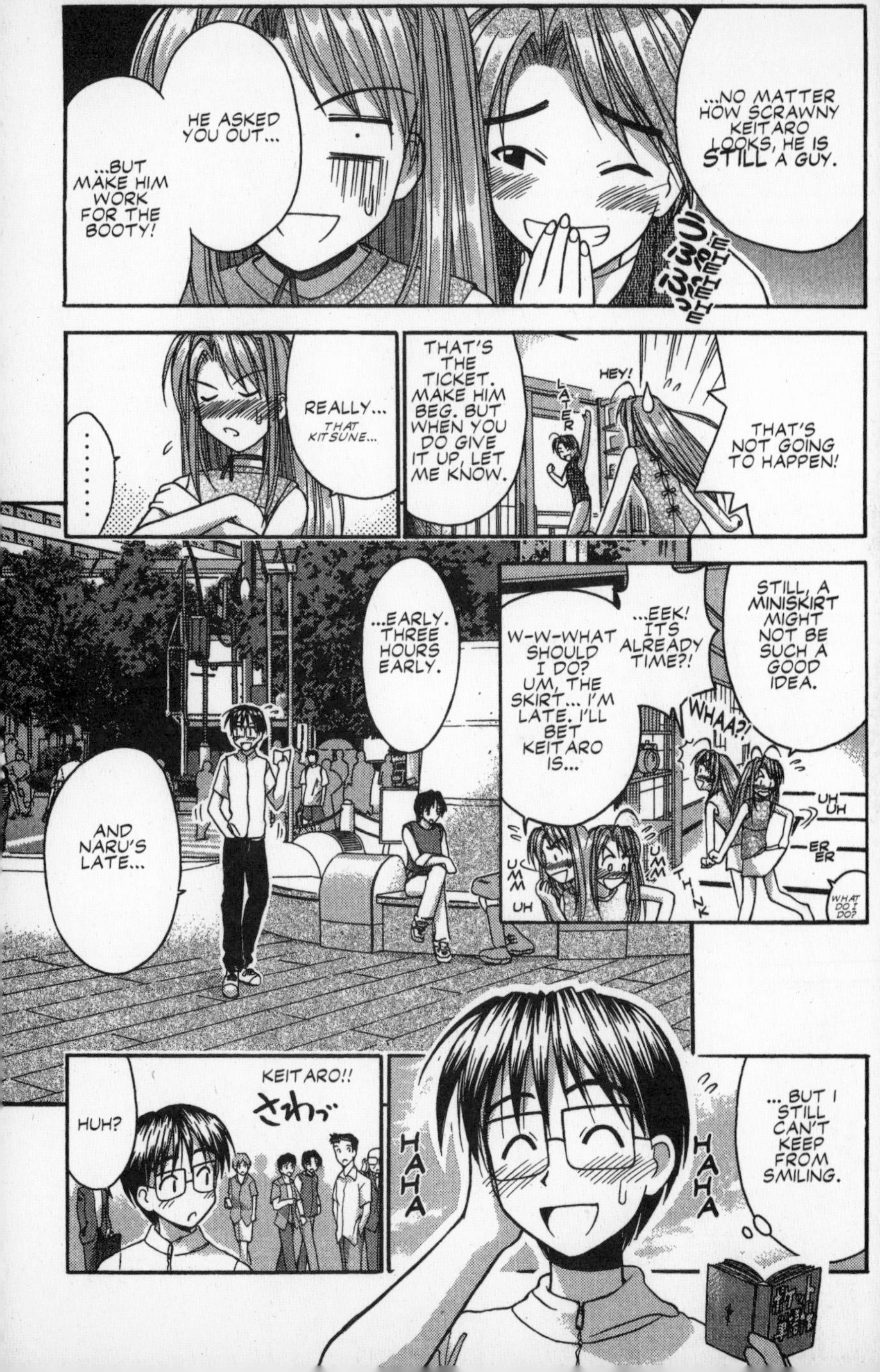
...NO MATTER HOW SCRAWNY KEITARO LOOKS, HE IS STILL A GUY.
うふふふ
HEHEHEHE
HE ASKED YOU OUT...
...BUT MAKE HIM WORK FOR THE BOOTY!
THAT'S THE TICKET. MAKE HIM BEG. BUT WHEN YOU DO GIVE IT UP, LET ME KNOW.
THAT'S NOT GOING TO HAPPEN!
HEY!
LATER-
REALLY... THAT KITSUNE...
....
STILL, A MINISKIRT MIGHT NOT BE SUCH A GOOD IDEA.
...EEK! ITS ALREADY TIME?!
WHAA?!
W-W-WHAT SHOULD I DO? UM, THE SKIRT... I'M LATE. I'LL BET KEITARO IS...
UH UH
ER ER
WHAT DO I DO?
THINK
UMM
UMM UH
...EARLY. THREE HOURS EARLY.
AND NARU'S LATE...
...BUT I STILL CAN'T KEEP FROM SMILING.
HAHA
HAHA
KEITARO!!
さわっ
HUH?

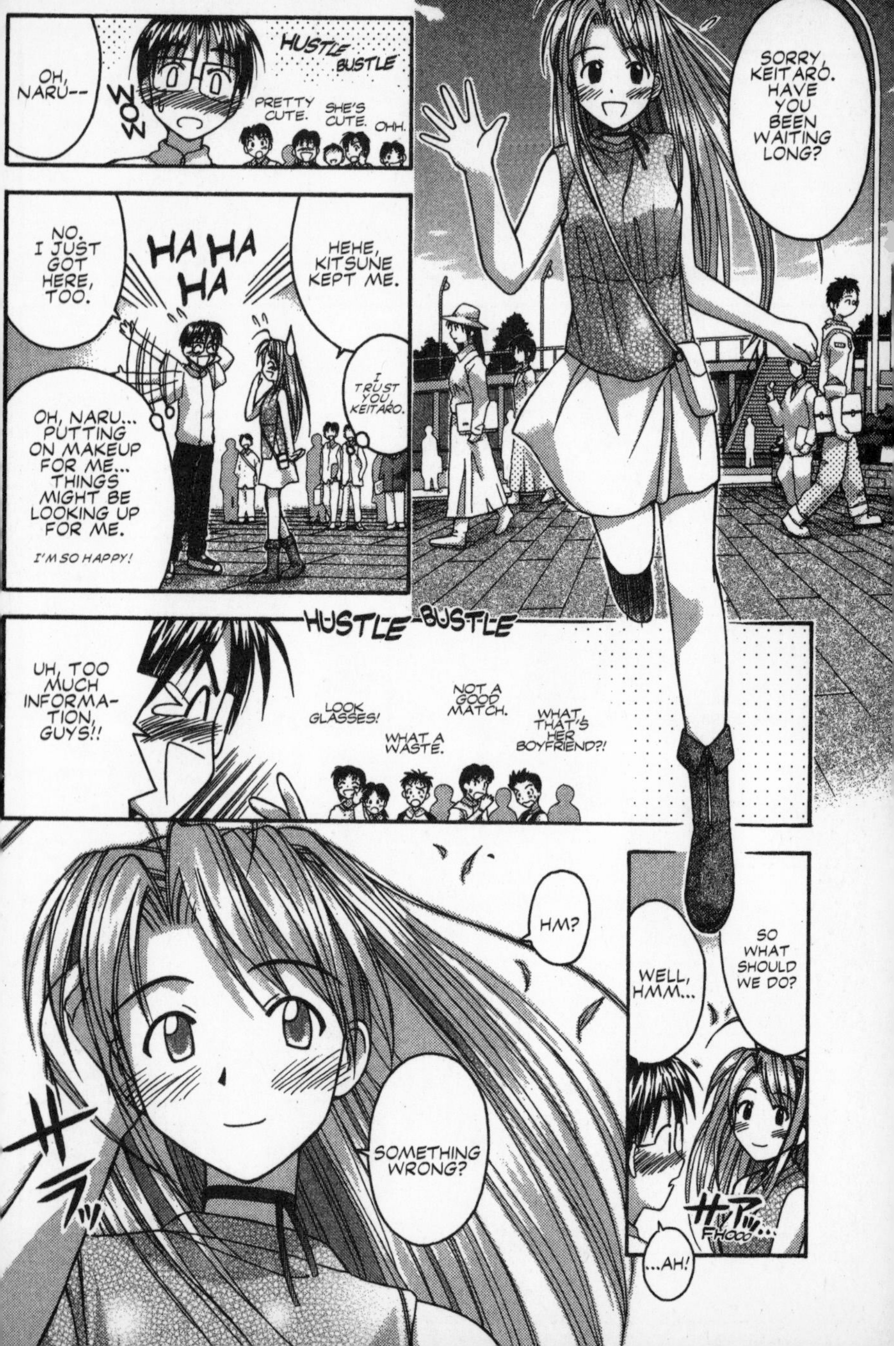
SORRY, KEITARO. HAVE YOU BEEN WAITING LONG?
OH, NARU--
HUSTLE BUSTLE
WOW
PRETTY CUTE.
SHE'S CUTE.
OHH.
HEHE, KITSUNE KEPT ME.
HA HA HA
NO. I JUST GOT HERE, TOO.
I TRUST YOU, KEITARO.
OH, NARU... PUTTING ON MAKEUP FOR ME... THINGS MIGHT BE LOOKING UP FOR ME.
I'M SO HAPPY!
HUSTLE-BUSTLE
WHAT, THAT'S HER BOYFRIEND?!
NOT A GOOD MATCH.
WHAT A WASTE.
LOOK GLASSES!
UH, TOO MUCH INFORMATION, GUYS!!
SO WHAT SHOULD WE DO?
WELL, HMM...
FHOOO...
...AH!
HM?
SOMETHING WRONG?

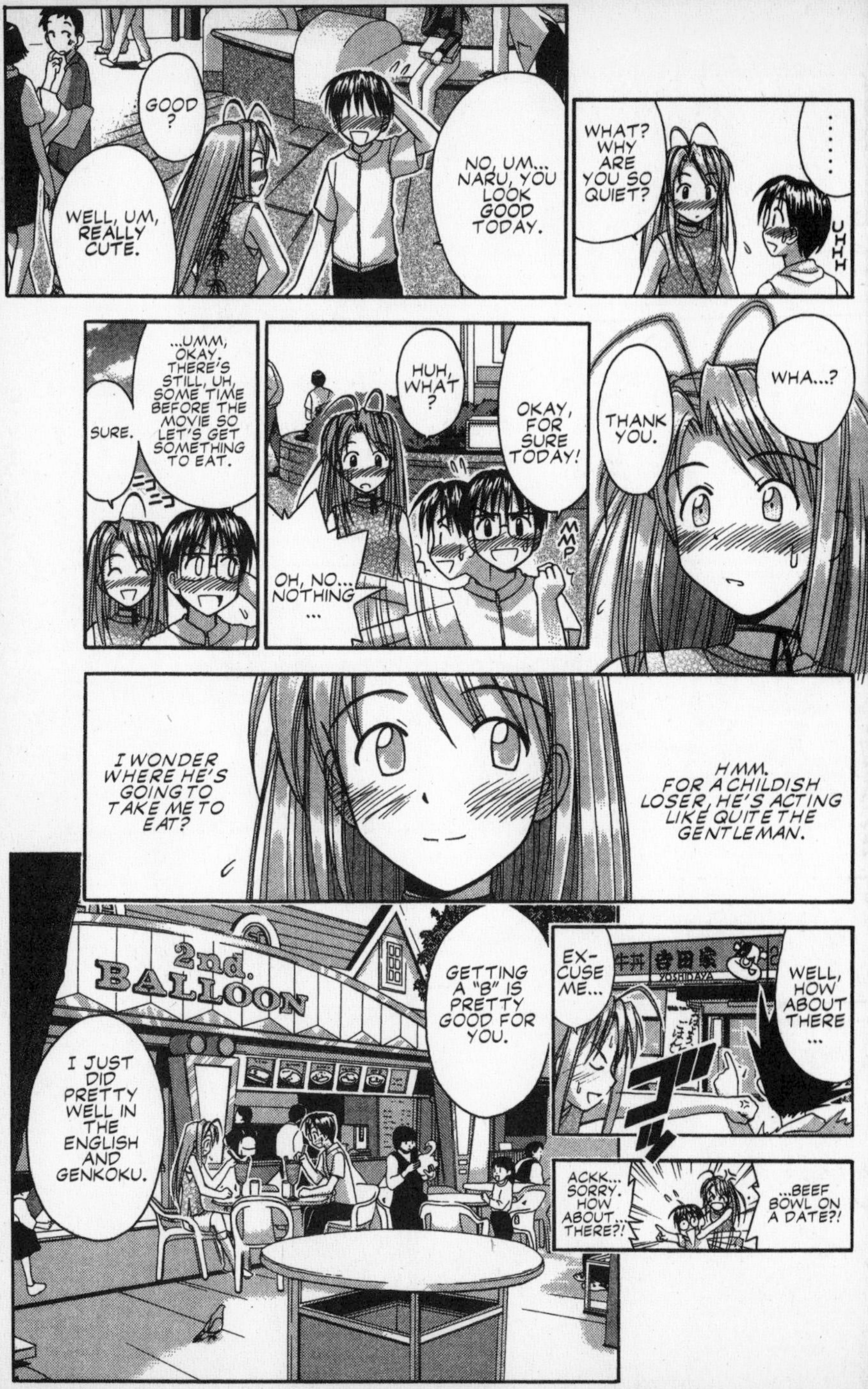
......
WHAT? WHY ARE YOU SO QUIET?
UHHH
NO, UM... NARU, YOU LOOK GOOD TODAY.
GOOD?
WELL, UM, REALLY CUTE.
WHA...?
THANK YOU.
OKAY, FOR SURE TODAY!
HUH, WHAT?
MMP
OH, NO... NOTHING...
...UMM, OKAY. THERE'S STILL, UH, SOME TIME BEFORE THE MOVIE SO LET'S GET SOMETHING TO EAT.
SURE.
HMM. FOR A CHILDISH LOSER, HE'S ACTING LIKE QUITE THE GENTLEMAN.
I WONDER WHERE HE'S GOING TO TAKE ME TO EAT?
WELL, HOW ABOUT THERE...
EX-CUSE ME...
YOSHIDAYA
...BEEF BOWL ON A DATE?!
ACKK... SORRY. HOW ABOUT THERE?!
2nd. BALLOON
GETTING A "B" IS PRETTY GOOD FOR YOU.
I JUST DID PRETTY WELL IN THE ENGLISH AND GENKOKU.

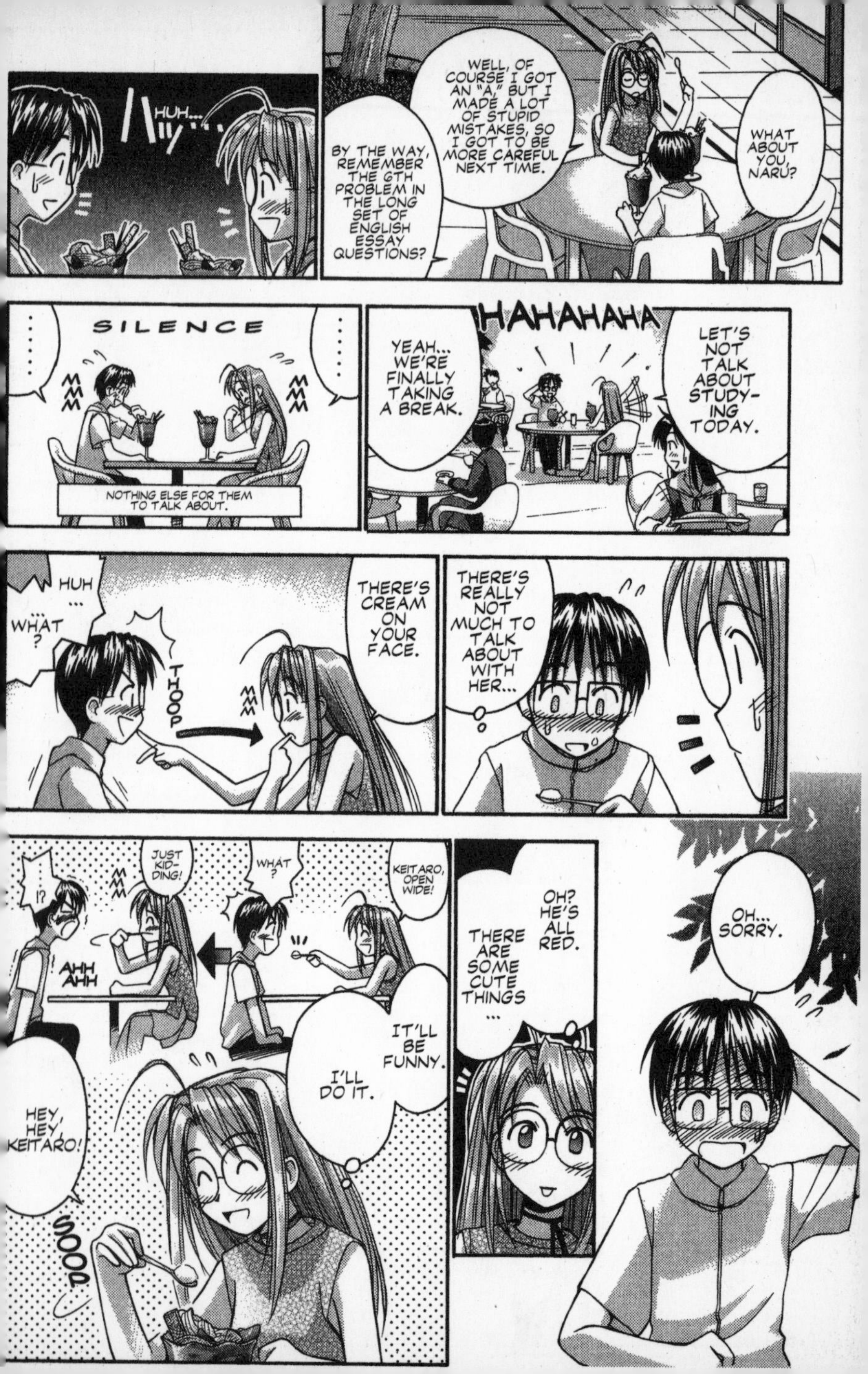
WHAT ABOUT YOU, NARU?
WELL, OF COURSE I GOT AN "A," BUT I MADE A LOT OF STUPID MISTAKES, SO I GOT TO BE MORE CAREFUL NEXT TIME.
BY THE WAY, REMEMBER THE 6TH PROBLEM IN THE LONG SET OF ENGLISH ESSAY QUESTIONS?
HUH...
HAHAHAHA
LET'S NOT TALK ABOUT STUDY-ING TODAY.
YEAH... WE'RE FINALLY TAKING A BREAK.
......
SILENCE
MMM
MMM
......
NOTHING ELSE FOR THEM TO TALK ABOUT.
THERE'S REALLY NOT MUCH TO TALK ABOUT WITH HER...
THERE'S CREAM ON YOUR FACE.
THOOP
MMM
HUH ... ... WHAT ?
OH... SORRY.
OH? HE'S ALL RED.
THERE ARE SOME CUTE THINGS ...
KEITARO, OPEN WIDE!
WHAT ?
JUST KID-DING!
MMM
!?
AHH AHH
IT'LL BE FUNNY.
I'LL DO IT.
HEY, HEY, KEITARO!
SOOP

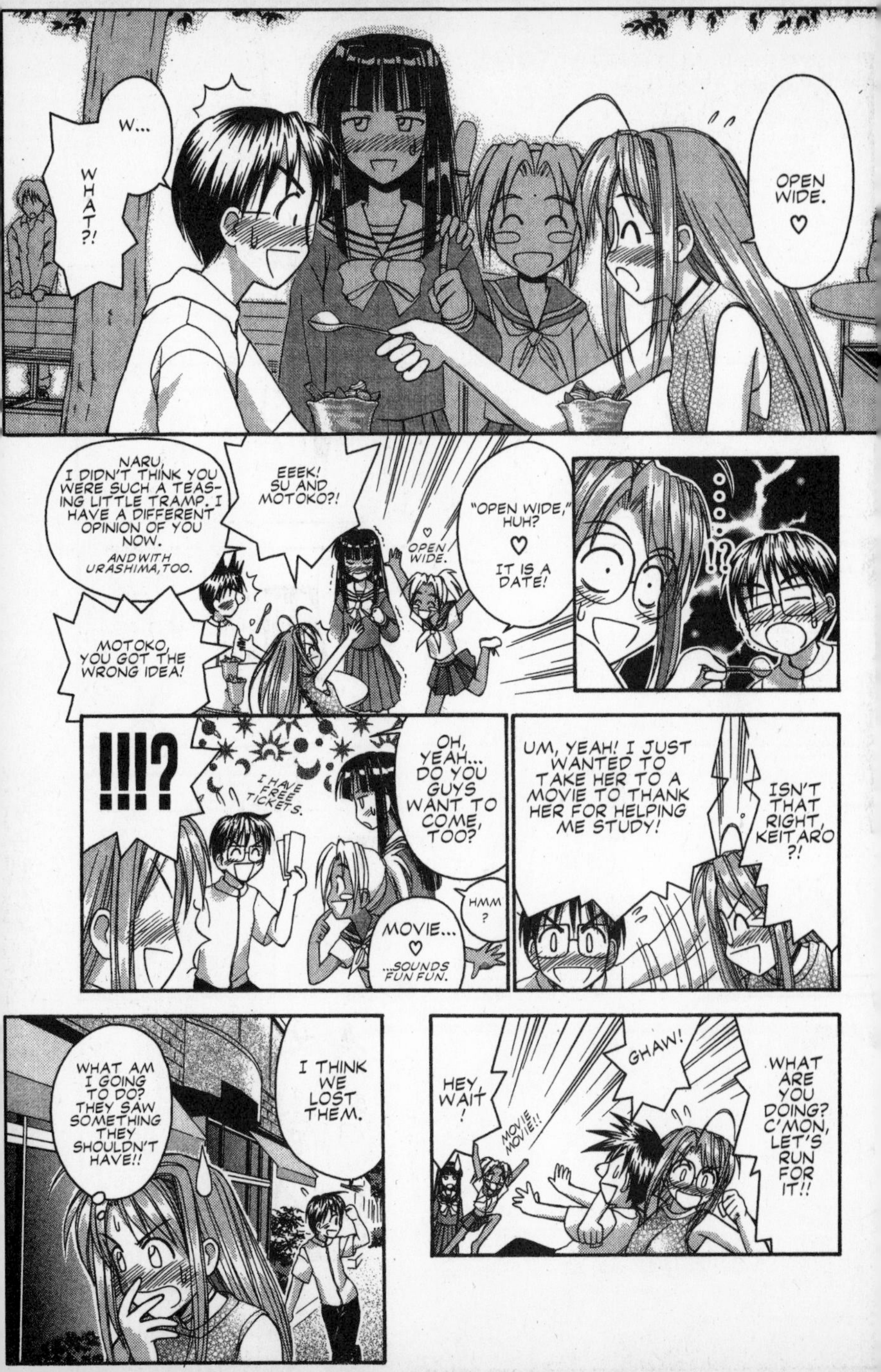
OPEN WIDE. ♡
W... WHAT?!
OOOO...!?
"OPEN WIDE," HUH? ♡ IT IS A DATE!
OPEN WIDE. ♡
EEEK! SU AND MOTOKO?!
NARU, I DIDN'T THINK YOU WERE SUCH A TEASING LITTLE TRAMP. I HAVE A DIFFERENT OPINION OF YOU NOW.
AND WITH URASHIMA, TOO.
MOTOKO, YOU GOT THE WRONG IDEA!
ISN'T THAT RIGHT, KEITARO?!
UM, YEAH! I JUST WANTED TO TAKE HER TO A MOVIE TO THANK HER FOR HELPING ME STUDY!
OH, YEAH... DO YOU GUYS WANT TO COME, TOO?
HMM?
MOVIE... ♡ ...SOUNDS FUN FUN.
I HAVE FREE TICKETS.
!!!?
WHAT ARE YOU DOING? C'MON, LET'S RUN FOR IT!!
GHAW!
HEY, WAIT!
MOVIE MOVIE!!
I THINK WE LOST THEM.
WHAT AM I GOING TO DO? THEY SAW SOMETHING THEY SHOULDN'T HAVE!!

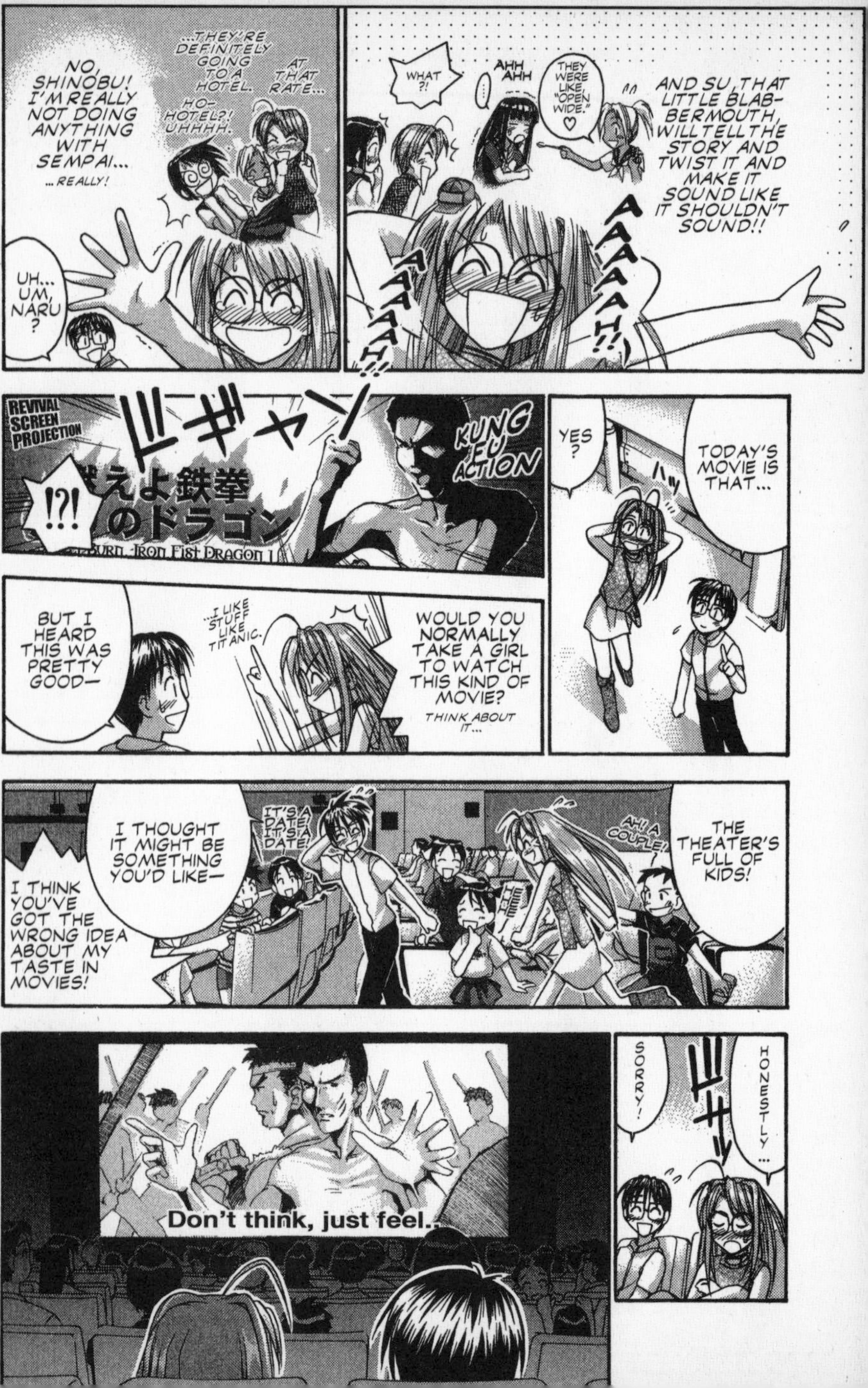

AND SU, THAT LITTLE BLABBERMOUTH, WILL TELL THE STORY AND TWIST IT AND MAKE IT SOUND LIKE IT SHOULDN'T SOUND!!
THEY WERE LIKE, "OPEN WIDE." ♡
AHH AHH
WHAT ?!
...
AAAAAH!!
AAAAH!!
...THEY'RE DEFINITELY GOING TO A HOTEL.
AT THAT RATE...
HO-HOTEL?! UHHHH.
NO, SHINOBU! I'M REALLY NOT DOING ANYTHING WITH SEMPAI... ...REALLY!
UH... UM, NARU?
TODAY'S MOVIE IS THAT...
ハッ
YES?
REVIVAL SCREEN PROJECTION
ドギャーン
KUNG FU ACTION
!?!
えよ鉄拳のドラゴン
BURN, IRON FIST DRAGON 1
WOULD YOU NORMALLY TAKE A GIRL TO WATCH THIS KIND OF MOVIE? THINK ABOUT IT...
...I LIKE STUFF LIKE TITANIC.
BUT I HEARD THIS WAS PRETTY GOOD—
THE THEATER'S FULL OF KIDS!
AH! A COUPLE!
IT'S A DATE! IT'S A DATE!
I THOUGHT IT MIGHT BE SOMETHING YOU'D LIKE—
I THINK YOU'VE GOT THE WRONG IDEA ABOUT MY TASTE IN MOVIES!
HONESTLY...
SORRY!
Don't think, just feel...

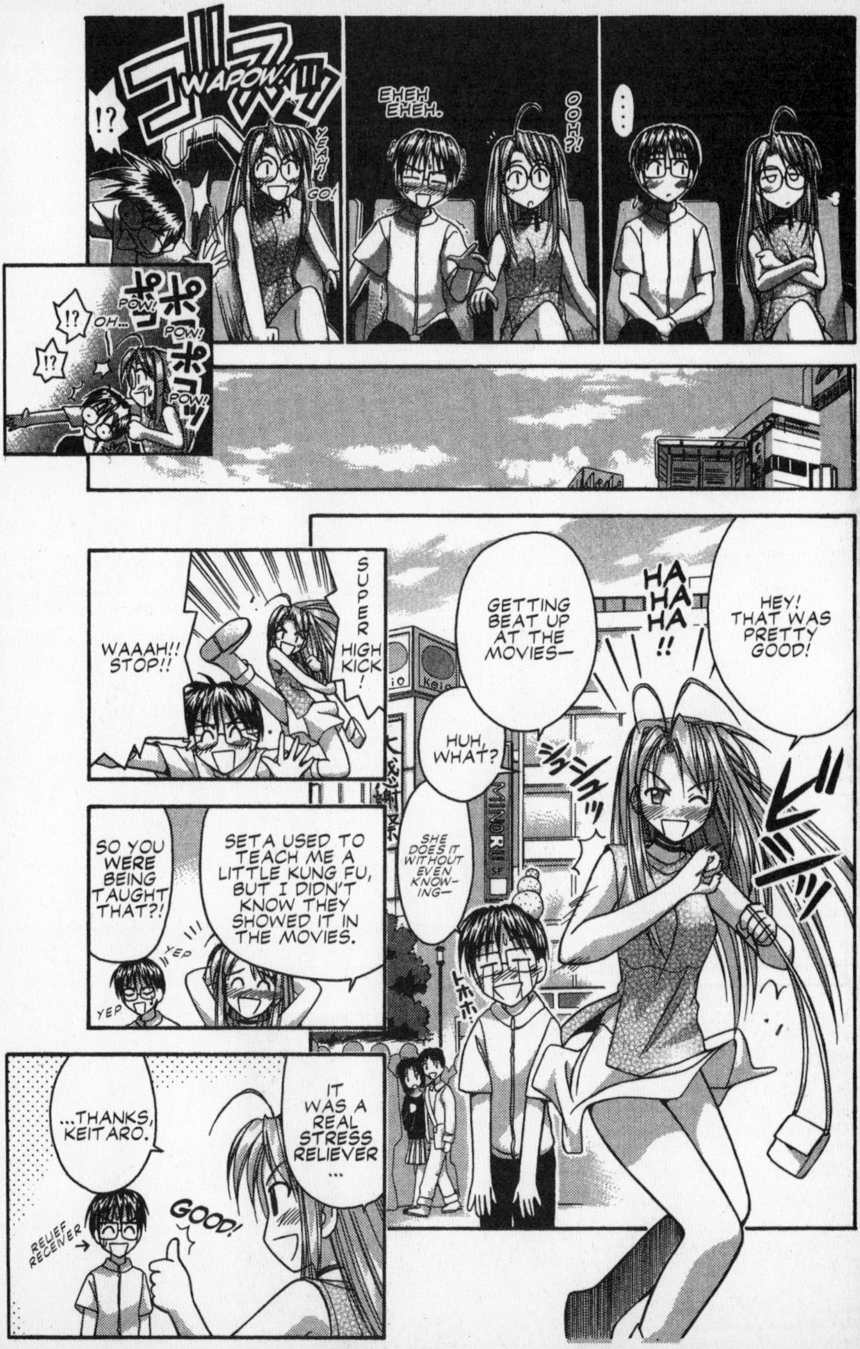
...
EHEH EHEH.
OOOH?!
WAPOW!
!?
YEAH! GO!
POW! POW! POW!
!? OH...
!?
HEY! THAT WAS PRETTY GOOD!
HA HA HA!!
GETTING BEAT UP AT THE MOVIES—
HUH, WHAT?
MINORU
SHE DOES IT WITHOUT EVEN KNOWING—
SUPER HIGH KICK!
WAAAH!! STOP!!
SETA USED TO TEACH ME A LITTLE KUNG FU, BUT I DIDN'T KNOW THEY SHOWED IT IN THE MOVIES.
SO YOU WERE BEING TAUGHT THAT?!
YEP
YEP
IT WAS A REAL STRESS RELIEVER ...
...THANKS, KEITARO.
GOOD!
RELIEF RECEIVER

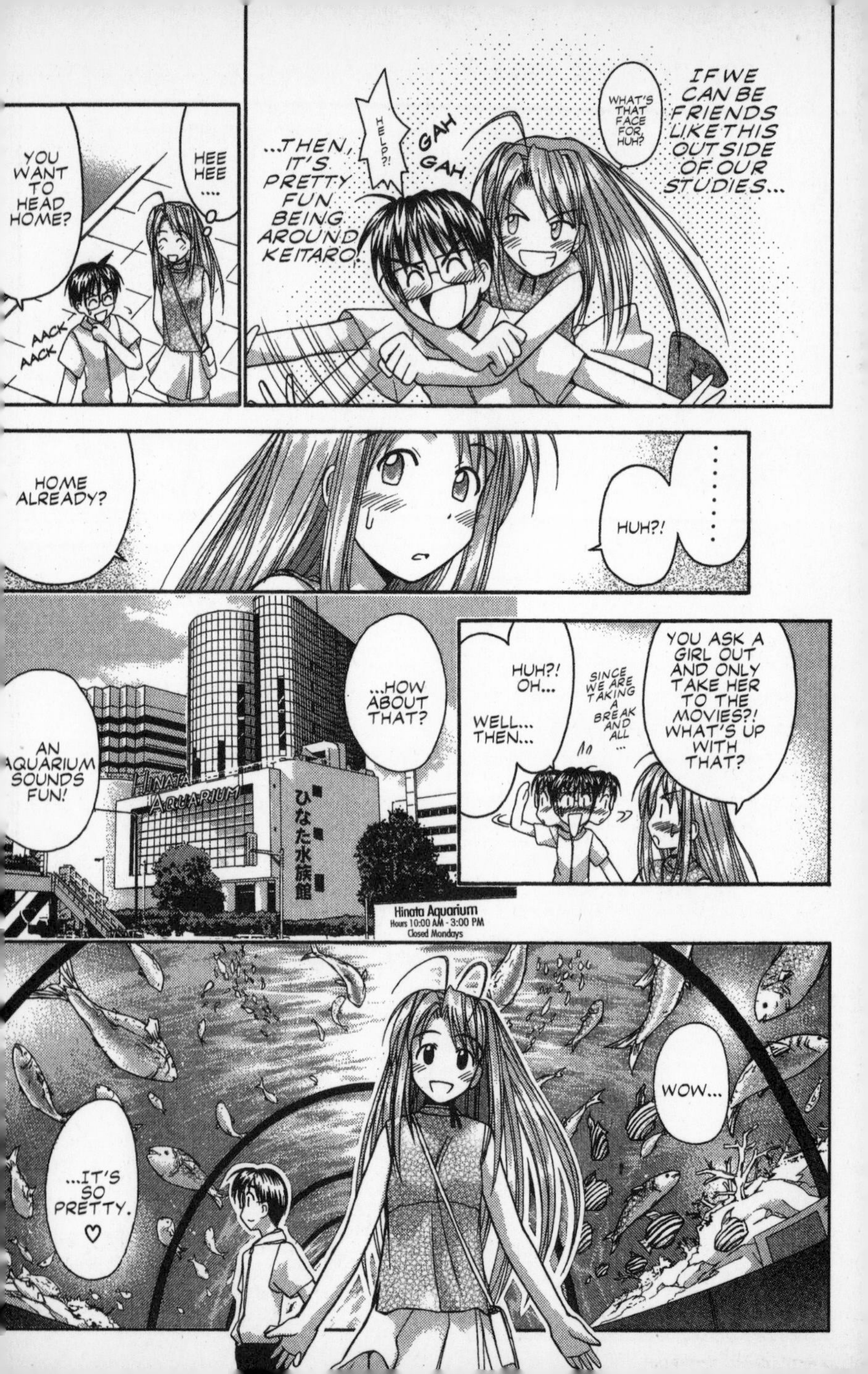
IF WE CAN BE FRIENDS LIKE THIS OUTSIDE OF OUR STUDIES...
WHAT'S THAT FACE FOR, HUH?
GAH GAH
HELP?!
...THEN, IT'S PRETTY FUN BEING AROUND KEITARO!
HEE HEE ....
YOU WANT TO HEAD HOME?
AACK AACK
......
HUH?!
HOME ALREADY?
YOU ASK A GIRL OUT AND ONLY TAKE HER TO THE MOVIES?! WHAT'S UP WITH THAT?
SINCE WE ARE TAKING A BREAK AND ALL ...
HUH?! OH...
WELL... THEN...
...HOW ABOUT THAT?
AN AQUARIUM SOUNDS FUN!
HINATA AQUARIUM
ひなた水族館
Hinata Aquarium Hours 10:00 AM - 3:00 PM Closed Mondays
WOW...
...IT'S SO PRETTY. ♡

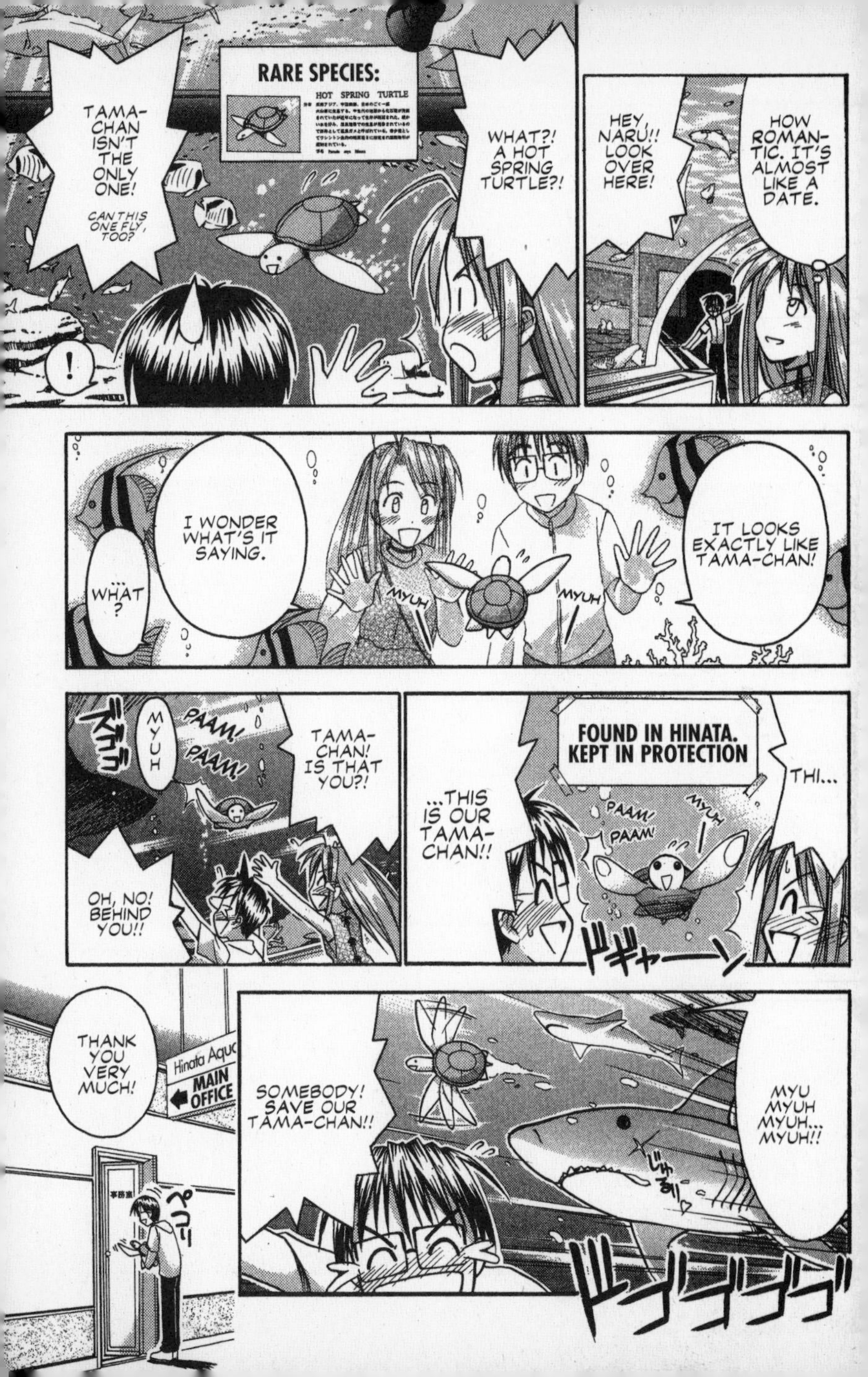

HOW ROMANTIC. IT'S ALMOST LIKE A DATE.
HEY, NARU!! LOOK OVER HERE!
WHAT?! A HOT SPRING TURTLE?!
RARE SPECIES:
HOT SPRING TURTLE
TAMA-CHAN ISN'T THE ONLY ONE!
CAN THIS ONE FLY, TOO?
!
IT LOOKS EXACTLY LIKE TAMA-CHAN!
MYUH
MYUH
I WONDER WHAT'S IT SAYING.
... WHAT?
THI...
FOUND IN HINATA. KEPT IN PROTECTION
MYUH
PAAM! PAAM!
...THIS IS OUR TAMA-CHAN!!
TAMA-CHAN! IS THAT YOU?!
PAAM! PAAM!
MYUH
OH, NO! BEHIND YOU!!
MYU MYUH MYUH... MYUH!!
SOMEBODY! SAVE OUR TAMA-CHAN!!
THANK YOU VERY MUCH!
Hinata Aqu
MAIN OFFICE

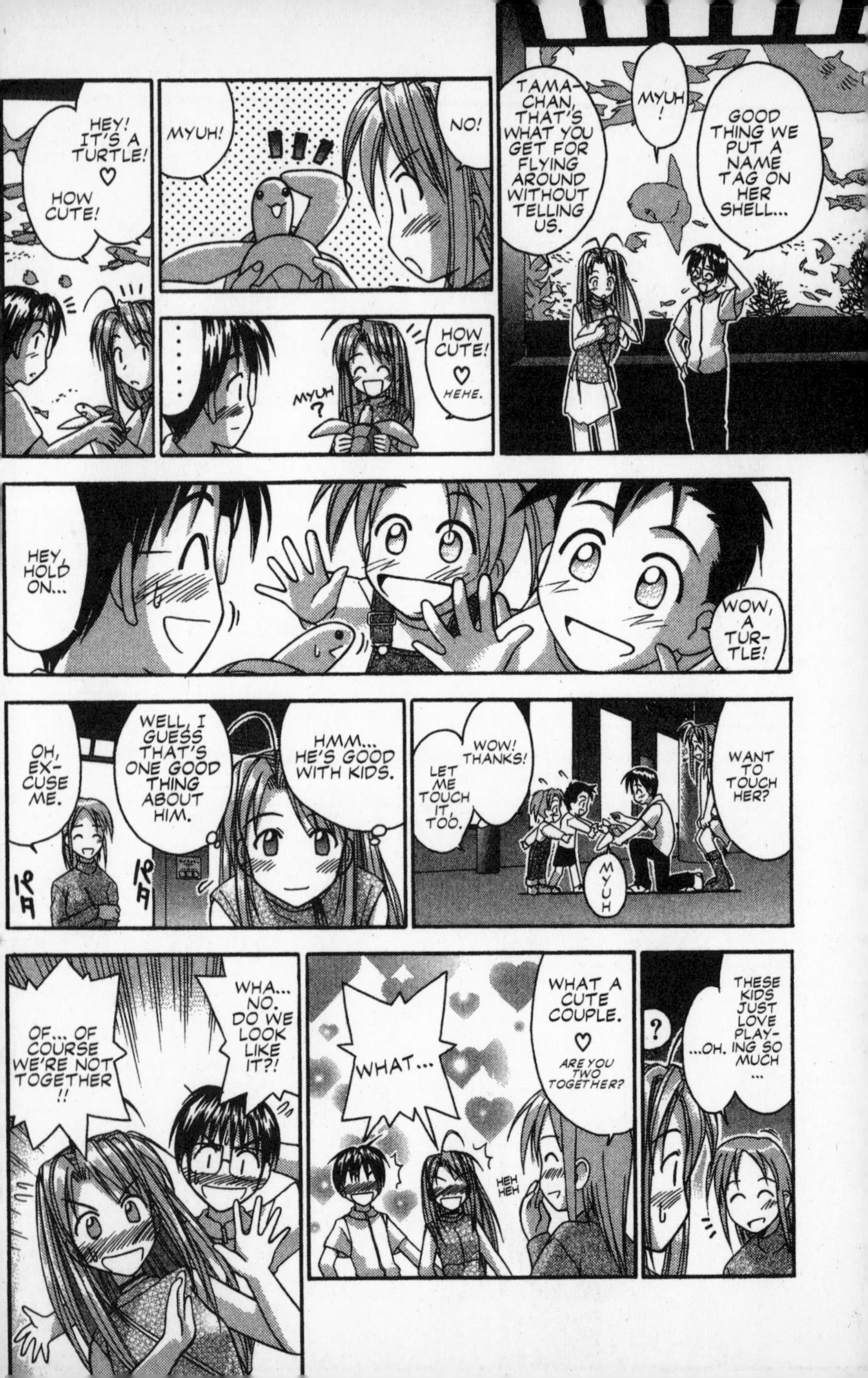
GOOD THING WE PUT A NAME TAG ON HER SHELL...
MYUH!
TAMA-CHAN, THAT'S WHAT YOU GET FOR FLYING AROUND WITHOUT TELLING US.
NO!
MYUH!
HOW CUTE! ♡ HEHE.
MYUH?
HEY! IT'S A TURTLE! ♡
HOW CUTE!
WOW, A TURTLE!
HEY, HOLD ON...
WANT TO TOUCH HER?
WOW! THANKS!
LET ME TOUCH IT, TOO.
MYUH
HMM... HE'S GOOD WITH KIDS.
WELL, I GUESS THAT'S ONE GOOD THING ABOUT HIM.
OH, EXCUSE ME.
パタ
パタ
THESE KIDS JUST LOVE PLAYING SO MUCH...
...OH.
?
WHAT A CUTE COUPLE. ♡
ARE YOU TWO TOGETHER?
HEH HEH
WHAT...
WHA... NO. DO WE LOOK LIKE IT?!
OF... OF COURSE WE'RE NOT TOGETHER!!

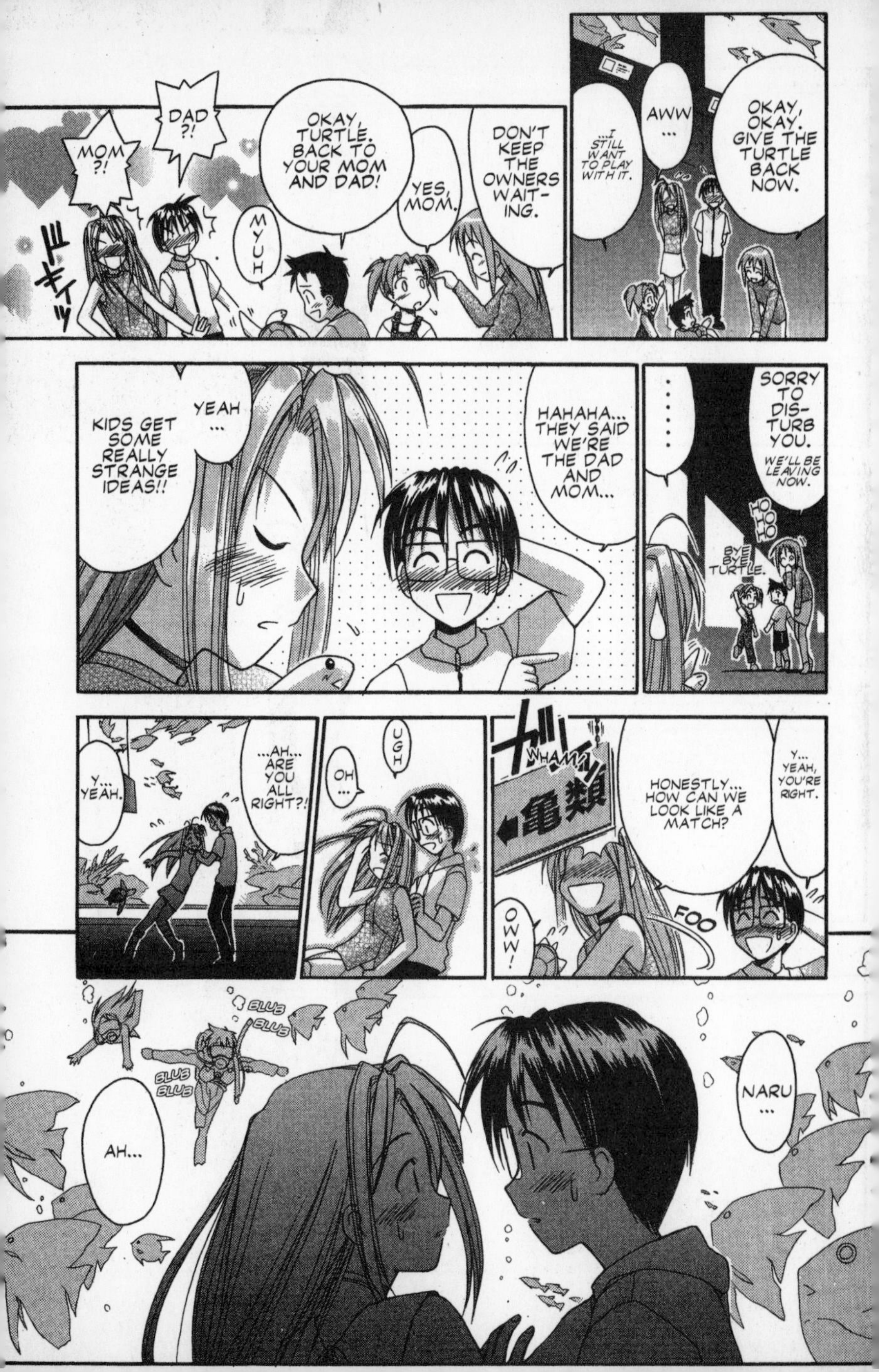
OKAY, OKAY. GIVE THE TURTLE BACK NOW.
AWW ...
...I STILL WANT TO PLAY WITH IT.
DON'T KEEP THE OWNERS WAIT-ING.
YES, MOM.
OKAY, TURTLE. BACK TO YOUR MOM AND DAD!
MYUH
DAD ?!
MOM ?!
ドキッ
SORRY TO DIS-TURB YOU.
WE'LL BE LEAVING NOW.
HO HO HO
......
BYE BYE TURTLE.
HAHAHA... THEY SAID WE'RE THE DAD AND MOM...
YEAH ...
KIDS GET SOME REALLY STRANGE IDEAS!!
Y... YEAH, YOU'RE RIGHT.
HONESTLY... HOW CAN WE LOOK LIKE A MATCH?
WHAM
亀類
FOO
OWW!
UGH
OH ...
...AH... ARE YOU ALL RIGHT?!
Y... YEAH.
NARU ...
AH...
BLUB BLUB
BLUB BLUB

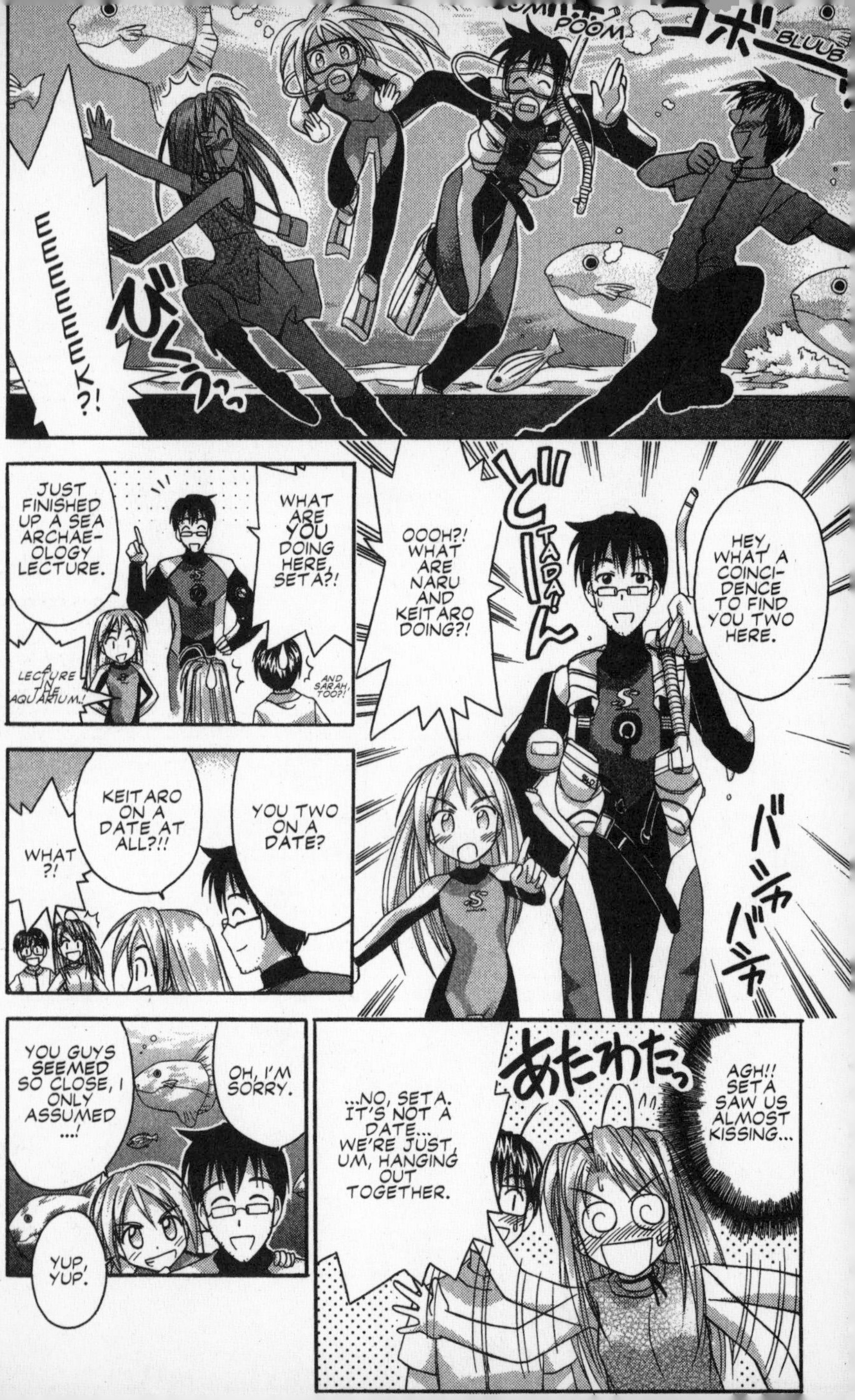
コポー
BLUUB
POOM
EEEEEEEEK?!
びくぅっ
HEY, WHAT A COINCIDENCE TO FIND YOU TWO HERE.
とーん
TADA
OOOH?! WHAT ARE NARU AND KEITARO DOING?!
バシャバシャ
WHAT ARE YOU DOING HERE, SETA?!
JUST FINISHED UP A SEA ARCHAEOLOGY LECTURE.
AND SARAH, TOO?!
A LECTURE IN THE AQUARIUM!
YOU TWO ON A DATE?
KEITARO ON A DATE AT ALL?!!
WHAT ?!
AGH!! SETA SAW US ALMOST KISSING...
あたわたっ
...NO, SETA. IT'S NOT A DATE... WE'RE JUST, UM, HANGING OUT TOGETHER.
OH, I'M SORRY.
YOU GUYS SEEMED SO CLOSE, I ONLY ASSUMED ...!
YUP, YUP.

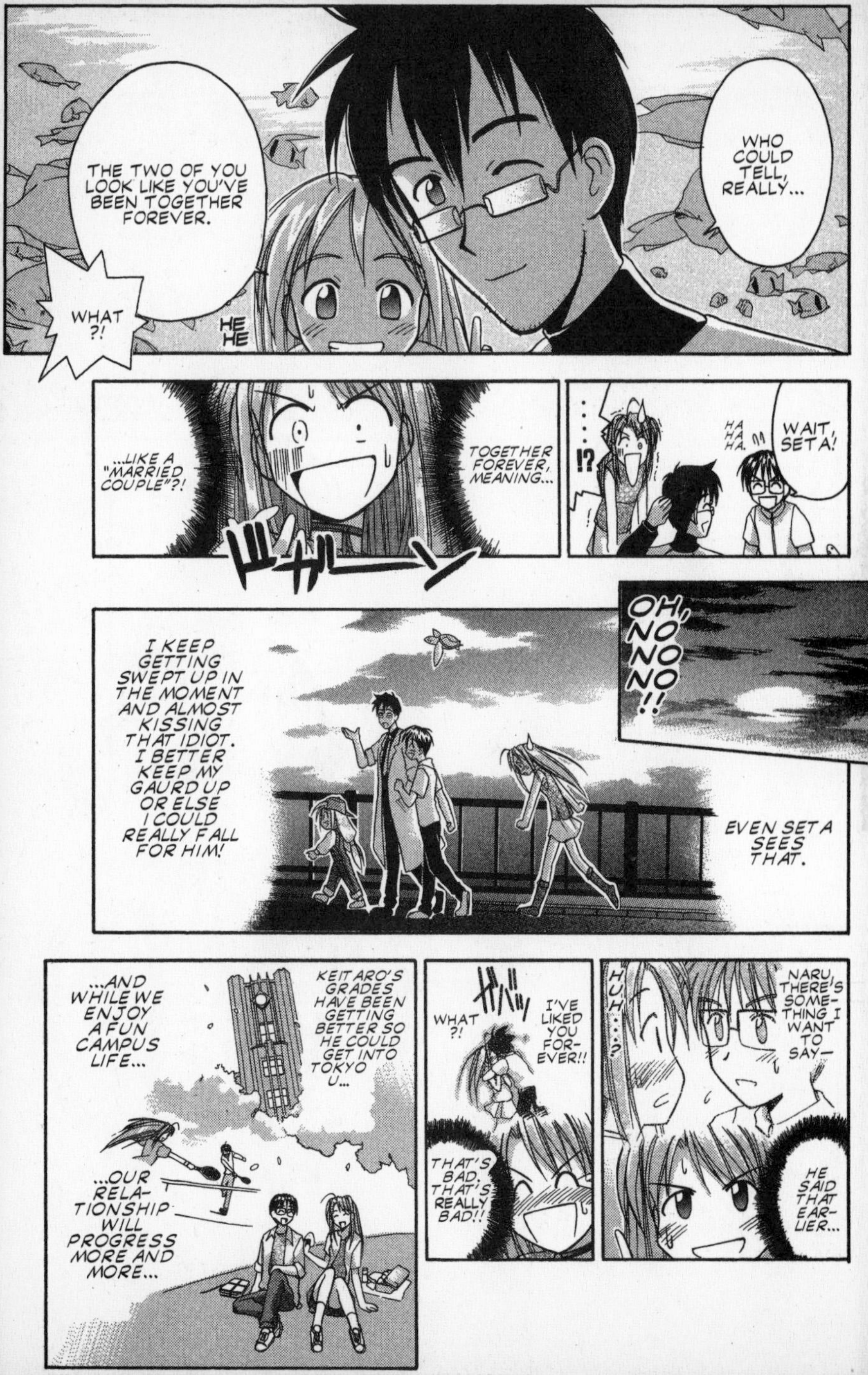
WHO COULD TELL, REALLY...
THE TWO OF YOU LOOK LIKE YOU'VE BEEN TOGETHER FOREVER.
HE HE
WHAT ?!
WAIT, SETA!
HA HA HA.
...!?
TOGETHER FOREVER, MEANING...
...LIKE A "MARRIED COUPLE"?!
ドガーン
OH, NO NO NO NO!!
EVEN SETA SEES THAT.
I KEEP GETTING SWEPT UP IN THE MOMENT AND ALMOST KISSING THAT IDIOT. I BETTER KEEP MY GAURD UP OR ELSE I COULD REALLY FALL FOR HIM!
NARU, THERE'S SOME-THING I WANT TO SAY—
HUH...?
HE SAID THAT EAR-LIER...
I'VE LIKED YOU FOR-EVER!!
ガバッ
WHAT ?!
THAT'S BAD. THAT'S REALLY BAD!!
KEITARO'S GRADES HAVE BEEN GETTING BETTER SO HE COULD GET INTO TOKYO U...
...AND WHILE WE ENJOY A FUN CAMPUS LIFE...
...OUR RELA-TIONSHIP WILL PROGRESS MORE AND MORE...

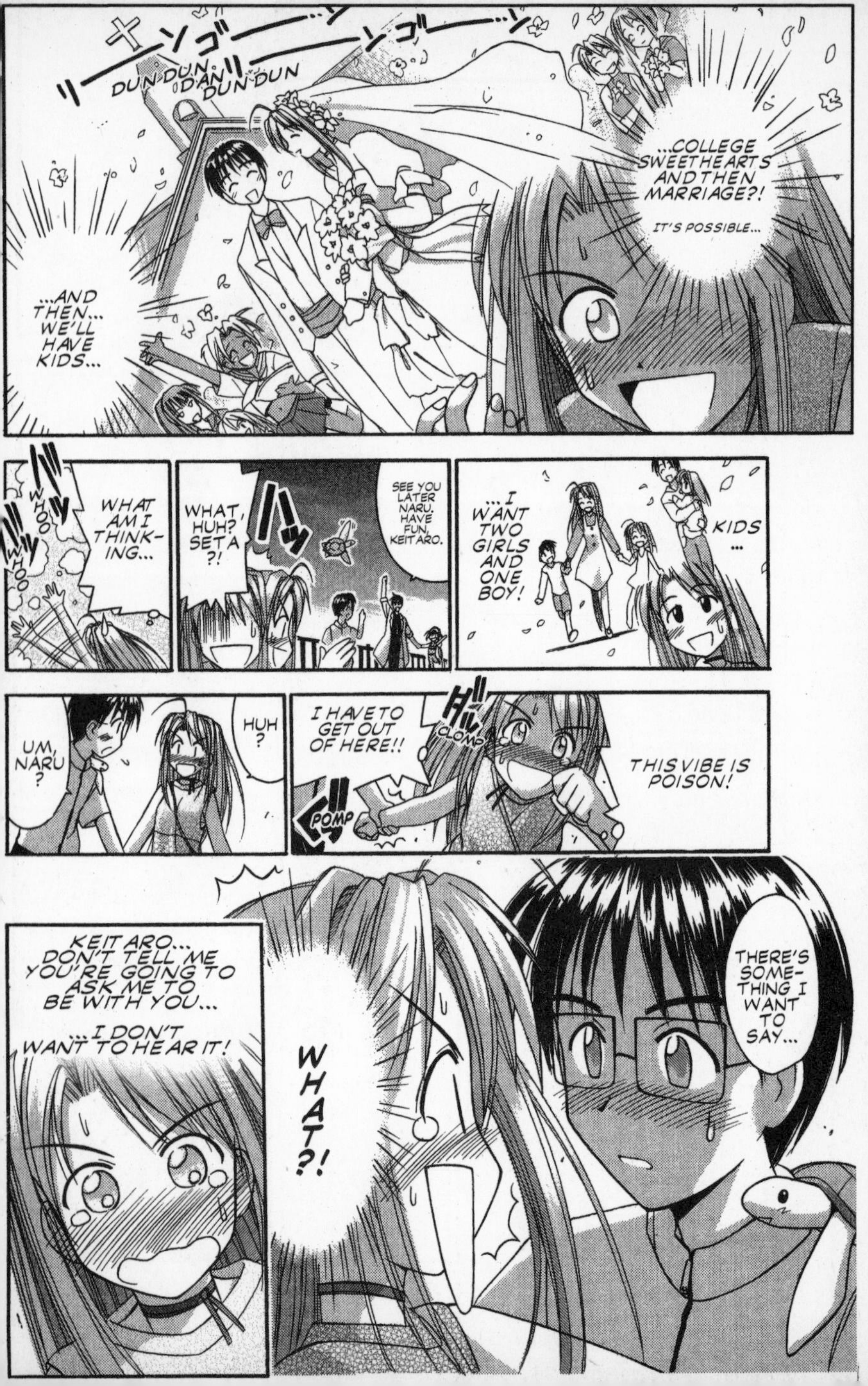
...COLLEGE SWEETHEARTS AND THEN MARRIAGE?!
IT'S POSSIBLE...
リーンゴーン リーンゴーン
DUN DUN DAN DUN DUN
...AND THEN... WE'LL HAVE KIDS...
...I WANT TWO GIRLS AND ONE BOY!
KIDS...
SEE YOU LATER NARU. HAVE FUN, KEITARO.
WHAT, HUH? SETA?!
WHAT AM I THINKING...
WHOOO
WHOOO
THIS VIBE IS POISON!
I HAVE TO GET OUT OF HERE!!
CLOMP
POMP
HUH?
UM, NARU?
THERE'S SOMETHING I WANT TO SAY...
WHAT?!
KEITARO... DON'T TELL ME YOU'RE GOING TO ASK ME TO BE WITH YOU...
...I DON'T WANT TO HEAR IT!

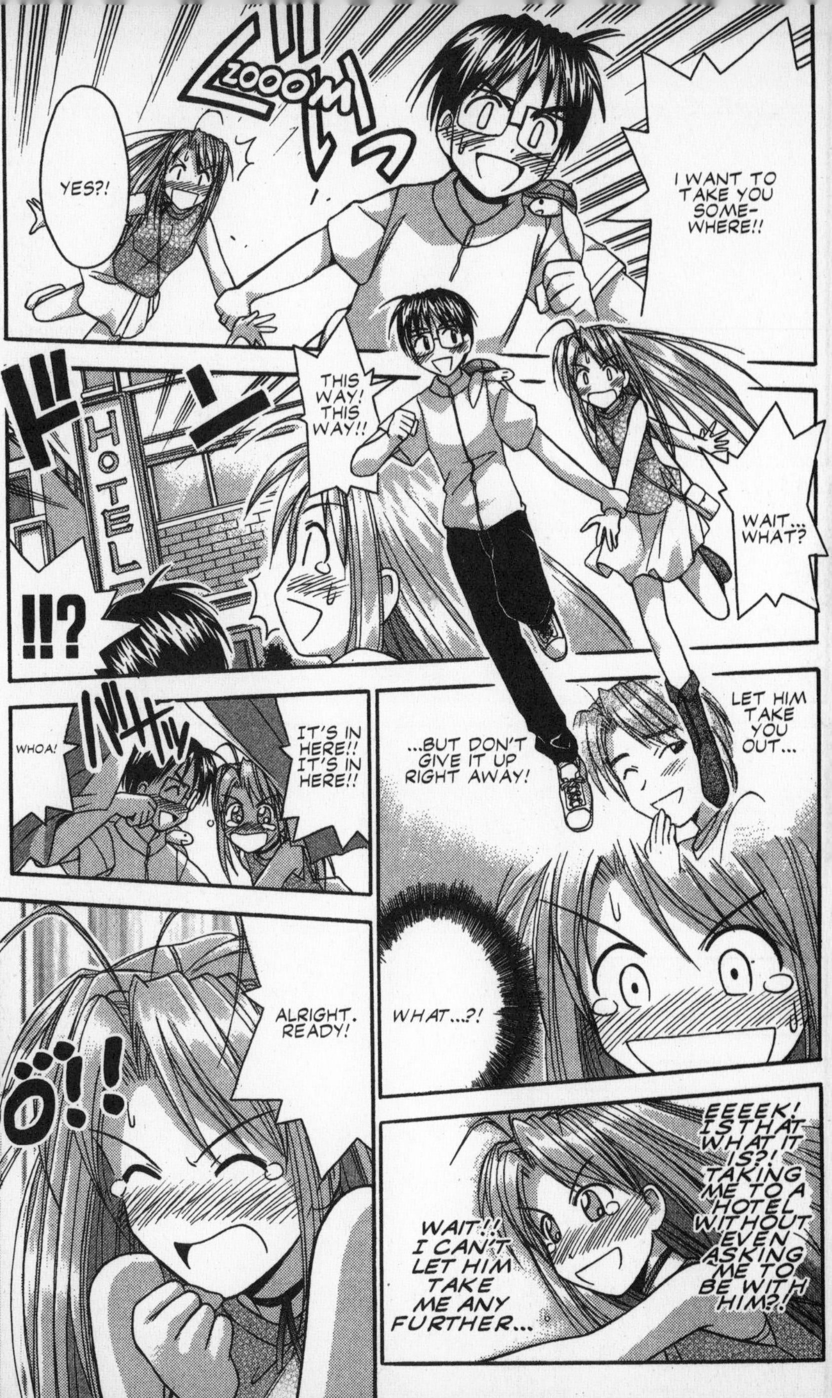
I WANT TO TAKE YOU SOME-WHERE!!
ZOOOM
YES?!
WAIT... WHAT?
THIS WAY! THIS WAY!!
HOTEL
!!?
LET HIM TAKE YOU OUT...
...BUT DON'T GIVE IT UP RIGHT AWAY!
IT'S IN HERE!! IT'S IN HERE!!
WHOA!
WHAT...?!
EEEEK! IS THAT WHAT IT IS?! TAKING ME TO A HOTEL WITHOUT EVEN ASKING ME TO BE WITH HIM?!
WAIT!! I CAN'T LET HIM TAKE ME ANY FURTHER...
ALRIGHT. READY!
NO!!

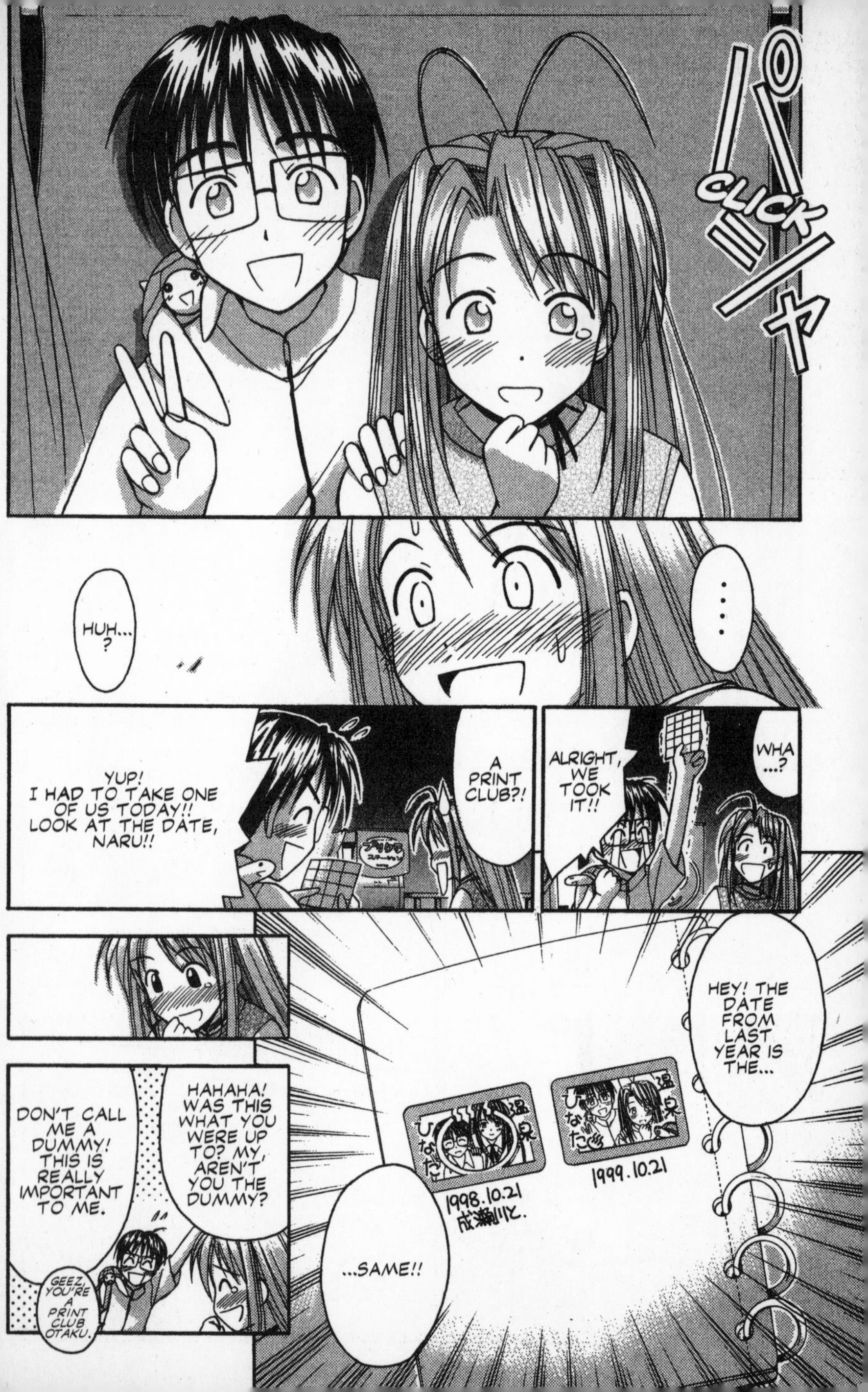
パシャ
CLICK
...
HUH...?
WHA...?
ALRIGHT, WE TOOK IT!!
A PRINT CLUB?!
YUP! I HAD TO TAKE ONE OF US TODAY!! LOOK AT THE DATE, NARU!!
HEY! THE DATE FROM LAST YEAR IS THE...
1999.10.21
1998.10.21
成瀬川と.
...SAME!!
HAHAHA! WAS THIS WHAT YOU WERE UP TO? MY, AREN'T YOU THE DUMMY?
DON'T CALL ME A DUMMY! THIS IS REALLY IMPORTANT TO ME.
GEEZ, YOU'RE A PRINT CLUB OTAKU.

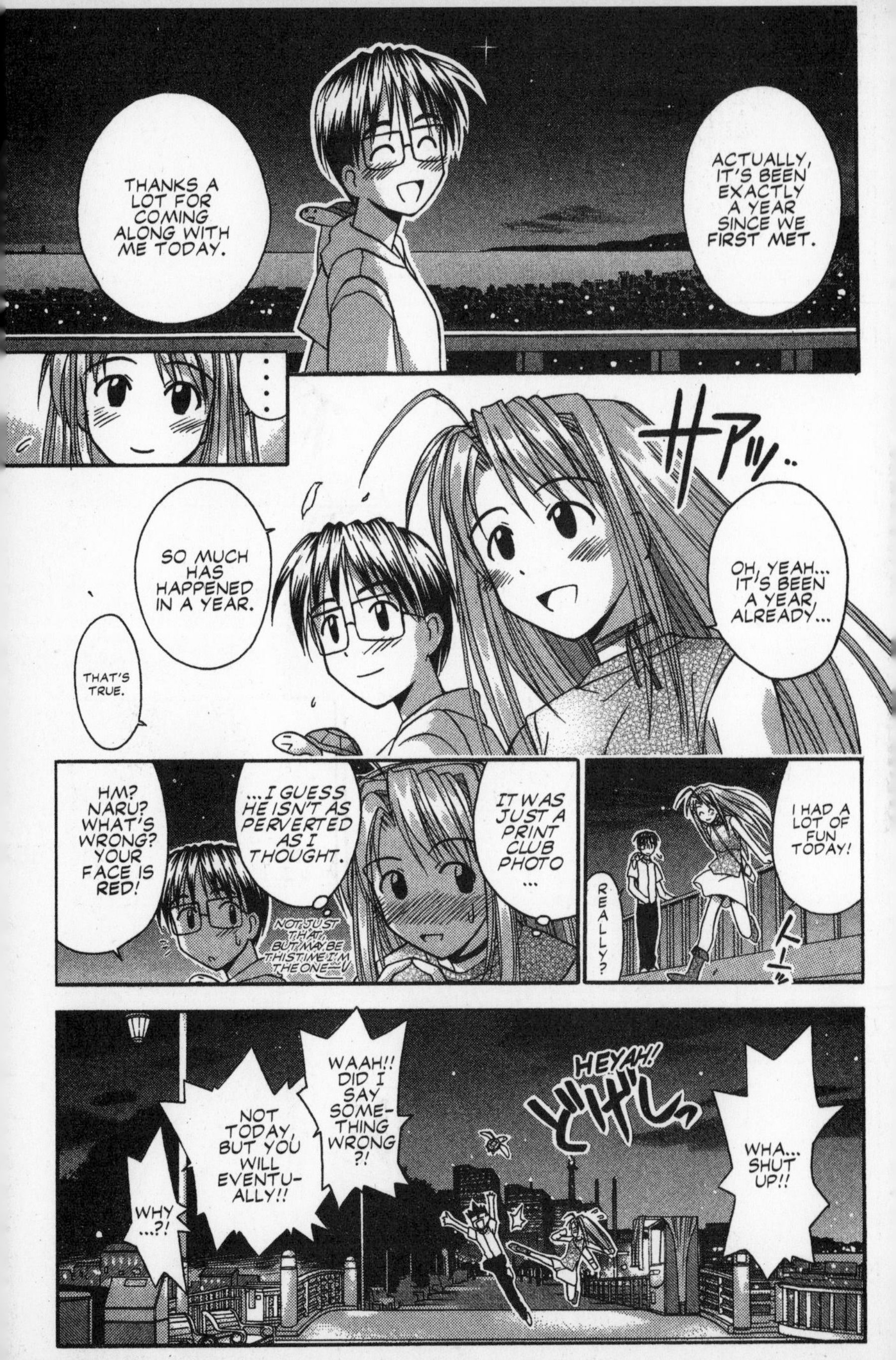
ACTUALLY, IT'S BEEN EXACTLY A YEAR SINCE WE FIRST MET.
THANKS A LOT FOR COMING ALONG WITH ME TODAY.
サァッ..
OH, YEAH... IT'S BEEN A YEAR, ALREADY...
SO MUCH HAS HAPPENED IN A YEAR.
THAT'S TRUE.
....
I HAD A LOT OF FUN TODAY!
REALLY?
トッ
IT WAS JUST A PRINT CLUB PHOTO ...
...I GUESS HE ISN'T AS PERVERTED AS I THOUGHT.
NOT JUST THAT, BUT MAYBE THIS TIME I'M THE ONE—
HM? NARU? WHAT'S WRONG? YOUR FACE IS RED!
WHA... SHUT UP!!
HEYAH!!
どげしっ
WAAH!! DID I SAY SOME-THING WRONG?!
NOT TODAY, BUT YOU WILL EVENTU-ALLY!!
WHY ...?!

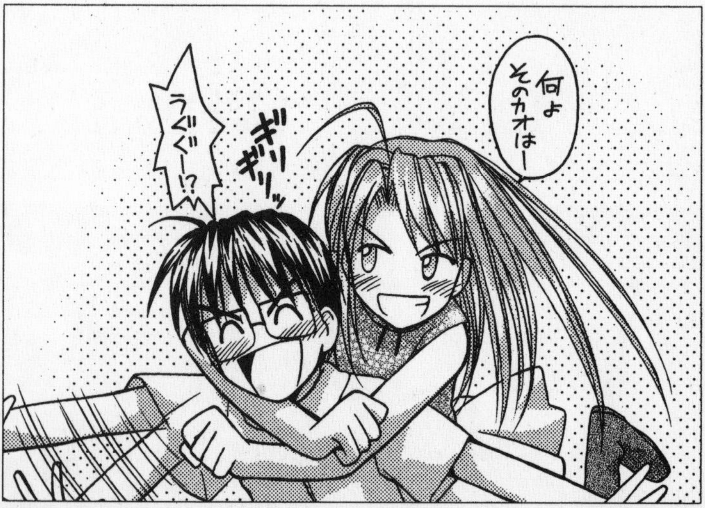
何よ
そのカオはー
ギリギリッ
うぐぐー!?

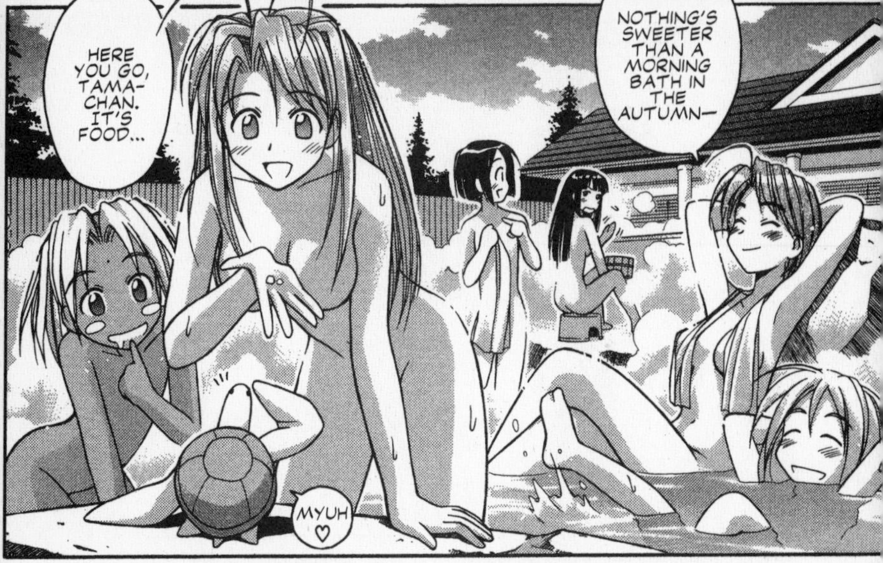
NOTHING'S SWEETER THAN A MORNING BATH IN THE AUTUMN—
HERE YOU GO, TAMA-CHAN. IT'S FOOD...
MYUH ♡

Love Hina

HINATA.45 The Sudden Goodbye...

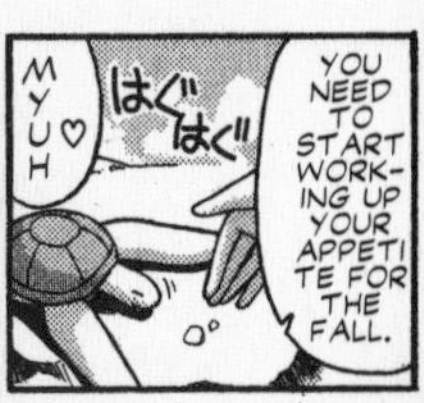
YOU NEED TO START WORKING UP YOUR APPETITE FOR THE FALL.
はぐはぐ
MYUH ♡

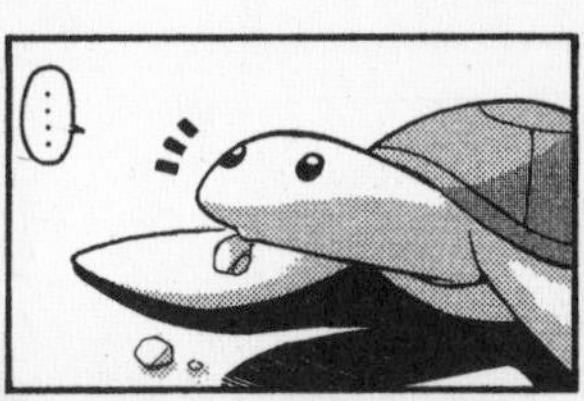
...

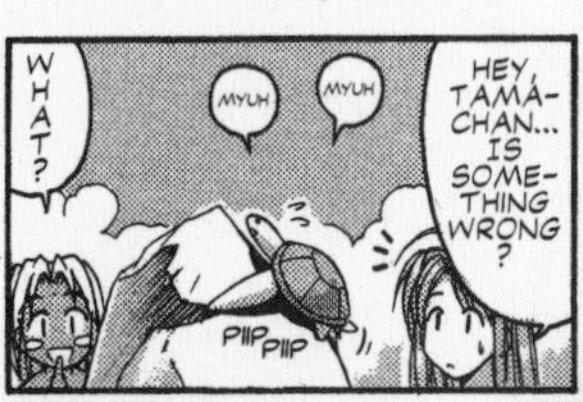
HEY, TAMA-CHAN... IS SOMETHING WRONG?
MYUH
MYUH
WHAT?
PIIP PIIP

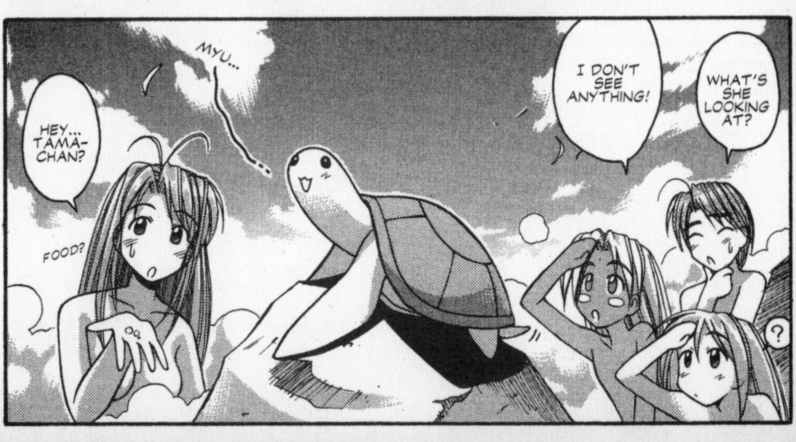
WHAT'S SHE LOOKING AT?
I DON'T SEE ANYTHING!
MYU...
HEY... TAMA-CHAN?
FOOD?
?

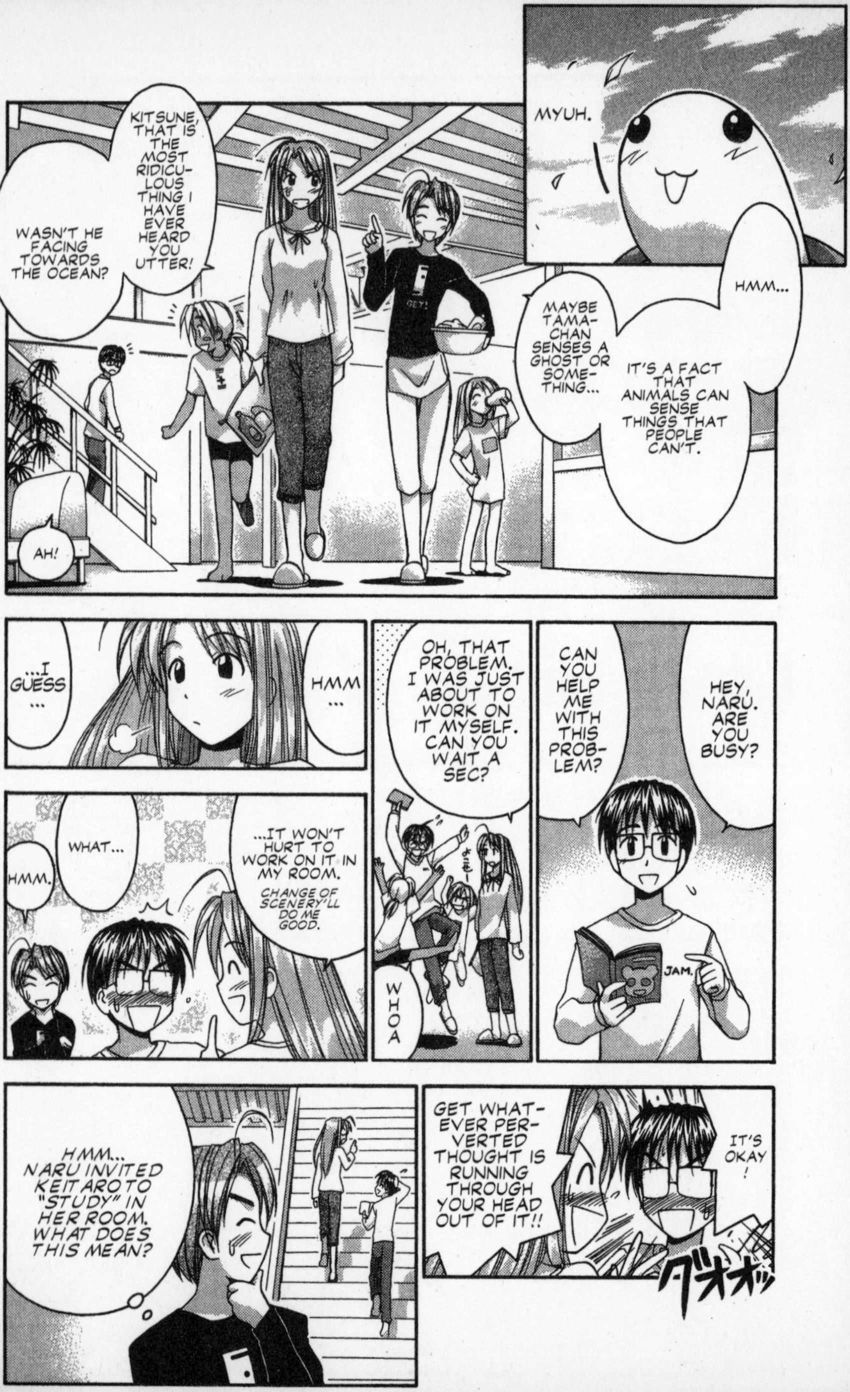
MYUH.
HMM...
IT'S A FACT THAT ANIMALS CAN SENSE THINGS THAT PEOPLE CAN'T.
MAYBE TAMA-CHAN SENSES A GHOST OR SOME-THING...
KITSUNE, THAT IS THE MOST RIDICU-LOUS THING I HAVE EVER HEARD YOU UTTER!
WASN'T HE FACING TOWARDS THE OCEAN?
AH!
HEY, NARU. ARE YOU BUSY?
CAN YOU HELP ME WITH THIS PROB-LEM?
JAM.
OH, THAT PROBLEM. I WAS JUST ABOUT TO WORK ON IT MYSELF. CAN YOU WAIT A SEC?
WHOA
HMM ...
...I GUESS ...
...IT WON'T HURT TO WORK ON IT IN MY ROOM.
CHANGE OF SCENERY'LL DO ME GOOD.
WHAT...
HMM.
IT'S OKAY!
GET WHAT-EVER PER-VERTED THOUGHT IS RUNNING THROUGH YOUR HEAD OUT OF IT!!
グオオッ
HMM... NARU INVITED KEITARO TO "STUDY" IN HER ROOM. WHAT DOES THIS MEAN?

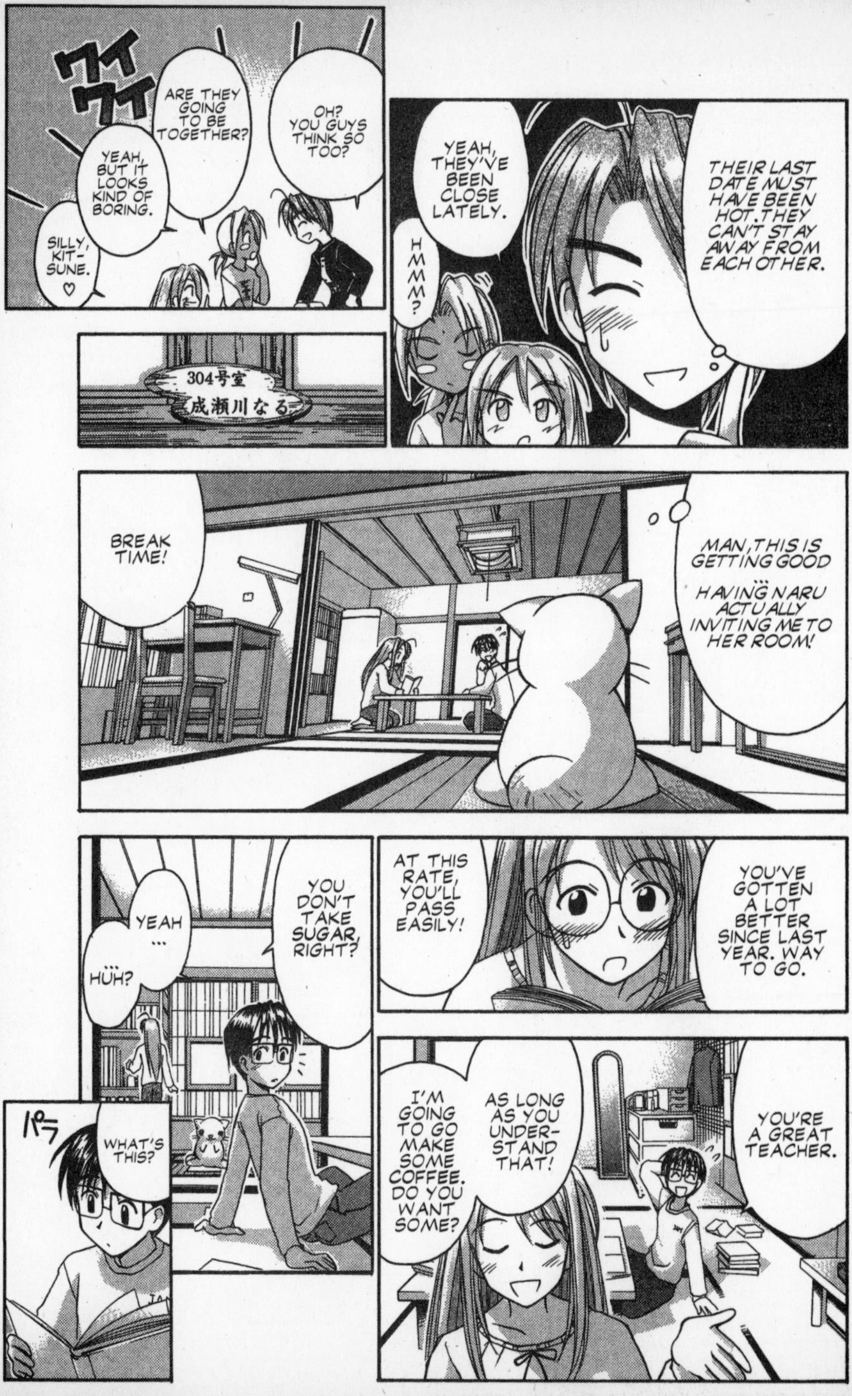
ワイワイ
ARE THEY GOING TO BE TOGETHER?
OH? YOU GUYS THINK SO TOO?
YEAH, BUT IT LOOKS KIND OF BORING.
SILLY, KIT-SUNE. ♡
THEIR LAST DATE MUST HAVE BEEN HOT. THEY CAN'T STAY AWAY FROM EACH OTHER.
YEAH, THEY'VE BEEN CLOSE LATELY.
HMMMM?
304号室
成瀬川なる
MAN, THIS IS GETTING GOOD
HAVING NARU ACTUALLY INVITING ME TO HER ROOM!
BREAK TIME!
YOU'VE GOTTEN A LOT BETTER SINCE LAST YEAR. WAY TO GO.
AT THIS RATE, YOU'LL PASS EASILY!
YOU'RE A GREAT TEACHER.
AS LONG AS YOU UNDER-STAND THAT!
I'M GOING TO GO MAKE SOME COFFEE. DO YOU WANT SOME?
YOU DON'T TAKE SUGAR, RIGHT?
YEAH ...
... HUH?
パラ
WHAT'S THIS?

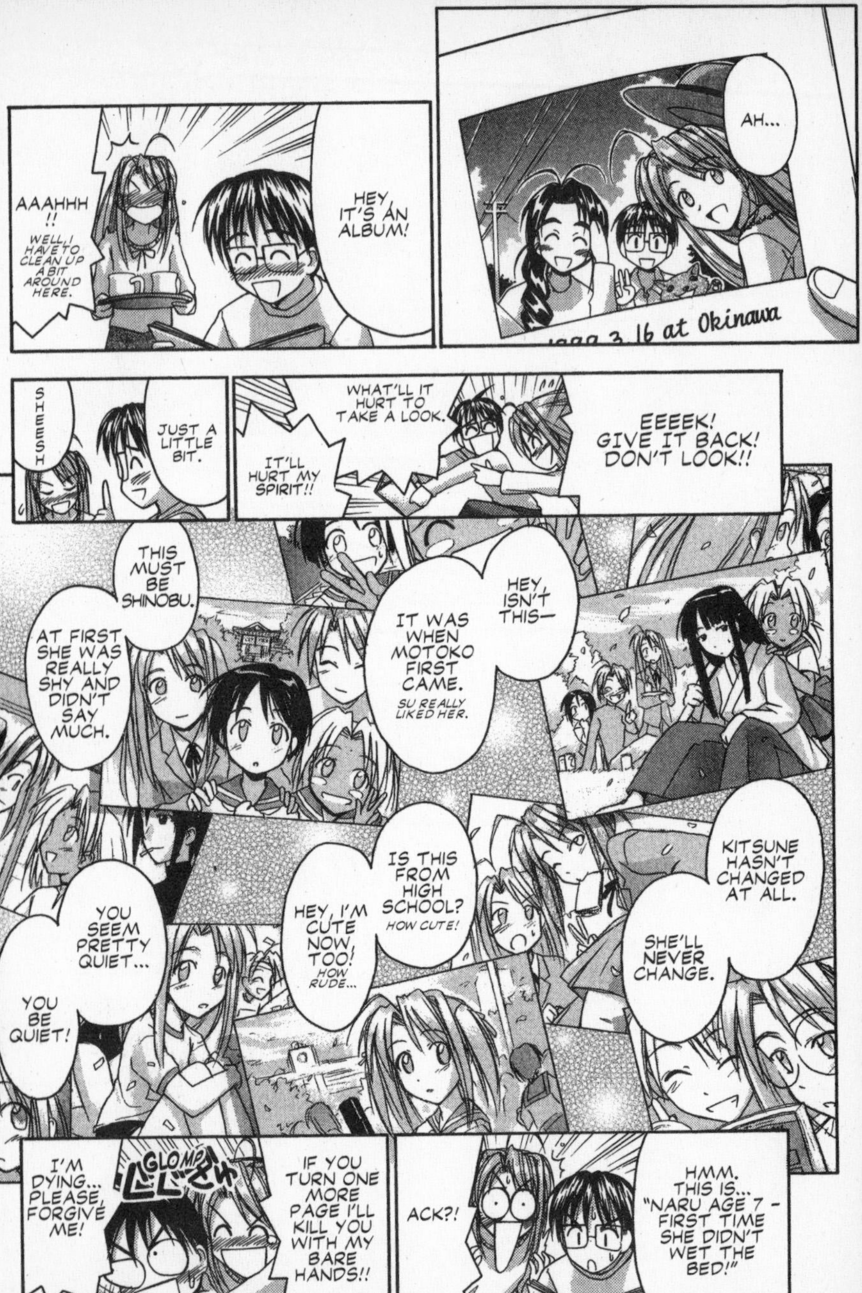
AH...
3.16 at Okinawa
HEY, IT'S AN ALBUM!
AAAHHH!!
WELL, I HAVE TO CLEAN UP A BIT AROUND HERE.
EEEEK! GIVE IT BACK! DON'T LOOK!!
WHAT'LL IT HURT TO TAKE A LOOK.
IT'LL HURT MY SPIRIT!!
JUST A LITTLE BIT.
SHEESH
HEY, ISN'T THIS—
IT WAS WHEN MOTOKO FIRST CAME.
SU REALLY LIKED HER.
THIS MUST BE SHINOBU.
AT FIRST SHE WAS REALLY SHY AND DIDN'T SAY MUCH.
KITSUNE HASN'T CHANGED AT ALL.
SHE'LL NEVER CHANGE.
IS THIS FROM HIGH SCHOOL?
HOW CUTE!
HEY, I'M CUTE NOW, TOO!
HOW RUDE...
YOU SEEM PRETTY QUIET...
YOU BE QUIET!
HMM. THIS IS... "NARU AGE 7 - FIRST TIME SHE DIDN'T WET THE BED!"
ACK?!
IF YOU TURN ONE MORE PAGE I'LL KILL YOU WITH MY BARE HANDS!!
GLOMP
I'M DYING... PLEASE, FORGIVE ME!

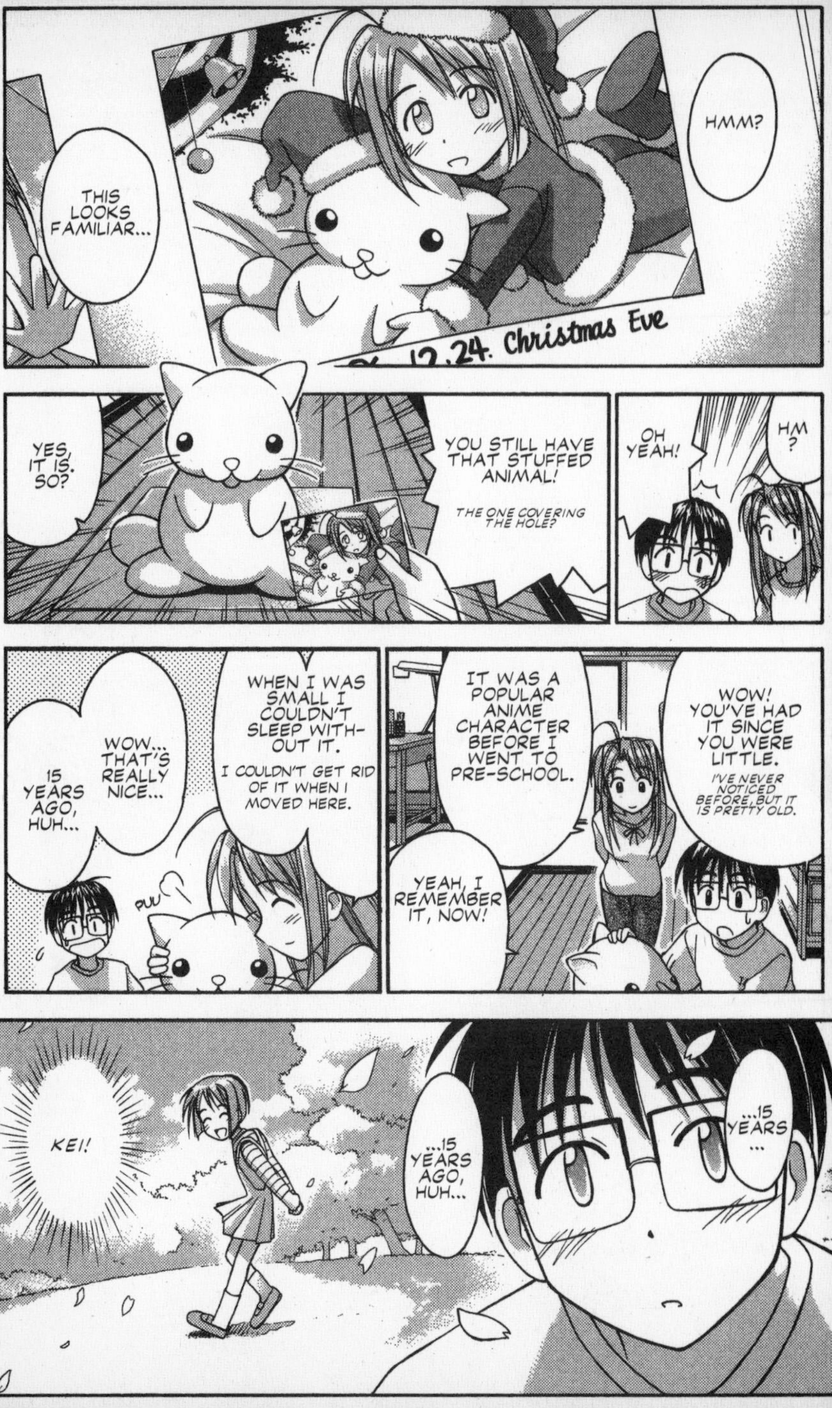
HMM?
THIS LOOKS FAMILIAR...
12.24. Christmas Eve
HM?
OH YEAH!
YOU STILL HAVE THAT STUFFED ANIMAL!
THE ONE COVERING THE HOLE?
YES, IT IS. SO?
WOW! YOU'VE HAD IT SINCE YOU WERE LITTLE.
I'VE NEVER NOTICED BEFORE, BUT IT IS PRETTY OLD.
IT WAS A POPULAR ANIME CHARACTER BEFORE I WENT TO PRE-SCHOOL.
YEAH, I REMEMBER IT, NOW!
WHEN I WAS SMALL I COULDN'T SLEEP WITH-OUT IT.
I COULDN'T GET RID OF IT WHEN I MOVED HERE.
WOW... THAT'S REALLY NICE...
15 YEARS AGO, HUH...
PUU
...15 YEARS...
...15 YEARS AGO, HUH...
KEI!

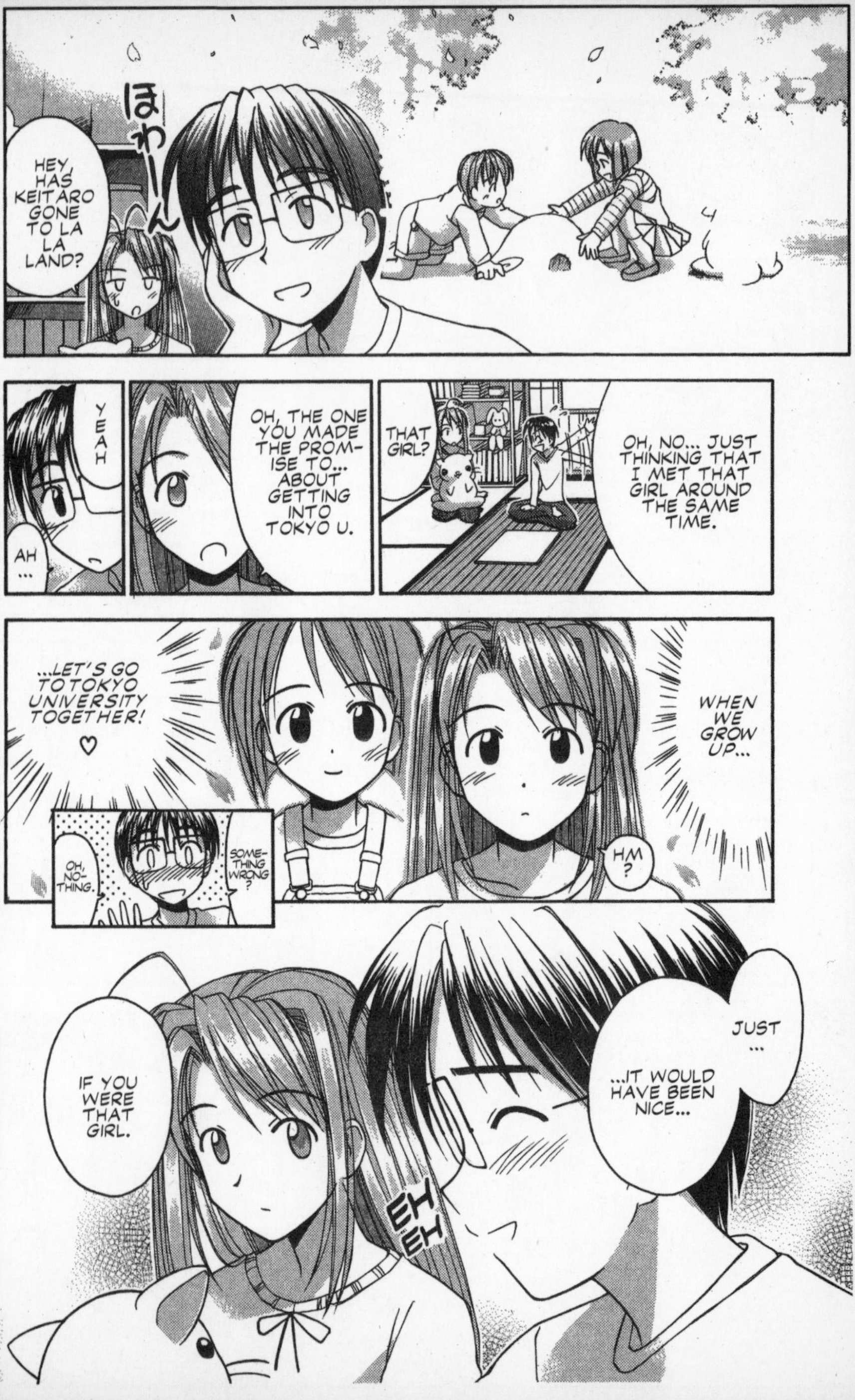
ほわーん
HEY, HAS KEITARO GONE TO LA LA LAND?
OH, NO... JUST THINKING THAT I MET THAT GIRL AROUND THE SAME TIME.
THAT GIRL?
OH, THE ONE YOU MADE THE PROMISE TO... ABOUT GETTING INTO TOKYO U.
YEAH
AH ...
WHEN WE GROW UP...
...LET'S GO TO TOKYO UNIVERSITY TOGETHER! ♡
HM ?
SOME-THING WRONG ?
OH, NO-THING.
JUST ...
...IT WOULD HAVE BEEN NICE...
EH EH
IF YOU WERE THAT GIRL.

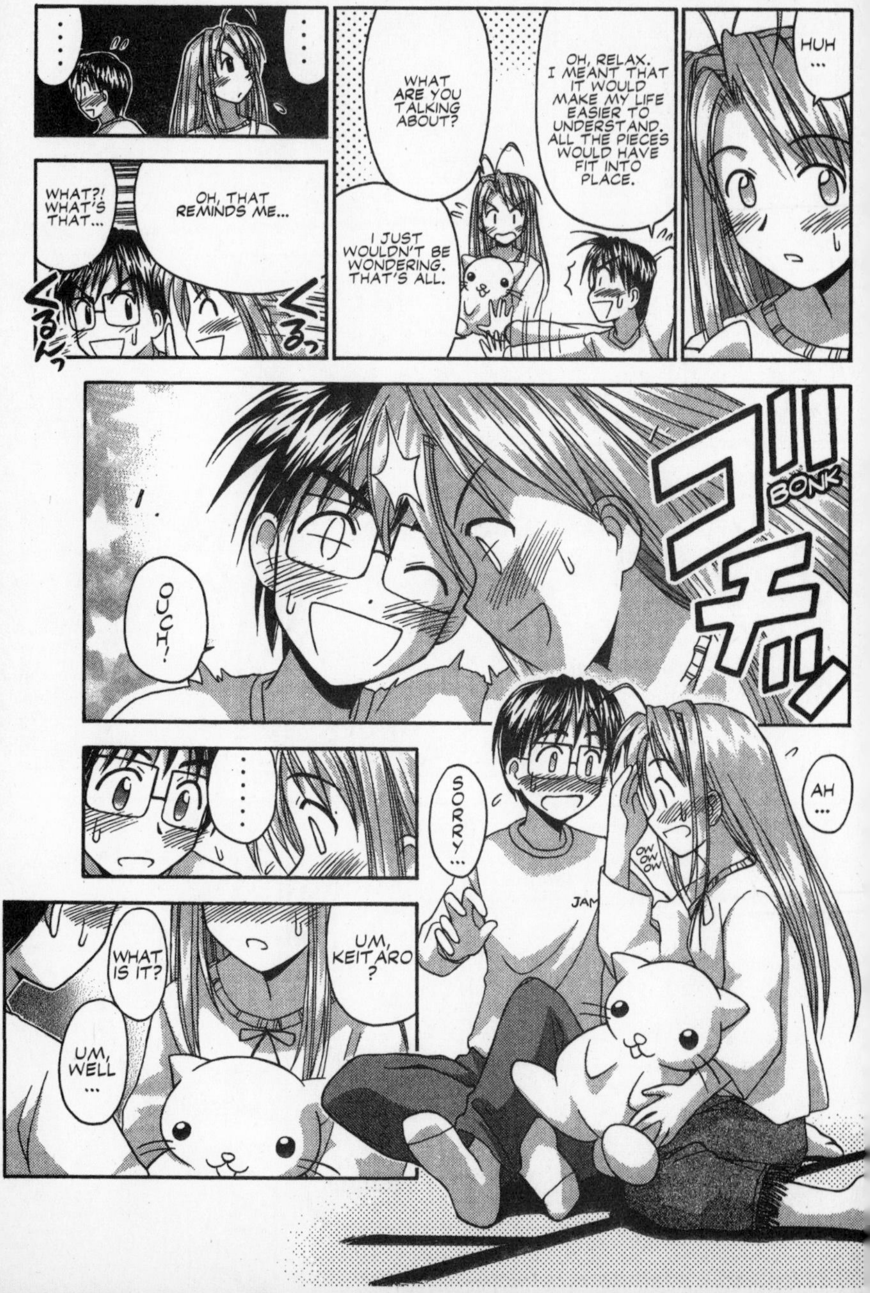
HUH ...
OH, RELAX. I MEANT THAT IT WOULD MAKE MY LIFE EASIER TO UNDERSTAND. ALL THE PIECES WOULD HAVE FIT INTO PLACE.
WHAT ARE YOU TALKING ABOUT?
I JUST WOULDN'T BE WONDERING. THAT'S ALL.
....
....
OH, THAT REMINDS ME...
WHAT?! WHAT'S THAT...
くるっ
くるんっ
ゴチッ
BONK
!
OUCH!
AH ...
OW OW OW
SORRY...
......
UM, KEITARO ?
WHAT IS IT?
UM, WELL ...

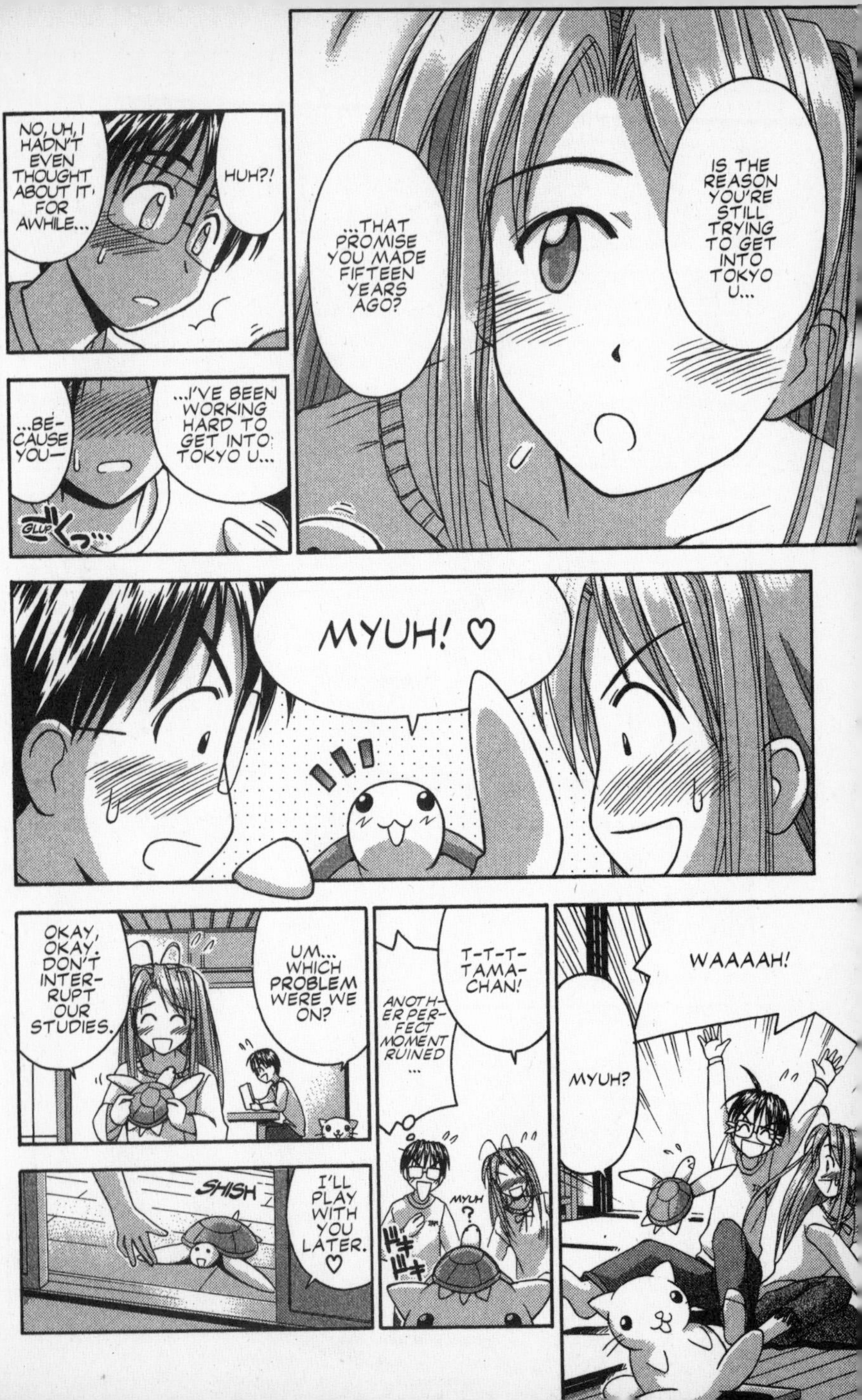
IS THE REASON YOU'RE STILL TRYING TO GET INTO TOKYO U...
...THAT PROMISE YOU MADE FIFTEEN YEARS AGO?
HUH?!
NO, UH, I HADN'T EVEN THOUGHT ABOUT IT FOR AWHILE...
...I'VE BEEN WORKING HARD TO GET INTO TOKYO U...
...BE-CAUSE YOU—
GLUP
MYUH! ♡
WAAAAH!
MYUH?
T-T-T-TAMA-CHAN!
ANOTHER PERFECT MOMENT RUINED...
MYUH ?
UM... WHICH PROBLEM WERE WE ON?
OKAY, OKAY. DON'T INTERRUPT OUR STUDIES.
I'LL PLAY WITH YOU LATER. ♡
SHISH

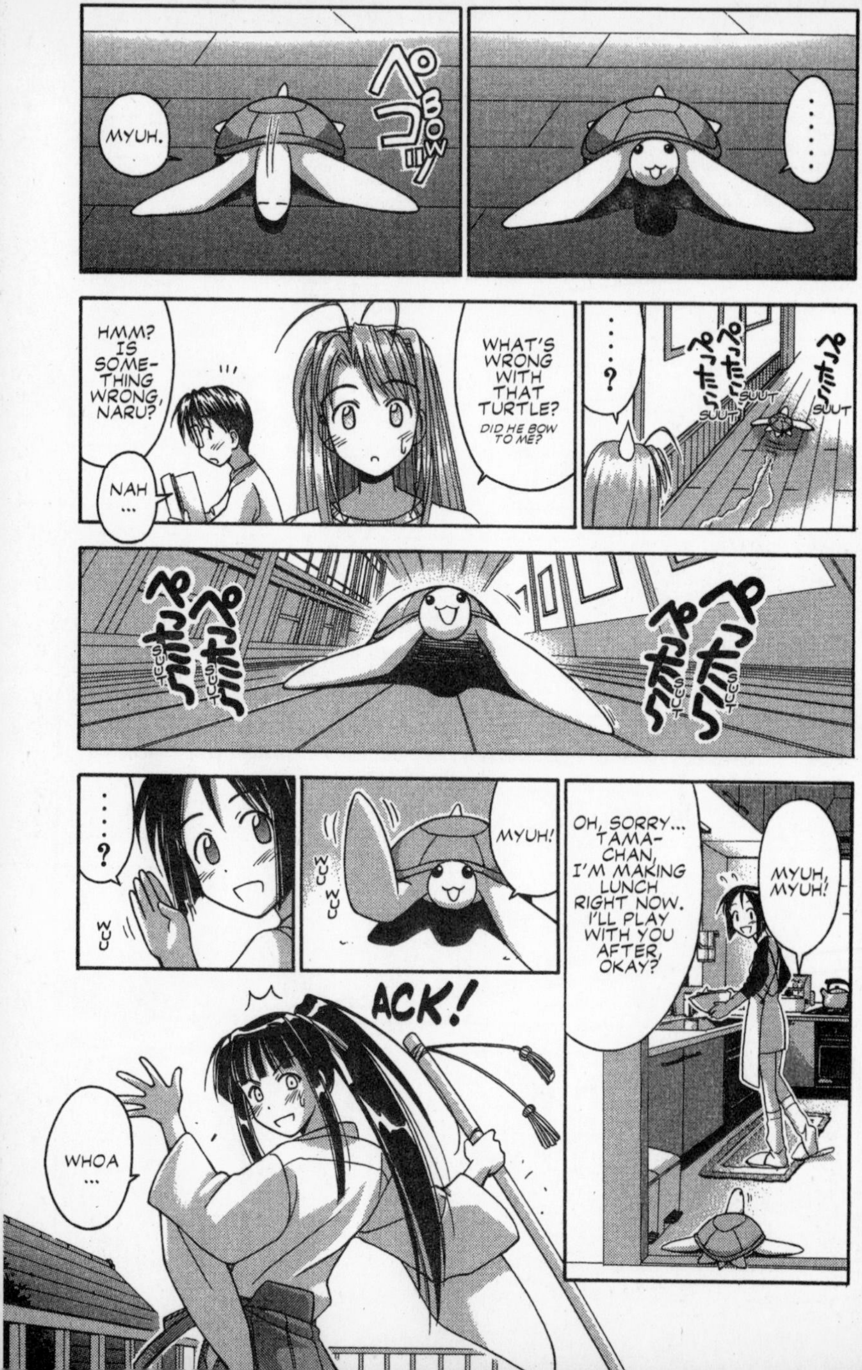
......
ペコ
BOW
MYUH.
....?
ぺったら
SUUT
ぺったら
SUUT
ぺったら
SUUT
WHAT'S WRONG WITH THAT TURTLE?
DID HE BOW TO ME?
HMM? IS SOME-THING WRONG, NARU?
NAH ...
ぺったら
SUUT
ぺったら
SUUT
ぺったら
SUUT
ぺったら
SUUT
MYUH, MYUH!
OH, SORRY... TAMA-CHAN, I'M MAKING LUNCH RIGHT NOW. I'LL PLAY WITH YOU AFTER, OKAY?
MYUH!
WUU WUU
....?
WUU
ACK!
WHOA ...

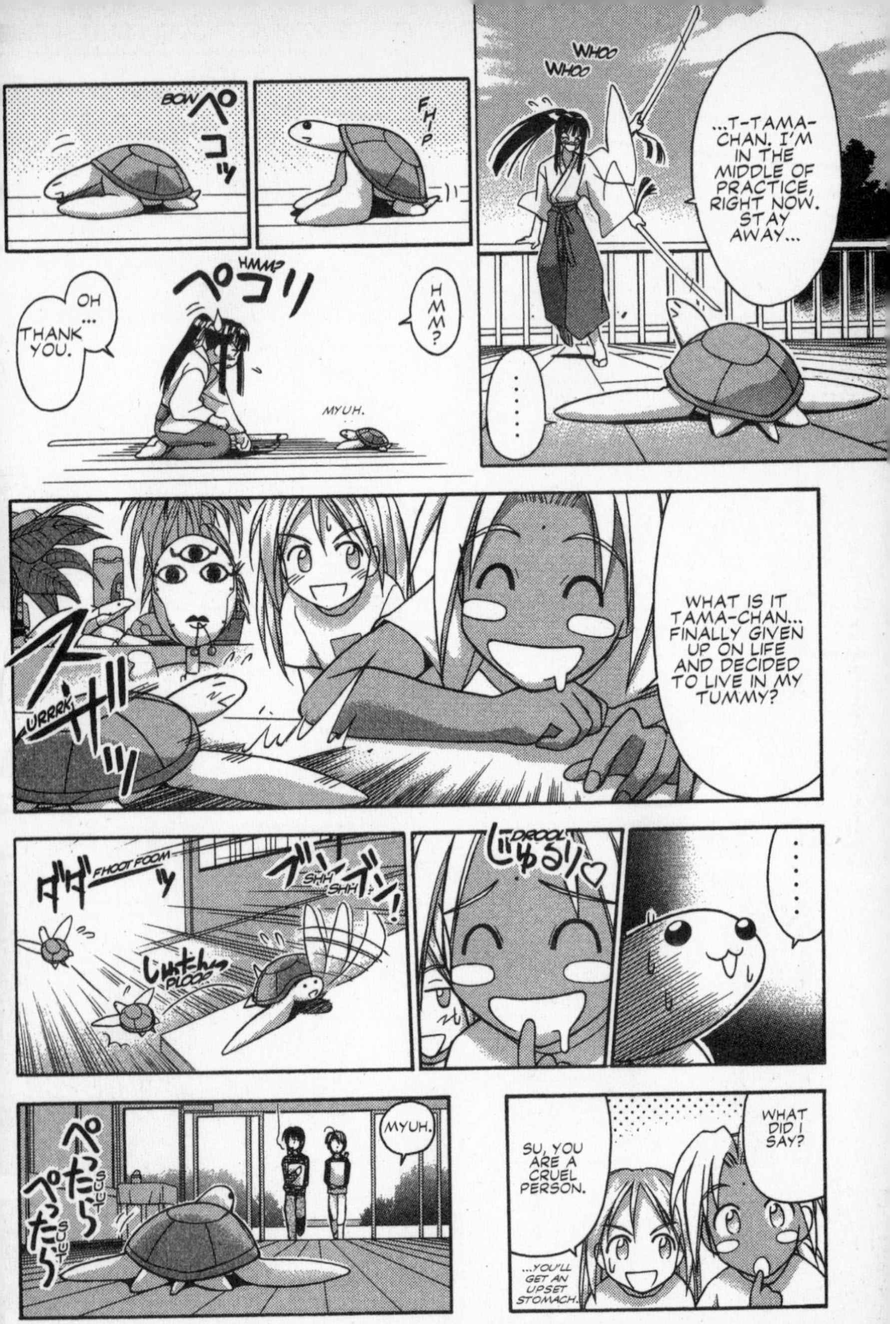
WHOO
WHOO
...T-TAMA-CHAN. I'M IN THE MIDDLE OF PRACTICE, RIGHT NOW. STAY AWAY...
......
FHIP
BON ペコッ
ペコリ HMM?
HMM?
OH... THANK YOU.
MYUH.
WHAT IS IT TAMA-CHAN... FINALLY GIVEN UP ON LIFE AND DECIDED TO LIVE IN MY TUMMY?
URRRK ザッ
......
じゅるり♡ DROOL
ブンブン! SHH SHH
ダダッ FHOOT FOOM
PLOOP
WHAT DID I SAY?
SU, YOU ARE A CRUEL PERSON.
...YOU'LL GET AN UPSET STOMACH.
MYUH.
ぺったらぺったら SUUT SUUT

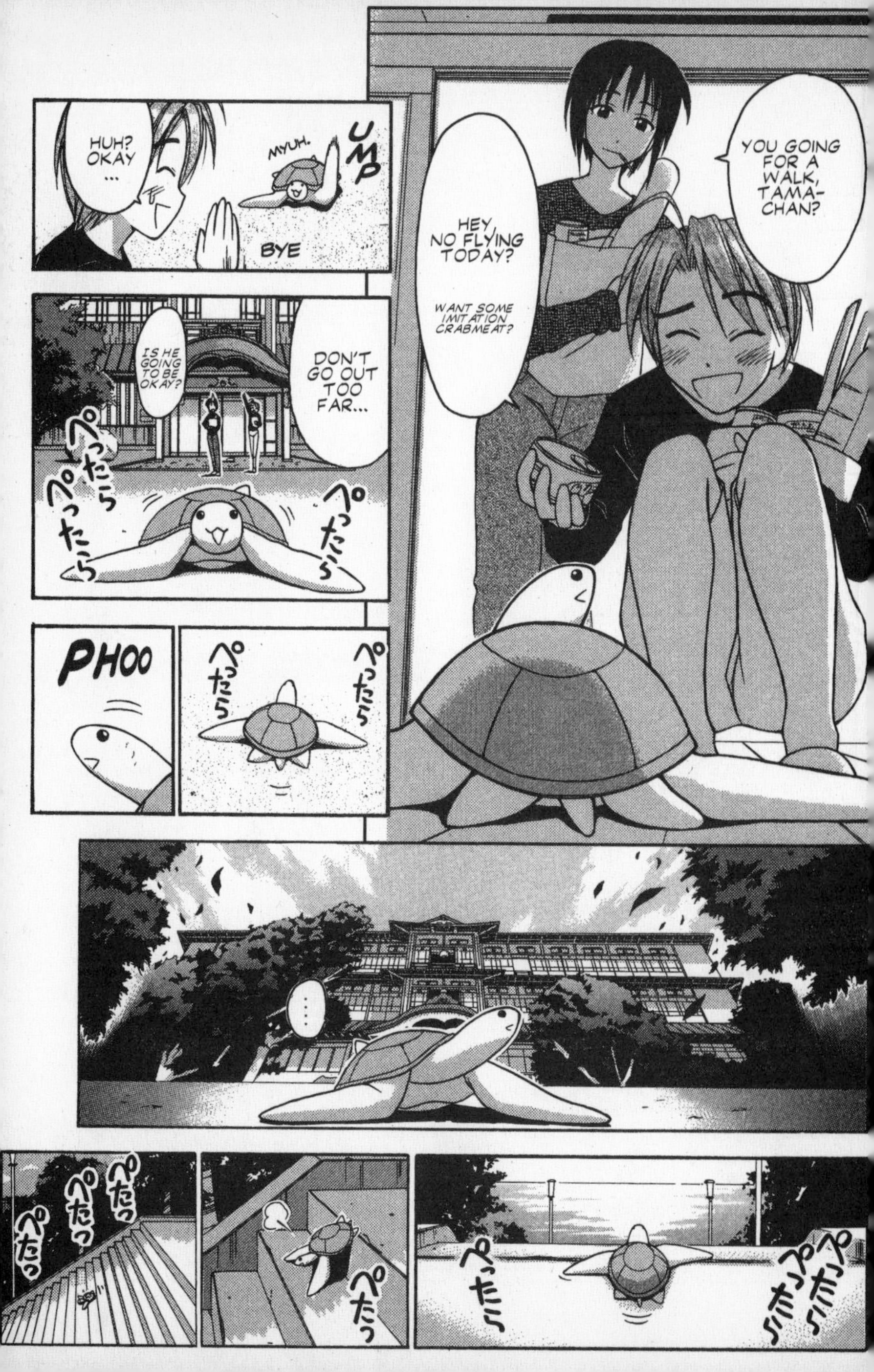
YOU GOING FOR A WALK, TAMA-CHAN?
HEY, NO FLYING TODAY?
WANT SOME IMITATION CRABMEAT?
UMP
MYUH.
HUH? OKAY ...
BYE
DON'T GO OUT TOO FAR...
IS HE GOING TO BE OKAY?
ぺったら
ぺったら
ぺったら
ぺったら
ぺったら
PHOO
....
ぺったら
ぺったら
ぺったら
ぺたっ
ぺたっ
ぺたっ
ぺたっ

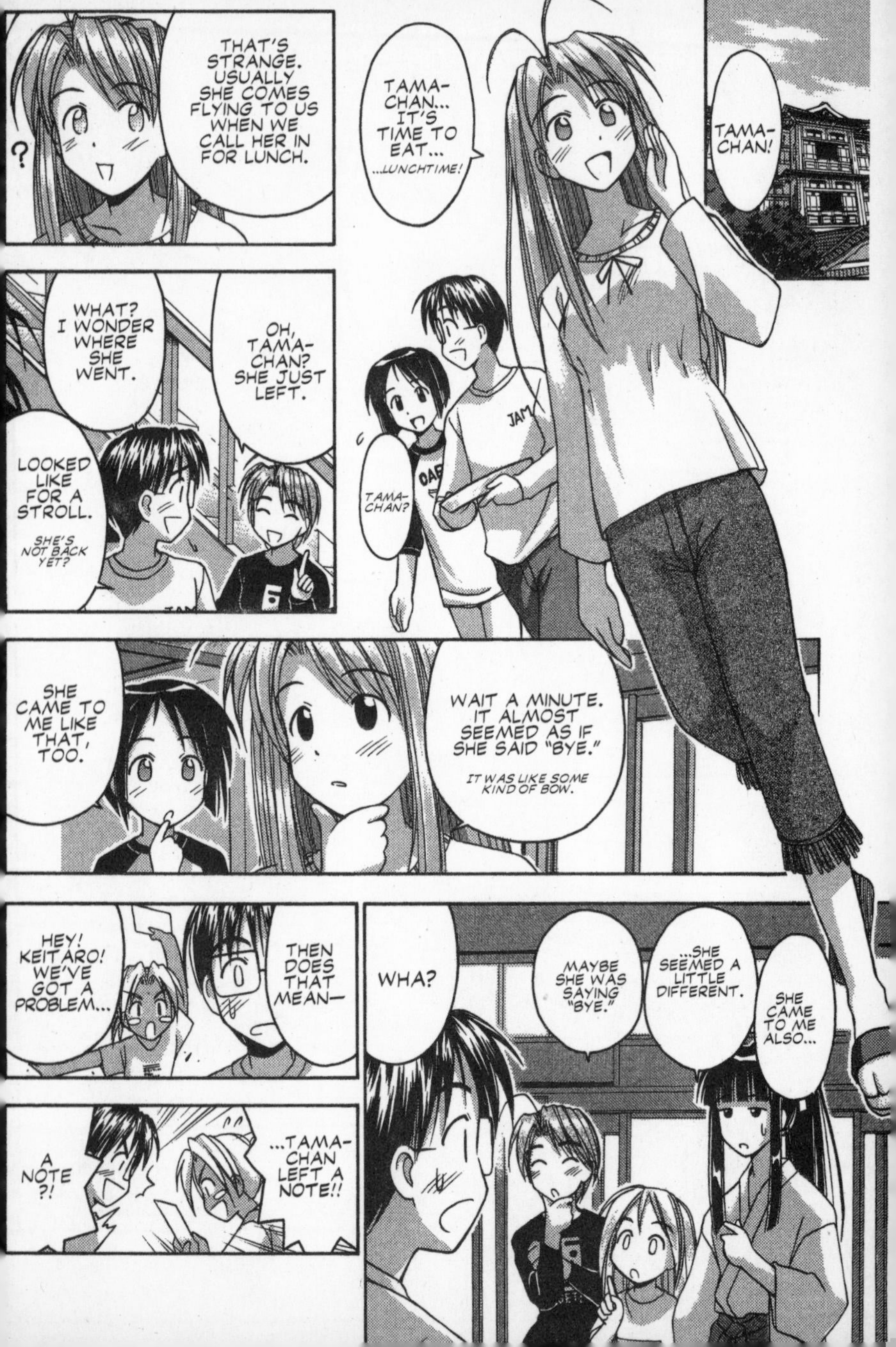
TAMA-CHAN!
TAMA-CHAN... IT'S TIME TO EAT...
...LUNCHTIME!
TAMA-CHAN?
THAT'S STRANGE. USUALLY SHE COMES FLYING TO US WHEN WE CALL HER IN FOR LUNCH.
?
OH, TAMA-CHAN? SHE JUST LEFT.
WHAT? I WONDER WHERE SHE WENT.
LOOKED LIKE FOR A STROLL.
SHE'S NOT BACK YET?
WAIT A MINUTE. IT ALMOST SEEMED AS IF SHE SAID "BYE."
IT WAS LIKE SOME KIND OF BOW.
SHE CAME TO ME LIKE THAT, TOO.
SHE CAME TO ME ALSO...
...SHE SEEMED A LITTLE DIFFERENT.
MAYBE SHE WAS SAYING "BYE."
WHA?
THEN DOES THAT MEAN—
HEY! KEITARO! WE'VE GOT A PROBLEM...
...TAMA-CHAN LEFT A NOTE!!
A NOTE?!

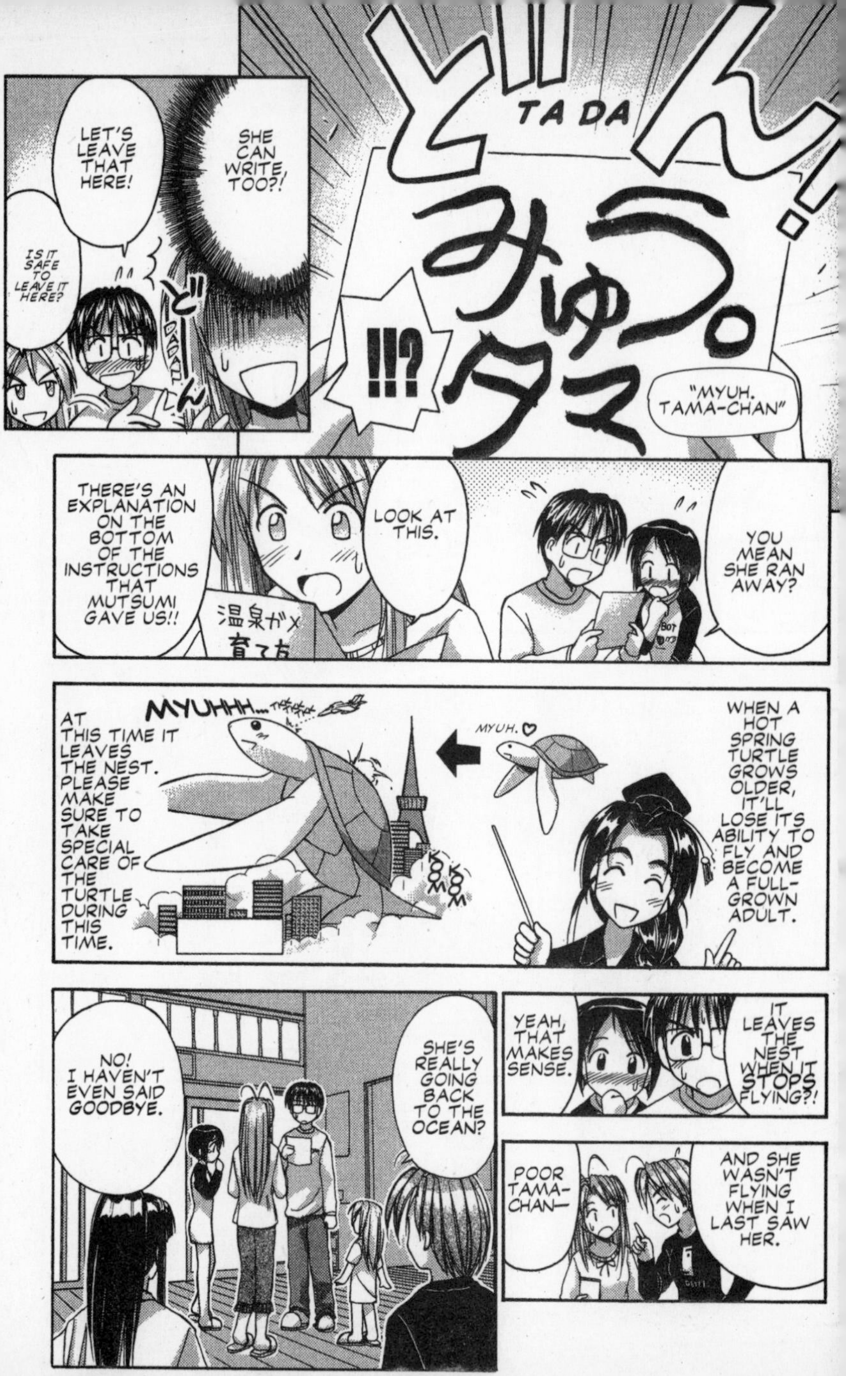
TA DA
どん!
みゅう。タマ
"MYUH. TAMA-CHAN"
!!?
SHE CAN WRITE, TOO?!
LET'S LEAVE THAT HERE!
IS IT SAFE TO LEAVE IT HERE?
DADA
YOU MEAN SHE RAN AWAY?
LOOK AT THIS.
THERE'S AN EXPLANATION ON THE BOTTOM OF THE INSTRUCTIONS THAT MUTSUMI GAVE US!!
温泉ガメ育て方
WHEN A HOT SPRING TURTLE GROWS OLDER, IT'LL LOSE ITS ABILITY TO FLY AND BECOME A FULL-GROWN ADULT.
MYUH.
MYUHHH...
AT THIS TIME IT LEAVES THE NEST. PLEASE MAKE SURE TO TAKE SPECIAL CARE OF THE TURTLE DURING THIS TIME.
KOM KOM
IT LEAVES THE NEST WHEN IT STOPS FLYING?!
YEAH, THAT MAKES SENSE.
AND SHE WASN'T FLYING WHEN I LAST SAW HER.
POOR TAMA-CHAN—
SHE'S REALLY GOING BACK TO THE OCEAN?
NO! I HAVEN'T EVEN SAID GOODBYE.

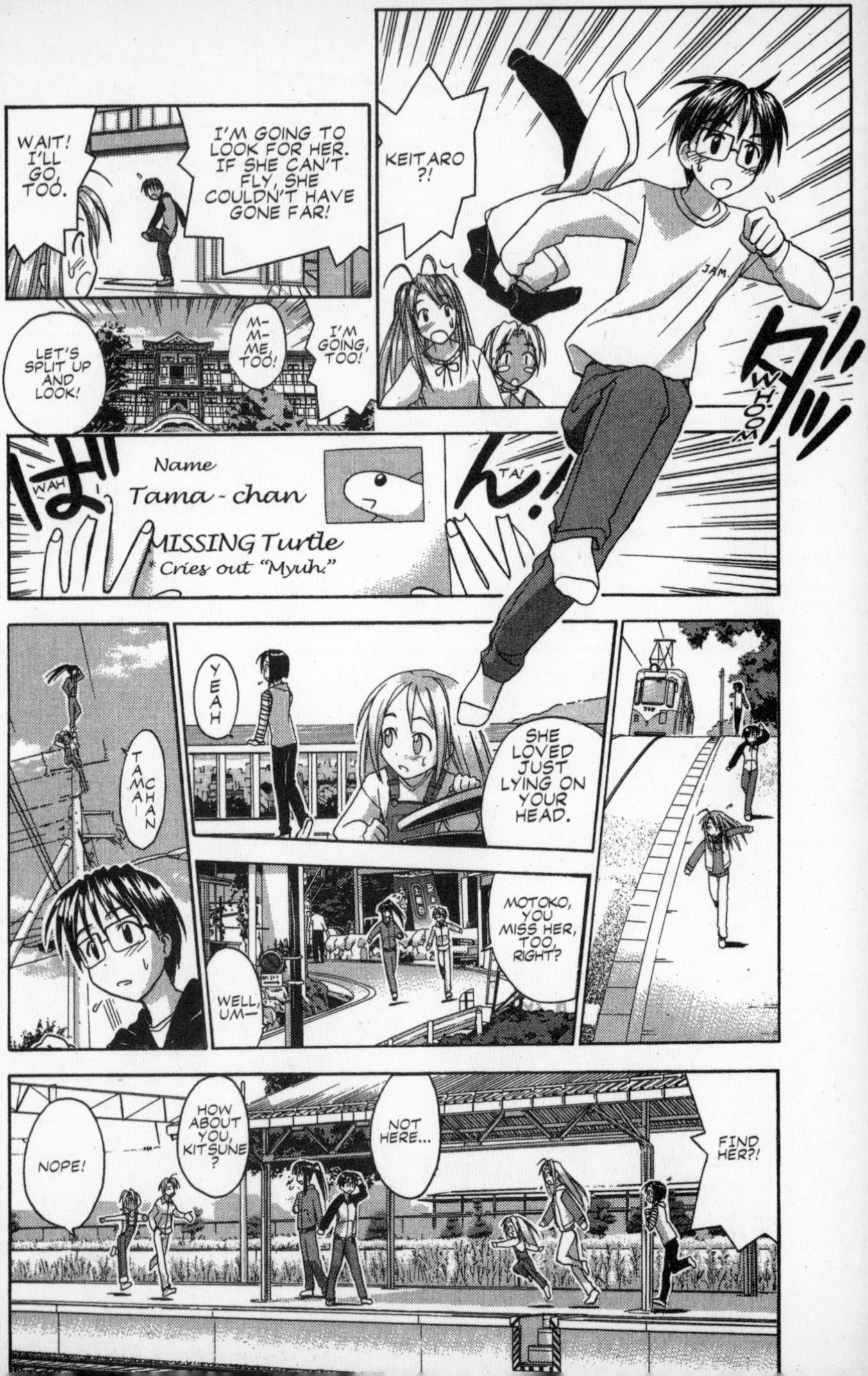
KEITARO ?!
WHOOM
I'M GOING TO LOOK FOR HER. IF SHE CAN'T FLY, SHE COULDN'T HAVE GONE FAR!
WAIT! I'LL GO, TOO.
I'M GOING, TOO!
M-M-ME, TOO!
LET'S SPLIT UP AND LOOK!
TA
Name
Tama-chan
MISSING Turtle
* Cries out "Myuh."
WAH
SHE LOVED JUST LYING ON YOUR HEAD.
YEAH
TAMA-CHAN
MOTOKO, YOU MISS HER, TOO, RIGHT?
WELL, UM—
FIND HER?!
NOT HERE...
HOW ABOUT YOU, KITSUNE?
NOPE!

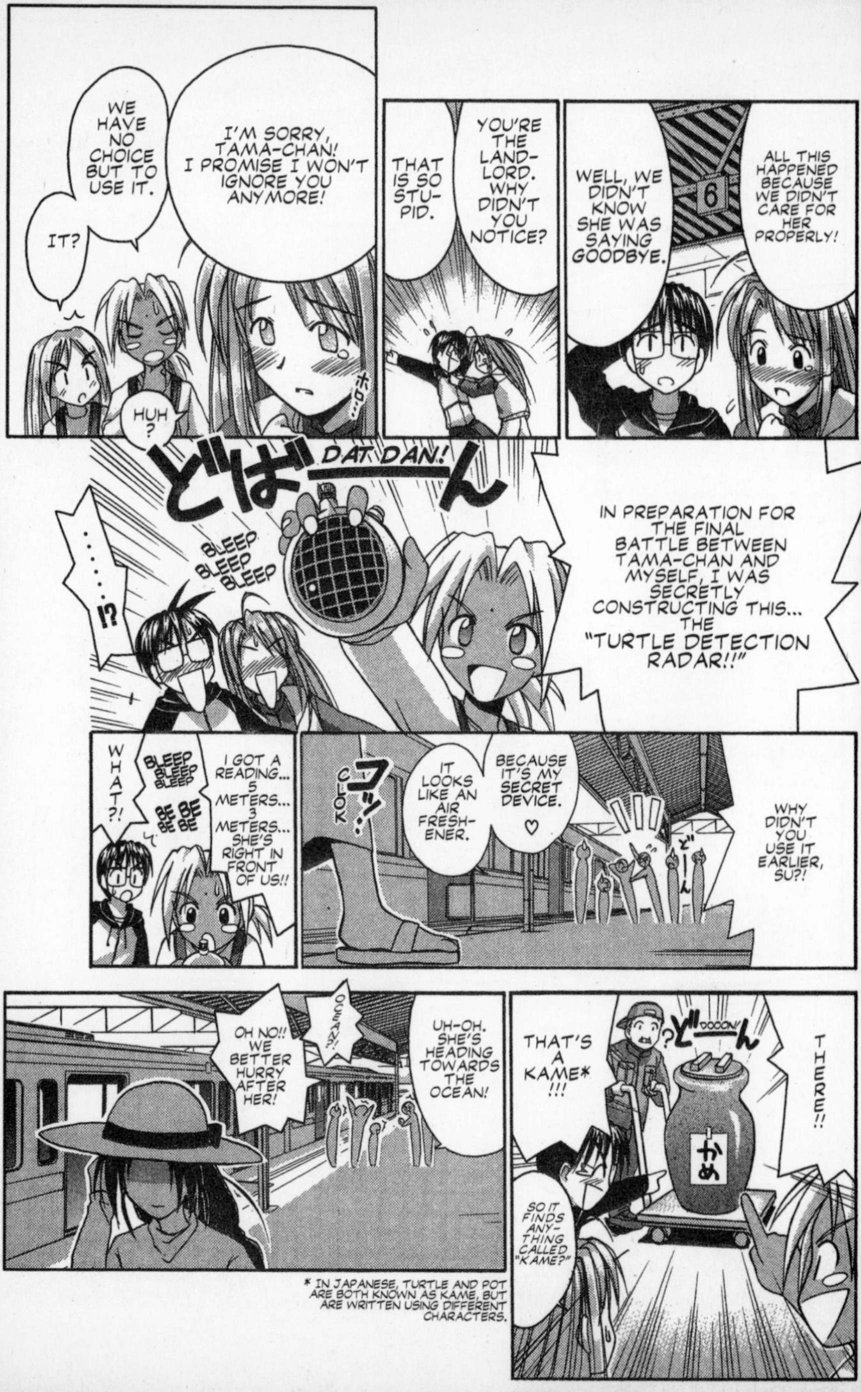
ALL THIS HAPPENED BECAUSE WE DIDN'T CARE FOR HER PROPERLY!
WELL, WE DIDN'T KNOW SHE WAS SAYING GOODBYE.
YOU'RE THE LANDLORD. WHY DIDN'T YOU NOTICE?
THAT IS SO STU-PID.
I'M SORRY, TAMA-CHAN! I PROMISE I WON'T IGNORE YOU ANYMORE!
WE HAVE NO CHOICE BUT TO USE IT.
IT?
HUH?
DAT DAN!
IN PREPARATION FOR THE FINAL BATTLE BETWEEN TAMA-CHAN AND MYSELF, I WAS SECRETLY CONSTRUCTING THIS... THE "TURTLE DETECTION RADAR!!"
BLEEP BLEEP BLEEP
......!?
WHY DIDN'T YOU USE IT EARLIER, SU?!
BECAUSE IT'S MY SECRET DEVICE. ♡
IT LOOKS LIKE AN AIR FRESHENER.
CLOK
I GOT A READING... 5 METERS... 3 METERS... SHE'S RIGHT IN FRONT OF US!!
BLEEP BLEEP BLEEP
BE BE BE BE
WHAT?!
THERE!!
DOOON!
THAT'S A KAME* !!!
かめ
SO IT FINDS ANYTHING CALLED "KAME?"
UH-OH. SHE'S HEADING TOWARDS THE OCEAN!
OCEAN?!
OH NO!! WE BETTER HURRY AFTER HER!

* IN JAPANESE, TURTLE AND POT ARE BOTH KNOWN AS KAME, BUT ARE WRITTEN USING DIFFERENT CHARACTERS.

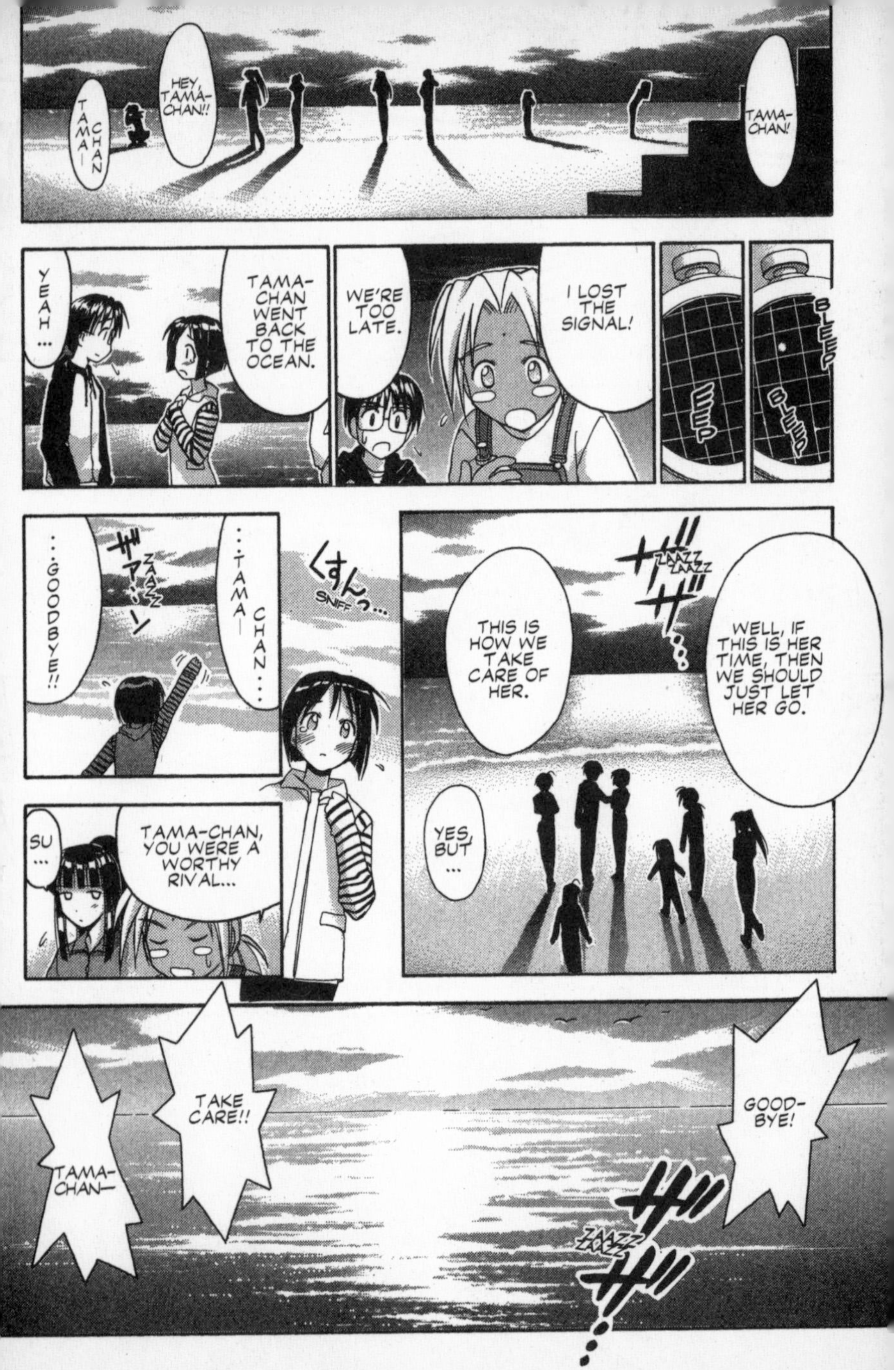
TAMA-CHAN!
HEY, TAMA-CHAN!!
TAMA-CHAN
BLEEP
BLEEP BLEEP
I LOST THE SIGNAL!
WE'RE TOO LATE.
TAMA-CHAN WENT BACK TO THE OCEAN.
YEAH...
WELL, IF THIS IS HER TIME, THEN WE SHOULD JUST LET HER GO.
ZAAZZ ZAAZZ
THIS IS HOW WE TAKE CARE OF HER.
YES, BUT...
くすん
SNIFF...
...TAMA-CHAN...
ZAAZZ
...GOODBYE!!
TAMA-CHAN, YOU WERE A WORTHY RIVAL...
SU...
GOOD-BYE!
ZAAZZ ZAAZZ
TAKE CARE!!
TAMA-CHAN—

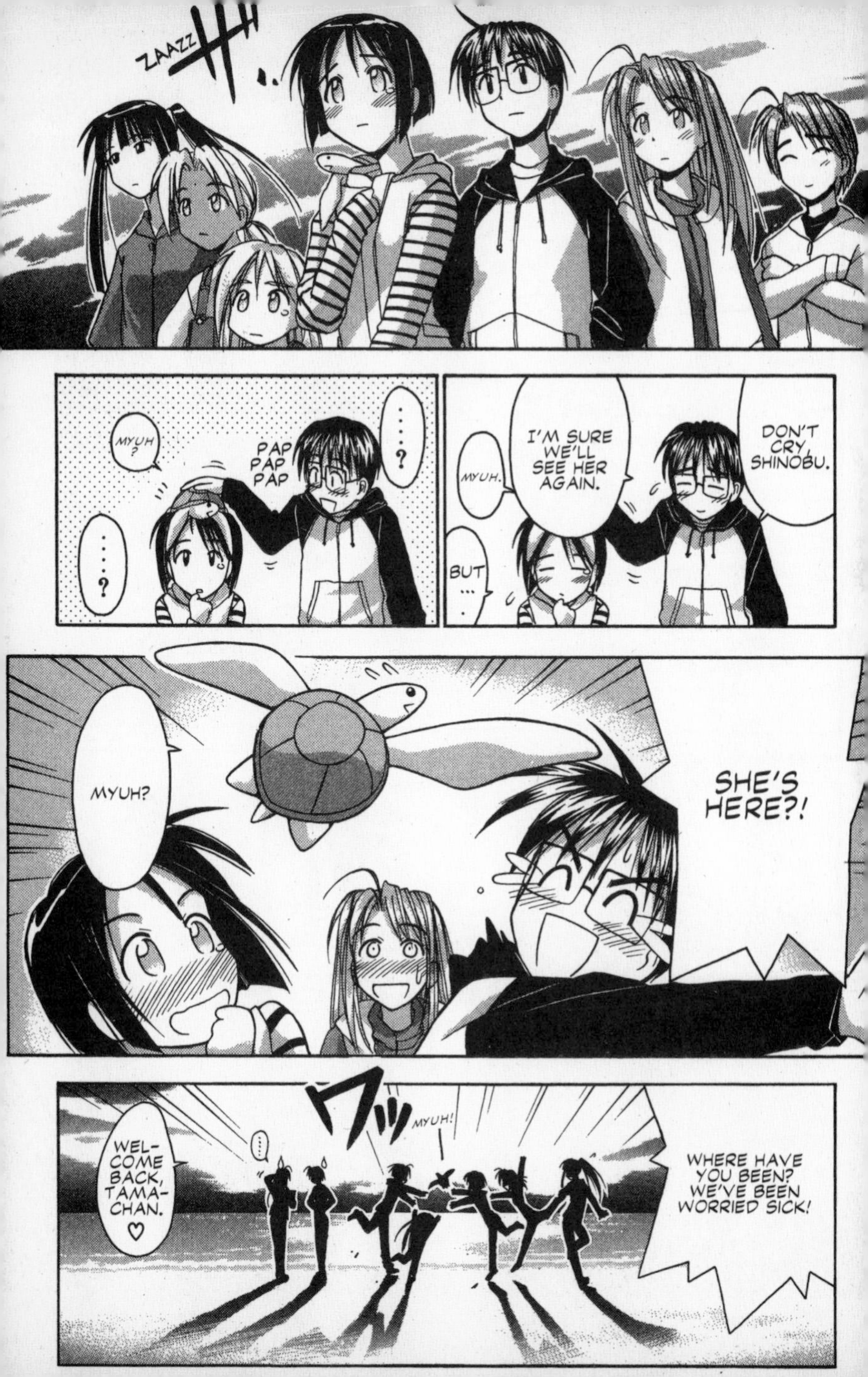
ZAAZZ
DON'T CRY, SHINOBU.
I'M SURE WE'LL SEE HER AGAIN.
MYUH.
BUT....
....?
PAP PAP PAP
MYUH ?
....?
SHE'S HERE?!
MYUH?
WHERE HAVE YOU BEEN? WE'VE BEEN WORRIED SICK!
MYUH!
....
WEL-COME BACK, TAMA-CHAN. ♡

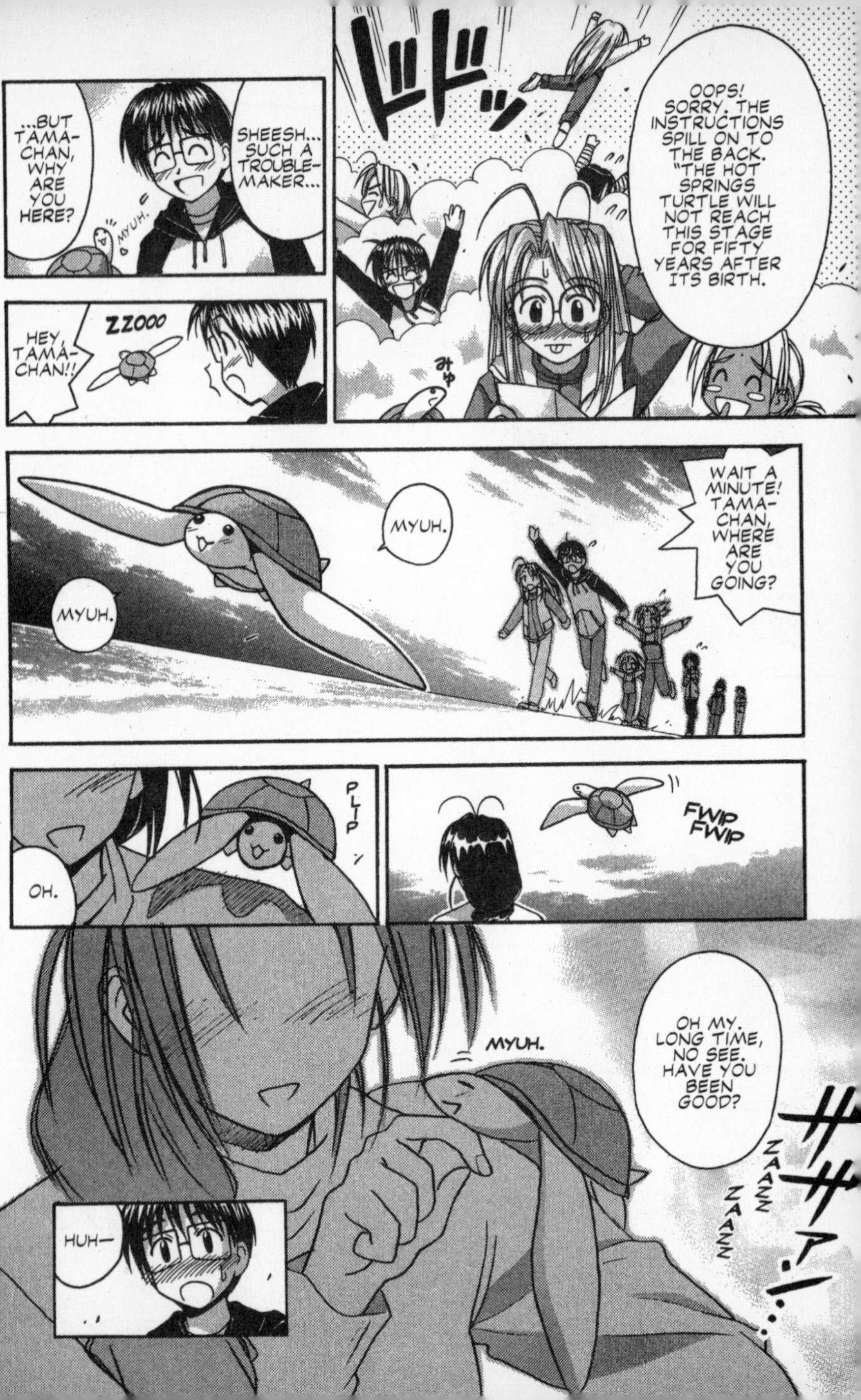
ドドッ
OOPS! SORRY. THE INSTRUCTIONS SPILL ON TO THE BACK. "THE HOT SPRINGS TURTLE WILL NOT REACH THIS STAGE FOR FIFTY YEARS AFTER ITS BIRTH.
みゅ
SHEESH... SUCH A TROUBLE-MAKER...
...BUT TAMA-CHAN, WHY ARE YOU HERE?
MYUH.
ZZOOO
HEY, TAMA-CHAN!!
WAIT A MINUTE! TAMA-CHAN, WHERE ARE YOU GOING?
MYUH.
MYUH.
FWIP FWIP
PLIP
OH.
ザザァ…!
ZAAZZ ZAAZZ
OH MY. LONG TIME, NO SEE. HAVE YOU BEEN GOOD?
MYUH.
HUH—

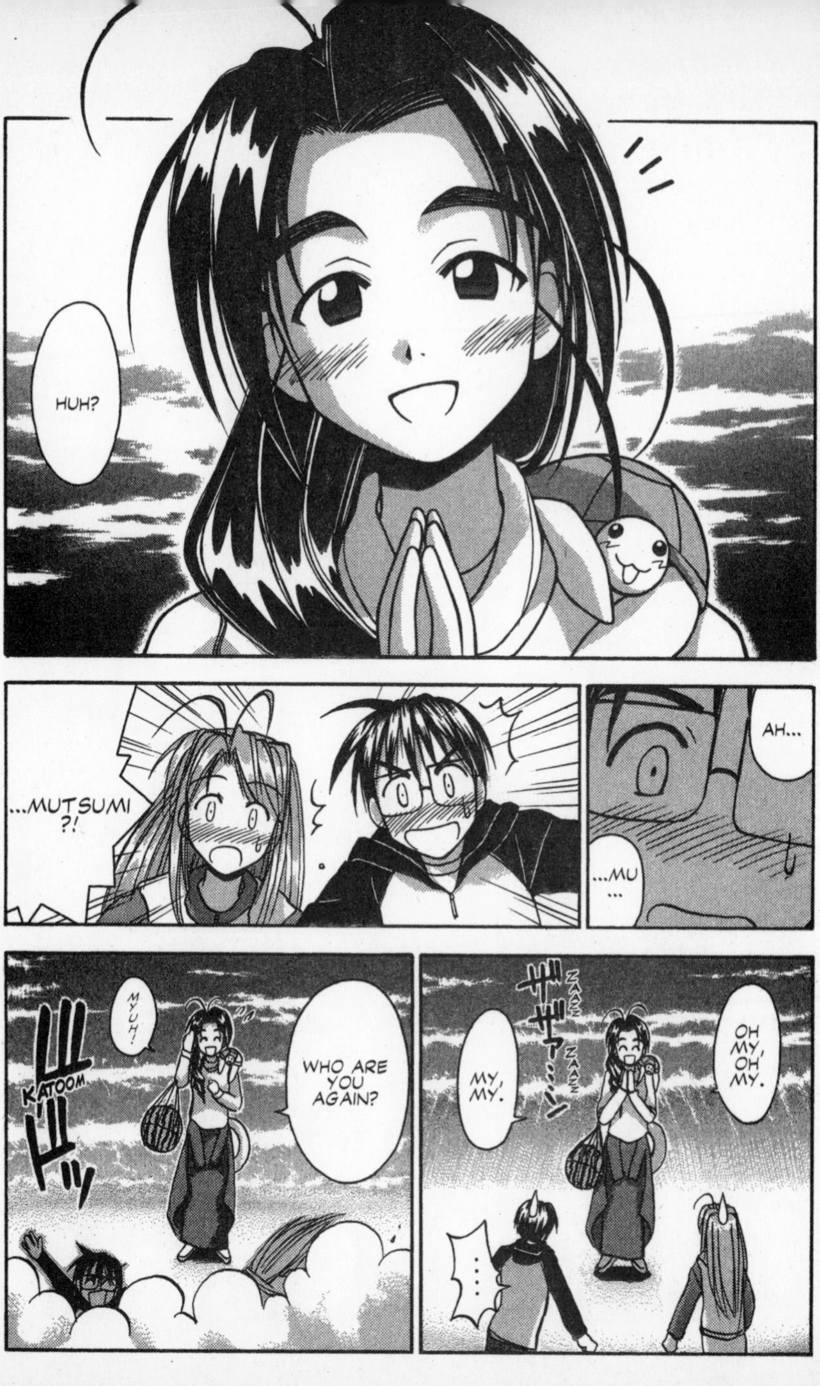
HUH?
AH...
...MU...
...MUTSUMI ?!
ZAAZ ZAAZ
OH MY, OH MY.
MY, MY.
....
MYUH!
WHO ARE YOU AGAIN?
KATOOM

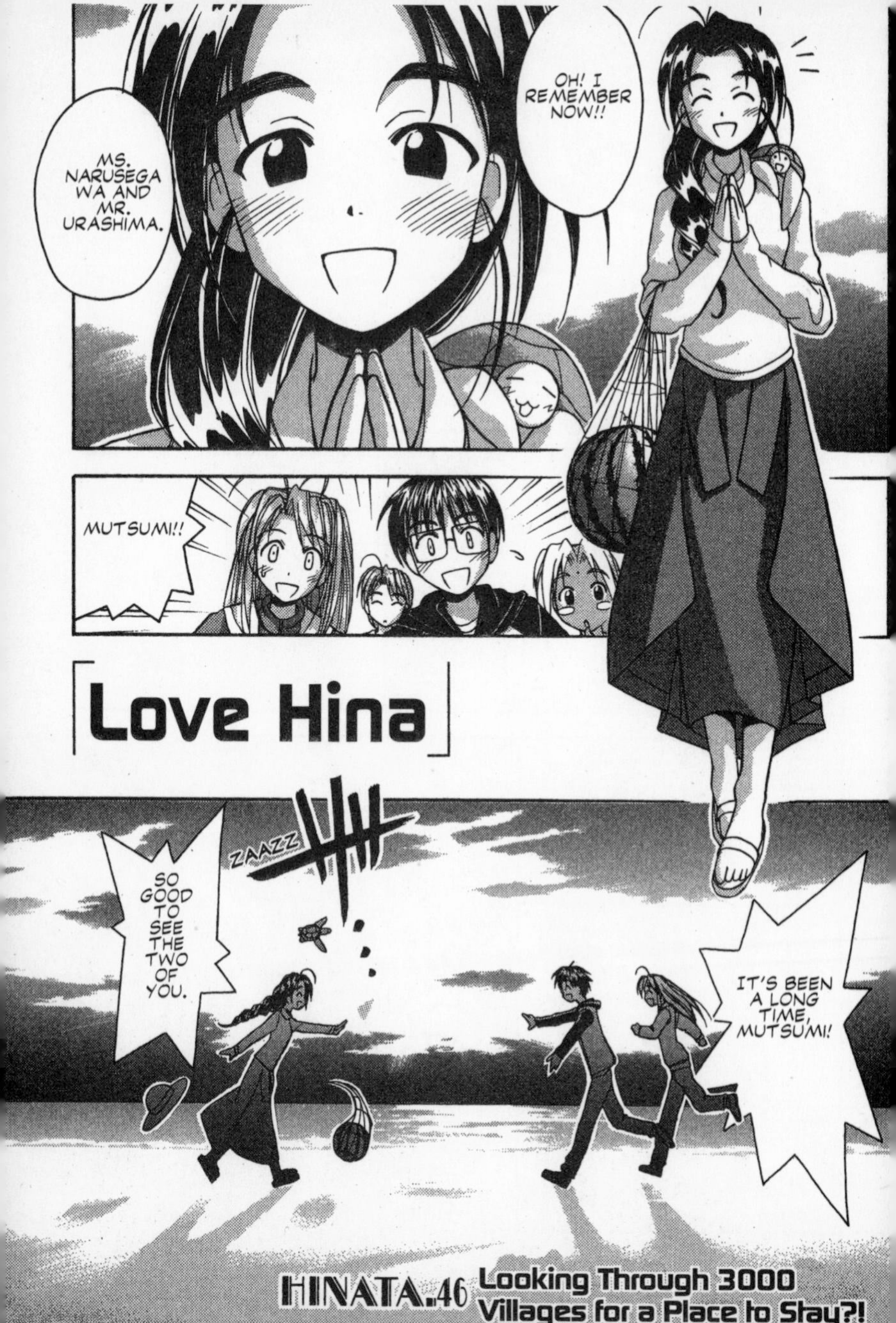
OH! I REMEMBER NOW!!
MS. NARUSEGAWA AND MR. URASHIMA.
MUTSUMI!!
Love Hina
IT'S BEEN A LONG TIME, MUTSUMI!
ZAAZZ
SO GOOD TO SEE THE TWO OF YOU.
HINATA.46 Looking Through 3000 Villages for a Place to Stay?!

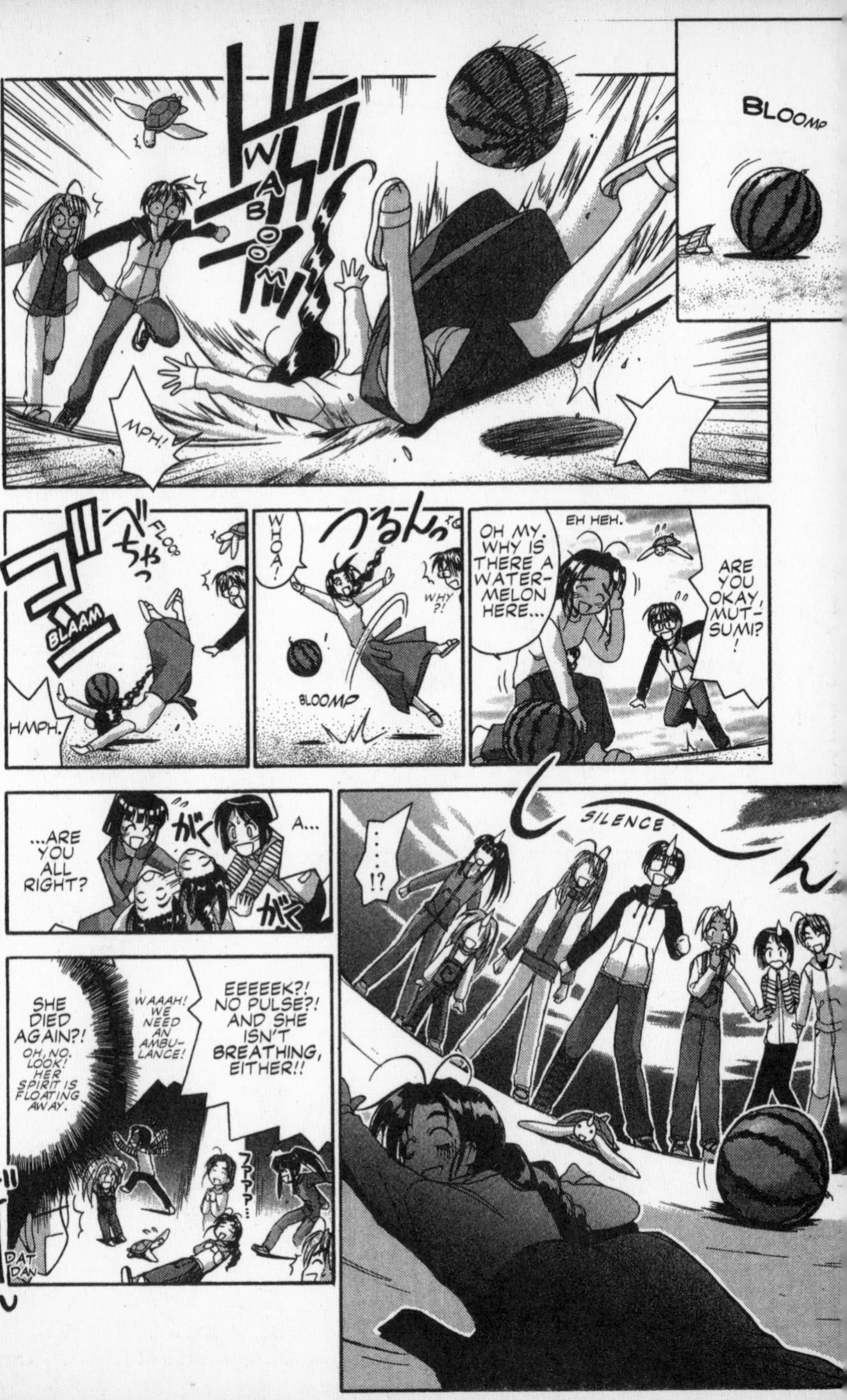
BLOOMP
WABOOM
MPH!
ARE YOU OKAY, MUTSUMI?!
EH HEH.
OH MY. WHY IS THERE A WATER-MELON HERE...
つるんっ
WHOA!
WHY?!
BLOOMP
べちゃっ
FLOOP
BLAAM
HMPH.
SILENCE
......!?
A...
...ARE YOU ALL RIGHT?
がく
がく
EEEEEK?! NO PULSE?! AND SHE ISN'T BREATHING, EITHER!!
WAAAH! WE NEED AN AMBULANCE!
SHE DIED AGAIN?!
OH, NO. LOOK! HER SPIRIT IS FLOATING AWAY.
どーん
DAT DAN

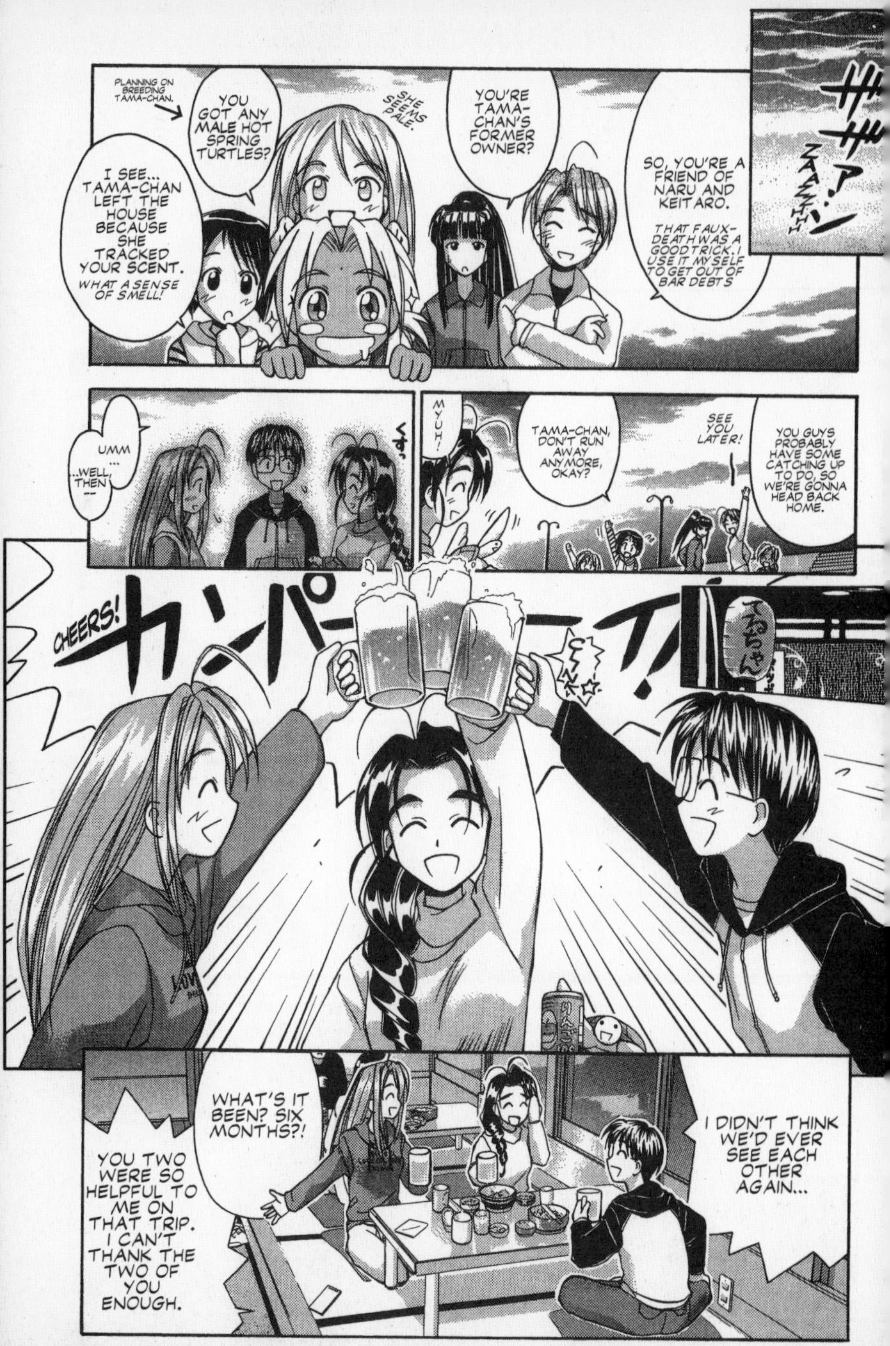
ザザァ…ン
ZAAAHN
SO, YOU'RE A FRIEND OF NARU AND KEITARO.
THAT FAUX-DEATH WAS A GOOD TRICK. I USE IT MYSELF TO GET OUT OF BAR DEBTS
YOU'RE TAMA-CHAN'S FORMER OWNER?
SHE SEEMS PALE.
YOU GOT ANY MALE HOT SPRING TURTLES?
PLANNING ON BREEDING TAMA-CHAN.
I SEE... TAMA-CHAN LEFT THE HOUSE BECAUSE SHE TRACKED YOUR SCENT.
WHAT A SENSE OF SMELL!
YOU GUYS PROBABLY HAVE SOME CATCHING UP TO DO, SO WE'RE GONNA HEAD BACK HOME.
SEE YOU LATER!
TAMA-CHAN, DON'T RUN AWAY ANYMORE, OKAY?
MYUH!
くすっ
UMM ...
...WELL, THEN --
CHEERS!
カンパーーイ!
CLINK!
I DIDN'T THINK WE'D EVER SEE EACH OTHER AGAIN...
WHAT'S IT BEEN? SIX MONTHS?!
YOU TWO WERE SO HELPFUL TO ME ON THAT TRIP. I CAN'T THANK THE TWO OF YOU ENOUGH.

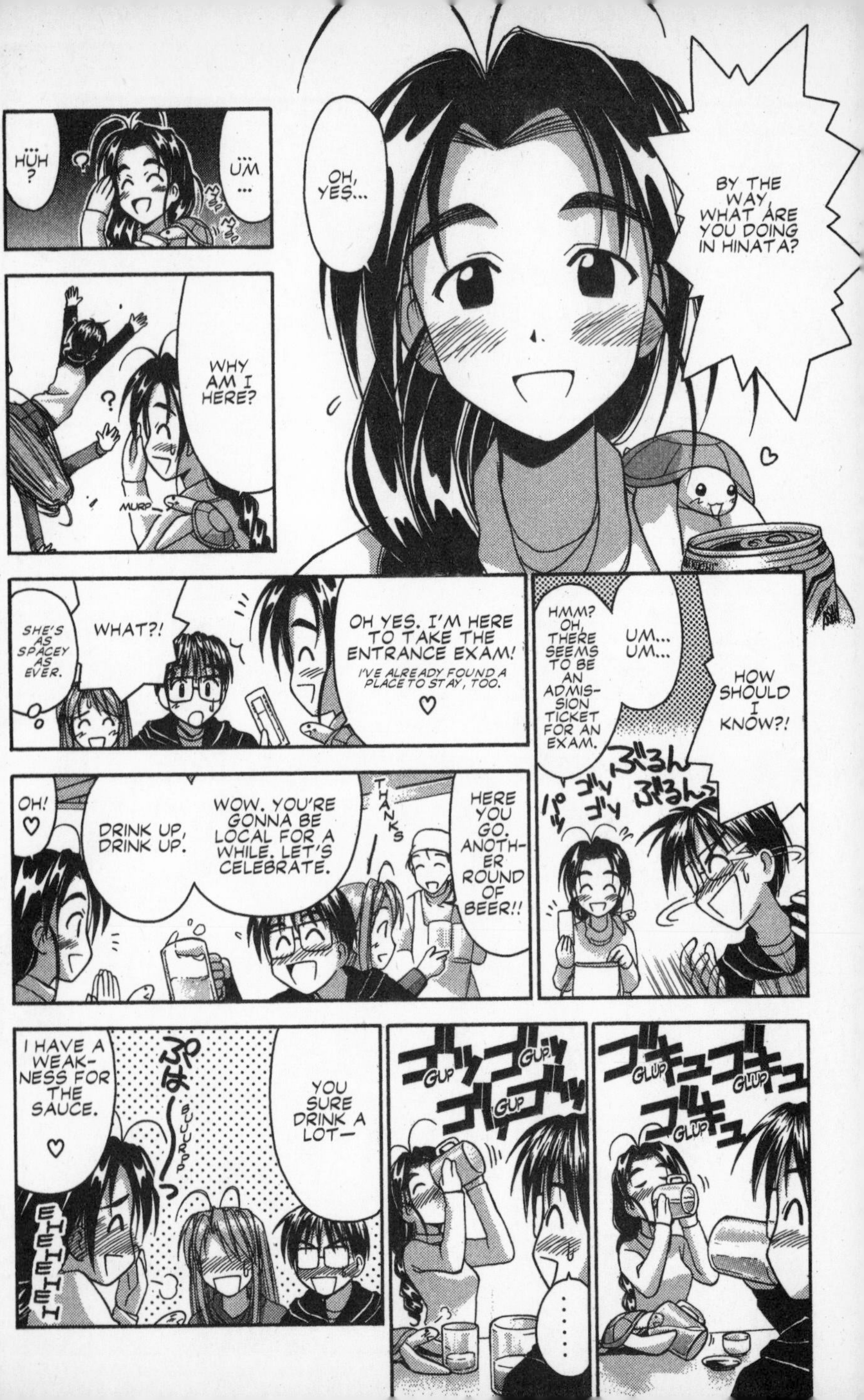
BY THE WAY, WHAT ARE YOU DOING IN HINATA?
OH, YES...
...UM...
MGO MGO
...HUH?
WHY AM I HERE?
MURP
HOW SHOULD I KNOW?!
UM... UM...
HMM? OH, THERE SEEMS TO BE AN ADMISSION TICKET FOR AN EXAM.
ぶるん ぶるん
ゴッ ゴッ
パッ
OH YES. I'M HERE TO TAKE THE ENTRANCE EXAM!
I'VE ALREADY FOUND A PLACE TO STAY, TOO. ♡
WHAT?!
SHE'S AS SPACEY AS EVER.
HERE YOU GO. ANOTHER ROUND OF BEER!!
THANKS
WOW. YOU'RE GONNA BE LOCAL FOR A WHILE. LET'S CELEBRATE.
DRINK UP, DRINK UP.
OH! ♡
ゴキュ ゴキュ ゴキュ GLUP GLUP GLUP
ゴッ ゴッ ゴッ ゴッ GUP GUP GUP GUP
......
YOU SURE DRINK A LOT—
ぷはー BUUURPP
I HAVE A WEAKNESS FOR THE SAUCE. ♡
EHEHEHEHEH

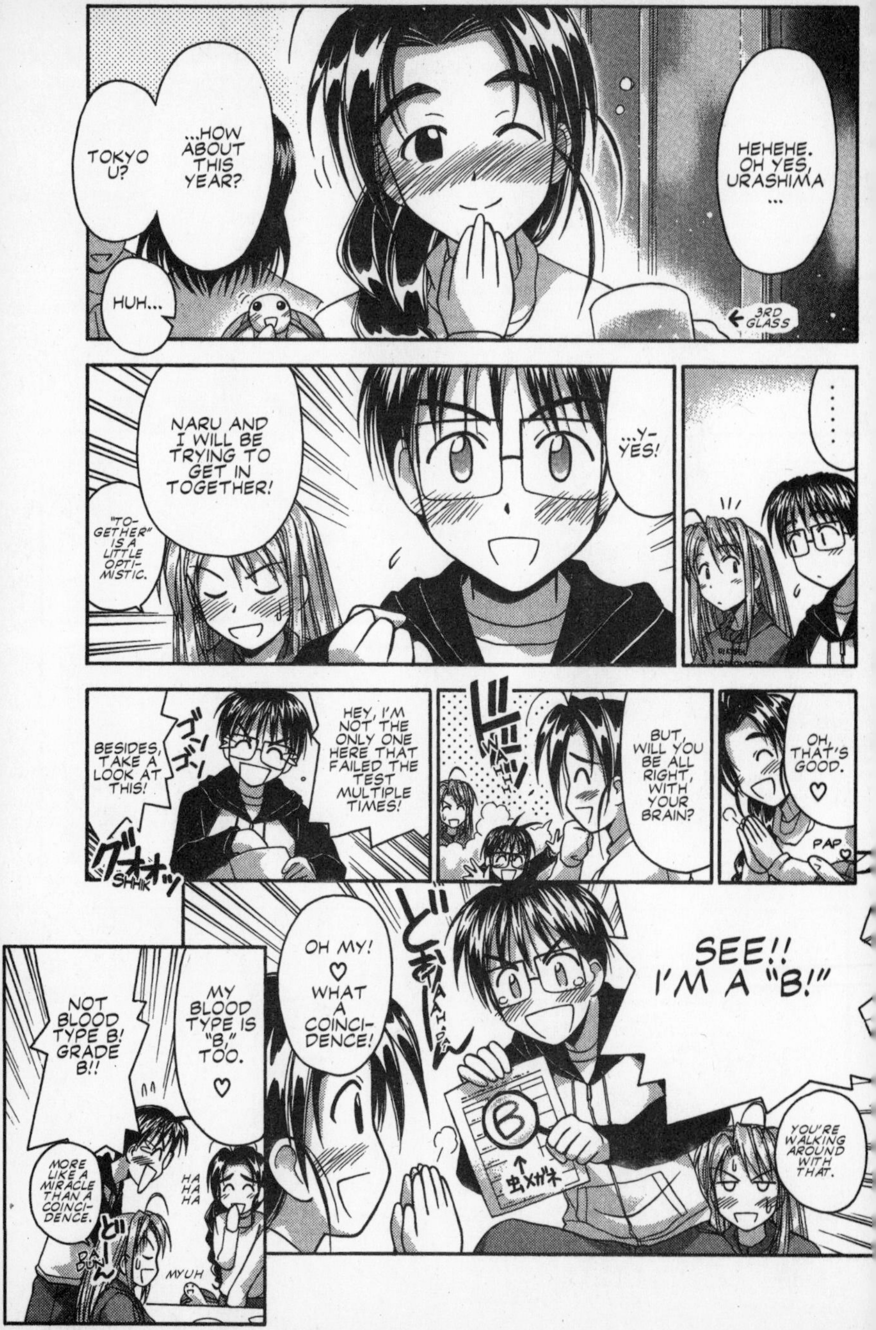
HEHEHE. OH YES, URASHIMA ...
3RD GLASS
...HOW ABOUT THIS YEAR?
TOKYO U?
HUH...
......
...Y-YES!
NARU AND I WILL BE TRYING TO GET IN TOGETHER!
"TO-GETHER" IS A LITTLE OPTI-MISTIC.
OH, THAT'S GOOD. ♡
PAP ♡
BUT, WILL YOU BE ALL RIGHT, WITH YOUR BRAIN?
WAHHH
HEY, I'M NOT THE ONLY ONE HERE THAT FAILED THE TEST MULTIPLE TIMES!
BESIDES, TAKE A LOOK AT THIS!
SHHIK
SEE!! I'M A "B!"
YOU'RE WALKING AROUND WITH THAT.
虫メガネ
OH MY! ♡ WHAT A COINCIDENCE!
MY BLOOD TYPE IS "B," TOO. ♡
NOT BLOOD TYPE B! GRADE B!!
HA HA HA
MORE LIKE A MIRACLE THAN A COINCIDENCE.
DA DUN
MYUH

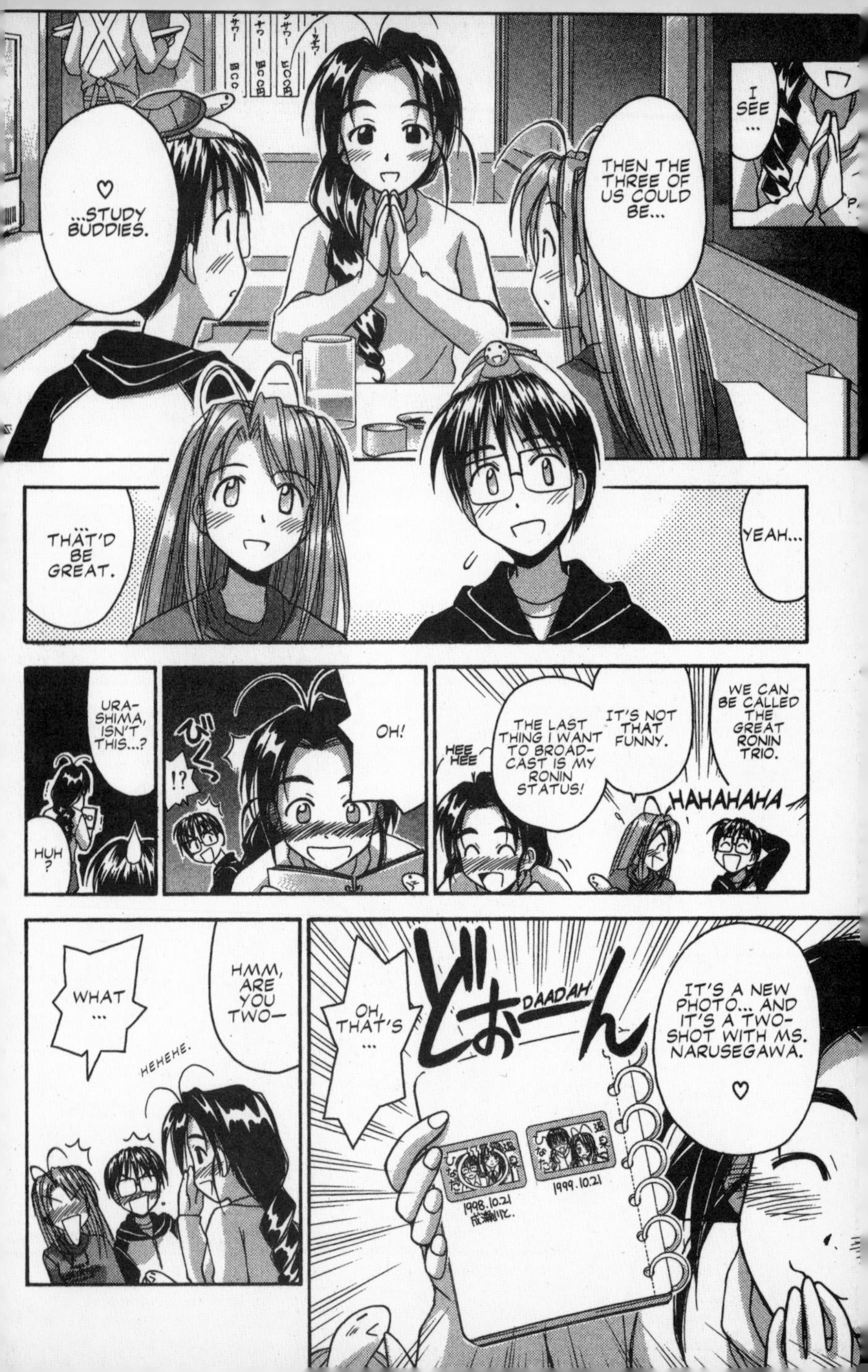
I SEE ...
THEN THE THREE OF US COULD BE...
♡ ...STUDY BUDDIES.
YEAH...
... THAT'D BE GREAT.
WE CAN BE CALLED THE GREAT RONIN TRIO.
HAHAHAHA
IT'S NOT THAT FUNNY.
THE LAST THING I WANT TO BROADCAST IS MY RONIN STATUS!
HEE HEE
OH!
びくっ
!?
URA-SHIMA, ISN'T THIS...?
HUH?
IT'S A NEW PHOTO... AND IT'S A TWO-SHOT WITH MS. NARUSEGAWA.
♡
どぉーん
DAADAH
OH, THAT'S ...
1999.10.21
1998.10.21
HMM, ARE YOU TWO—
WHAT ...
HEHEHE.

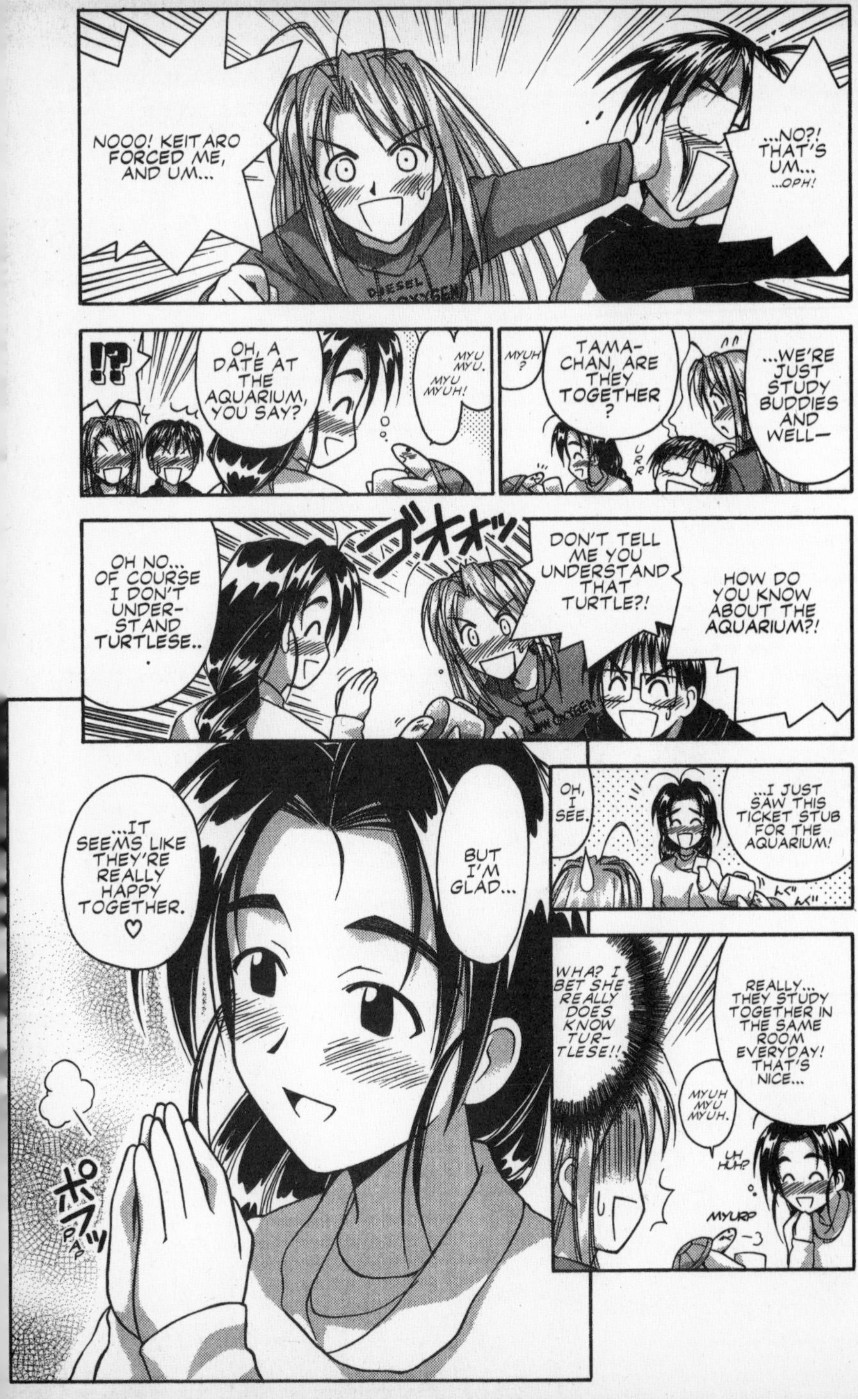
...NO?! THAT'S UM... ...OPH!
NOOO! KEITARO FORCED ME, AND UM...
DIESEL OXYGEN
...WE'RE JUST STUDY BUDDIES AND WELL—
TAMA-CHAN, ARE THEY TOGETHER?
MYUH?
URR
MYU MYU. MYU MYUH!
OH, A DATE AT THE AQUARIUM, YOU SAY?
!?
HOW DO YOU KNOW ABOUT THE AQUARIUM?!
DON'T TELL ME YOU UNDERSTAND THAT TURTLE?!
ゴオオッ
OH NO... OF COURSE I DON'T UNDER-STAND TURTLESE...
...I JUST SAW THIS TICKET STUB FOR THE AQUARIUM!
OH, I SEE.
んぐんぐ
REALLY... THEY STUDY TOGETHER IN THE SAME ROOM EVERYDAY! THAT'S NICE...
MYUH MYU MYUH.
WHA? I BET SHE REALLY DOES KNOW TUR-TLESE!!
UH HUH?
MYURP
BUT I'M GLAD...
...IT SEEMS LIKE THEY'RE REALLY HAPPY TOGETHER. ♡
ポフッ
PAP

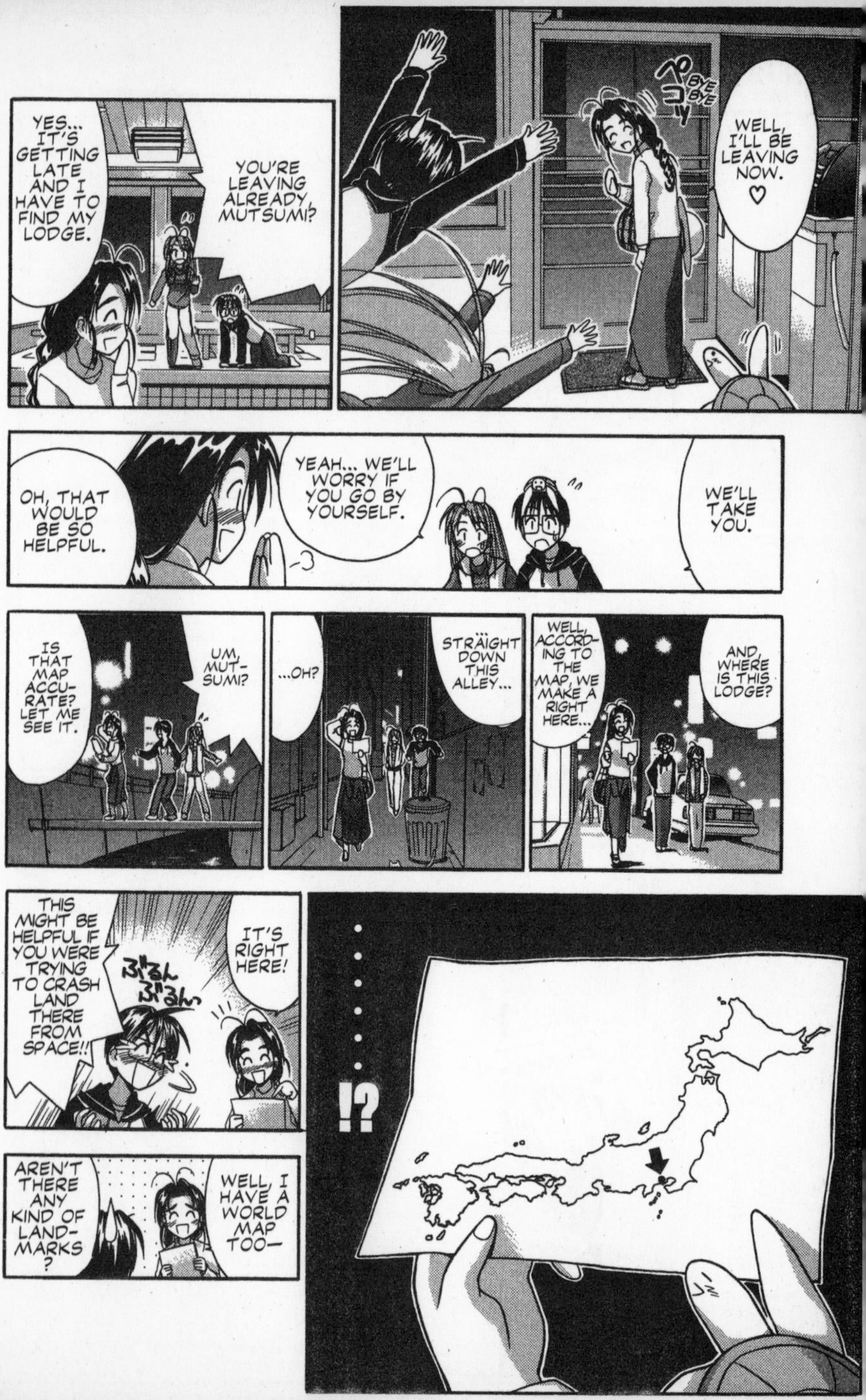

ペコッ BYE BYE
WELL, I'LL BE LEAVING NOW. ♡
YOU'RE LEAVING ALREADY, MUTSUMI?
YES... IT'S GETTING LATE AND I HAVE TO FIND MY LODGE.
WE'LL TAKE YOU.
YEAH... WE'LL WORRY IF YOU GO BY YOURSELF.
OH, THAT WOULD BE SO HELPFUL.
AND, WHERE IS THIS LODGE?
WELL, ACCORDING TO THE MAP, WE MAKE A RIGHT HERE...
...STRAIGHT DOWN THIS ALLEY...
...OH?
UM, MUTSUMI?
IS THAT MAP ACCURATE? LET ME SEE IT.
!?
IT'S RIGHT HERE!
ぶるんぶるんっ
THIS MIGHT BE HELPFUL IF YOU WERE TRYING TO CRASH LAND THERE FROM SPACE!!
AREN'T THERE ANY KIND OF LANDMARKS?
WELL, I HAVE A WORLD MAP TOO—

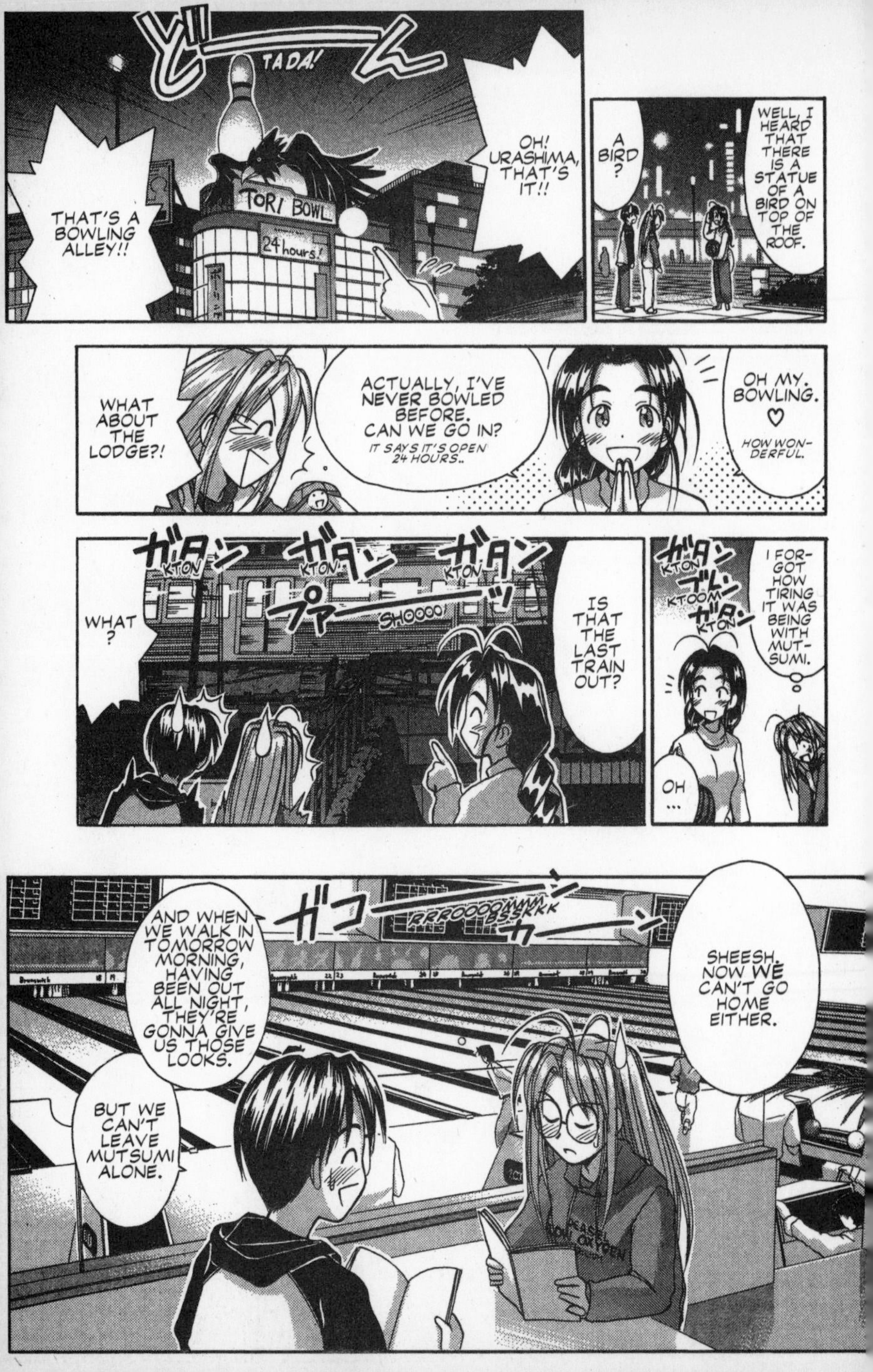
WELL, I HEARD THAT THERE IS A STATUE OF A BIRD ON TOP OF THE ROOF.
A BIRD?
TADA!
OH! URASHIMA, THAT'S IT!!
TORI BOWL
24 hours.!
THAT'S A BOWLING ALLEY!!
OH MY. BOWLING. ♥
HOW WONDERFUL.
ACTUALLY, I'VE NEVER BOWLED BEFORE. CAN WE GO IN?
IT SAYS IT'S OPEN 24 HOURS..
WHAT ABOUT THE LODGE?!
KTON
KTOOM
KTON
I FORGOT HOW TIRING IT WAS BEING WITH MUTSUMI.
OH ...
KTON
KTON
KTON
SHOOOO!
IS THAT THE LAST TRAIN OUT?
WHAT?
RRROOOOMMM
BSSKKK
SHEESH. NOW WE CAN'T GO HOME EITHER.
AND WHEN WE WALK IN TOMORROW MORNING, HAVING BEEN OUT ALL NIGHT, THEY'RE GONNA GIVE US THOSE LOOKS.
BUT WE CAN'T LEAVE MUTSUMI ALONE.

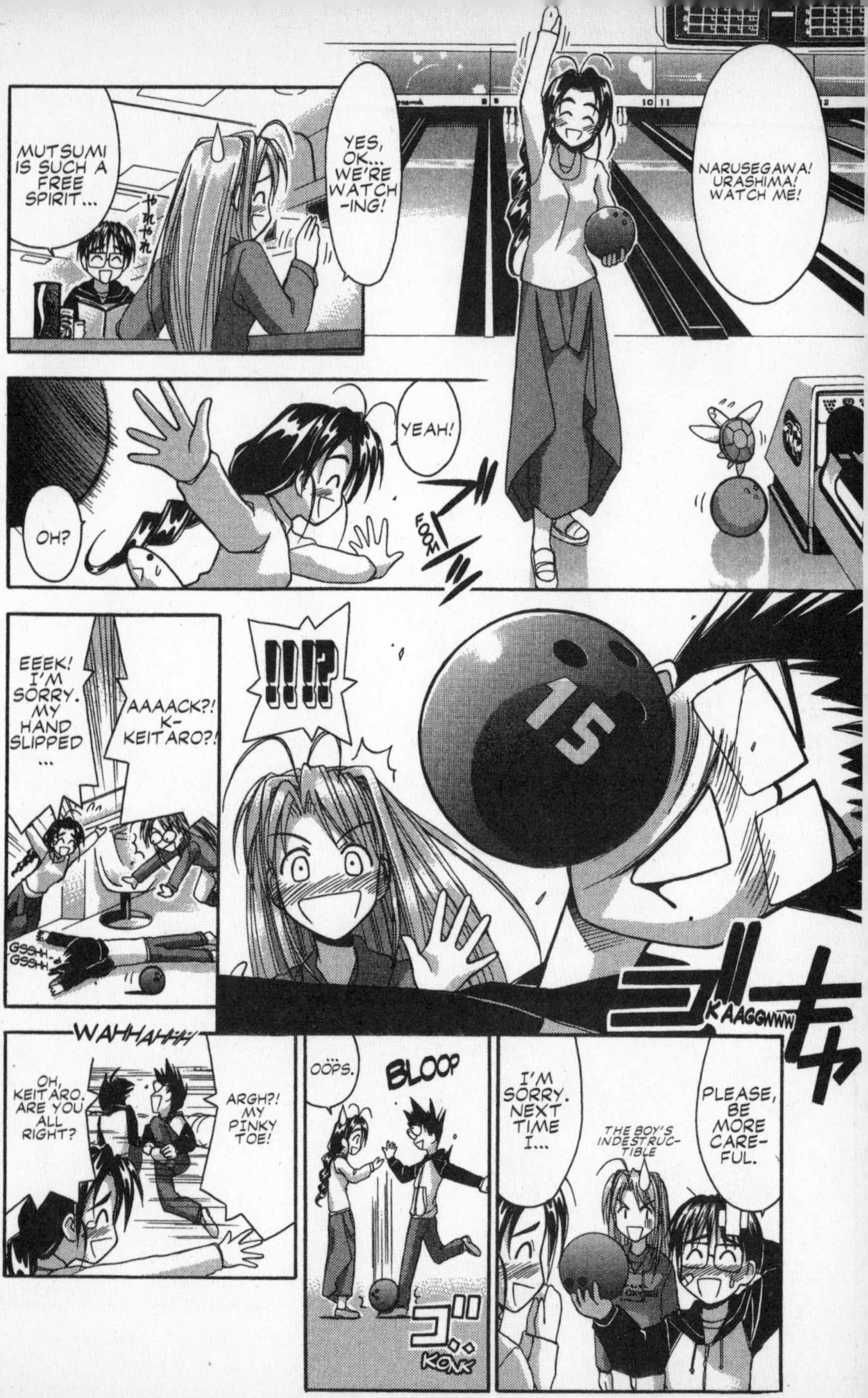
NARUSEGAWA! URASHIMA! WATCH ME!
YES, OK... WE'RE WATCH-ING!
MUTSUMI IS SUCH A FREE SPIRIT...
YEAH!
FOOM
OH?
!!!?
KAAGGWWW
AAAACK?! K-KEITARO?!
EEEK! I'M SORRY. MY HAND SLIPPED ...
GSSHH GSSHH
PLEASE, BE MORE CARE-FUL.
THE BOY'S INDESTRUC-TIBLE
I'M SORRY. NEXT TIME I...
BLOOP
OOPS.
KONK
WAHHAHHH
ARGH?! MY PINKY TOE!
OH, KEITARO. ARE YOU ALL RIGHT?

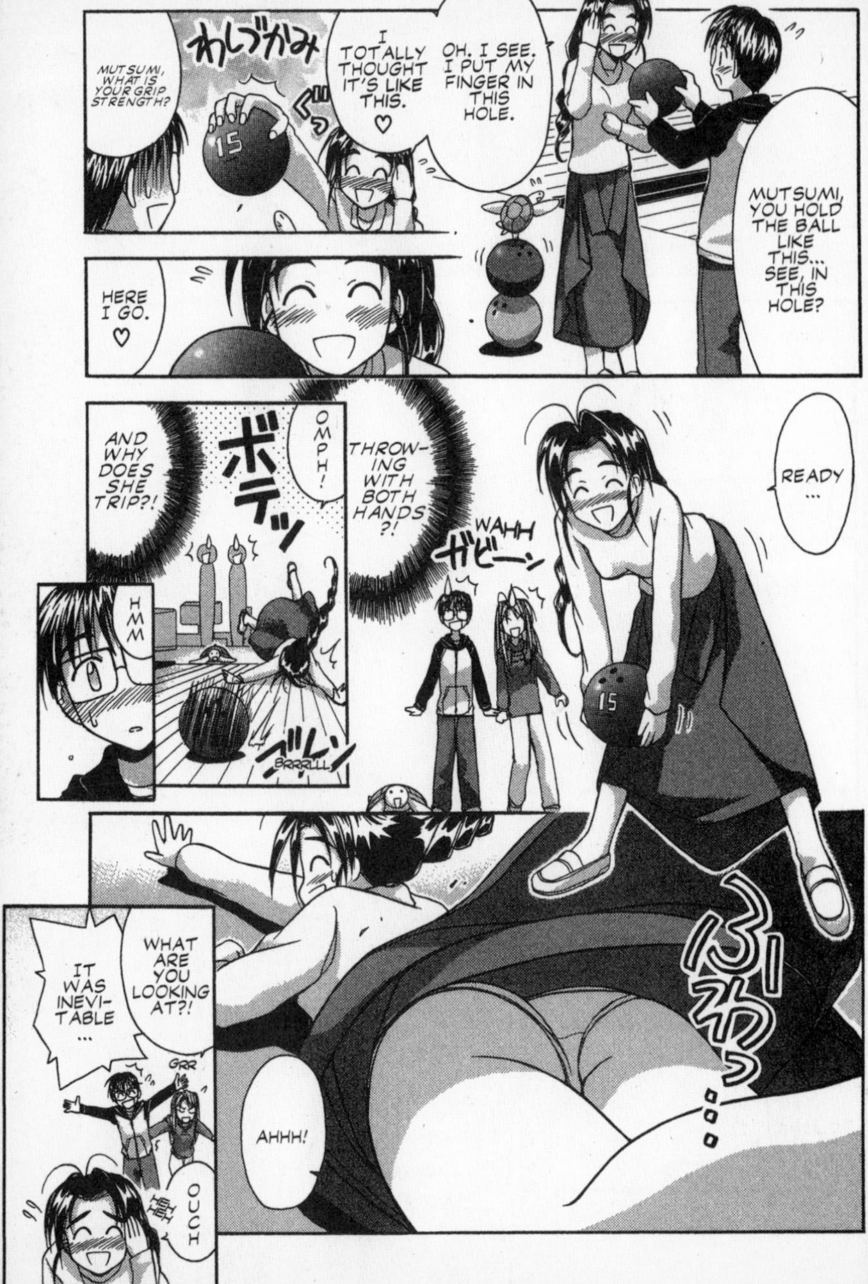
MUTSUMI, YOU HOLD THE BALL LIKE THIS... SEE, IN THIS HOLE?
OH. I SEE. I PUT MY FINGER IN THIS HOLE.
I TOTALLY THOUGHT IT'S LIKE THIS. ♡
わしづかみ
ぐっ
MUTSUMI, WHAT IS YOUR GRIP STRENGTH?
HERE I GO. ♡
READY ...
WAHH
ガビーン
THROWING WITH BOTH HANDS?!
OMPH!
ボテッ
AND WHY DOES SHE TRIP?!
BRRRLLL
HMM
ふわっ...
AHHH!
WHAT ARE YOU LOOKING AT?!
IT WAS INEVI-TABLE ...
GRR
OUCH
HEH HEH

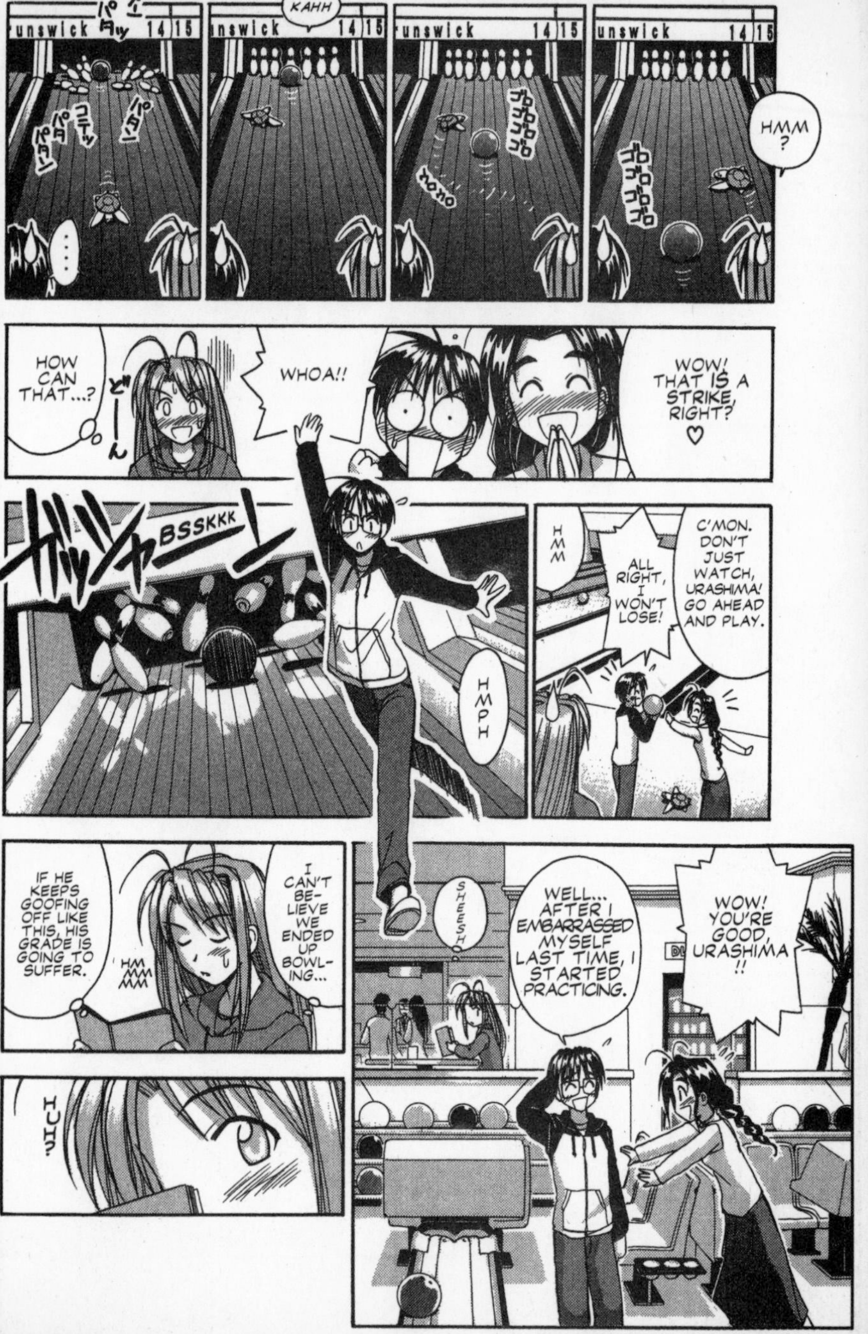
HMM ?
ゴロゴロゴロ
KAHH
. . . .
WOW! THAT IS A STRIKE, RIGHT? ♡
WHOA!!
HOW CAN THAT...?
どーん
C'MON. DON'T JUST WATCH, URASHIMA! GO AHEAD AND PLAY.
ALL RIGHT, I WON'T LOSE!
HMM
HMPH
BSSKKK
WOW! YOU'RE GOOD, URASHIMA !!
WELL... AFTER I EMBARRASSED MYSELF LAST TIME, I STARTED PRACTICING.
SHEESH
I CAN'T BE-LIEVE WE ENDED UP BOWL-ING...
HM MM MM
IF HE KEEPS GOOFING OFF LIKE THIS, HIS GRADE IS GOING TO SUFFER.
HUH?

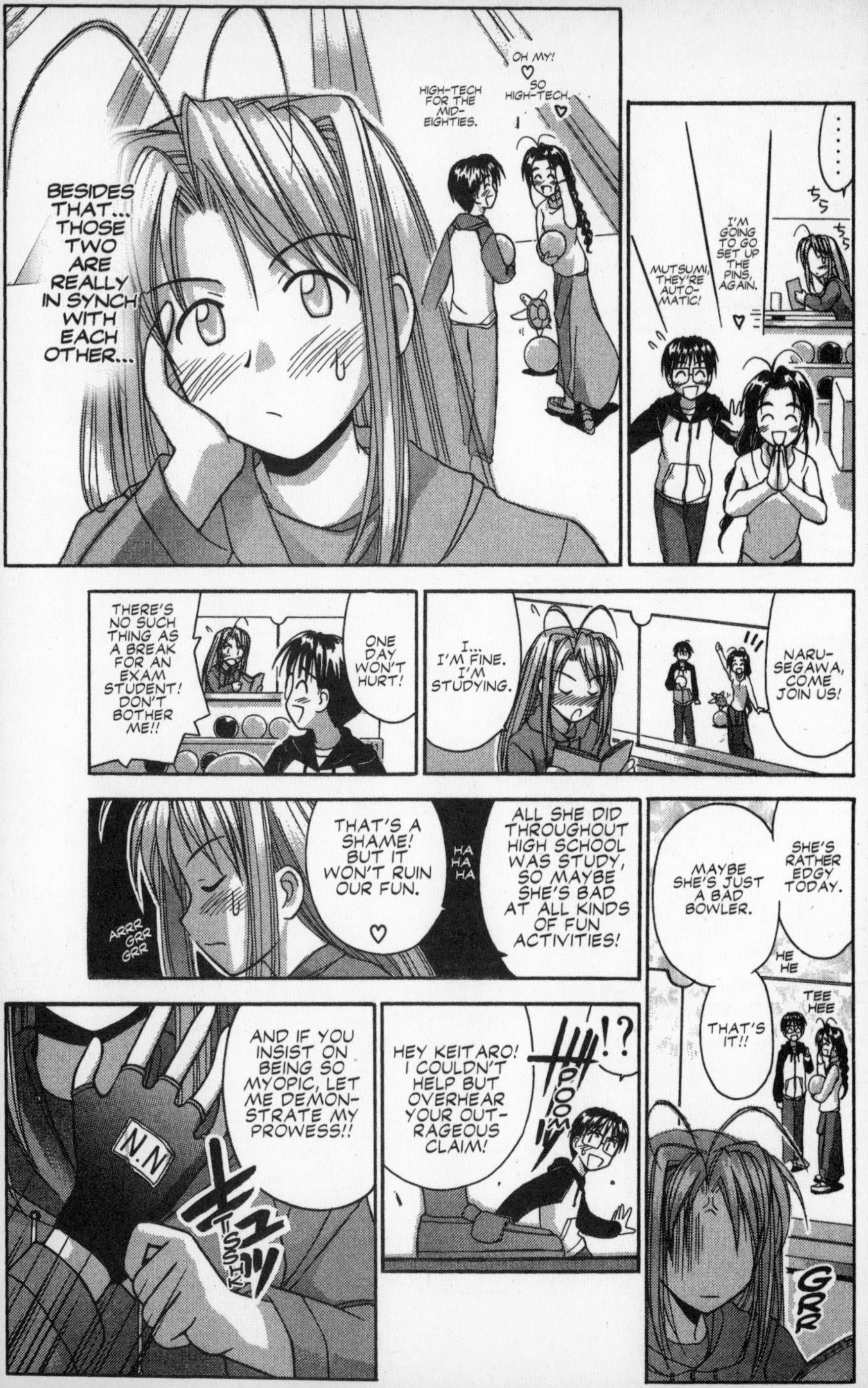
......
I'M GOING TO GO SET UP THE PINS, AGAIN.
MUTSUMI, THEY'RE AUTO-MATIC!
OH MY! SO HIGH-TECH.
HIGH-TECH FOR THE MID-EIGHTIES.
BESIDES THAT... THOSE TWO ARE REALLY IN SYNCH WITH EACH OTHER...
NARU-SEGAWA, COME JOIN US!
I... I'M FINE. I'M STUDYING.
ONE DAY WON'T HURT!
THERE'S NO SUCH THING AS A BREAK FOR AN EXAM STUDENT! DON'T BOTHER ME!!
SHE'S RATHER EDGY TODAY.
MAYBE SHE'S JUST A BAD BOWLER.
HE HE
TEE HEE
THAT'S IT!!
GRR
ALL SHE DID THROUGHOUT HIGH SCHOOL WAS STUDY, SO MAYBE SHE'S BAD AT ALL KINDS OF FUN ACTIVITIES!
HA HA HA
THAT'S A SHAME! BUT IT WON'T RUIN OUR FUN.
ARRR GRR GRR
!?
POOM
HEY KEITARO! I COULDN'T HELP BUT OVERHEAR YOUR OUT-RAGEOUS CLAIM!
AND IF YOU INSIST ON BEING SO MYOPIC, LET ME DEMON-STRATE MY PROWESS!!
N.N
TSHK

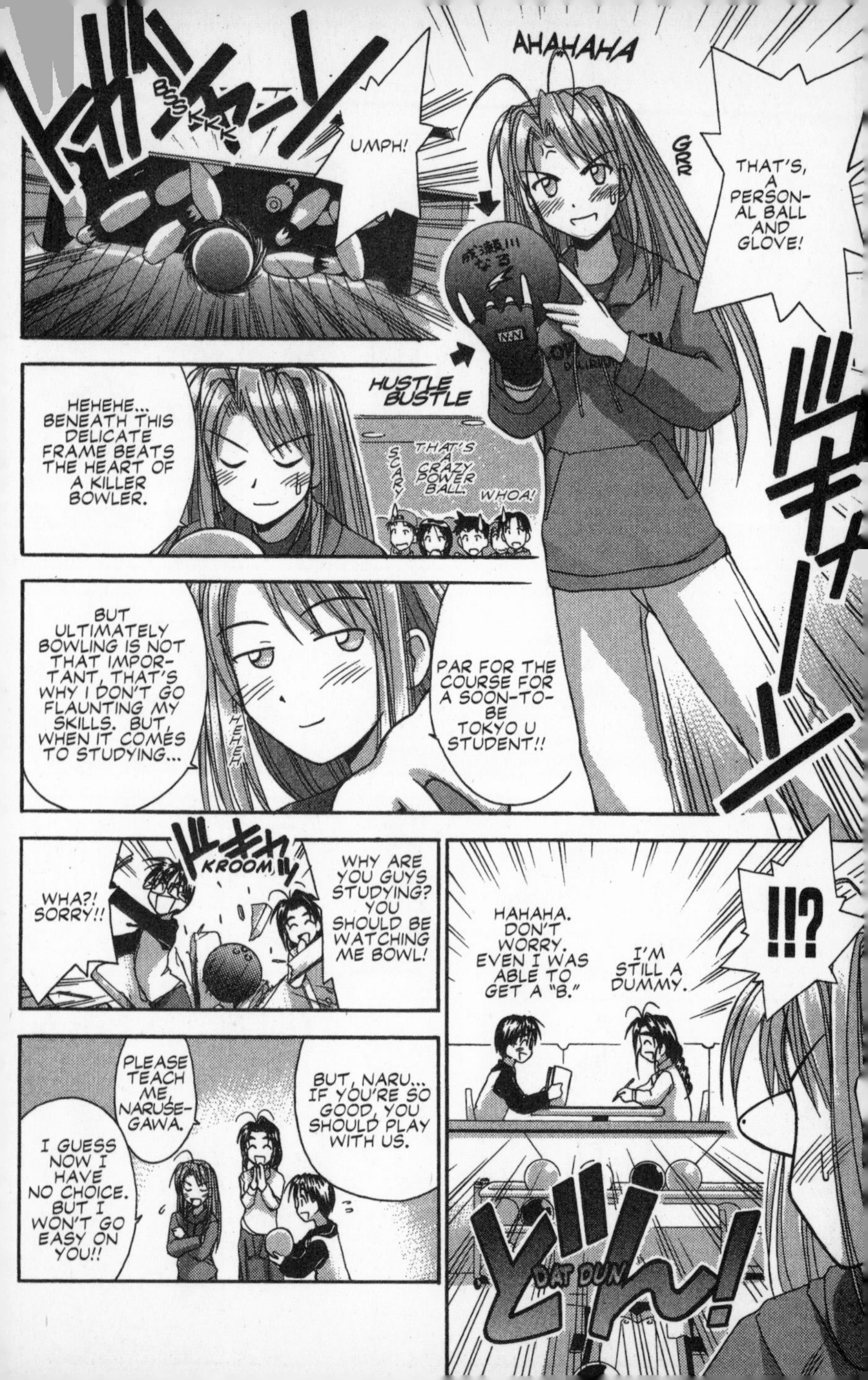

BSSKKK
UMPH!
AHAHAHA
GRR
THAT'S, A PERSONAL BALL AND GLOVE!
HUSTLE BUSTLE
HEHEHE... BENEATH THIS DELICATE FRAME BEATS THE HEART OF A KILLER BOWLER.
THAT'S CRAZY POWER BALL.
SCARY
WHOA!
PAR FOR THE COURSE FOR A SOON-TO-BE TOKYO U STUDENT!!
BUT ULTIMATELY BOWLING IS NOT THAT IMPORTANT, THAT'S WHY I DON'T GO FLAUNTING MY SKILLS. BUT, WHEN IT COMES TO STUDYING...
HEHEHEH
!!?
I'M STILL A DUMMY.
HAHAHA. DON'T WORRY. EVEN I WAS ABLE TO GET A "B."
DAT DUN
KROOM
WHY ARE YOU GUYS STUDYING? YOU SHOULD BE WATCHING ME BOWL!
WHA?! SORRY!!
BUT, NARU... IF YOU'RE SO GOOD, YOU SHOULD PLAY WITH US.
PLEASE TEACH ME, NARUSEGAWA.
I GUESS NOW I HAVE NO CHOICE. BUT I WON'T GO EASY ON YOU!!

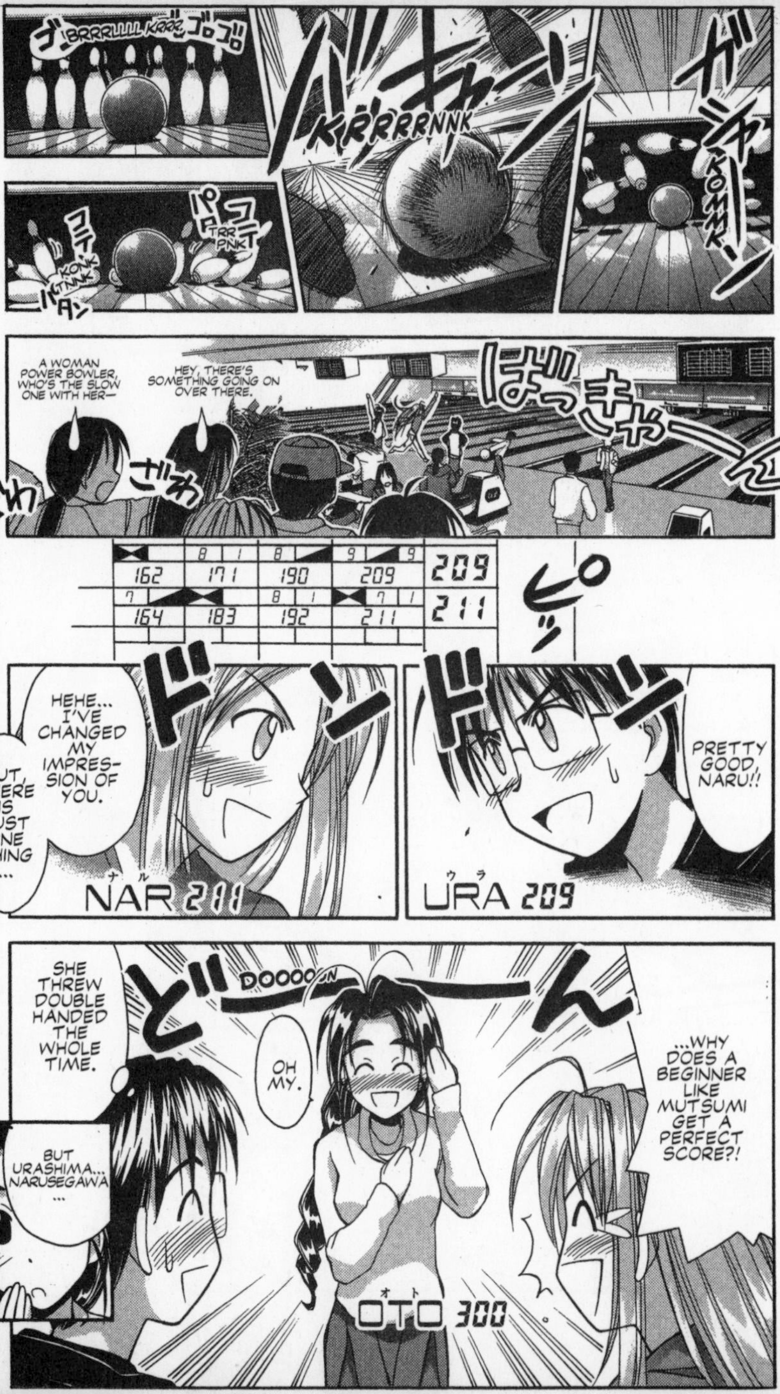
ガシャ
KOMMK
バガァーン
KRRRRRNNK
ゴロゴロ
BRRRULLL KRRR
コテ
TRR PNK
パタ
コテ
KONK TNNK
パタン
ばっきゃーん
HEY, THERE'S SOMETHING GOING ON OVER THERE.
A WOMAN POWER BOWLER, WHO'S THE SLOW ONE WITH HER—
ざわ
ざわ
209
211
162 171 190 209
164 183 192 211
ピッ
ドン
PRETTY GOOD, NARU!!
URA 209
HEHE... I'VE CHANGED MY IMPRESSION OF YOU.
BUT, THERE IS JUST ONE THING...
NAR 211
...WHY DOES A BEGINNER LIKE MUTSUMI GET A PERFECT SCORE?!
どーん
DOOOOON
OH MY.
SHE THREW DOUBLE HANDED THE WHOLE TIME.
BUT URASHIMA... NARUSEGAWA...
OTO 300

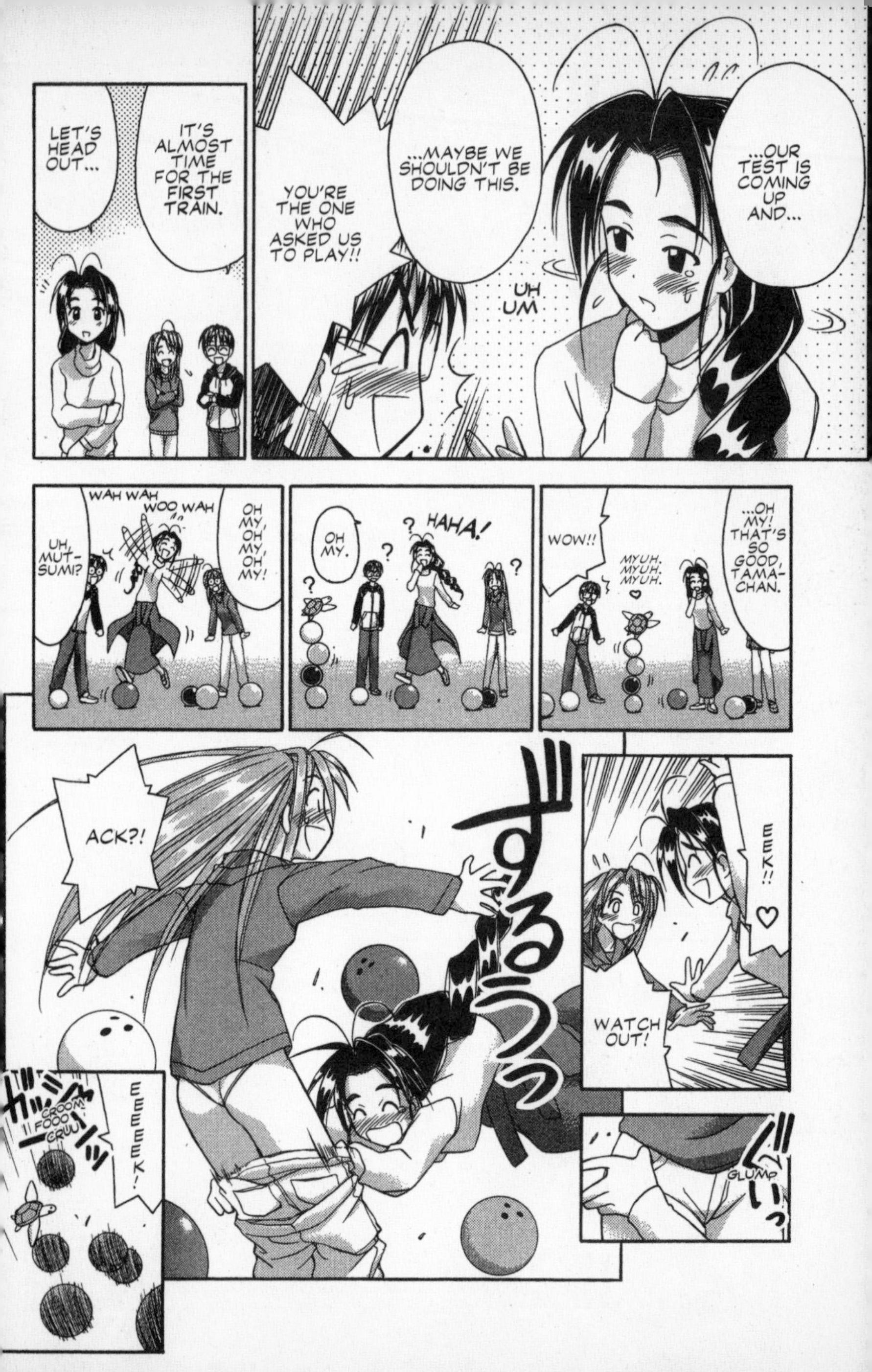
...OUR TEST IS COMING UP AND...
UH UM
...MAYBE WE SHOULDN'T BE DOING THIS.
YOU'RE THE ONE WHO ASKED US TO PLAY!!
IT'S ALMOST TIME FOR THE FIRST TRAIN.
LET'S HEAD OUT...
...OH MY! THAT'S SO GOOD, TAMA-CHAN.
MYUH. MYUH. MYUH.
WOW!!
HAHA!
OH MY.
OH MY, OH MY, OH MY!
WOO WAH
WAH WAH
UH, MUT-SUMI?
EEEK!!
WATCH OUT!
GLUMP
ACK?!
EEEEEK!
CROOM FOOO CRUU

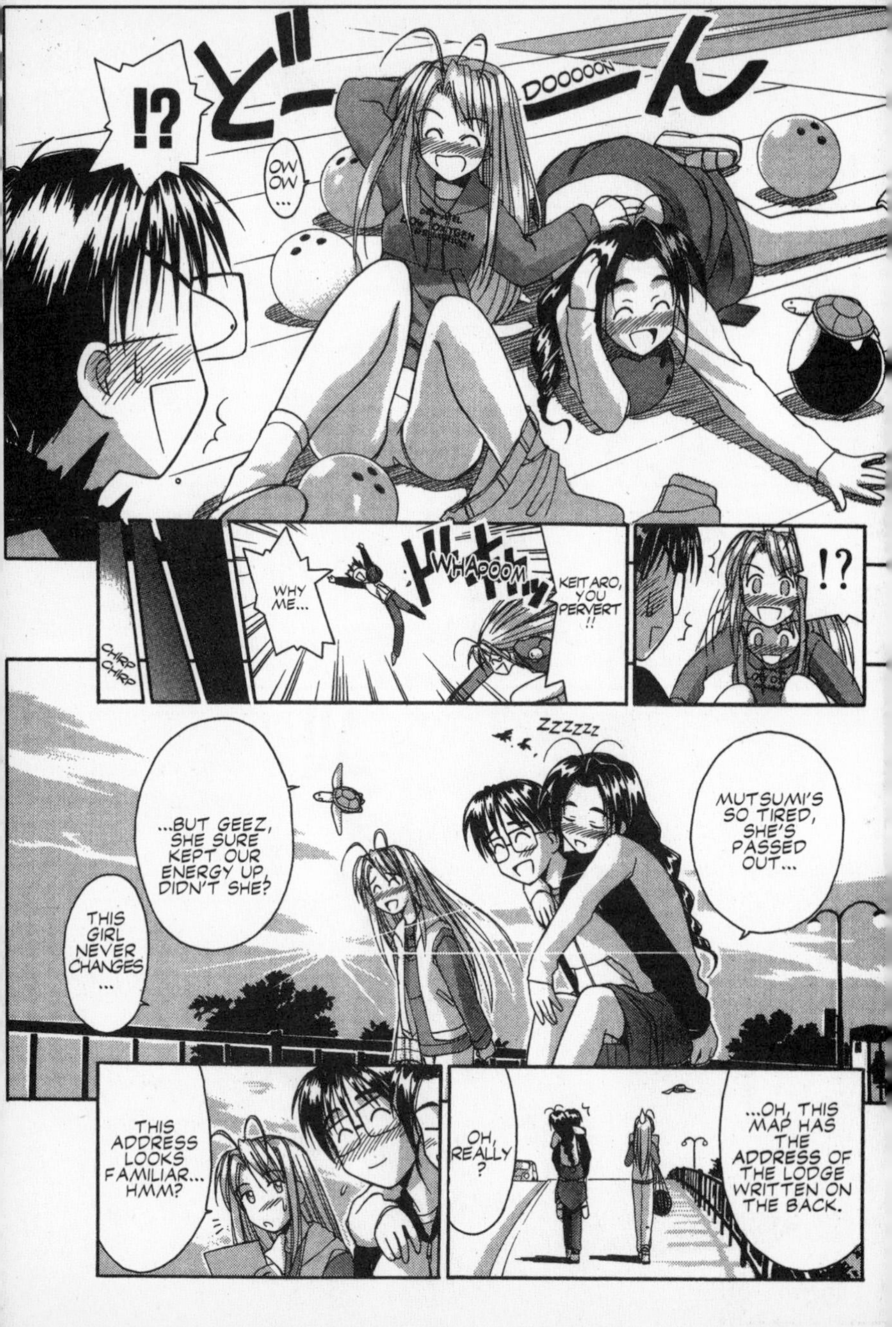
どーん
DOOOOON
!?
OW OW ...
!?
KEITARO, YOU PERVERT !!
WHAPOOM
WHY ME...
CHIRP CHIRP
MUTSUMI'S SO TIRED, SHE'S PASSED OUT...
ZZZZZZ
...BUT GEEZ, SHE SURE KEPT OUR ENERGY UP, DIDN'T SHE?
THIS GIRL NEVER CHANGES ...
...OH, THIS MAP HAS THE ADDRESS OF THE LODGE WRITTEN ON THE BACK.
OH, REALLY ?
THIS ADDRESS LOOKS FAMILIAR... HMM?

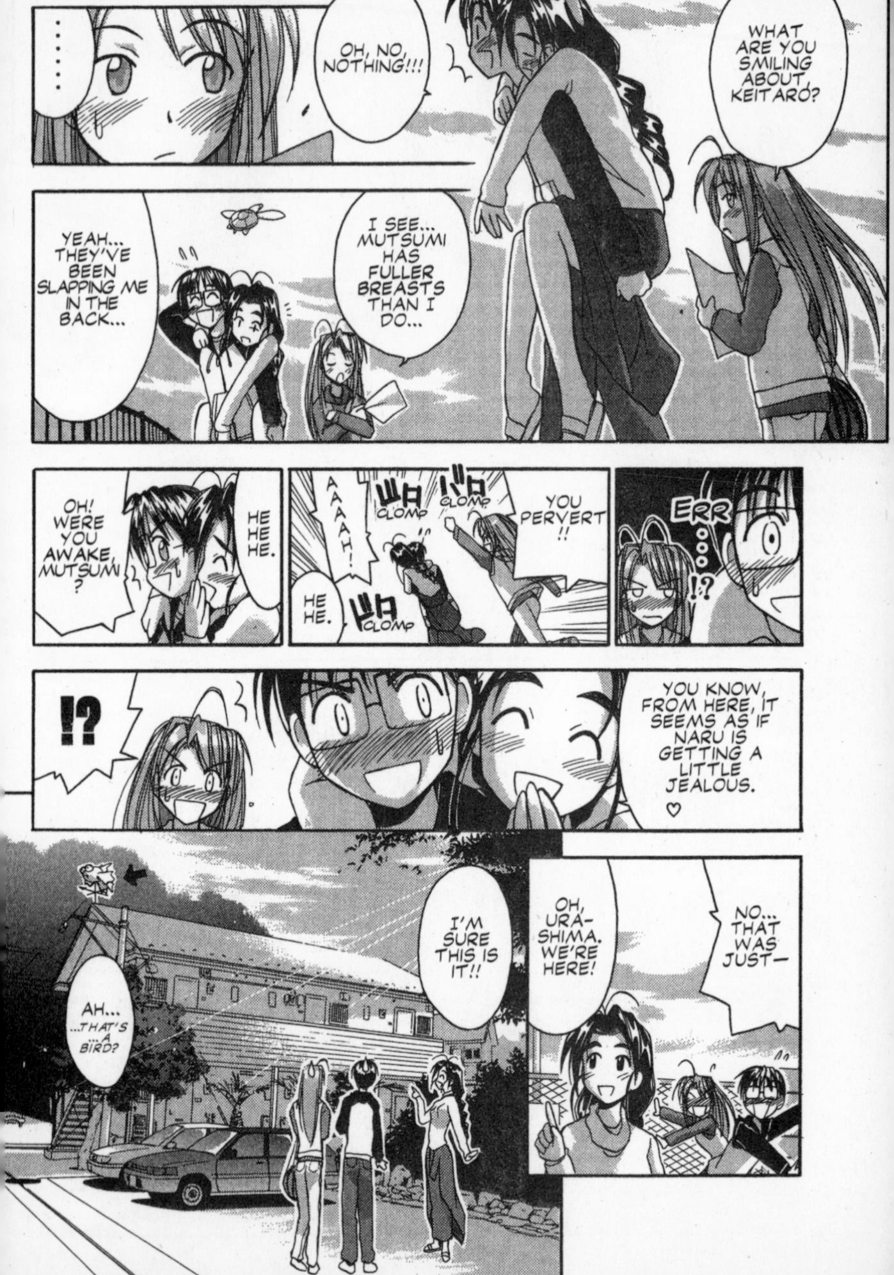
WHAT ARE YOU SMILING ABOUT, KEITARO?
OH, NO, NOTHING!!!
......
I SEE... MUTSUMI HAS FULLER BREASTS THAN I DO...
YEAH... THEY'VE BEEN SLAPPING ME IN THE BACK...
ERR
OOOO
!?
YOU PERVERT!!
CLOMP
CLOMP
AAAAH!
HE HE.
CLOMP
HE HE HE.
OH! WERE YOU AWAKE, MUTSUMI?
YOU KNOW, FROM HERE, IT SEEMS AS IF NARU IS GETTING A LITTLE JEALOUS. ♡
!?
NO... THAT WAS JUST—
OH, URASHIMA. WE'RE HERE!
I'M SURE THIS IS IT!!
AH... ...THAT'S ...A BIRD?

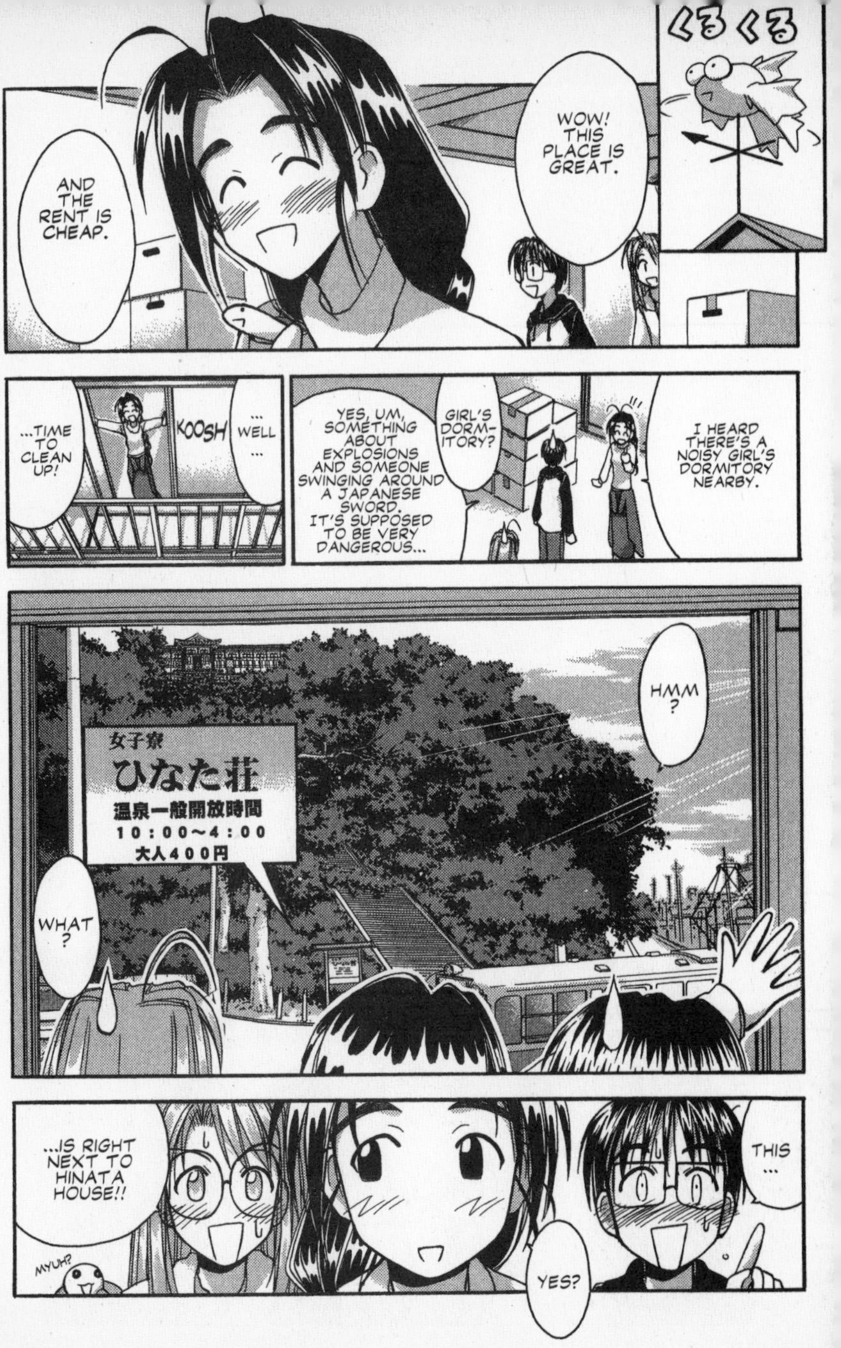
くるくる
WOW! THIS PLACE IS GREAT.
AND THE RENT IS CHEAP.
I HEARD THERE'S A NOISY GIRL'S DORMITORY NEARBY.
GIRL'S DORMITORY?
YES, UM, SOMETHING ABOUT EXPLOSIONS AND SOMEONE SWINGING AROUND A JAPANESE SWORD. IT'S SUPPOSED TO BE VERY DANGEROUS...
... WELL ...
KOOSH
...TIME TO CLEAN UP!
HMM?
女子寮
ひなた荘
温泉一般開放時間
10:00~4:00
大人400円
WHAT?
THIS ...
YES?
...IS RIGHT NEXT TO HINATA HOUSE!!
MYUH?

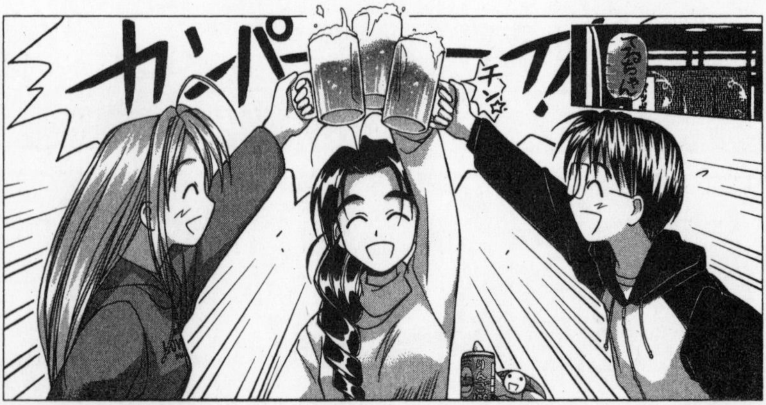
カンパーイ!
チン☆

Love Hina

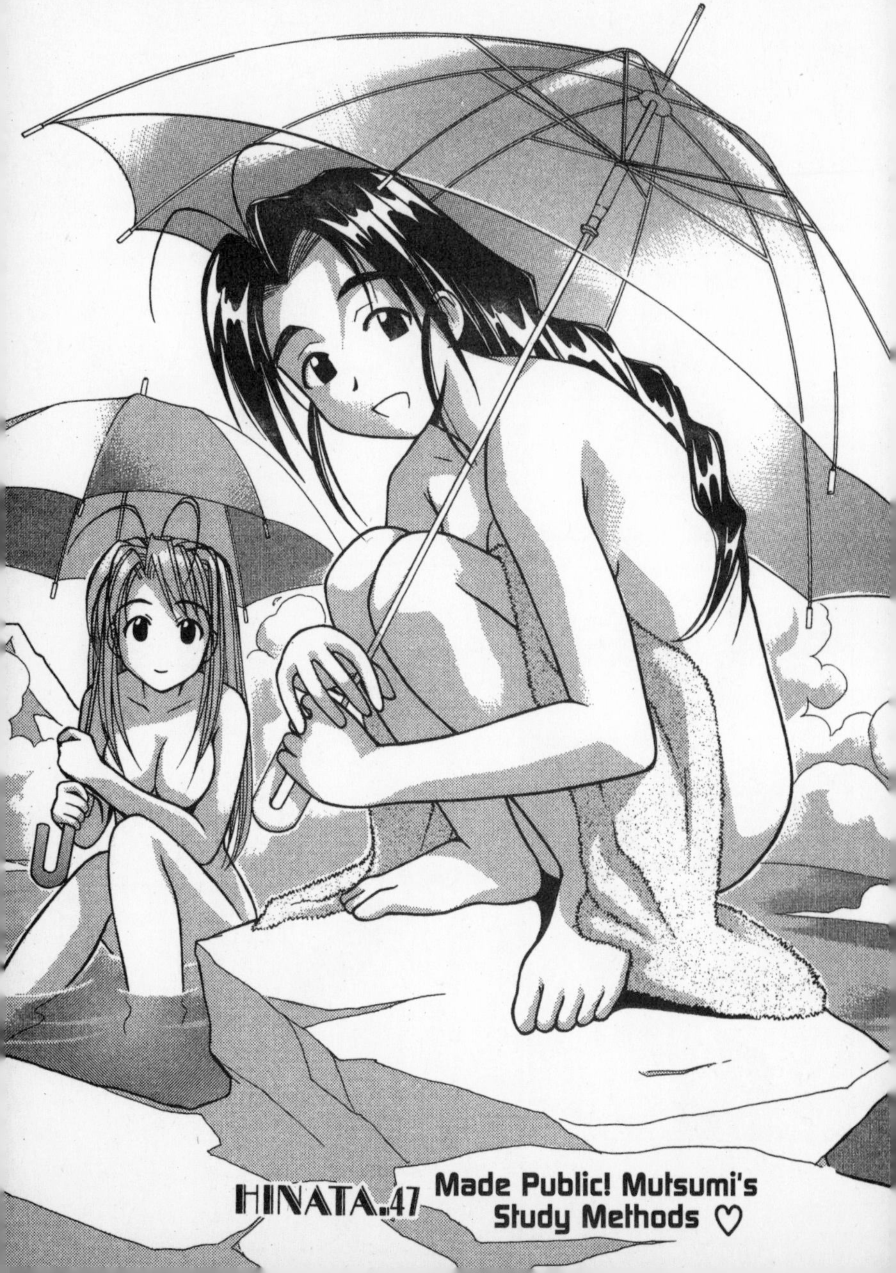

HINATA.47 Made Public! Mutsumi's Study Methods ♡

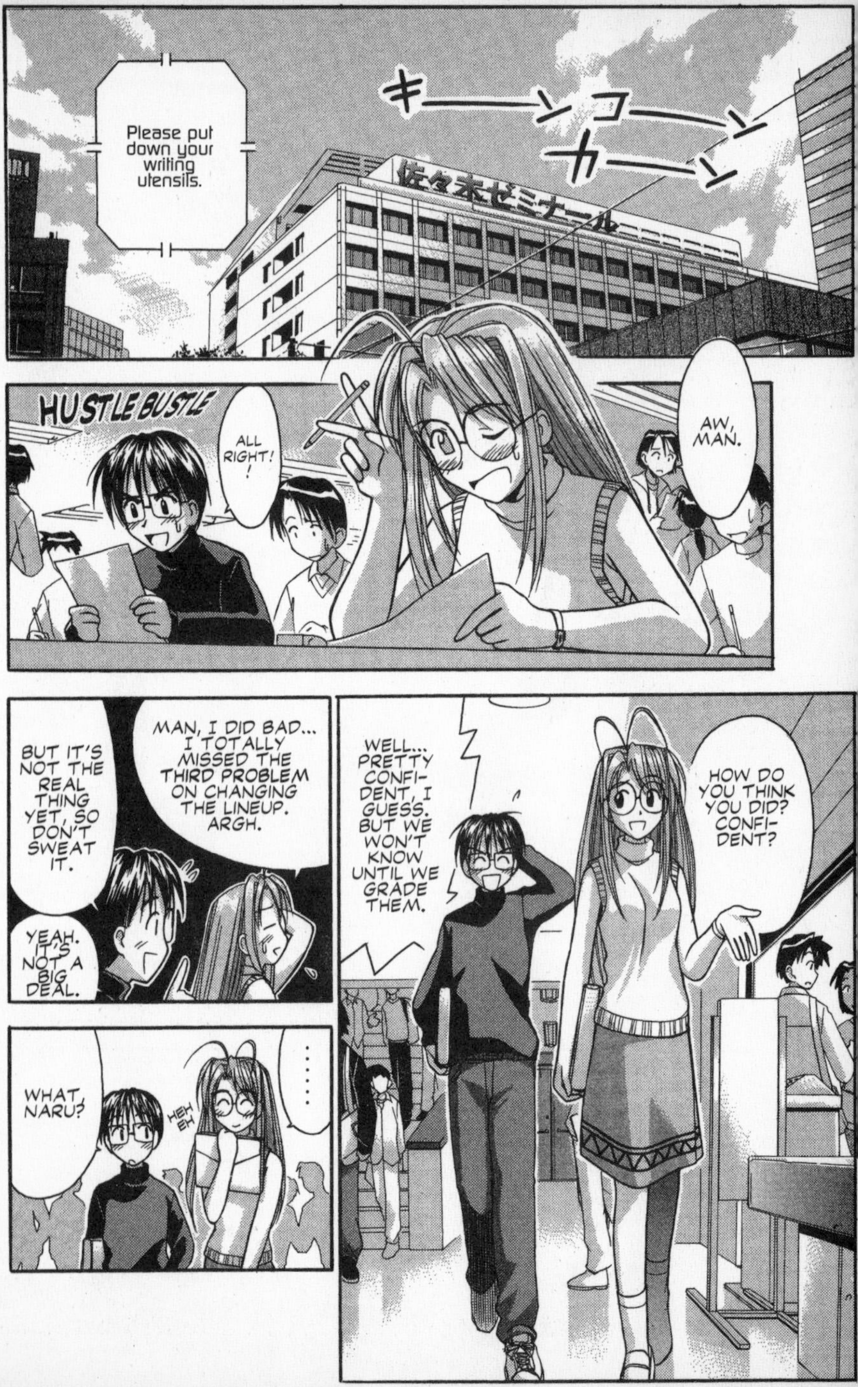

Please put down your writing utensils.
キーンコーン
カーン
佐々木ゼミナール
AW, MAN.
ALL RIGHT!!
HUSTLE BUSTLE
HOW DO YOU THINK YOU DID? CONFIDENT?
WELL... PRETTY CONFIDENT, I GUESS. BUT WE WON'T KNOW UNTIL WE GRADE THEM.
MAN, I DID BAD... I TOTALLY MISSED THE THIRD PROBLEM ON CHANGING THE LINEUP. ARGH.
BUT IT'S NOT THE REAL THING YET, SO DON'T SWEAT IT.
YEAH. IT'S NOT A BIG DEAL.
......
HEH EH
WHAT, NARU?

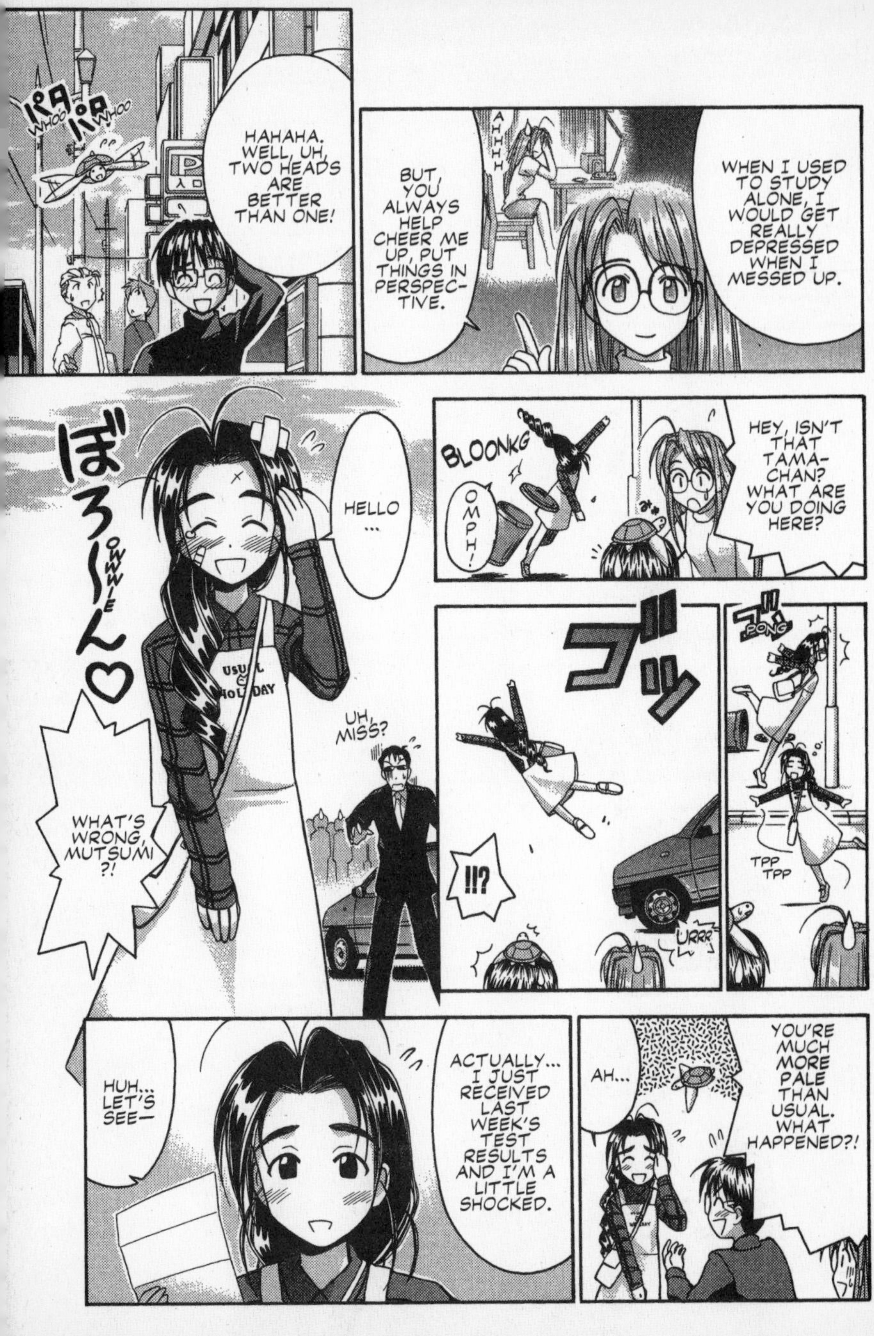
WHEN I USED TO STUDY ALONE, I WOULD GET REALLY DEPRESSED WHEN I MESSED UP.
AHHHH
BUT, YOU ALWAYS HELP CHEER ME UP, PUT THINGS IN PERSPEC-TIVE.
HAHAHA. WELL, UH, TWO HEADS ARE BETTER THAN ONE!
パタ WHOO パタ WHOO
HEY, ISN'T THAT TAMA-CHAN? WHAT ARE YOU DOING HERE?
BLOONKG
OMPH!
PONG
TPP TPP
URRR
ゴッ
!!?
HELLO ...
ぼろ〜ん♡
OWWIE
UH, MISS?
WHAT'S WRONG, MUTSUMI?!
YOU'RE MUCH MORE PALE THAN USUAL. WHAT HAPPENED?!
AH...
ACTUALLY... I JUST RECEIVED LAST WEEK'S TEST RESULTS AND I'M A LITTLE SHOCKED.
HUH... LET'S SEE—

Name: Otohime Mutsumi "Sasaki Seminar Scho

Intended Study	Results	Percentile	Comment
Tokyo University III	Z	-100%	*Please, at least write your name.
Tokyo University I	Z	-100%	*Please, at least

IF YOU DON'T TAKE THIS MORE SERIOUSLY YOU'RE NOT GONNA GET IN!

MUTSUMI, IT'S ALREADY NOVEMBER.

OH MY...

...THAT IS TRUE...

YES.

YOU HAVE TO MAKE SURE YOU AT LEAST WRITE YOUR NAME CORRECTLY!!

AH... I JUST GOT SO NERVOUS —

Z —!?

WHAT SHOULD WE DO? THERE ARE ONLY TWO AND A HALF MONTHS BEFORE THE NEXT TEST. IF YOU DON'T PASS IT, YOU'LL BE A FOURTH-YEAR RONIN!

I DON'T KNOW...

NOT IF YOU DON'T STUDY.

THINGS JUST MAY WORK THEM- SELVES OUT.

...OH YEAH!

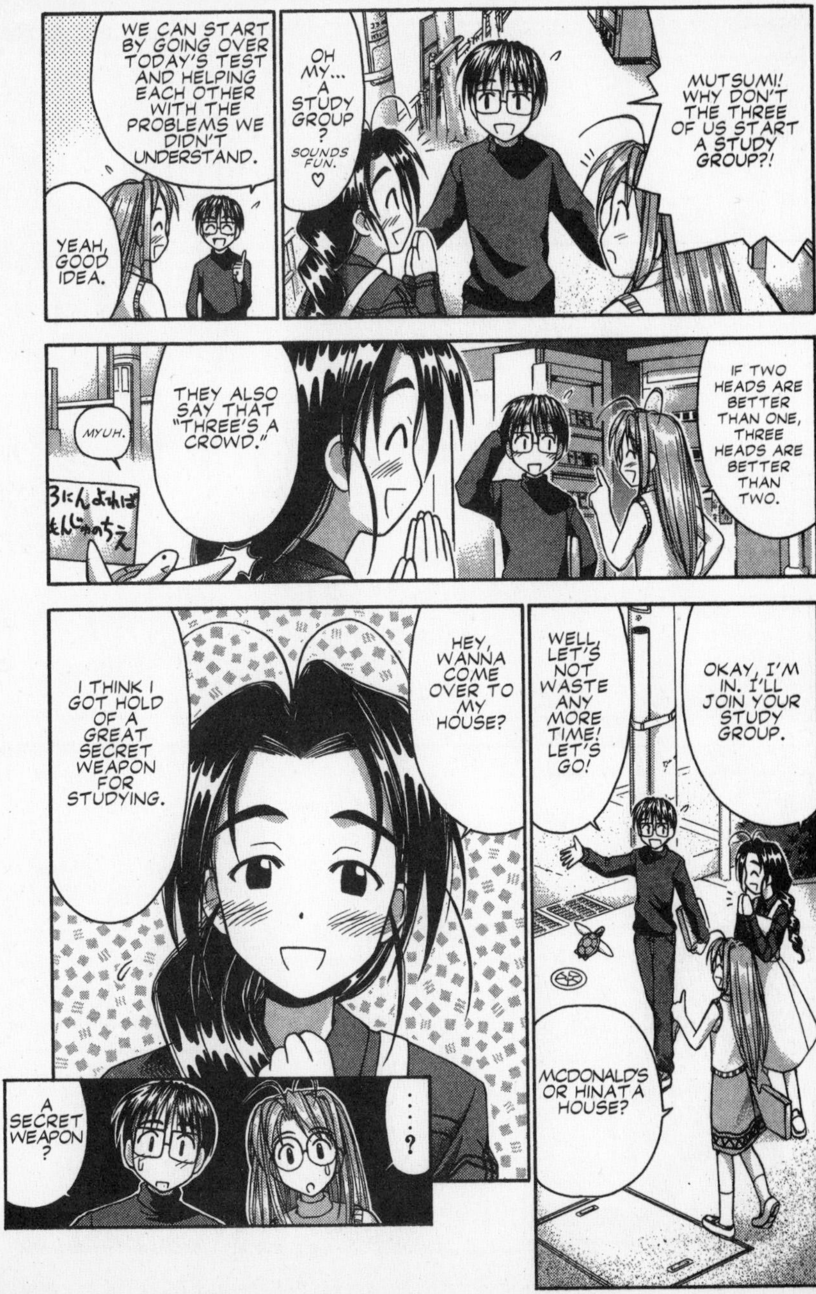
MUTSUMI! WHY DON'T THE THREE OF US START A STUDY GROUP?!
OH MY... A STUDY GROUP?
SOUNDS FUN. ♡
WE CAN START BY GOING OVER TODAY'S TEST AND HELPING EACH OTHER WITH THE PROBLEMS WE DIDN'T UNDERSTAND.
YEAH, GOOD IDEA.
IF TWO HEADS ARE BETTER THAN ONE, THREE HEADS ARE BETTER THAN TWO.
THEY ALSO SAY THAT "THREE'S A CROWD."
MYUH.
3にんよればもんじゅのちえ
OKAY, I'M IN. I'LL JOIN YOUR STUDY GROUP.
WELL, LET'S NOT WASTE ANY MORE TIME! LET'S GO!
MCDONALD'S OR HINATA HOUSE?
HEY, WANNA COME OVER TO MY HOUSE?
I THINK I GOT HOLD OF A GREAT SECRET WEAPON FOR STUDYING.
....?
A SECRET WEAPON?

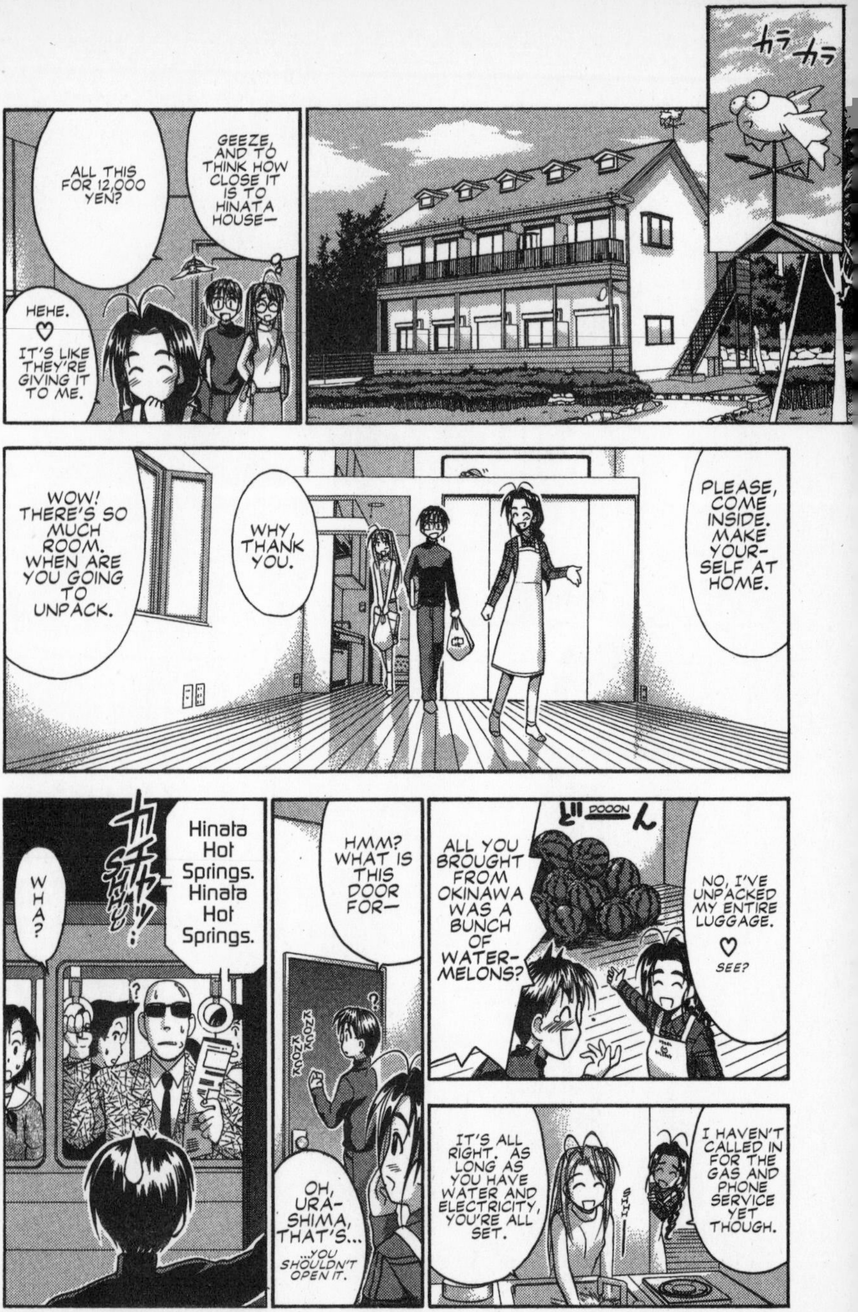
カラ カラ
GEEZE, AND TO THINK HOW CLOSE IT IS TO HINATA HOUSE—
ALL THIS FOR 12,000 YEN?
HEHE. ♡ IT'S LIKE THEY'RE GIVING IT TO ME.
PLEASE, COME INSIDE. MAKE YOUR-SELF AT HOME.
WHY, THANK YOU.
WOW! THERE'S SO MUCH ROOM. WHEN ARE YOU GOING TO UNPACK.
NO, I'VE UNPACKED MY ENTIRE LUGGAGE. ♡ SEE?
どーん DOOON
ALL YOU BROUGHT FROM OKINAWA WAS A BUNCH OF WATER-MELONS?
I HAVEN'T CALLED IN FOR THE GAS AND PHONE SERVICE YET THOUGH.
SHH—
IT'S ALL RIGHT. AS LONG AS YOU HAVE WATER AND ELECTRICITY, YOU'RE ALL SET.
HMM? WHAT IS THIS DOOR FOR—
KNOCK KNOCK
OH, URA-SHIMA, THAT'S...
...YOU SHOULDN'T OPEN IT.
Hinata Hot Springs. Hinata Hot Springs.
SHAK
WHA?

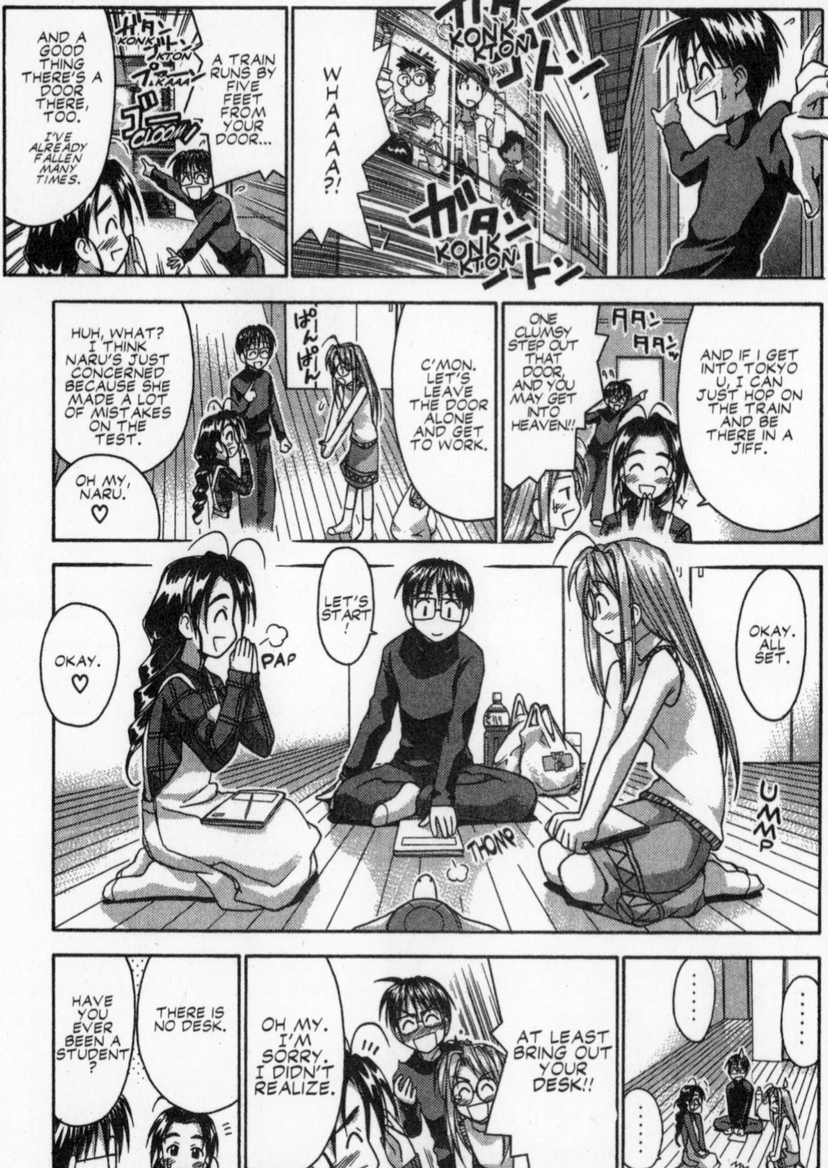
ガタン
KONK
KTON
ゴトン
WHAAAAA?!
ガタン
KONK
KTON
ゴトン
A TRAIN RUNS BY FIVE FEET FROM YOUR DOOR...
ガタン KONK
ゴトン KTON
プァーン KAAAN
ゴー CLOOM
AND A GOOD THING THERE'S A DOOR THERE, TOO.
I'VE ALREADY FALLEN MANY TIMES.
AND IF I GET INTO TOKYO U, I CAN JUST HOP ON THE TRAIN AND BE THERE IN A JIFF.
タタン タタン
ONE CLUMSY STEP OUT THAT DOOR, AND YOU MAY GET INTO HEAVEN!!
C'MON. LET'S LEAVE THE DOOR ALONE AND GET TO WORK.
ぱんぱーん
HUH, WHAT? I THINK NARU'S JUST CONCERNED BECAUSE SHE MADE A LOT OF MISTAKES ON THE TEST.
OH MY, NARU. ♡
OKAY. ALL SET.
UMMP
THOMP
LET'S START!
PAP
OKAY. ♡
......
......
......
AT LEAST BRING OUT YOUR DESK!!
OH MY. I'M SORRY. I DIDN'T REALIZE.
THERE IS NO DESK.
HAVE YOU EVER BEEN A STUDENT?

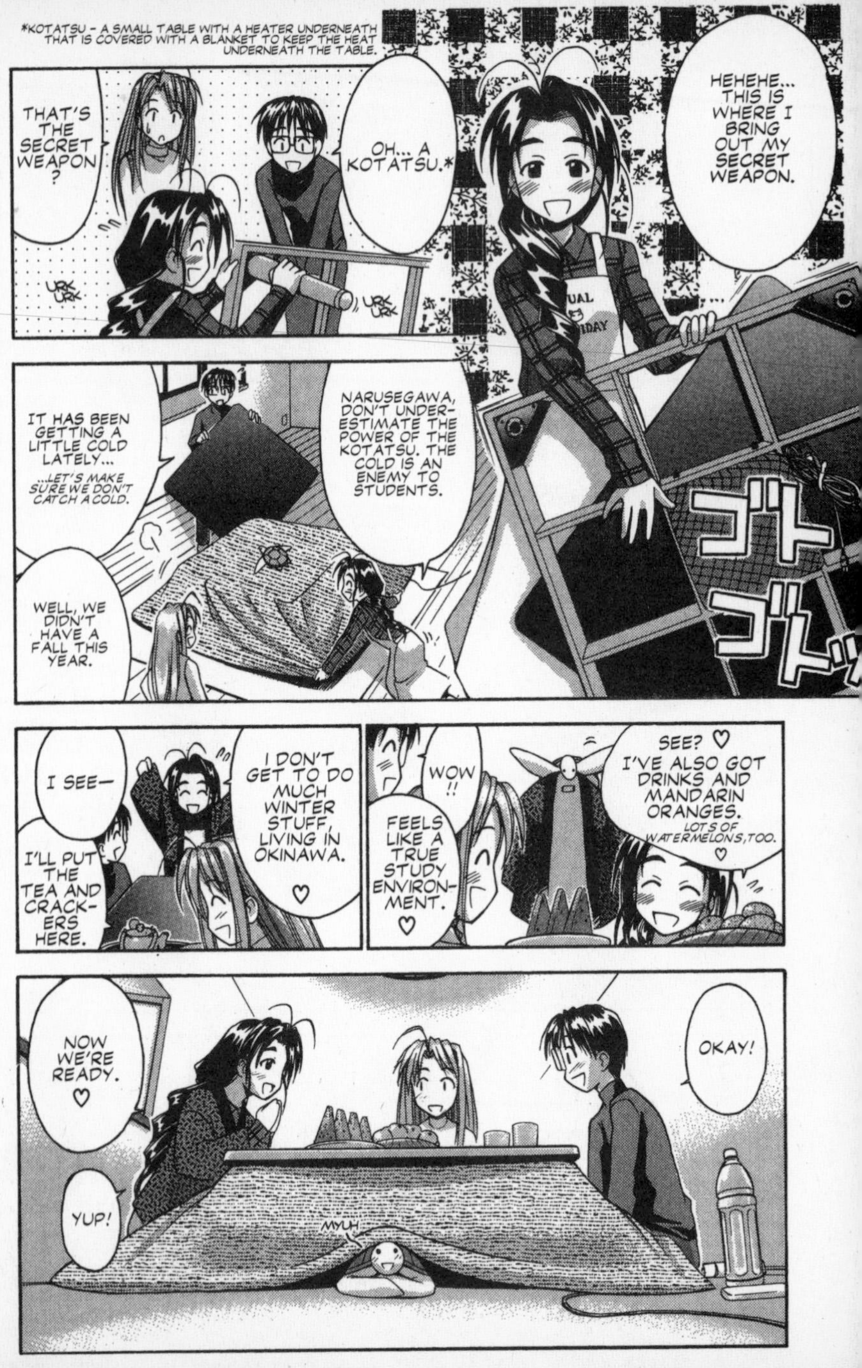
*KOTATSU - A SMALL TABLE WITH A HEATER UNDERNEATH THAT IS COVERED WITH A BLANKET TO KEEP THE HEAT UNDERNEATH THE TABLE.
HEHEHE... THIS IS WHERE I BRING OUT MY SECRET WEAPON.
ゴトゴトッ
OH... A KOTATSU.*
THAT'S THE SECRET WEAPON?
URK URK
URK URK
NARUSEGAWA, DON'T UNDER-ESTIMATE THE POWER OF THE KOTATSU. THE COLD IS AN ENEMY TO STUDENTS.
IT HAS BEEN GETTING A LITTLE COLD LATELY...
...LET'S MAKE SURE WE DON'T CATCH A COLD.
WELL, WE DIDN'T HAVE A FALL THIS YEAR.
SEE? ♡ I'VE ALSO GOT DRINKS AND MANDARIN ORANGES.
LOTS OF WATERMELONS, TOO. ♡
WOW!!
FEELS LIKE A TRUE STUDY ENVIRONMENT. ♡
I DON'T GET TO DO MUCH WINTER STUFF, LIVING IN OKINAWA. ♡
I SEE—
I'LL PUT THE TEA AND CRACKERS HERE.
OKAY!
NOW WE'RE READY. ♡
YUP!
MYUH

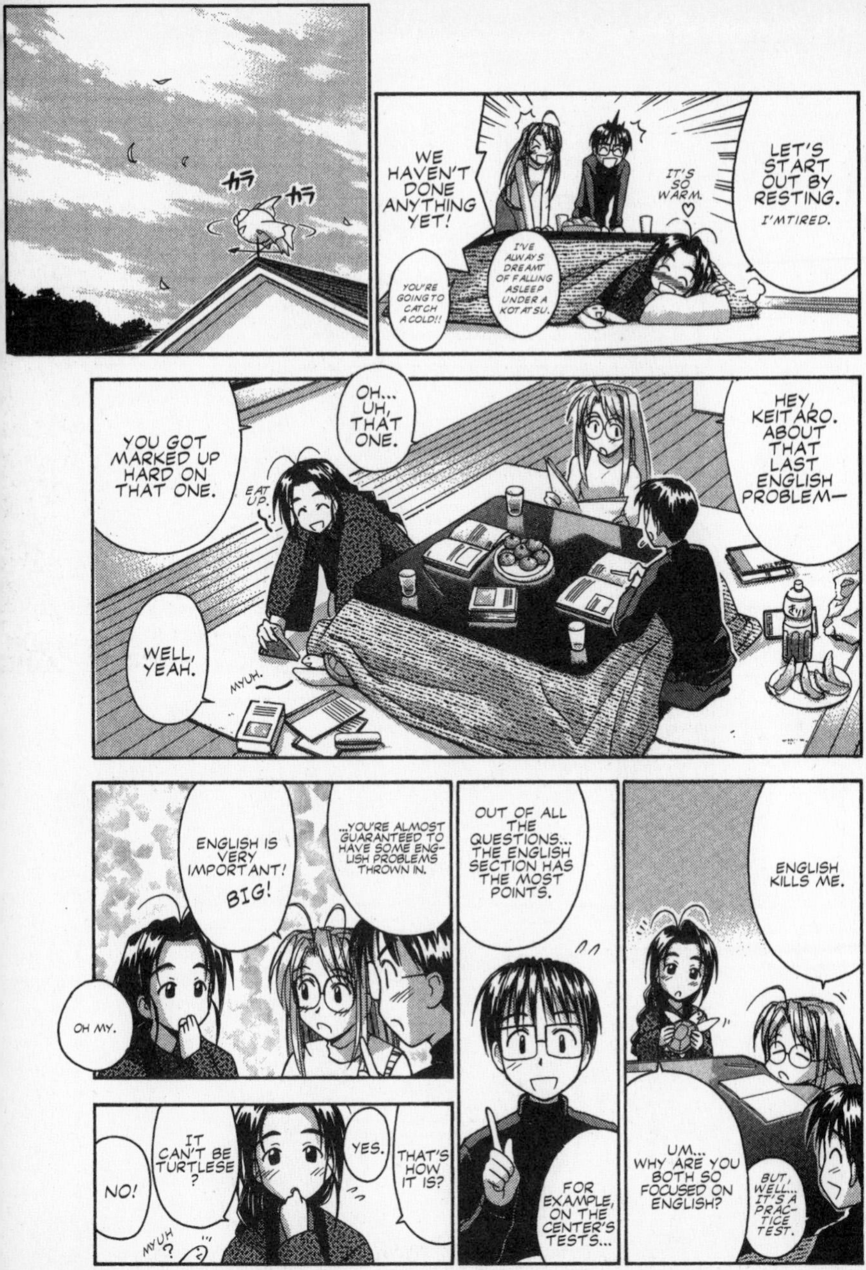
LET'S START OUT BY RESTING.
I'M TIRED.
IT'S SO WARM. ♡
WE HAVEN'T DONE ANYTHING YET!
I'VE ALWAYS DREAMT OF FALLING ASLEEP UNDER A KOTATSU.
YOU'RE GOING TO CATCH A COLD!!
カラ
カラ
HEY, KEITARO. ABOUT THAT LAST ENGLISH PROBLEM—
OH... UH, THAT ONE.
YOU GOT MARKED UP HARD ON THAT ONE.
EAT UP.
WELL, YEAH.
MYUH.
ENGLISH KILLS ME.
UM... WHY ARE YOU BOTH SO FOCUSED ON ENGLISH?
BUT, WELL... IT'S A PRACTICE TEST.
OUT OF ALL THE QUESTIONS... THE ENGLISH SECTION HAS THE MOST POINTS.
FOR EXAMPLE, ON THE CENTER'S TESTS...
...YOU'RE ALMOST GUARANTEED TO HAVE SOME ENGLISH PROBLEMS THROWN IN.
ENGLISH IS VERY IMPORTANT! BIG!
OH MY.
THAT'S HOW IT IS?
YES.
IT CAN'T BE TURTLESE?
NO!
MYUH?

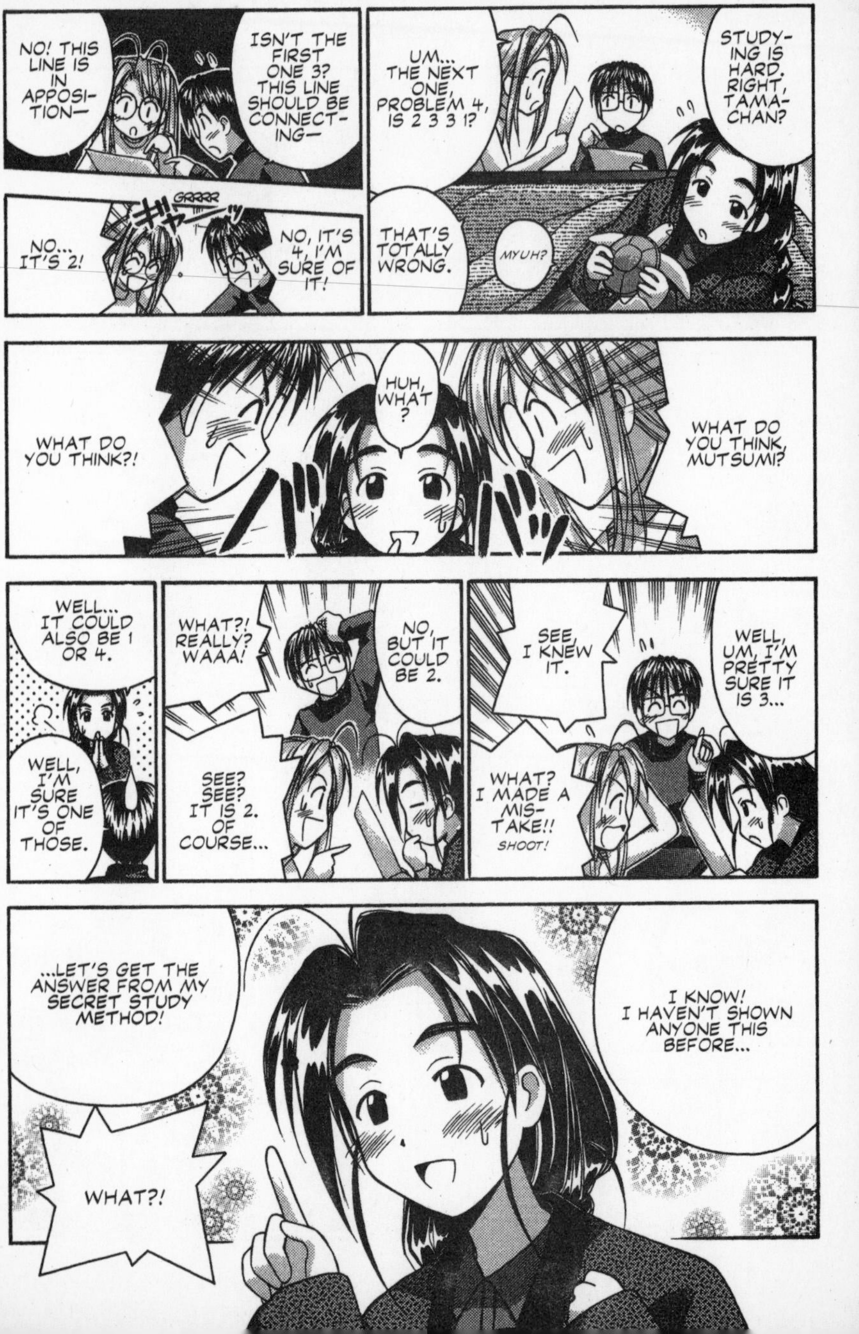
STUDYING IS HARD, RIGHT, TAMA-CHAN?
UM... THE NEXT ONE, PROBLEM 4, IS 2 3 3 1?
ISN'T THE FIRST ONE 3? THIS LINE SHOULD BE CONNECTING—
NO! THIS LINE IS IN APPOSITION—
MYUH?
THAT'S TOTALLY WRONG.
GRRRR
NO, IT'S 4, I'M SURE OF IT!
NO... IT'S 2!
WHAT DO YOU THINK, MUTSUMI?
HUH, WHAT?
WHAT DO YOU THINK?!
WELL, UM, I'M PRETTY SURE IT IS 3...
SEE, I KNEW IT.
WHAT? I MADE A MISTAKE!!
SHOOT!
NO, BUT IT COULD BE 2.
WHAT?! REALLY? WAAA!
SEE? SEE? IT IS 2. OF COURSE...
WELL... IT COULD ALSO BE 1 OR 4.
WELL, I'M SURE IT'S ONE OF THOSE.
I KNOW! I HAVEN'T SHOWN ANYONE THIS BEFORE...
...LET'S GET THE ANSWER FROM MY SECRET STUDY METHOD!
WHAT?!

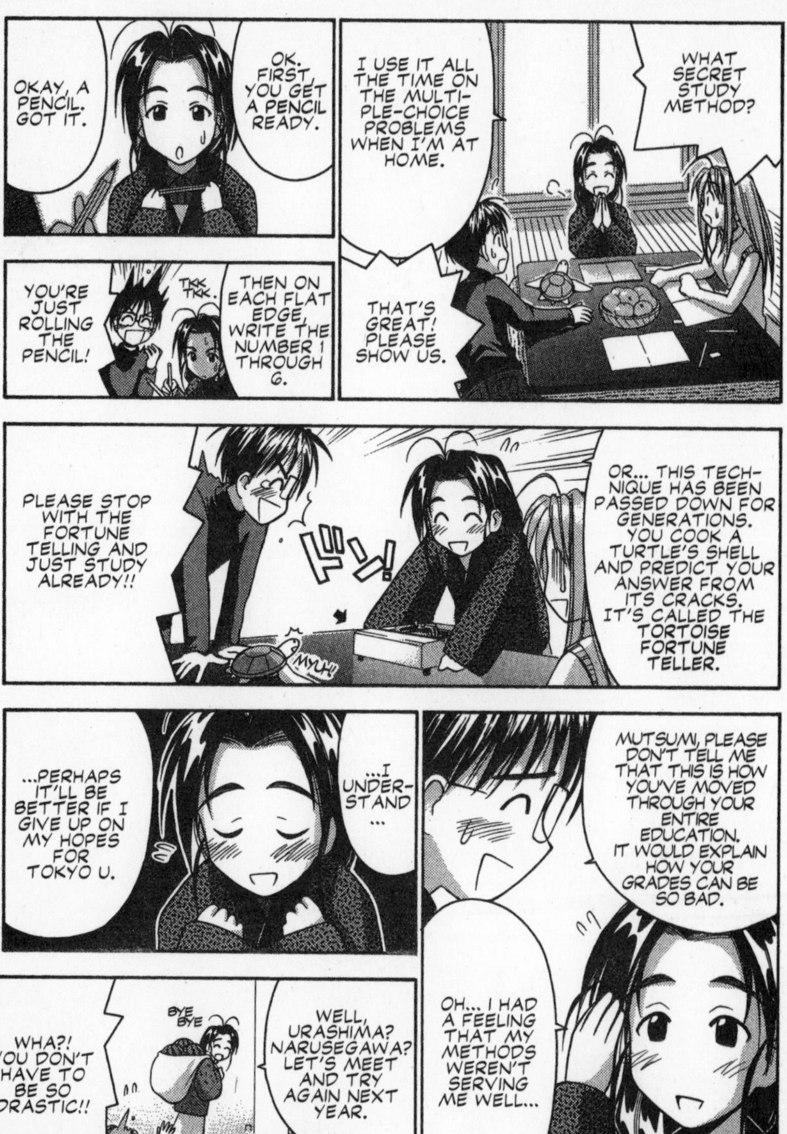
WHAT SECRET STUDY METHOD?
I USE IT ALL THE TIME ON THE MULTI-PLE-CHOICE PROBLEMS WHEN I'M AT HOME.
THAT'S GREAT! PLEASE SHOW US.
OK. FIRST, YOU GET A PENCIL READY.
OKAY, A PENCIL. GOT IT.
THEN ON EACH FLAT EDGE, WRITE THE NUMBER 1 THROUGH 6.
TKK TKK.
YOU'RE JUST ROLLING THE PENCIL!
OR... THIS TECH-NIQUE HAS BEEN PASSED DOWN FOR GENERATIONS. YOU COOK A TURTLE'S SHELL AND PREDICT YOUR ANSWER FROM ITS CRACKS. IT'S CALLED THE TORTOISE FORTUNE TELLER.
ドン!
MYUH!
PLEASE STOP WITH THE FORTUNE TELLING AND JUST STUDY ALREADY!!
MUTSUMI, PLEASE DON'T TELL ME THAT THIS IS HOW YOU'VE MOVED THROUGH YOUR ENTIRE EDUCATION. IT WOULD EXPLAIN HOW YOUR GRADES CAN BE SO BAD.
OH... I HAD A FEELING THAT MY METHODS WEREN'T SERVING ME WELL...
...I UNDER-STAND...
...PERHAPS IT'LL BE BETTER IF I GIVE UP ON MY HOPES FOR TOKYO U.
WELL, URASHIMA? NARUSEGAWA? LET'S MEET AND TRY AGAIN NEXT YEAR.
BYE BYE
WHA?! YOU DON'T HAVE TO BE SO DRASTIC!!

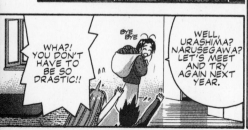

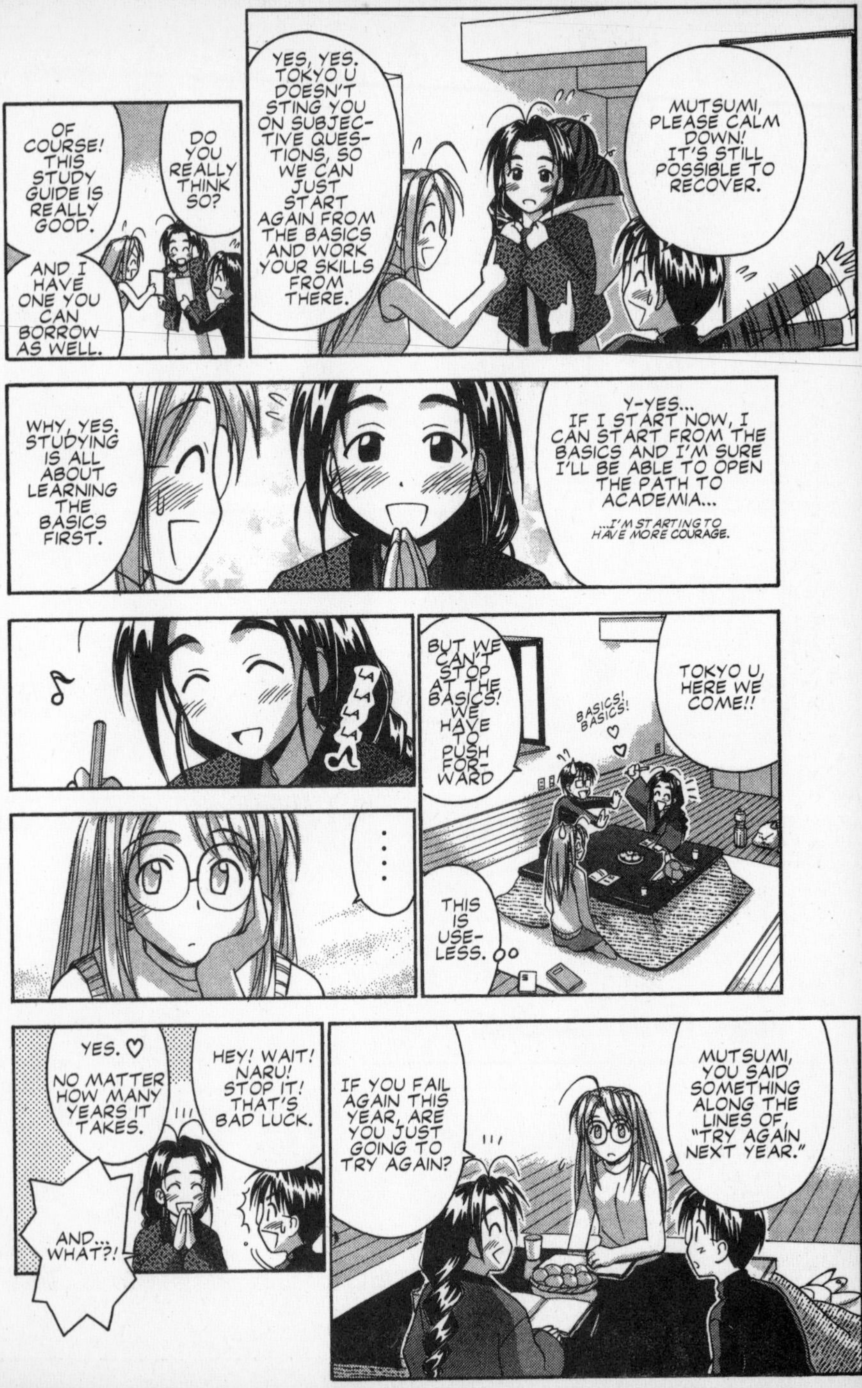

MUTSUMI, PLEASE CALM DOWN! IT'S STILL POSSIBLE TO RECOVER.
YES, YES. TOKYO U DOESN'T STING YOU ON SUBJECTIVE QUESTIONS, SO WE CAN JUST START AGAIN FROM THE BASICS AND WORK YOUR SKILLS FROM THERE.
DO YOU REALLY THINK SO?
OF COURSE! THIS STUDY GUIDE IS REALLY GOOD.
AND I HAVE ONE YOU CAN BORROW AS WELL.
Y-YES... IF I START NOW, I CAN START FROM THE BASICS AND I'M SURE I'LL BE ABLE TO OPEN THE PATH TO ACADEMIA...
...I'M STARTING TO HAVE MORE COURAGE.
WHY, YES. STUDYING IS ALL ABOUT LEARNING THE BASICS FIRST.
TOKYO U, HERE WE COME!!
BASICS! BASICS! ♡
BUT WE CAN'T STOP AT THE BASICS! WE HAVE TO PUSH FORWARD
THIS IS USELESS.
LA LA LA LA
....
MUTSUMI, YOU SAID SOMETHING ALONG THE LINES OF, "TRY AGAIN NEXT YEAR."
IF YOU FAIL AGAIN THIS YEAR, ARE YOU JUST GOING TO TRY AGAIN?
YES. ♡ NO MATTER HOW MANY YEARS IT TAKES.
HEY! WAIT! NARU! STOP IT! THAT'S BAD LUCK.
AND... WHAT?!

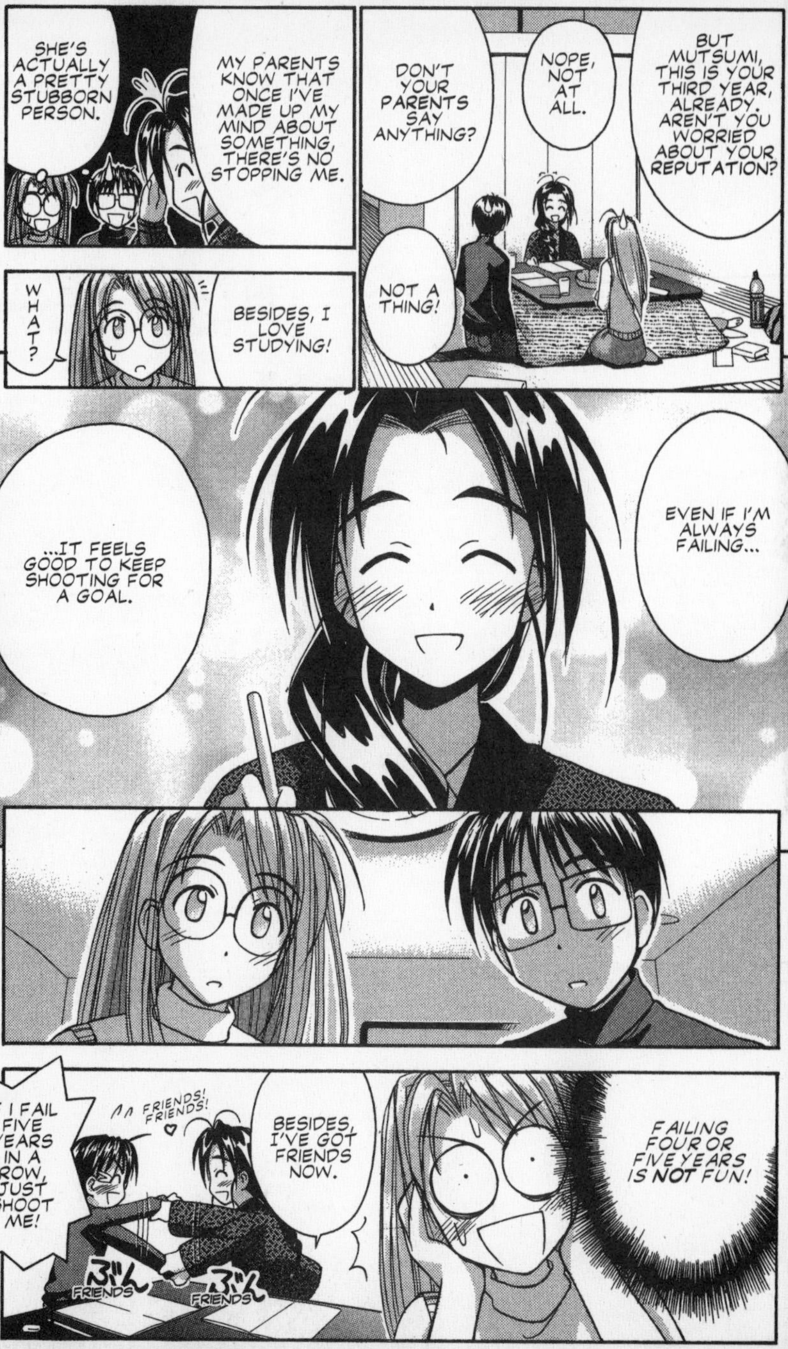
BUT MUTSUMI, THIS IS YOUR THIRD YEAR, ALREADY. AREN'T YOU WORRIED ABOUT YOUR REPUTATION?
NOPE, NOT AT ALL.
DON'T YOUR PARENTS SAY ANYTHING?
NOT A THING!
MY PARENTS KNOW THAT ONCE I'VE MADE UP MY MIND ABOUT SOMETHING, THERE'S NO STOPPING ME.
SHE'S ACTUALLY A PRETTY STUBBORN PERSON.
BESIDES, I LOVE STUDYING!
WHAT?
EVEN IF I'M ALWAYS FAILING...
...IT FEELS GOOD TO KEEP SHOOTING FOR A GOAL.
FAILING FOUR OR FIVE YEARS IS **NOT** FUN!
BESIDES, I'VE GOT FRIENDS NOW.
FRIENDS! FRIENDS!
IF I FAIL FIVE YEARS IN A ROW, JUST SHOOT ME!
ぶん FRIENDS
ぶん FRIENDS

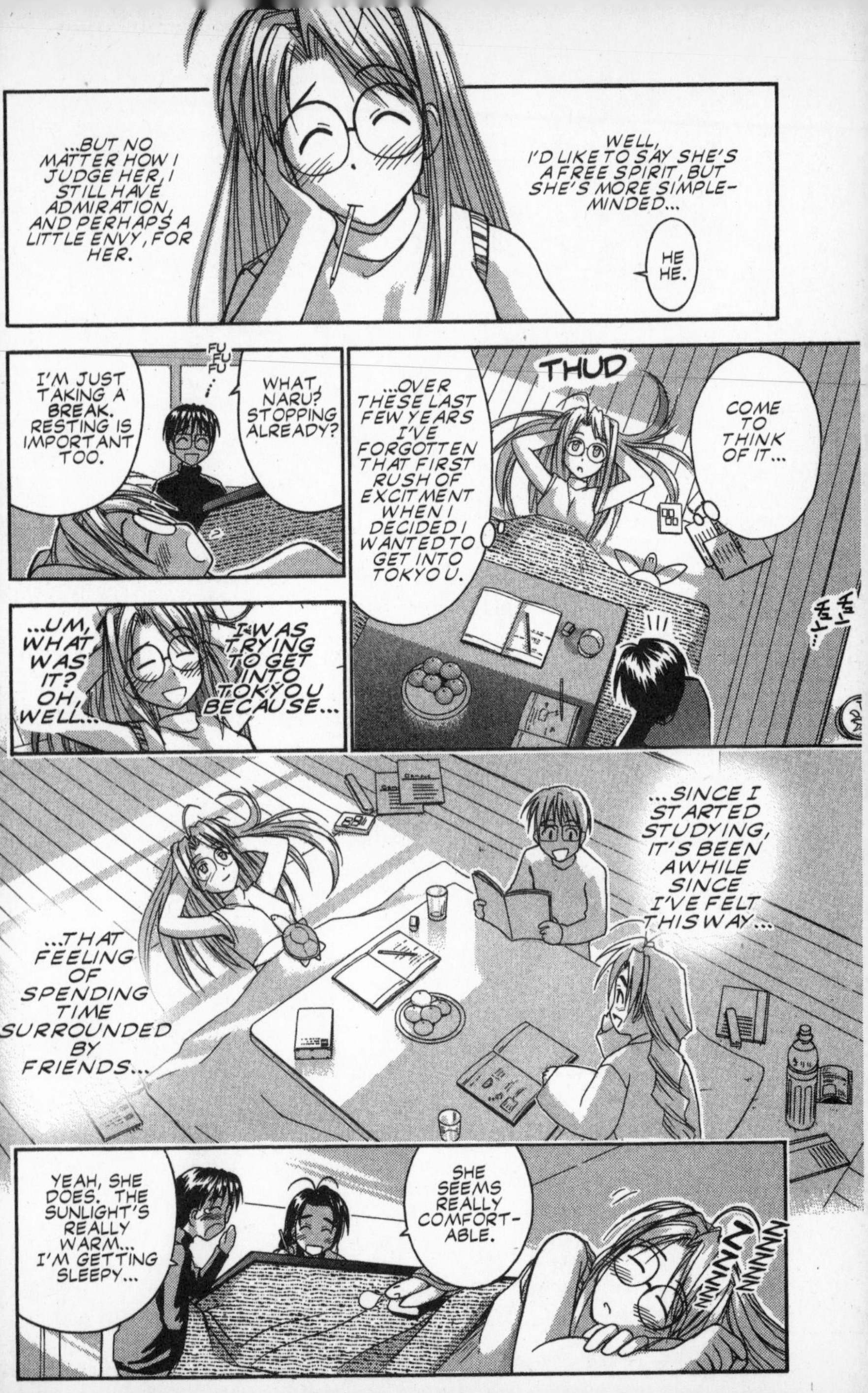
WELL, I'D LIKE TO SAY SHE'S A FREE SPIRIT, BUT SHE'S MORE SIMPLE-MINDED...
HE HE.
...BUT NO MATTER HOW I JUDGE HER, I STILL HAVE ADMIRATION, AND PERHAPS A LITTLE ENVY, FOR HER.
THUD
COME TO THINK OF IT...
...OVER THESE LAST FEW YEARS I'VE FORGOTTEN THAT FIRST RUSH OF EXCITMENT WHEN I DECIDED I WANTED TO GET INTO TOKYO U.
WHAT, NARU? STOPPING ALREADY?
FU FU FU...
I'M JUST TAKING A BREAK. RESTING IS IMPORTANT TOO.
I WAS TRYING TO GET INTO TOKYO U BECAUSE...
...UM, WHAT WAS IT? OH, WELL...
...SINCE I STARTED STUDYING, IT'S BEEN AWHILE SINCE I'VE FELT THIS WAY...
...THAT FEELING OF SPENDING TIME SURROUNDED BY FRIENDS...
NNNNNNNNNNN
SHE SEEMS REALLY COMFORTABLE.
YEAH, SHE DOES. THE SUNLIGHT'S REALLY WARM... I'M GETTING SLEEPY...

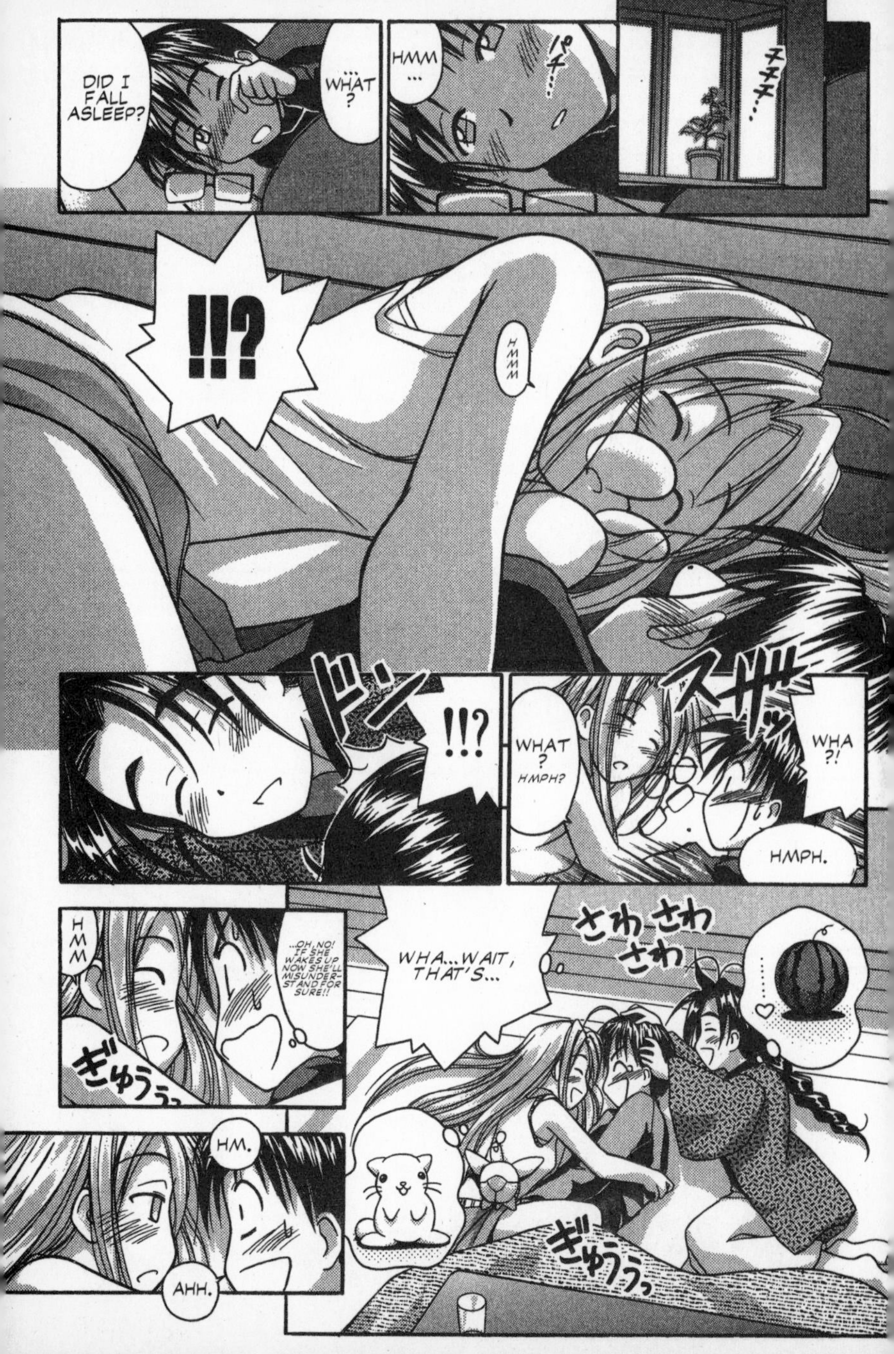
チチチ…
パチ…
HMM…
…WHAT?
DID I FALL ASLEEP?
!!?
HMMM
スザッ
WHA ?!
WHAT? HMPH?
HMPH.
ドン
!!?
さわ さわ さわ
WHA...WAIT, THAT'S...
ぎゅううっ
HMM
...OH, NO! IF SHE WAKES UP NOW SHE'LL MISUNDER-STAND FOR SURE!!
ぎゅううっ
HM.
AHH.

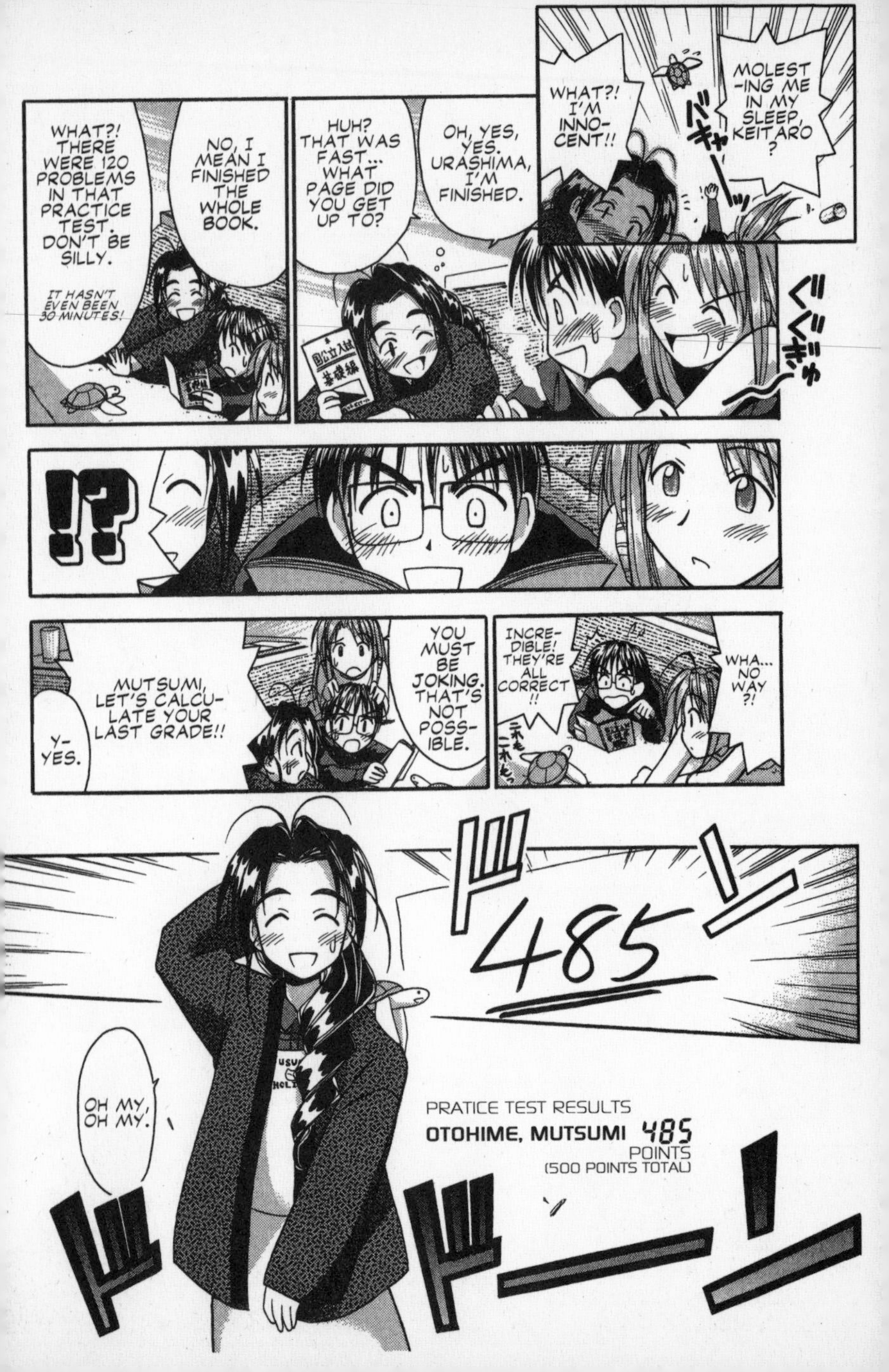

MOLEST-ING ME IN MY SLEEP, KEITARO?
WHAT?! I'M INNO-CENT!!
バキャーッ
OH, YES, YES. URASHIMA, I'M FINISHED.
HUH? THAT WAS FAST... WHAT PAGE DID YOU GET UP TO?
NO, I MEAN I FINISHED THE WHOLE BOOK.
WHAT?! THERE WERE 120 PROBLEMS IN THAT PRACTICE TEST. DON'T BE SILLY.
IT HASN'T EVEN BEEN 30 MINUTES!
!?
WHA... NO WAY?!
INCRE-DIBLE! THEY'RE ALL CORRECT!!
YOU MUST BE JOKING. THAT'S NOT POSS-IBLE.
MUTSUMI, LET'S CALCU-LATE YOUR LAST GRADE!!
Y-YES.
485
OH MY, OH MY.
PRATICE TEST RESULTS
OTOHIME, MUTSUMI 485
POINTS
(500 POINTS TOTAL)

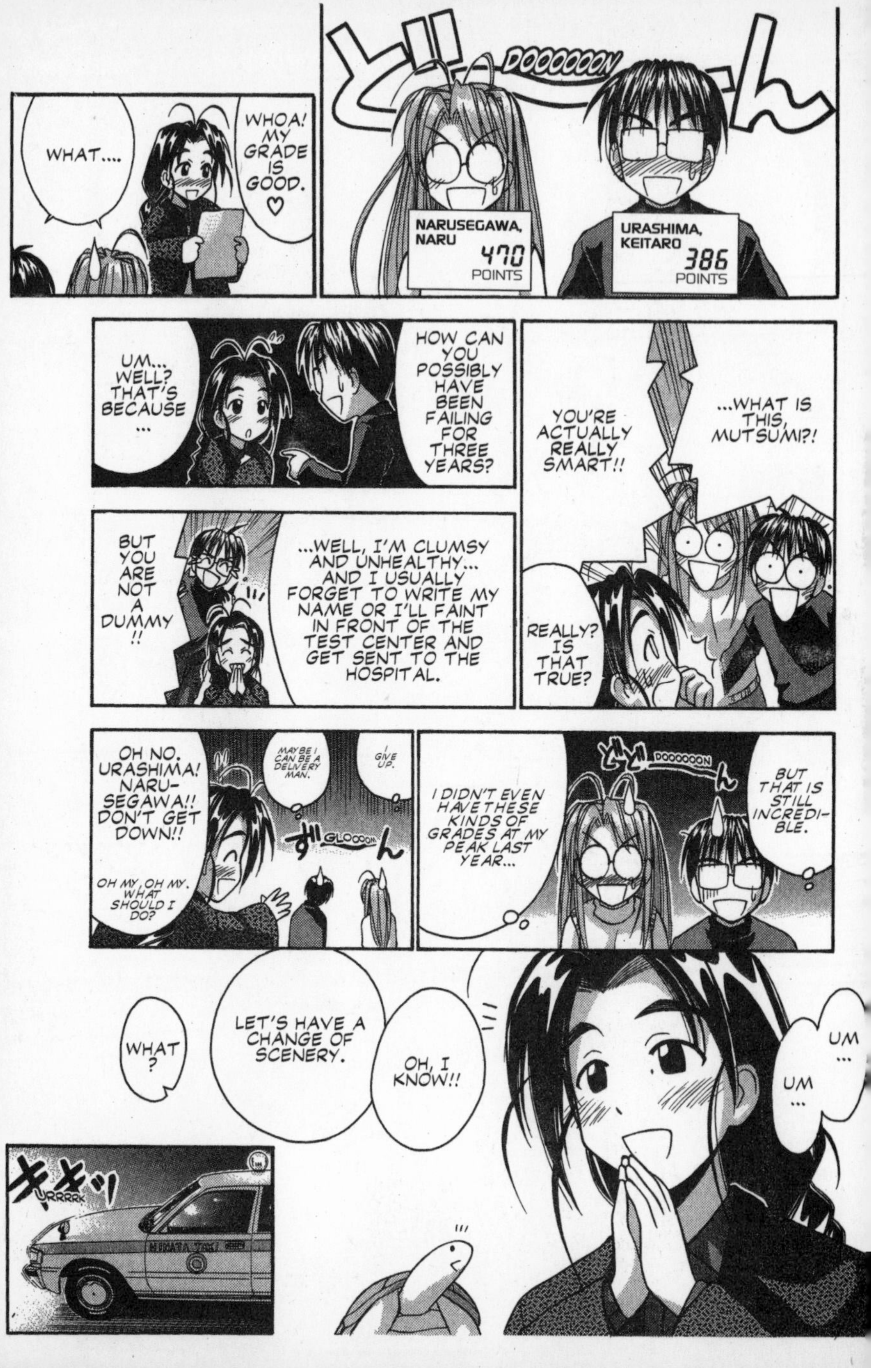
DOOOOOON
NARUSEGAWA, NARU 470 POINTS
URASHIMA, KEITARO 386 POINTS
WHOA! MY GRADE IS GOOD. ♡
WHAT....
...WHAT IS THIS, MUTSUMI?!
YOU'RE ACTUALLY REALLY SMART!!
REALLY? IS THAT TRUE?
HOW CAN YOU POSSIBLY HAVE BEEN FAILING FOR THREE YEARS?
UM... WELL? THAT'S BECAUSE ...
...WELL, I'M CLUMSY AND UNHEALTHY... AND I USUALLY FORGET TO WRITE MY NAME OR I'LL FAINT IN FRONT OF THE TEST CENTER AND GET SENT TO THE HOSPITAL.
BUT YOU ARE NOT A DUMMY!!
BUT THAT IS STILL INCREDIBLE.
DOOOOOON
I DIDN'T EVEN HAVE THESE KINDS OF GRADES AT MY PEAK LAST YEAR...
I GIVE UP.
MAYBE I CAN BE A DELIVERY MAN.
GLOOOOM
OH NO. URASHIMA! NARU-SEGAWA!! DON'T GET DOWN!!
OH MY, OH MY. WHAT SHOULD I DO?
UM ...
UM ...
OH, I KNOW!!
LET'S HAVE A CHANGE OF SCENERY.
WHAT?
URRRRK

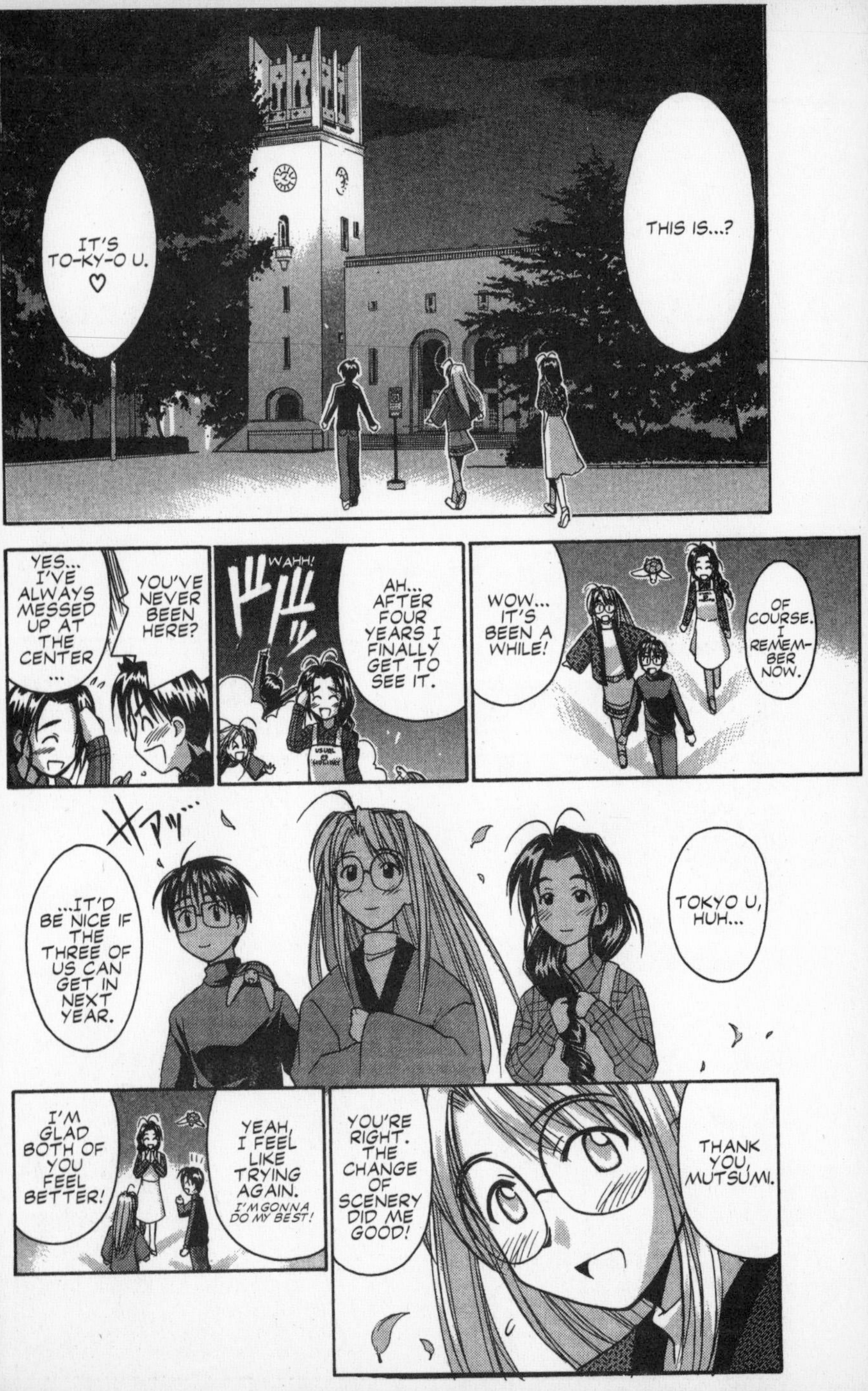
THIS IS...?
IT'S TO-KY-O U. ♡
OF COURSE. I REMEM-BER NOW.
WOW... IT'S BEEN A WHILE!
WAHH!
AH... AFTER FOUR YEARS I FINALLY GET TO SEE IT.
YOU'VE NEVER BEEN HERE?
YES... I'VE ALWAYS MESSED UP AT THE CENTER ...
TOKYO U, HUH...
...IT'D BE NICE IF THE THREE OF US CAN GET IN NEXT YEAR.
THANK YOU, MUTSUMI.
YOU'RE RIGHT. THE CHANGE OF SCENERY DID ME GOOD!
YEAH, I FEEL LIKE TRYING AGAIN. I'M GONNA DO MY BEST!
I'M GLAD BOTH OF YOU FEEL BETTER!

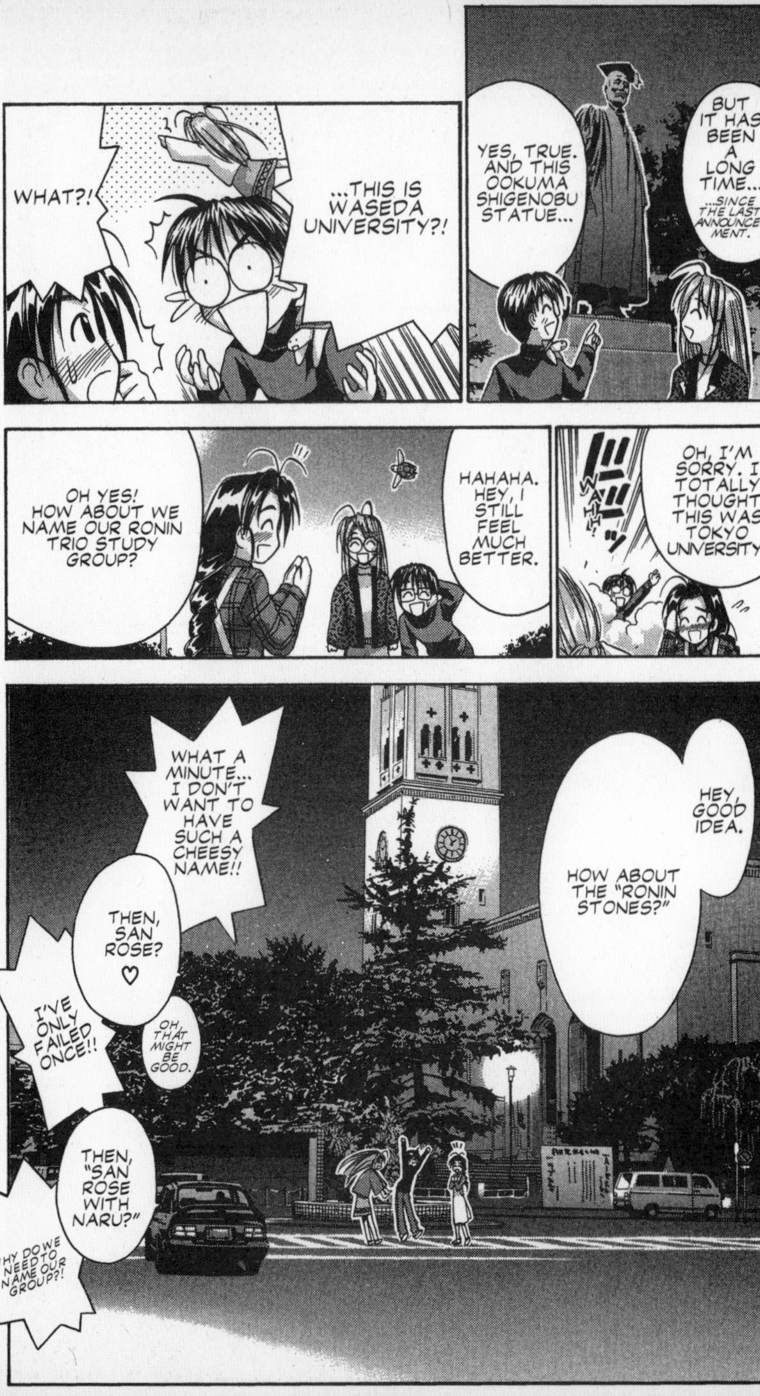
BUT IT HAS BEEN A LONG TIME...
...SINCE THE LAST ANNOUNCEMENT.
YES, TRUE. AND THIS OOKUMA SHIGENOBU STATUE...
...THIS IS WASEDA UNIVERSITY?!
WHAT?!
OH, I'M SORRY. I TOTALLY THOUGHT THIS WAS TOKYO UNIVERSITY.
WAHH!
HAHAHA. HEY, I STILL FEEL MUCH BETTER.
OH YES! HOW ABOUT WE NAME OUR RONIN TRIO STUDY GROUP?
HEY, GOOD IDEA.
HOW ABOUT THE "RONIN STONES?"
WHAT A MINUTE... I DON'T WANT TO HAVE SUCH A CHEESY NAME!!
THEN, SAN ROSE? ♡
OH, THAT MIGHT BE GOOD.
I'VE ONLY FAILED ONCE!!
THEN, "SAN ROSE WITH NARU?"
WHY DO WE NEED TO NAME OUR GROUP?!

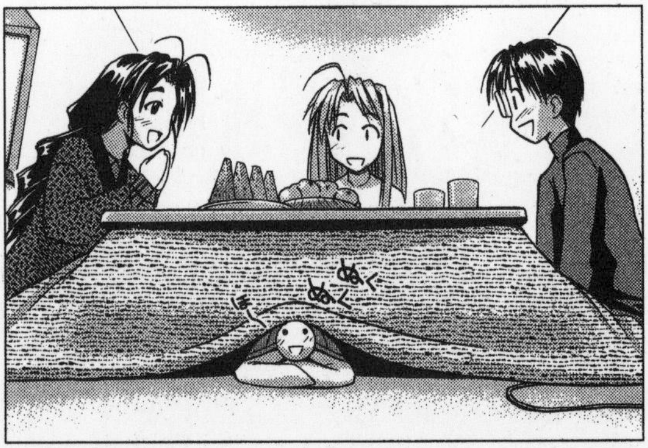
ぬくぬく
ほー

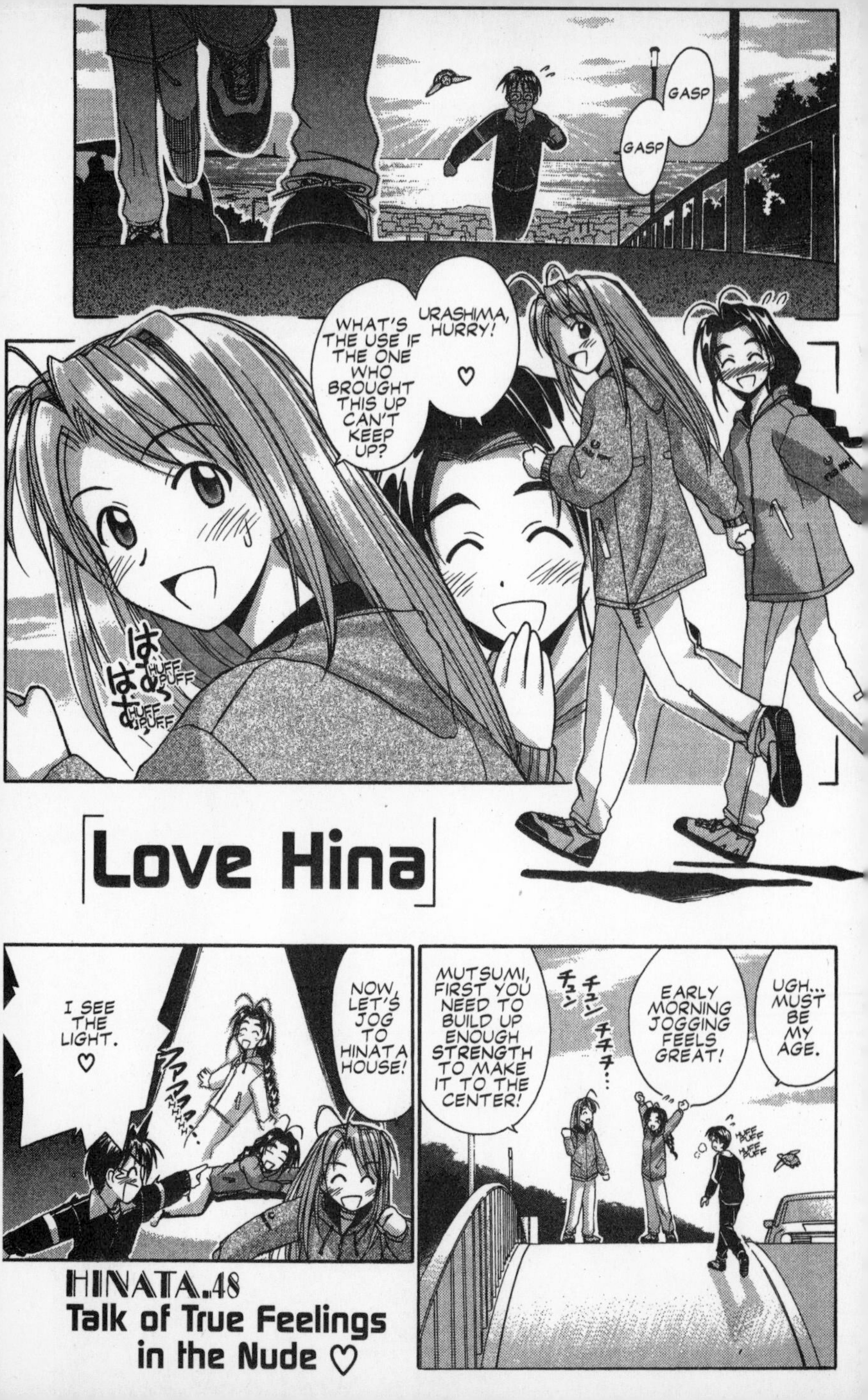
GASP
GASP
URASHIMA, HURRY! ♡
WHAT'S THE USE IF THE ONE WHO BROUGHT THIS UP CAN'T KEEP UP?
HUFF PUFF
HUFF PUFF
Love Hina
UGH... MUST BE MY AGE.
EARLY MORNING JOGGING FEELS GREAT!
HUFF PUFF
HUFF PUFF
MUTSUMI, FIRST YOU NEED TO BUILD UP ENOUGH STRENGTH TO MAKE IT TO THE CENTER!
NOW, LET'S JOG TO HINATA HOUSE!
I SEE THE LIGHT. ♡
AHHHH
HINATA.48
Talk of True Feelings in the Nude ♡

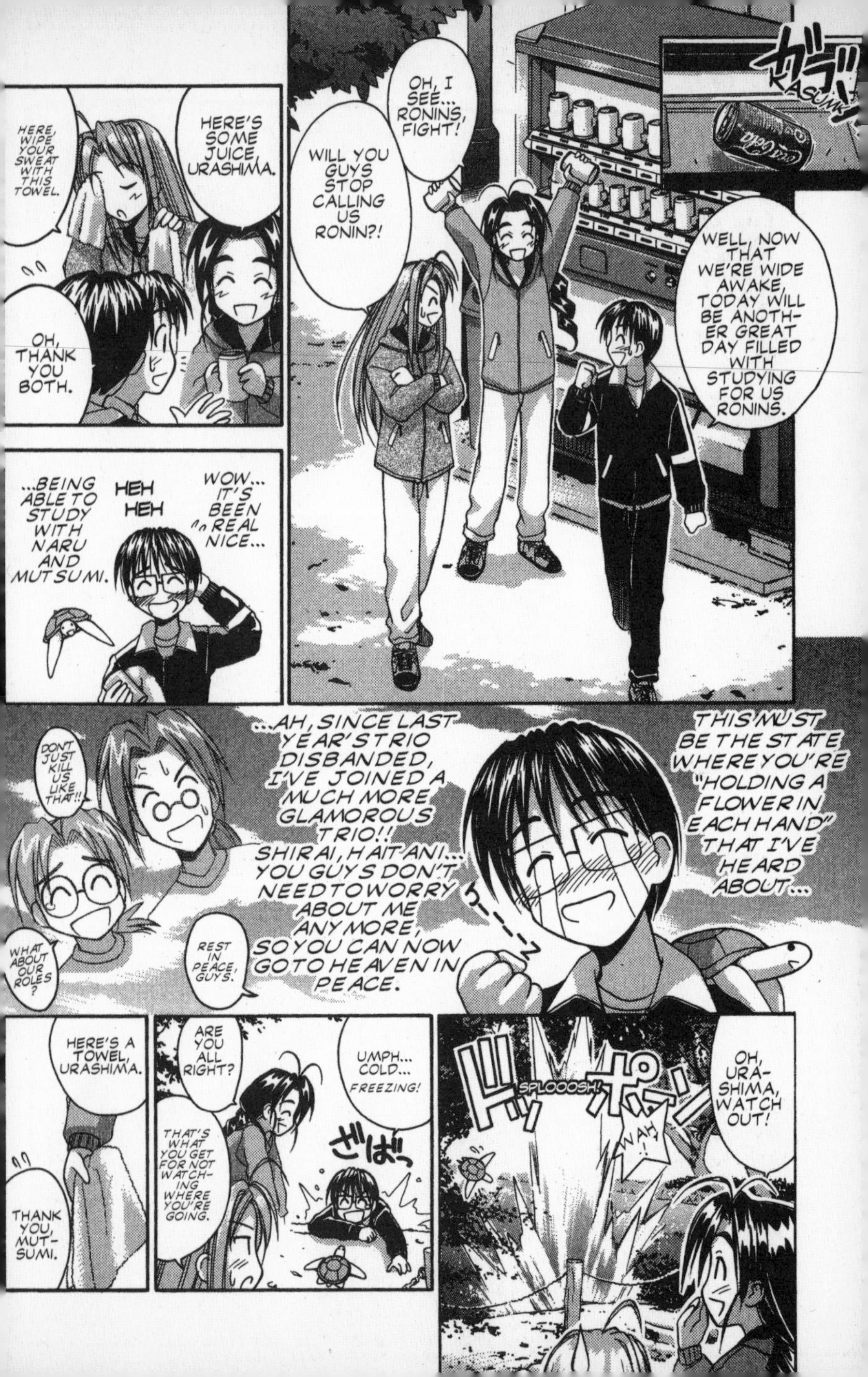
KASUNK!
WELL, NOW THAT WE'RE WIDE AWAKE, TODAY WILL BE ANOTHER GREAT DAY FILLED WITH STUDYING FOR US RONINS.
OH, I SEE... RONINS, FIGHT!
WILL YOU GUYS STOP CALLING US RONIN?!
HERE'S SOME JUICE, URASHIMA.
HERE, WIPE YOUR SWEAT WITH THIS TOWEL.
OH, THANK YOU BOTH.
WOW... IT'S BEEN REAL NICE...
HEH HEH
...BEING ABLE TO STUDY WITH NARU AND MUTSUMI.
THIS MUST BE THE STATE WHERE YOU'RE "HOLDING A FLOWER IN EACH HAND" THAT I'VE HEARD ABOUT...
...AH, SINCE LAST YEAR'S TRIO DISBANDED, I'VE JOINED A MUCH MORE GLAMOROUS TRIO!! SHIRAI, HAITANI... YOU GUYS DON'T NEED TO WORRY ABOUT ME ANYMORE, SO YOU CAN NOW GO TO HEAVEN IN PEACE.
REST IN PEACE, GUYS.
DON'T JUST KILL US LIKE THAT!!
WHAT ABOUT OUR ROLES?
OH, URA-SHIMA, WATCH OUT!
WAH!
SPLOOOOSH!
UMPH... COLD... FREEZING!
ARE YOU ALL RIGHT?
THAT'S WHAT YOU GET FOR NOT WATCH-ING WHERE YOU'RE GOING.
HERE'S A TOWEL, URASHIMA.
THANK YOU, MUT-SUMI.

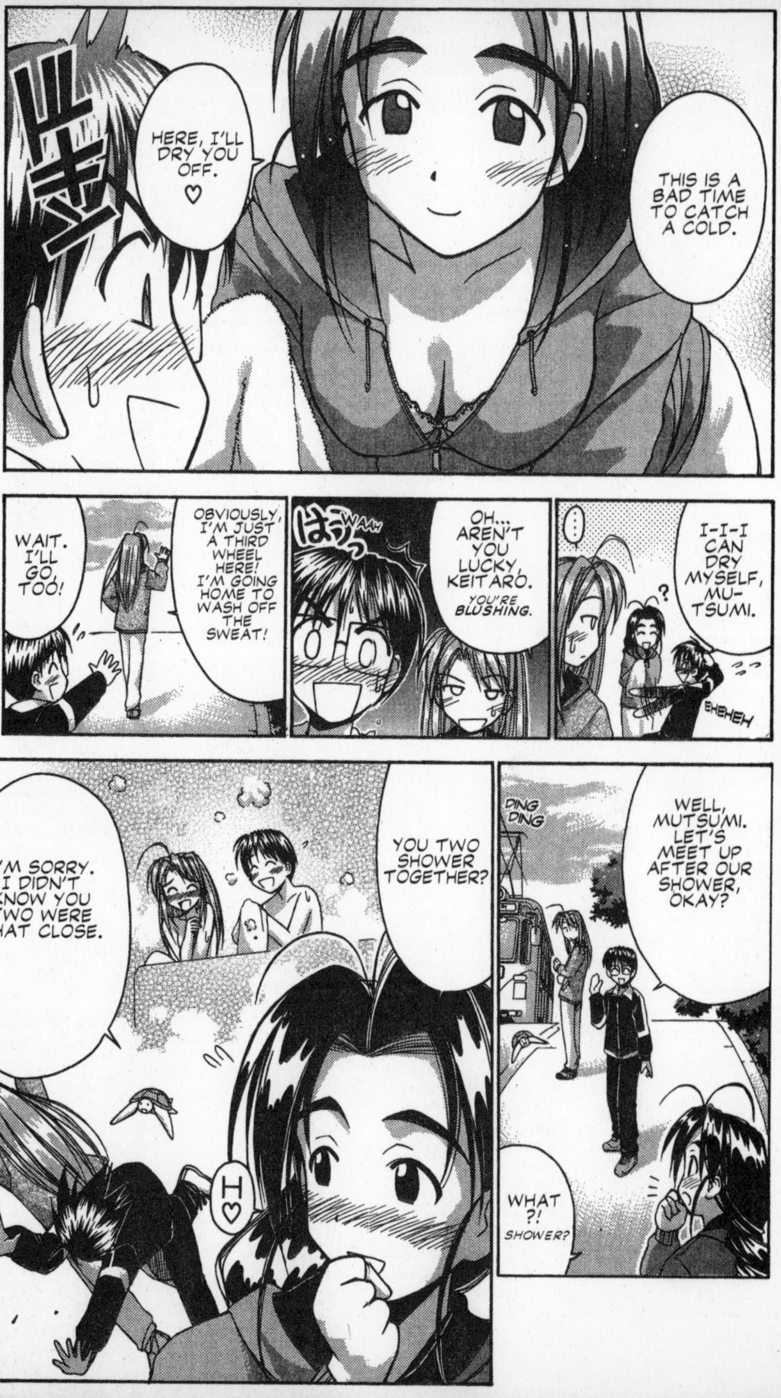
THIS IS A BAD TIME TO CATCH A COLD.
HERE, I'LL DRY YOU OFF. ♡
...
I-I-I CAN DRY MYSELF, MU-TSUMI.
?
EHEHEH
OH... AREN'T YOU LUCKY, KEITARO.
YOU'RE BLUSHING.
WAAH
OBVIOUSLY, I'M JUST A THIRD WHEEL HERE! I'M GOING HOME TO WASH OFF THE SWEAT!
WAIT. I'LL GO, TOO!
DING DING
WELL, MUTSUMI. LET'S MEET UP AFTER OUR SHOWER, OKAY?
WHAT?!
SHOWER?
YOU TWO SHOWER TOGETHER?
I'M SORRY. I DIDN'T KNOW YOU TWO WERE THAT CLOSE.
H ♡

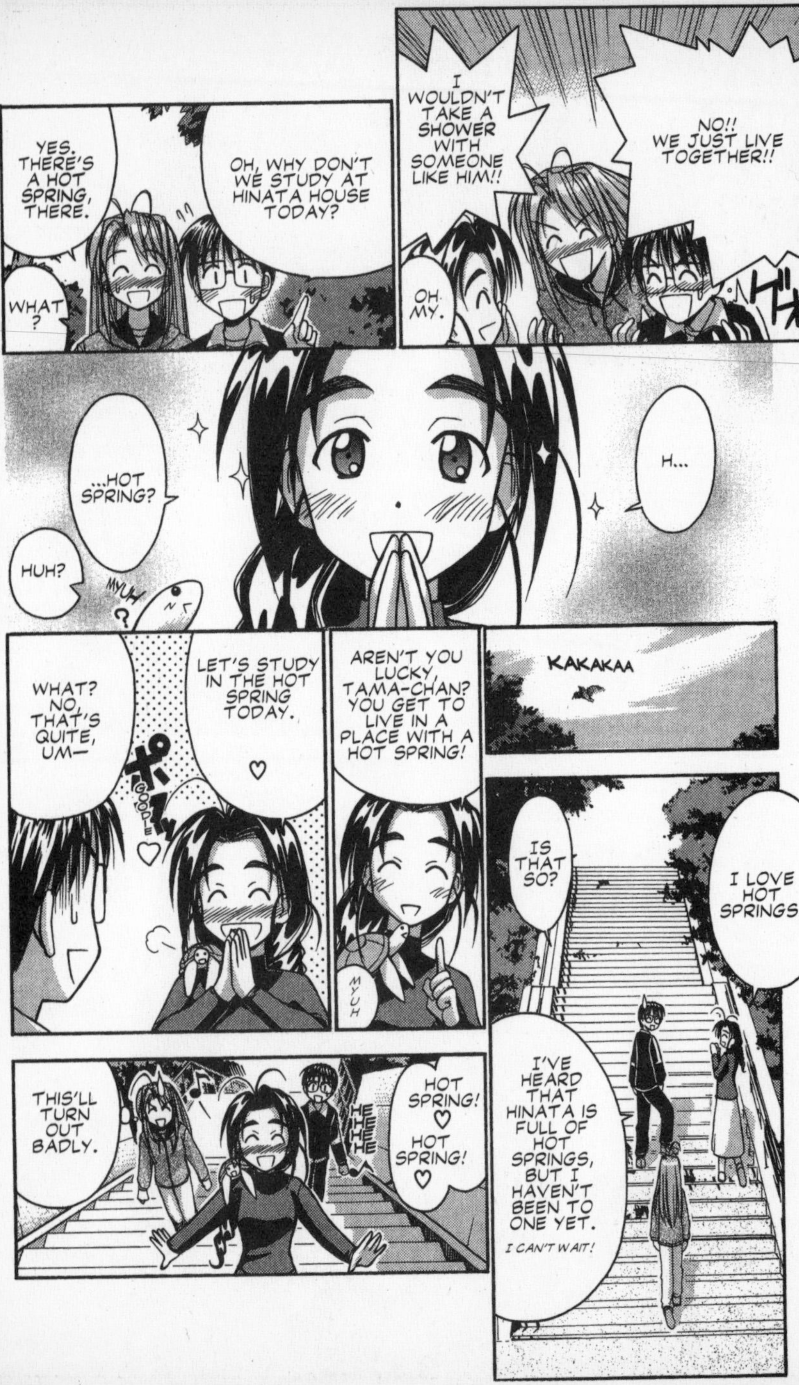
NO!! WE JUST LIVE TOGETHER!!
I WOULDN'T TAKE A SHOWER WITH SOMEONE LIKE HIM!!
OH. MY.
OH, WHY DON'T WE STUDY AT HINATA HOUSE TODAY?
YES. THERE'S A HOT SPRING, THERE.
WHAT?
H...
...HOT SPRING?
HUH?
MYUH ?
KAKAKAA
I LOVE HOT SPRINGS!
IS THAT SO?
I'VE HEARD THAT HINATA IS FULL OF HOT SPRINGS, BUT I HAVEN'T BEEN TO ONE YET.
I CAN'T WAIT!
AREN'T YOU LUCKY, TAMA-CHAN? YOU GET TO LIVE IN A PLACE WITH A HOT SPRING!
MYUH
LET'S STUDY IN THE HOT SPRING TODAY. ♡
GOODIE
WHAT? NO, THAT'S QUITE, UM—
HOT SPRING! ♡
HOT SPRING! ♡
HEHEHEHE
THIS'LL TURN OUT BADLY.

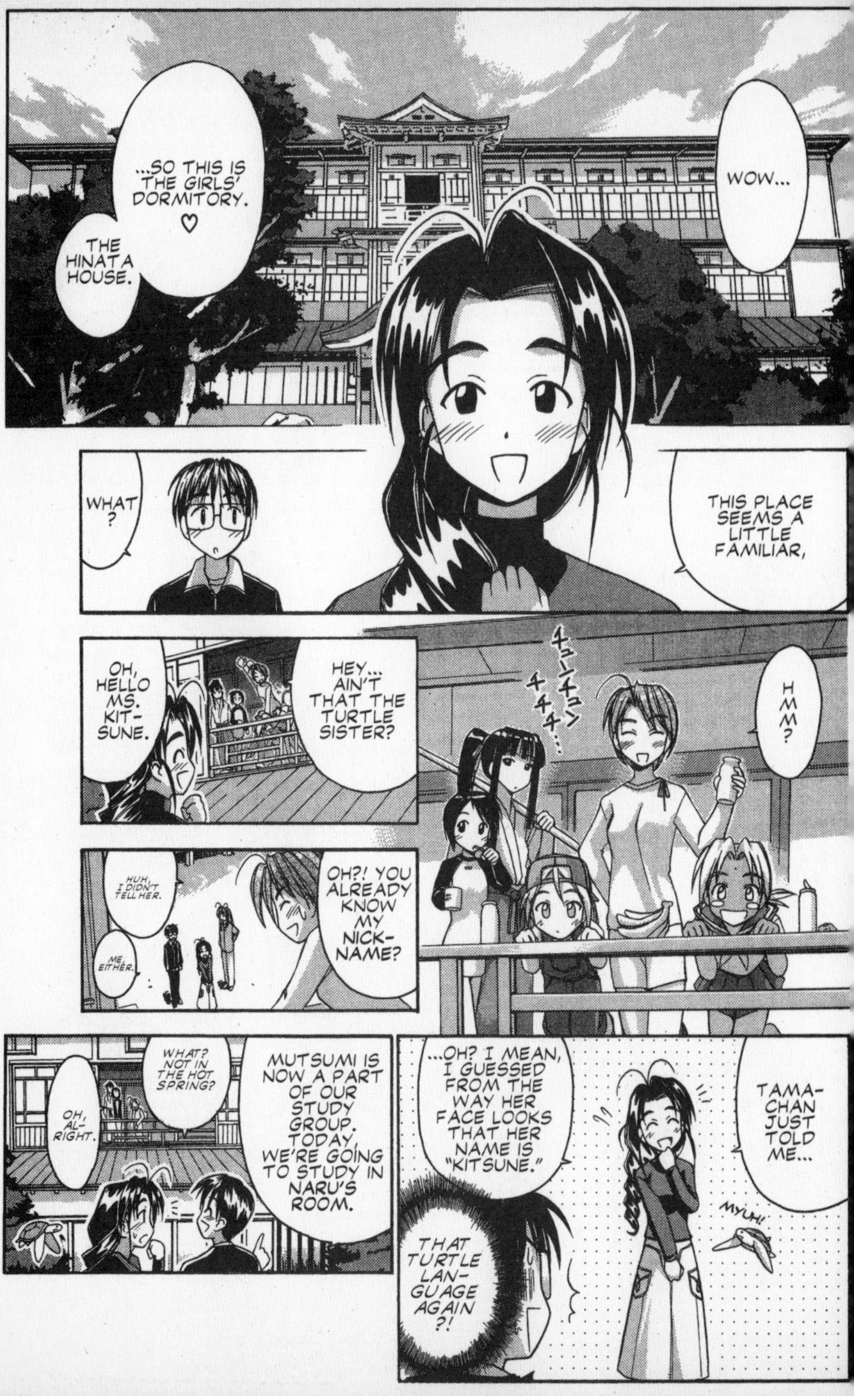
WOW...
...SO THIS IS THE GIRLS' DORMITORY. ♥
THE HINATA HOUSE.
THIS PLACE SEEMS A LITTLE FAMILIAR,
WHAT?
HMM?
チューチュン チチチ…
HEY... AIN'T THAT THE TURTLE SISTER?
OH, HELLO MS. KIT-SUNE.
OH?! YOU ALREADY KNOW MY NICK-NAME?
HUH, I DIDN'T TELL HER.
ME, EITHER.
TAMA-CHAN JUST TOLD ME...
...OH? I MEAN, I GUESSED FROM THE WAY HER FACE LOOKS THAT HER NAME IS "KITSUNE."
MYUH!
THAT TURTLE LAN-GUAGE AGAIN?!
MUTSUMI IS NOW A PART OF OUR STUDY GROUP. TODAY, WE'RE GOING TO STUDY IN NARU'S ROOM.
WHAT? NOT IN THE HOT SPRING?
OH, AL-RIGHT.

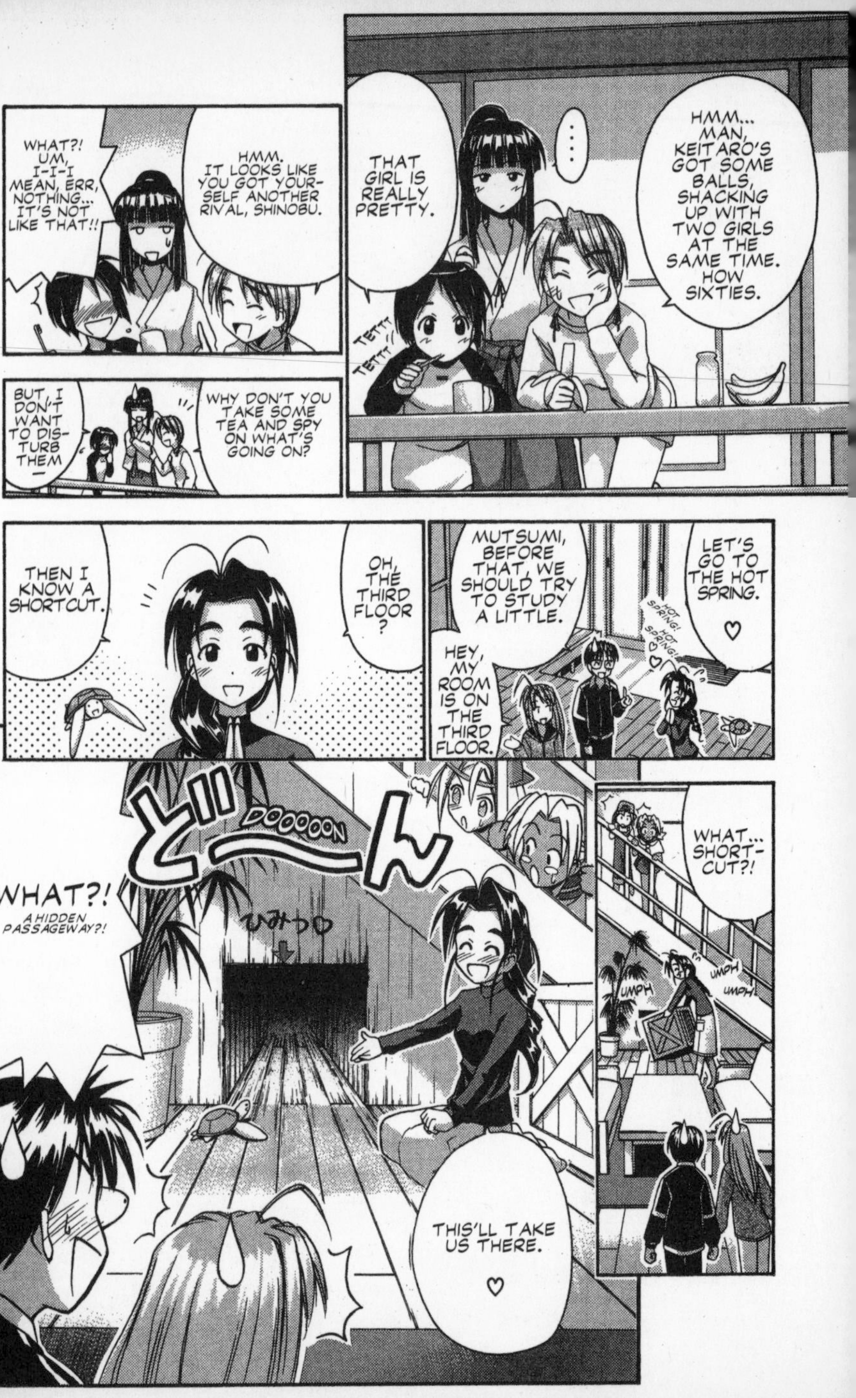
HMM... MAN, KEITARO'S GOT SOME BALLS, SHACKING UP WITH TWO GIRLS AT THE SAME TIME. HOW SIXTIES.
...
THAT GIRL IS REALLY PRETTY.
TETTT TETTT
HMM. IT LOOKS LIKE YOU GOT YOURSELF ANOTHER RIVAL, SHINOBU.
WHAT?! UM, I-I-I MEAN, ERR, NOTHING... IT'S NOT LIKE THAT!!
WHY DON'T YOU TAKE SOME TEA AND SPY ON WHAT'S GOING ON?
BUT, I DON'T WANT TO DISTURB THEM—
LET'S GO TO THE HOT SPRING. ♡
HOT SPRING! HOT SPRING! ♡
MUTSUMI, BEFORE THAT, WE SHOULD TRY TO STUDY A LITTLE.
HEY, MY ROOM IS ON THE THIRD FLOOR.
OH, THE THIRD FLOOR?
THEN I KNOW A SHORTCUT.
WHAT... SHORT-CUT?!
UMPH
UMPH
UMPH
どーん
DOOOOON
ひみつ♡
THIS'LL TAKE US THERE. ♡
WHAT?! A HIDDEN PASSAGEWAY?!

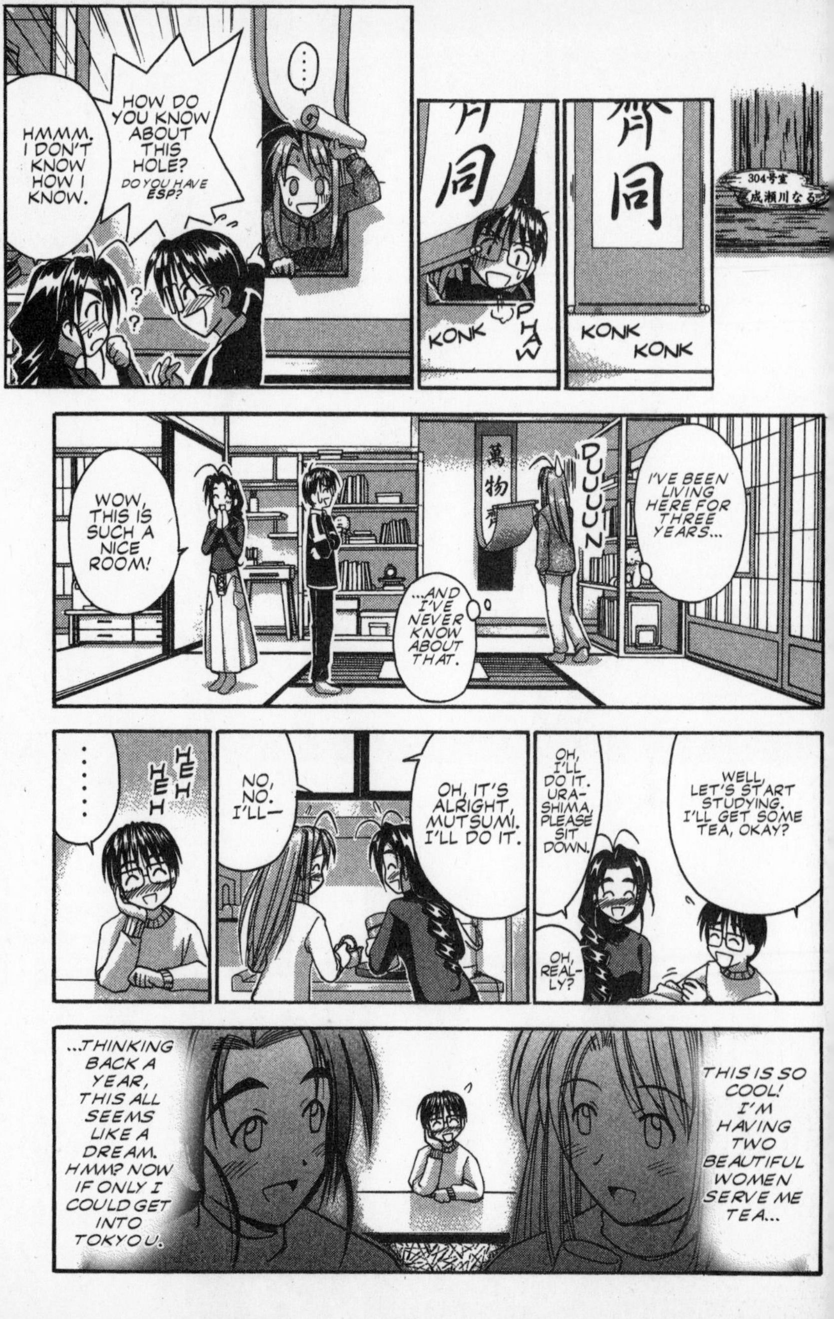
304号室
成瀬川なる
KONK
KONK
KONK
PHAW
...
HOW DO YOU KNOW ABOUT THIS HOLE? DO YOU HAVE ESP?
HMMM. I DON'T KNOW HOW I KNOW.
?
?
I'VE BEEN LIVING HERE FOR THREE YEARS...
DUUUUN
...AND I'VE NEVER KNOW ABOUT THAT.
WOW, THIS IS SUCH A NICE ROOM!
WELL, LET'S START STUDYING. I'LL GET SOME TEA, OKAY?
OH, I'LL DO IT. URA-SHIMA, PLEASE SIT DOWN.
OH, REAL-LY?
OH, IT'S ALRIGHT, MUTSUMI. I'LL DO IT.
NO, NO. I'LL—
HEH HEH HEH
......
THIS IS SO COOL! I'M HAVING TWO BEAUTIFUL WOMEN SERVE ME TEA...
...THINKING BACK A YEAR, THIS ALL SEEMS LIKE A DREAM. HMM? NOW IF ONLY I COULD GET INTO TOKYO U.

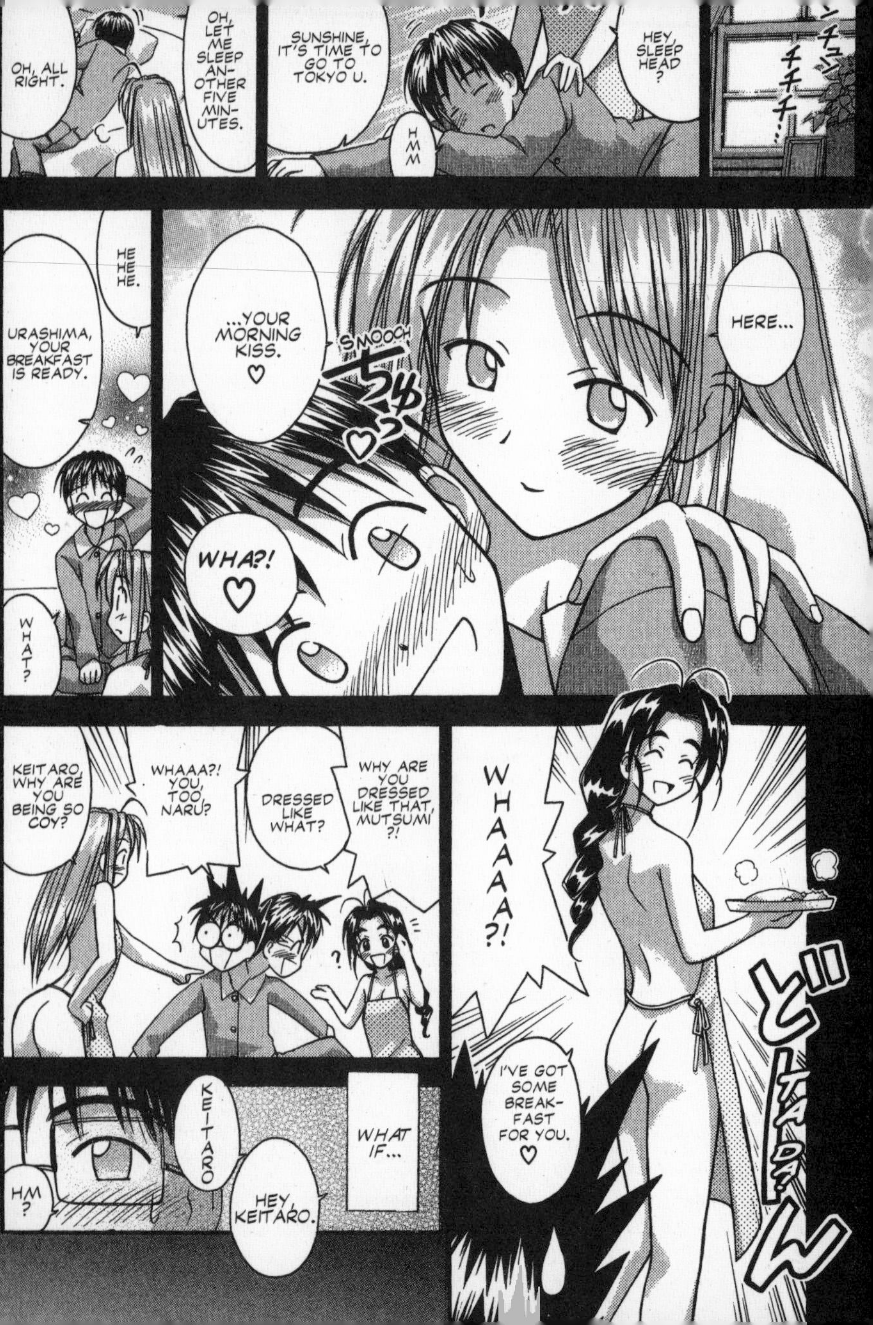
チチチ...
HEY, SLEEP HEAD?
SUNSHINE, IT'S TIME TO GO TO TOKYO U.
HMM
OH, LET ME SLEEP AN-OTHER FIVE MIN-UTES.
OH, ALL RIGHT.
HERE...
...YOUR MORNING KISS. ♡
SMOOCH
ちゅっ♡
WHA?! ♡
HE HE HE.
URASHIMA, YOUR BREAKFAST IS READY.
WHAT?
WHAAAA?!
I'VE GOT SOME BREAK-FAST FOR YOU. ♡
TA DA!
WHY ARE YOU DRESSED LIKE THAT, MUTSUMI?!
DRESSED LIKE WHAT?
WHAAA?! YOU, TOO, NARU?
KEITARO, WHY ARE YOU BEING SO COY?
WHAT IF...
KEITARO
HEY, KEITARO.
HM?

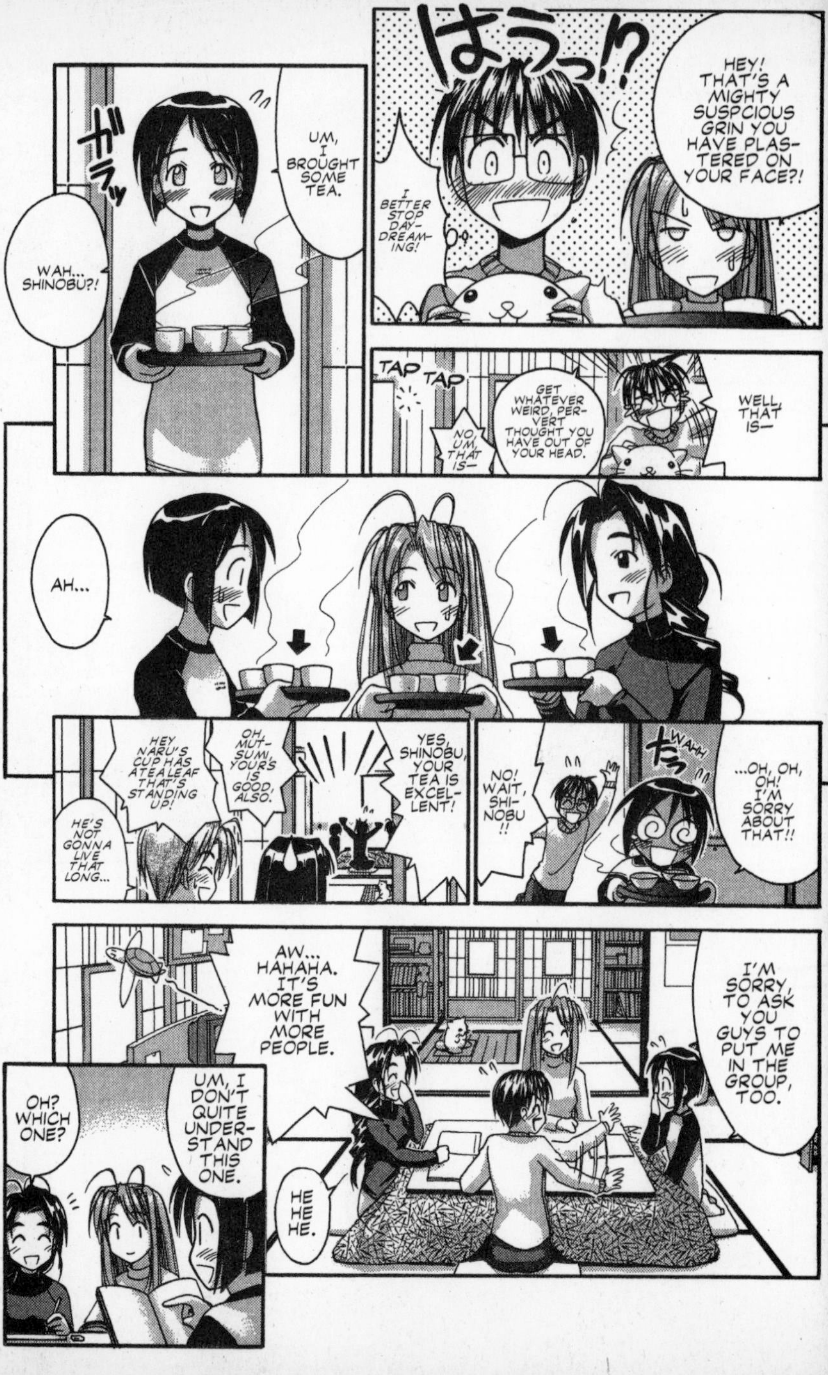
はうっ!?
HEY! THAT'S A MIGHTY SUSPCIOUS GRIN YOU HAVE PLAS-TERED ON YOUR FACE?!
I BETTER STOP DAY-DREAM-ING!
WELL, THAT IS—
GET WHATEVER WEIRD, PER-VERT THOUGHT YOU HAVE OUT OF YOUR HEAD.
NO, UM, THAT IS—
TAP TAP
UM, I BROUGHT SOME TEA.
ガラッ
WAH... SHINOBU?!
AH...
...OH, OH, OH! I'M SORRY ABOUT THAT!!
WAHH
NO! WAIT, SHI-NOBU!!
YES, SHINOBU, YOUR TEA IS EXCEL-LENT!
OH, MUT-SUMI, YOUR'S IS GOOD, ALSO.
HEY NARU'S CUP HAS ATEALEAF THAT'S STANDING UP!
HE'S NOT GONNA LIVE THAT LONG...
I'M SORRY, TO ASK YOU GUYS TO PUT ME IN THE GROUP, TOO.
AW... HAHAHA. IT'S MORE FUN WITH MORE PEOPLE.
HE HE HE.
UM, I DON'T QUITE UNDER-STAND THIS ONE.
OH? WHICH ONE?

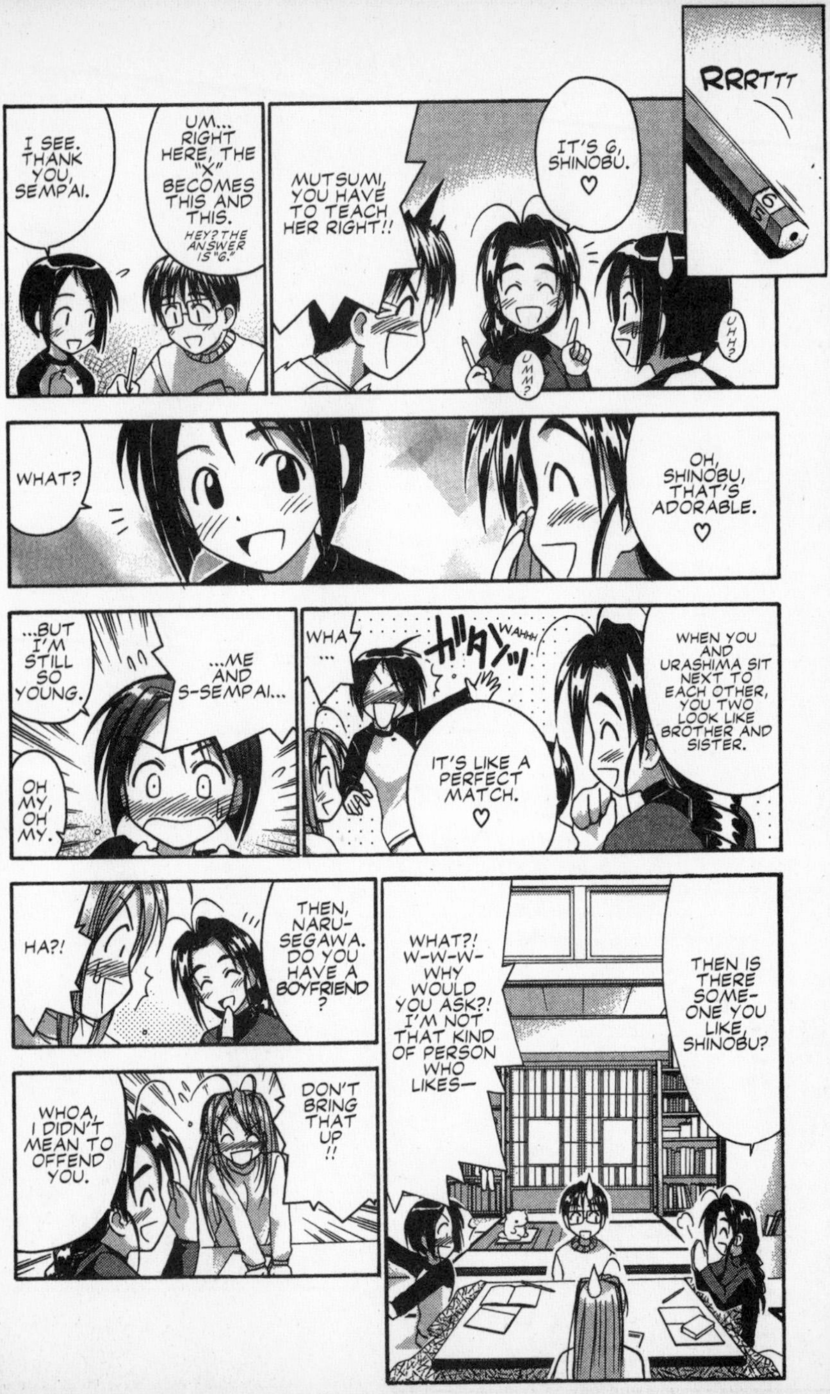
RRRTTT
IT'S 6, SHINOBU. ♡
UHH?
MUTSUMI, YOU HAVE TO TEACH HER RIGHT!!
UMM?
UM... RIGHT HERE, THE "X" BECOMES THIS AND THIS.
HEY? THE ANSWER IS "6."
I SEE. THANK YOU, SEMPAI.
OH, SHINOBU, THAT'S ADORABLE. ♡
WHAT?
WHEN YOU AND URASHIMA SIT NEXT TO EACH OTHER, YOU TWO LOOK LIKE BROTHER AND SISTER.
WAHHH
ガタッ
WHA ...
IT'S LIKE A PERFECT MATCH. ♡
...ME AND S-SEMPAI...
...BUT I'M STILL SO YOUNG.
OH MY, OH MY.
THEN IS THERE SOME-ONE YOU LIKE, SHINOBU?
WHAT?! W-W-W-WHY WOULD YOU ASK?! I'M NOT THAT KIND OF PERSON WHO LIKES—
THEN, NARU-SEGAWA. DO YOU HAVE A BOYFRIEND?
HA?!
DON'T BRING THAT UP!!
WHOA, I DIDN'T MEAN TO OFFEND YOU.

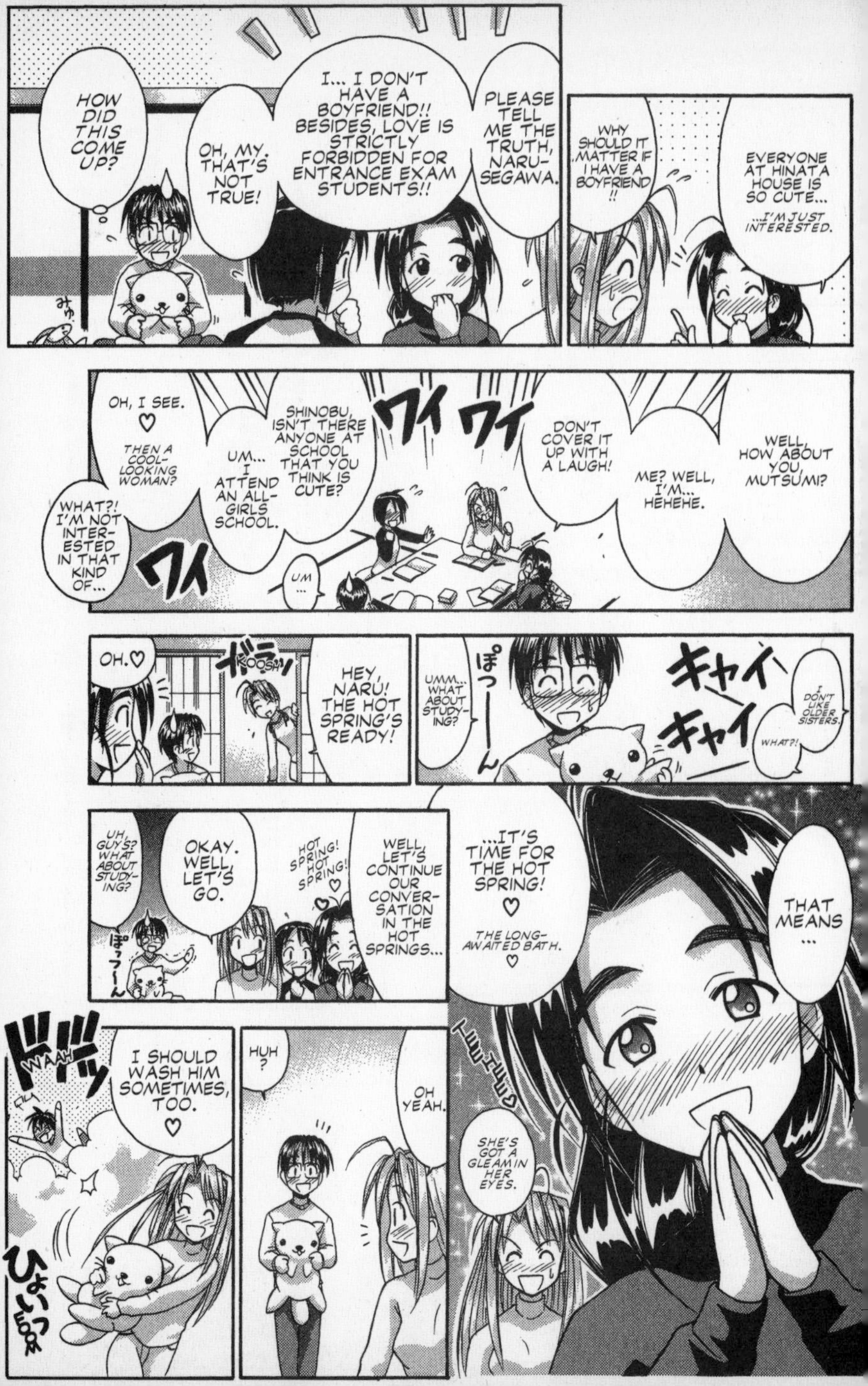
EVERYONE AT HINATA HOUSE IS SO CUTE...
...I'M JUST INTERESTED.
WHY SHOULD IT MATTER IF I HAVE A BOYFRIEND!!
PLEASE TELL ME THE TRUTH, NARU-SEGAWA.
I... I DON'T HAVE A BOYFRIEND!! BESIDES, LOVE IS STRICTLY FORBIDDEN FOR ENTRANCE EXAM STUDENTS!!
OH, MY. THAT'S NOT TRUE!
HOW DID THIS COME UP?
みゅ
WELL, HOW ABOUT YOU, MUTSUMI?
ME? WELL, I'M... HEHEHE.
DON'T COVER IT UP WITH A LAUGH!
ワイ ワイ
SHINOBU, ISN'T THERE ANYONE AT SCHOOL THAT YOU THINK IS CUTE?
UM... I ATTEND AN ALL-GIRLS SCHOOL.
UM ...
OH, I SEE. ♡
THEN A COOL-LOOKING WOMAN?
WHAT?! I'M NOT INTER-ESTED IN THAT KIND OF...
ワイ
キャイ キャイ
I DON'T LIKE OLDER SISTERS.
WHAT?!
ぽっ〜ん
UMM... WHAT ABOUT STUDYING?
HEY, NARU! THE HOT SPRING'S READY!
KOOSH
OH.♡
THAT MEANS ...
...IT'S TIME FOR THE HOT SPRING! ♡
THE LONG-AWAITED BATH. ♡
SHE'S GOT A GLEAM IN HER EYES.
WELL, LET'S CONTINUE OUR CONVERSATION IN THE HOT SPRINGS...
HOT SPRING! HOT SPRING! ♡
OKAY. WELL, LET'S GO.
UH, GUYS? WHAT ABOUT STUDYING?
ぽっ〜ん
OH YEAH.
HUH?
I SHOULD WASH HIM SOMETIMES, TOO. ♡
WAAH
FLOP

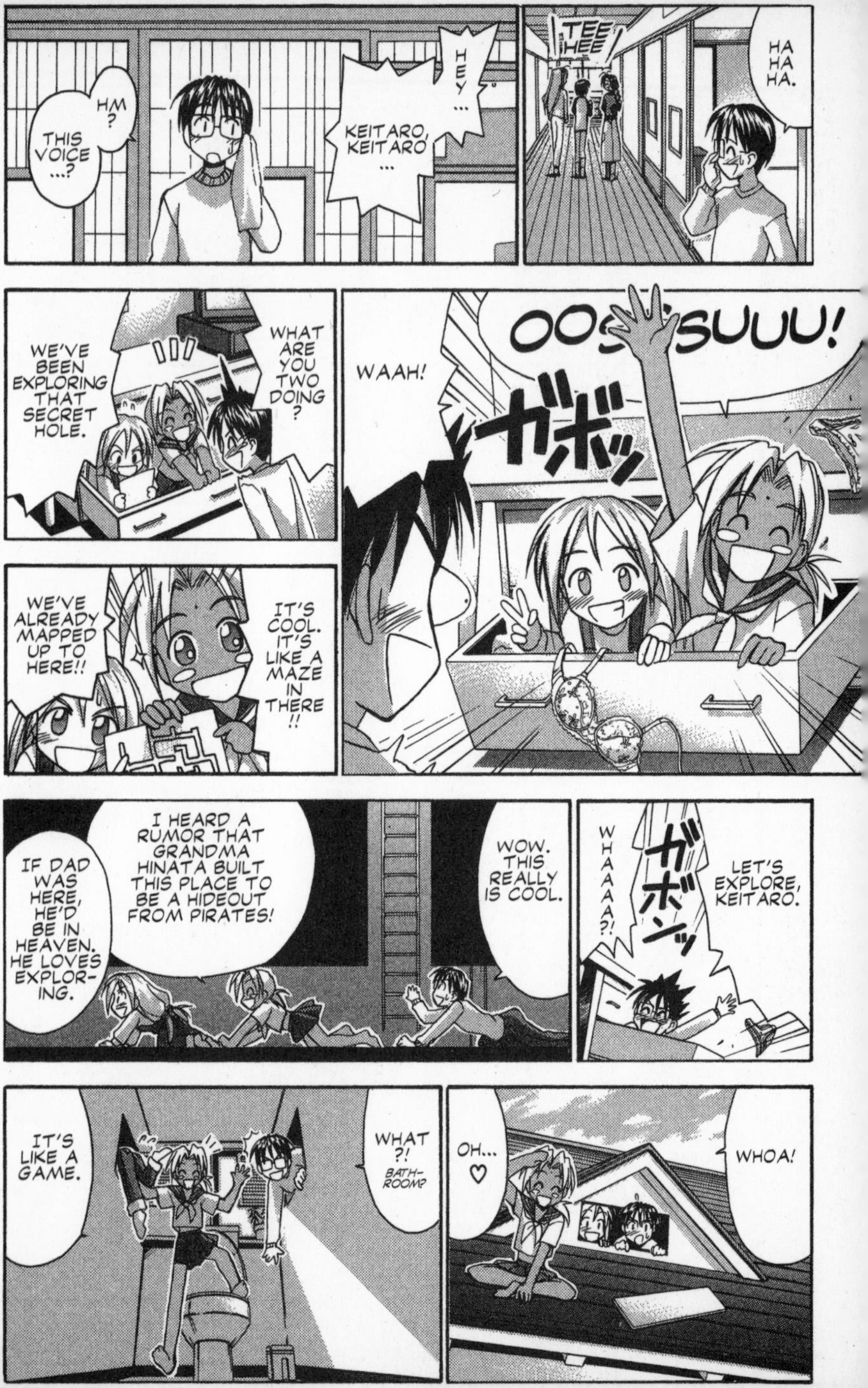
TEE HEE
HA HA HA.
HEY... KEITARO, KEITARO...
HM? THIS VOICE...?
OOS SUUU!
ガボッ
WAAH!
WHAT ARE YOU TWO DOING?
WE'VE BEEN EXPLORING THAT SECRET HOLE.
IT'S COOL. IT'S LIKE A MAZE IN THERE!!
WE'VE ALREADY MAPPED UP TO HERE!!
LET'S EXPLORE, KEITARO.
WHAAAAA?!
ガボンッ
WOW. THIS REALLY IS COOL.
I HEARD A RUMOR THAT GRANDMA HINATA BUILT THIS PLACE TO BE A HIDEOUT FROM PIRATES!
IF DAD WAS HERE, HE'D BE IN HEAVEN. HE LOVES EXPLOR-ING.
WHOA!
OH... ♡
WHAT?! BATH-ROOM?
IT'S LIKE A GAME.

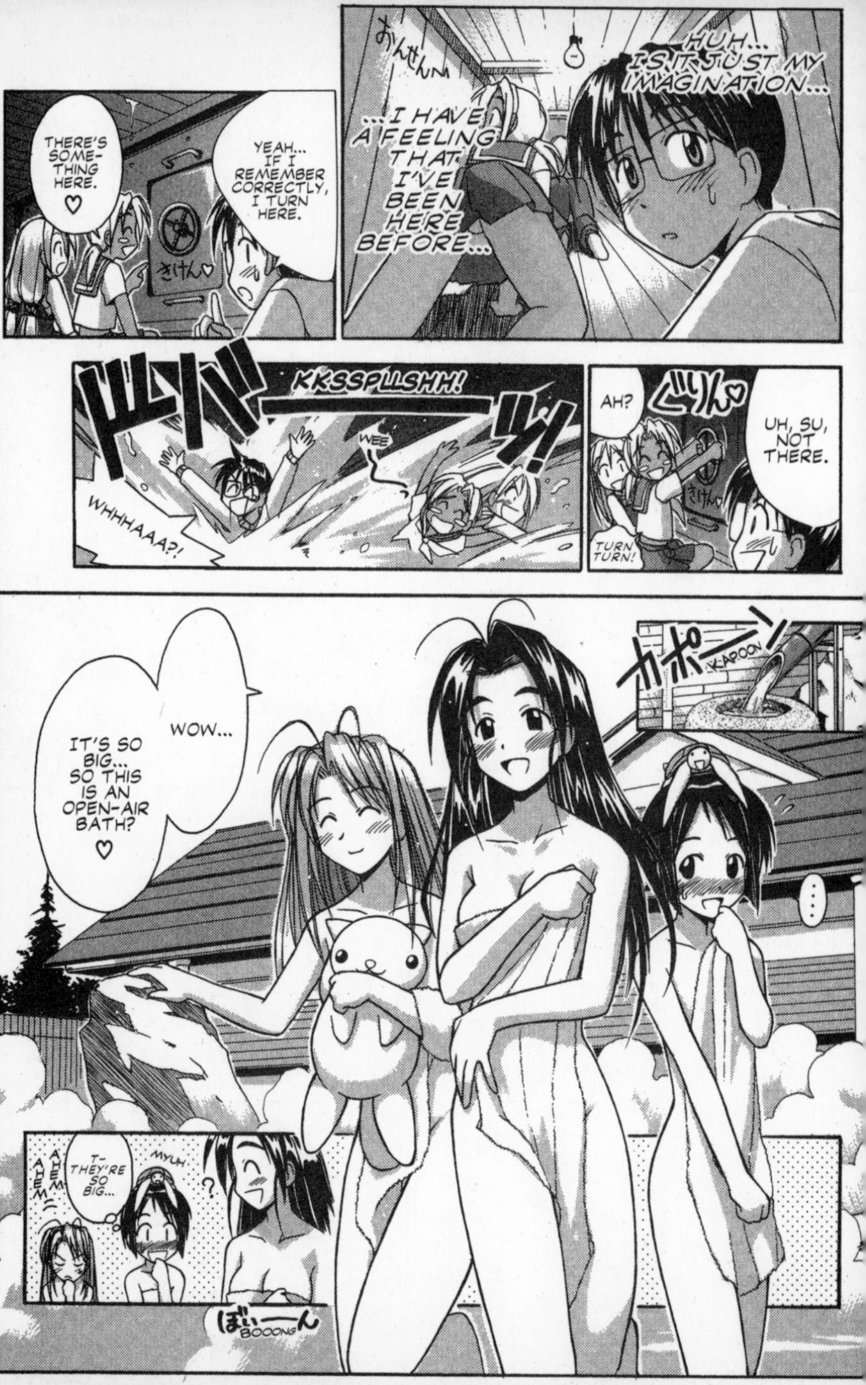
おんせん
HUH... IS IT JUST MY IMAGINATION...
...I HAVE A FEELING THAT I'VE BEEN HERE BEFORE...
YEAH... IF I REMEMBER CORRECTLY, I TURN HERE.
THERE'S SOMETHING HERE. ♡
きけん♡
UH, SU, NOT THERE.
ぐりん♡
AH?
きけん
TURN TURN!
ドバッ
KKSSPLUSHH!
WEE
WHHHAAA?!
カポーン
K-APOON
WOW...
IT'S SO BIG... SO THIS IS AN OPEN-AIR BATH? ♡
...
MYUH
T-THEY'RE SO BIG...
?
AHEM AHEM
ぼいーん
BOOONG

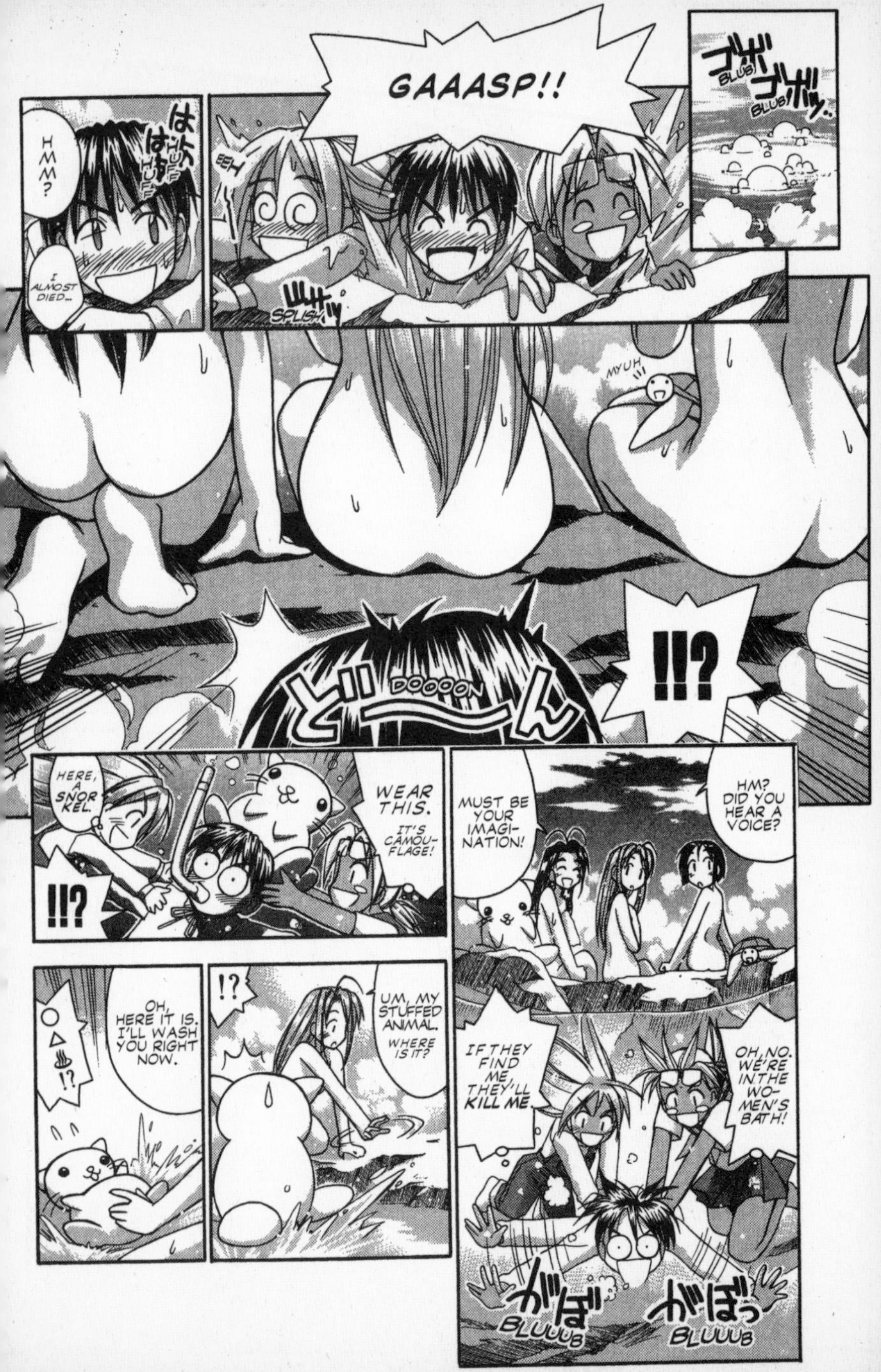
ゴボゴボッ
BLUB BLUB
GAAASP!!
EEH
ザザッ
SPLISH
はぁはぁ
HUFF HUFF
HMM?
I ALMOST DIED...
MYUH
どーーん
DOOOON
!!?
HM? DID YOU HEAR A VOICE?
MUST BE YOUR IMAGINATION!
OH, NO. WE'RE IN THE WOMEN'S BATH!
IF THEY FIND ME, THEY'LL KILL ME.
がぼっ
BLUUUB
がぼ
BLUUUB
WEAR THIS.
IT'S CAMOUFLAGE!
HERE, A SNORKEL.
!!?
UM, MY STUFFED ANIMAL.
WHERE IS IT?
!?
OH, HERE IT IS. I'LL WASH YOU RIGHT NOW.
○△♨!?

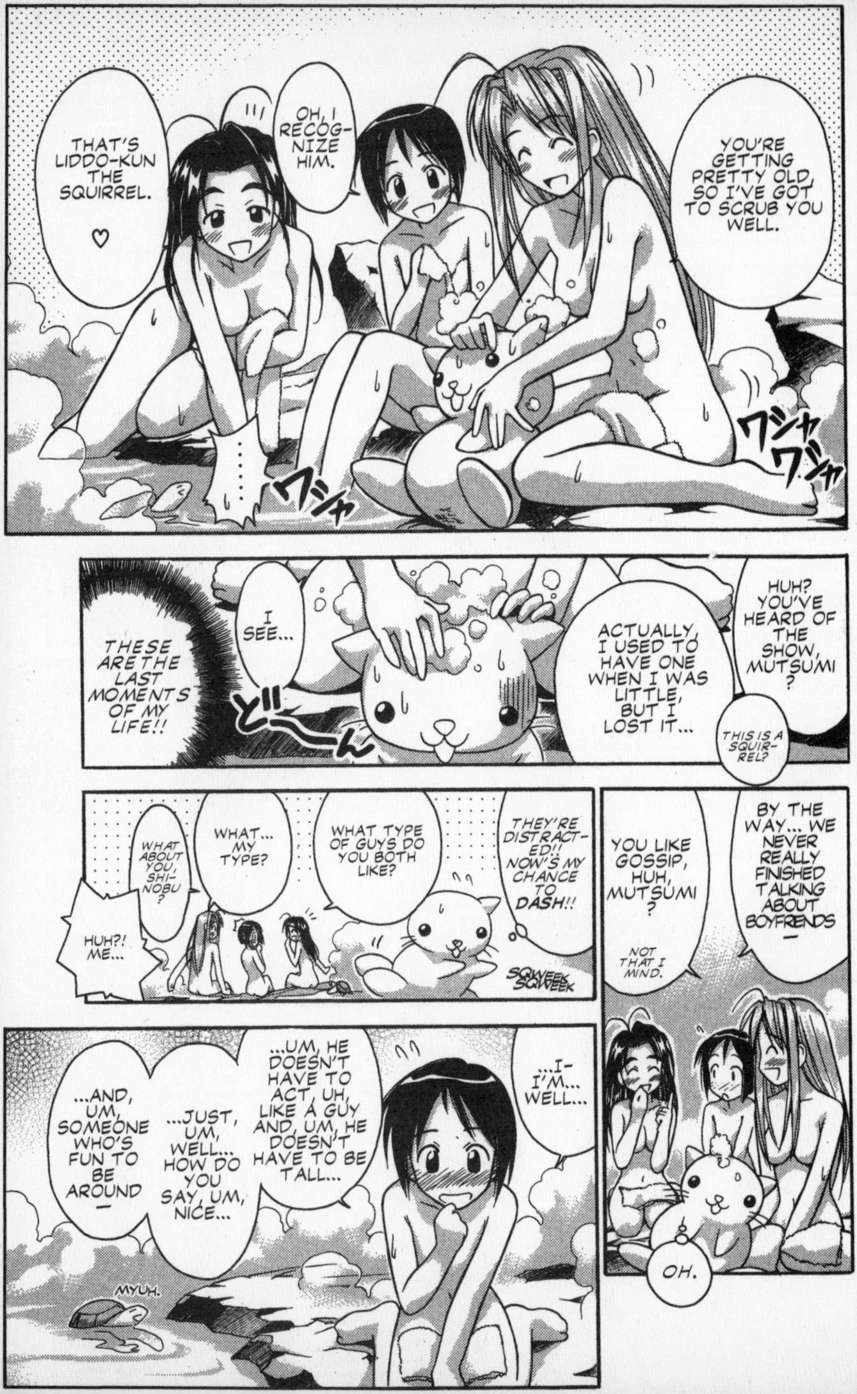
YOU'RE GETTING PRETTY OLD, SO I'VE GOT TO SCRUB YOU WELL.
OH, I RECOGNIZE HIM.
THAT'S LIDDO-KUN THE SQUIRREL. ♡
ワシャワシャ
......
ワシャ
HUH? YOU'VE HEARD OF THE SHOW, MUTSUMI?
THIS IS A SQUIRREL?
ACTUALLY, I USED TO HAVE ONE WHEN I WAS LITTLE, BUT I LOST IT...
I SEE...
どーん
THESE ARE THE LAST MOMENTS OF MY LIFE!!
BY THE WAY... WE NEVER REALLY FINISHED TALKING ABOUT BOYFRENDS—
YOU LIKE GOSSIP, HUH, MUTSUMI?
NOT THAT I MIND.
OH.
THEY'RE DISTRACTED!! NOW'S MY CHANCE TO DASH!!
WHAT TYPE OF GUYS DO YOU BOTH LIKE?
WHAT... MY TYPE?
WHAT ABOUT YOU, SHINOBU?
HUH?! ME...
SQWEEK SQWEEK
...I- I'M... WELL...
...UM, HE DOESN'T HAVE TO ACT, UH, LIKE A GUY AND, UM, HE DOESN'T HAVE TO BE TALL...
...JUST, UM, WELL... HOW DO YOU SAY, UM, NICE...
...AND, UM, SOMEONE WHO'S FUN TO BE AROUND—
MYUH.

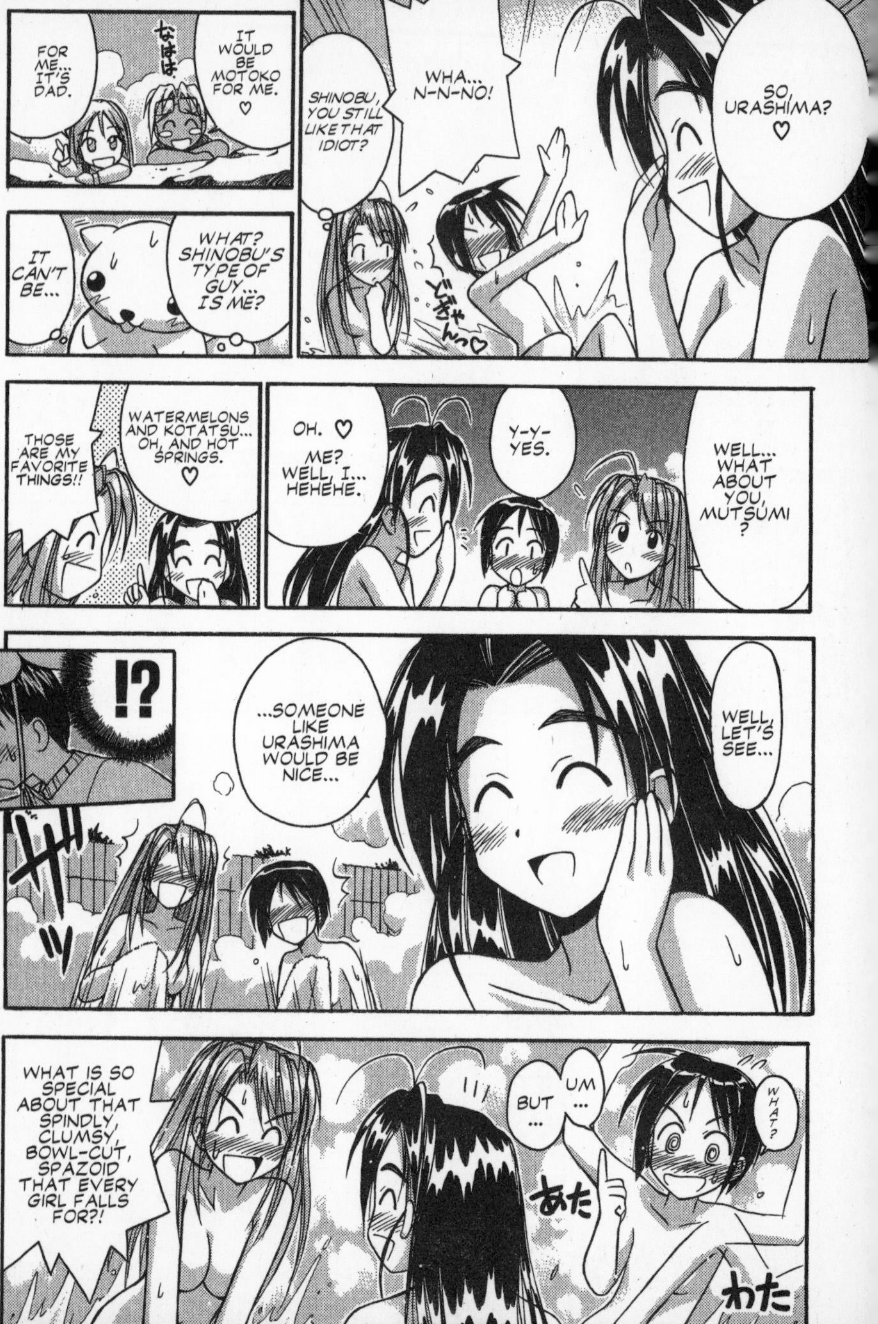
SO URASHIMA? ♡
WHA... N-N-NO!
SHINOBU, YOU STILL LIKE THAT IDIOT?
どぎゃんっ♡
IT WOULD BE MOTOKO FOR ME. ♡
なはは
FOR ME... IT'S DAD.
WHAT? SHINOBU'S TYPE OF GUY... IS ME?
IT CAN'T BE...
WELL... WHAT ABOUT YOU, MUTSUMI?
Y-Y-YES.
OH. ♡
ME? WELL, I... HEHEHE.
WATERMELONS AND KOTATSU... OH, AND HOT SPRINGS. ♡
THOSE ARE MY FAVORITE THINGS!!
WELL, LET'S SEE...
...SOMEONE LIKE URASHIMA WOULD BE NICE...
!?
WHAT?
UM...
BUT...
あた
わた
WHAT IS SO SPECIAL ABOUT THAT SPINDLY, CLUMSY, BOWL-CUT, SPAZOID THAT EVERY GIRL FALLS FOR?!

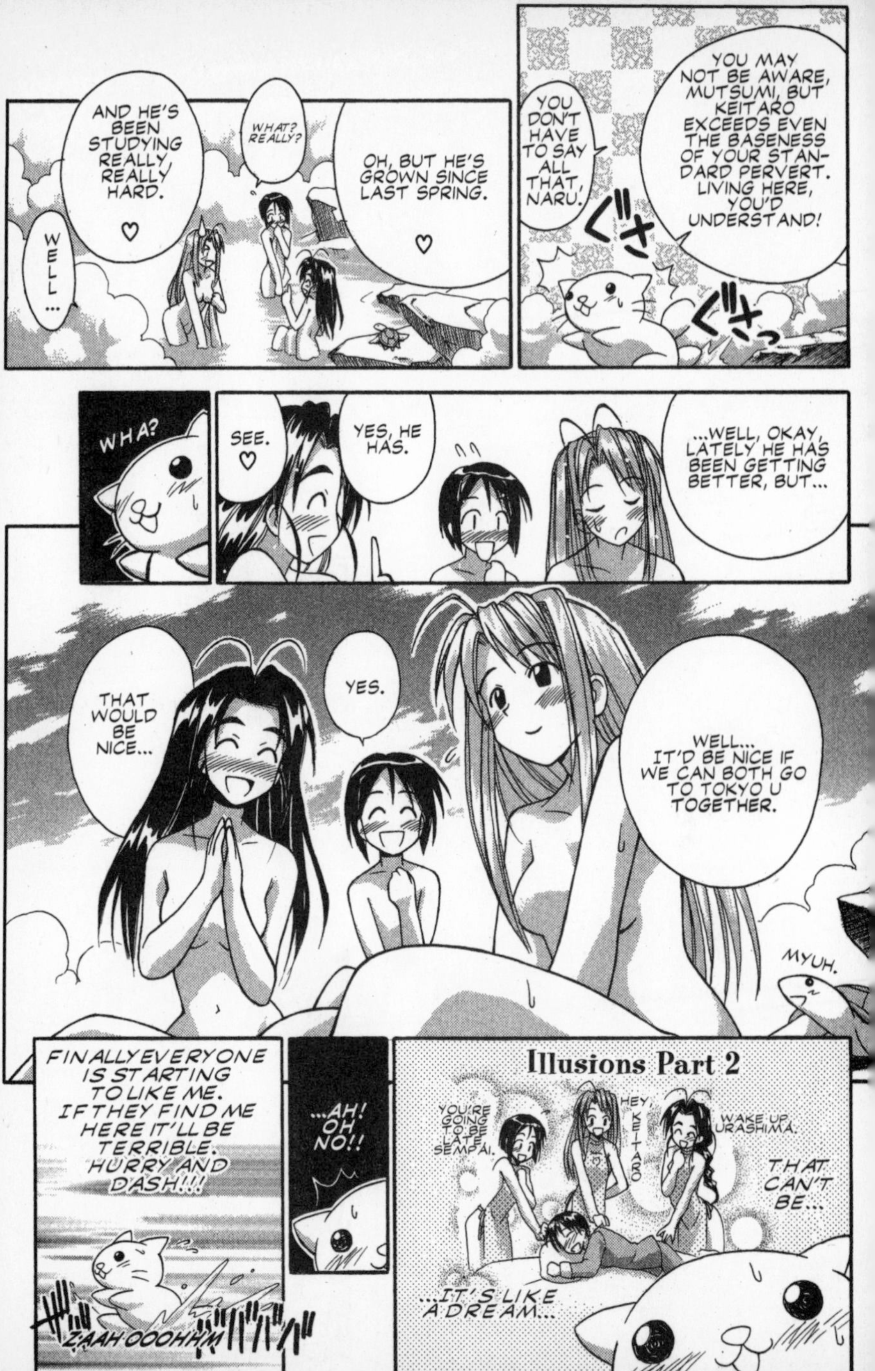
YOU MAY NOT BE AWARE, MUTSUMI, BUT KEITARO EXCEEDS EVEN THE BASENESS OF YOUR STAN-DARD PERVERT. LIVING HERE, YOU'D UNDERSTAND!
YOU DON'T HAVE TO SAY ALL THAT, NARU.
ぐさ
ぐさっ
OH, BUT HE'S GROWN SINCE LAST SPRING. ♡
WHAT? REALLY?
AND HE'S BEEN STUDYING REALLY, REALLY HARD. ♡
WELL...
...WELL, OKAY, LATELY HE HAS BEEN GETTING BETTER, BUT...
YES, HE HAS.
SEE. ♡
WHA?
WELL... IT'D BE NICE IF WE CAN BOTH GO TO TOKYO U TOGETHER.
YES.
THAT WOULD BE NICE...
MYUH.
Illusions Part 2
WAKE UP, URASHIMA.
HEY, KEITARO
YOU'RE GOING TO BE LATE, SEMPAI.
THAT CAN'T BE...
...IT'S LIKE A DREAM...
...AH! OH NO!!
FINALLY EVERYONE IS STARTING TO LIKE ME. IF THEY FIND ME HERE IT'LL BE TERRIBLE. HURRY AND DASH!!!
ZAAH OOOHHM

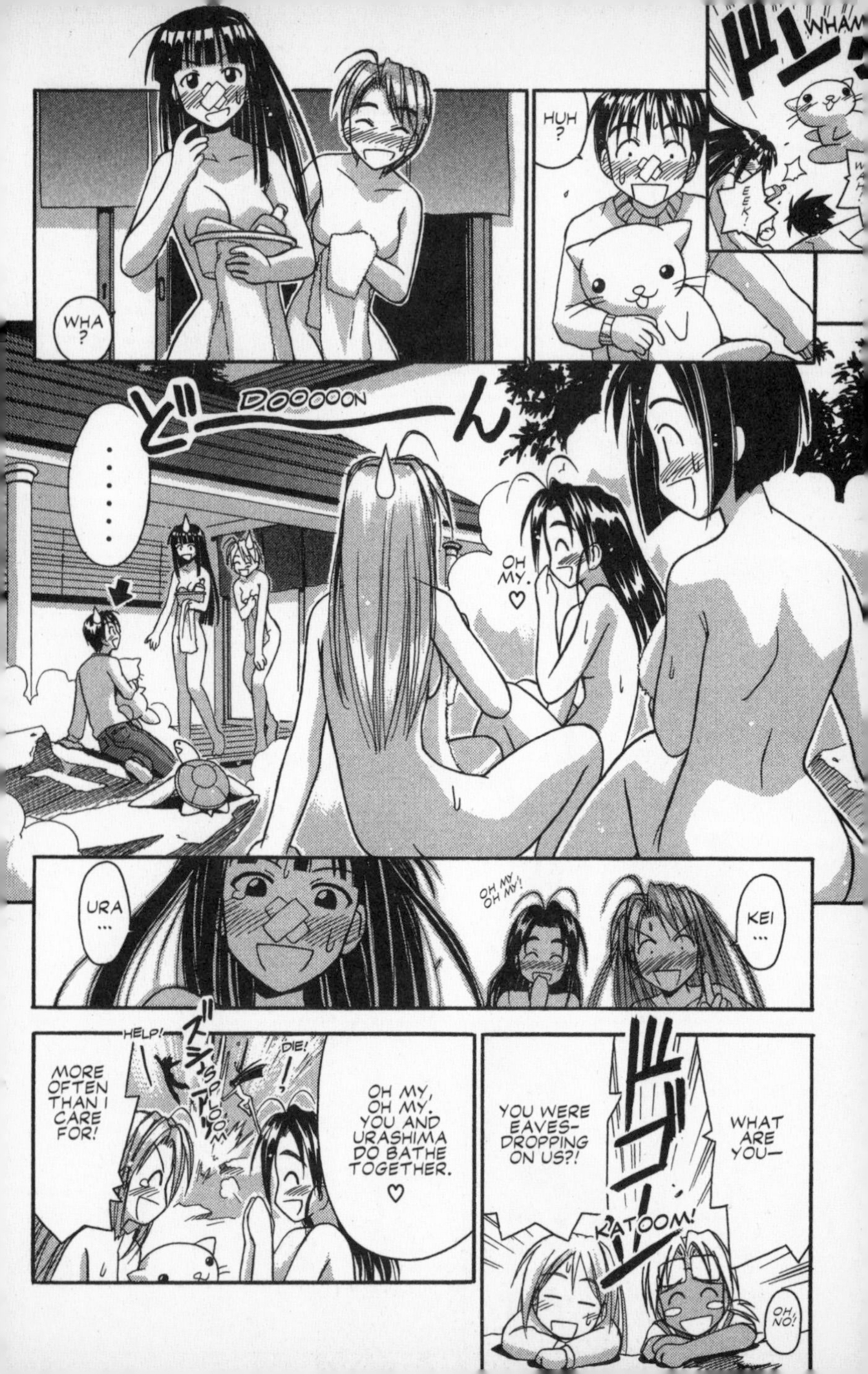
WHAM
EEK!
WAH!
HUH ?
WHA ?
DOOOOON
. . . .
OH MY. ♡
KEI ...
OH MY OH MY!
URA ...
WHAT ARE YOU—
YOU WERE EAVES-DROPPING ON US?!
KATOOM!
OH, NO!
OH MY, OH MY. YOU AND URASHIMA DO BATHE TOGETHER. ♡
DIE!
SPLOOM
HELP!
MORE OFTEN THAN I CARE FOR!

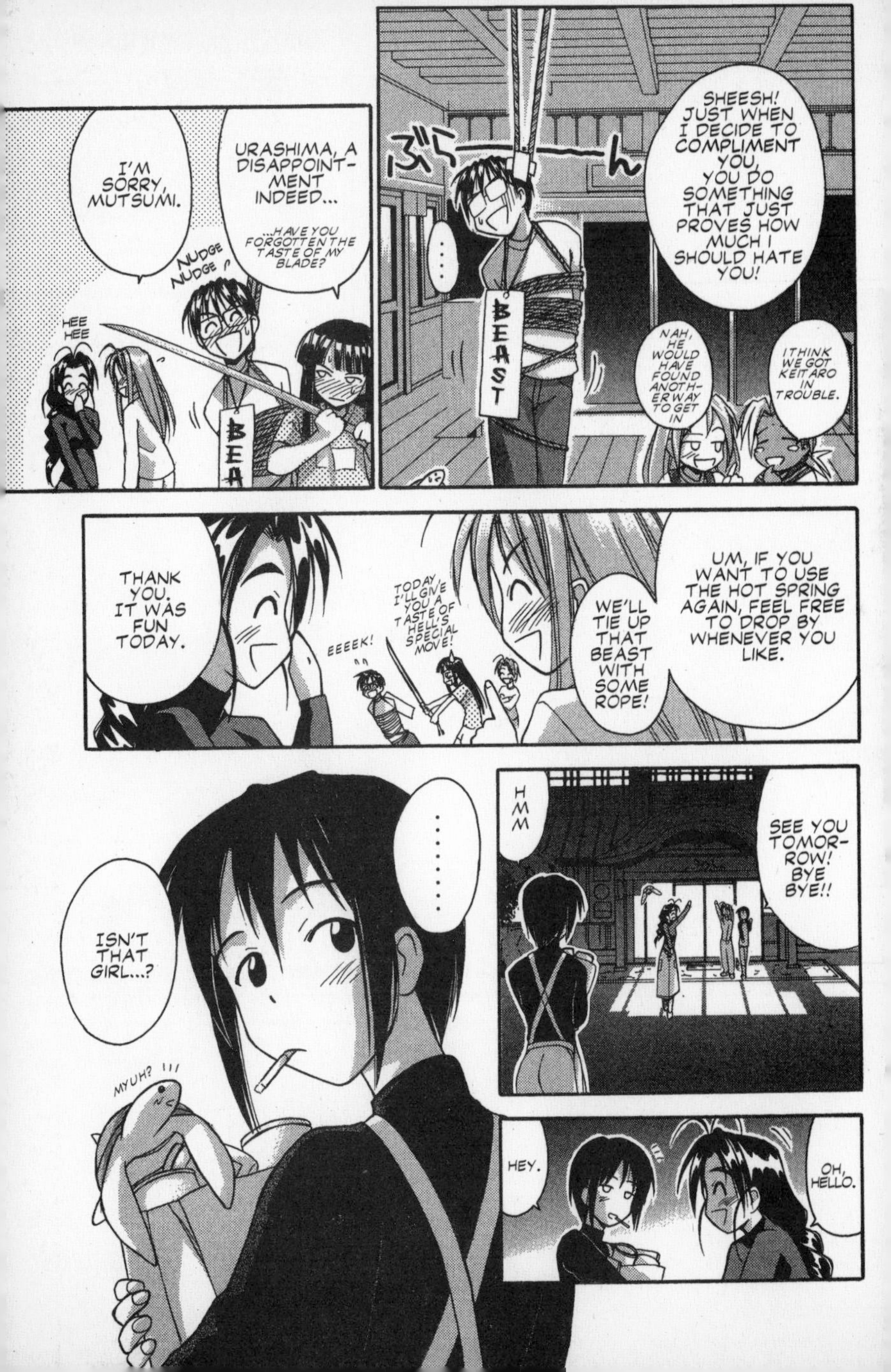
SHEESH! JUST WHEN I DECIDE TO COMPLIMENT YOU, YOU DO SOMETHING THAT JUST PROVES HOW MUCH I SHOULD HATE YOU!
ぶら――――ん
...
BEAST
I THINK WE GOT KEITARO IN TROUBLE.
NAH, HE WOULD HAVE FOUND ANOTHER WAY TO GET IN
URASHIMA, A DISAPPOINTMENT INDEED...
...HAVE YOU FORGOTTEN THE TASTE OF MY BLADE?
I'M SORRY, MUTSUMI.
NUDGE NUDGE
BEA
HEE HEE
UM, IF YOU WANT TO USE THE HOT SPRING AGAIN, FEEL FREE TO DROP BY WHENEVER YOU LIKE.
WE'LL TIE UP THAT BEAST WITH SOME ROPE!
TODAY, I'LL GIVE YOU A TASTE OF HELL'S SPECIAL MOVE!
EEEEK!
THANK YOU. IT WAS FUN TODAY.
SEE YOU TOMORROW! BYE BYE!!
HMM
....
ISN'T THAT GIRL...?
MYUH?
OH, HELLO.
HEY.

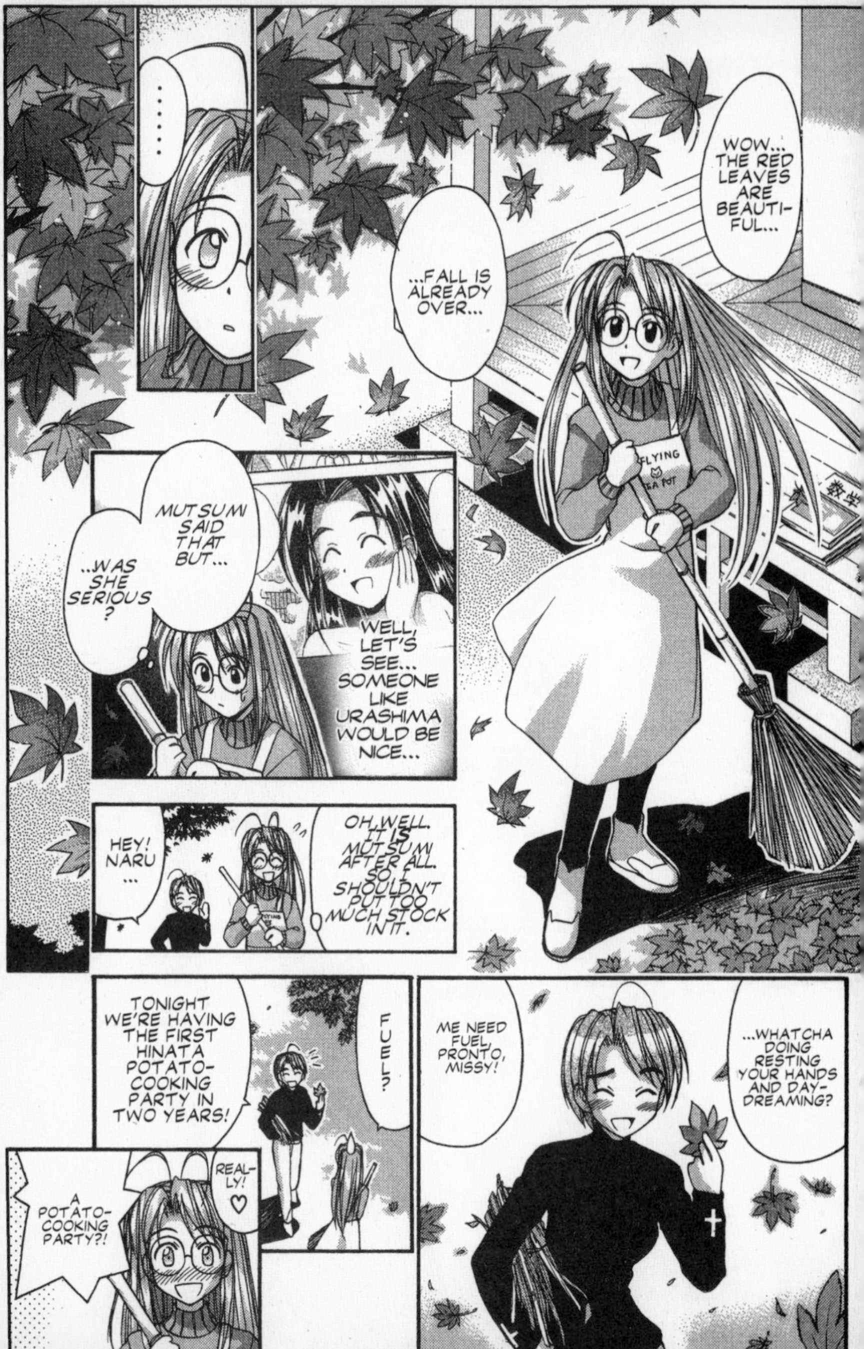
WOW... THE RED LEAVES ARE BEAUTIFUL...
...FALL IS ALREADY OVER...
......
MUTSUMI SAID THAT BUT...
...WAS SHE SERIOUS?
WELL, LET'S SEE... SOMEONE LIKE URASHIMA WOULD BE NICE...
OH WELL. IT IS MUTSUMI AFTER ALL. SO I SHOULDN'T PUT TOO MUCH STOCK IN IT.
HEY! NARU...
...WHATCHA DOING RESTING YOUR HANDS AND DAY-DREAMING?
ME NEED FUEL, PRONTO, MISSY!
FUEL?
TONIGHT WE'RE HAVING THE FIRST HINATA POTATO-COOKING PARTY IN TWO YEARS!
REALLY! ♥
A POTATO-COOKING PARTY?!

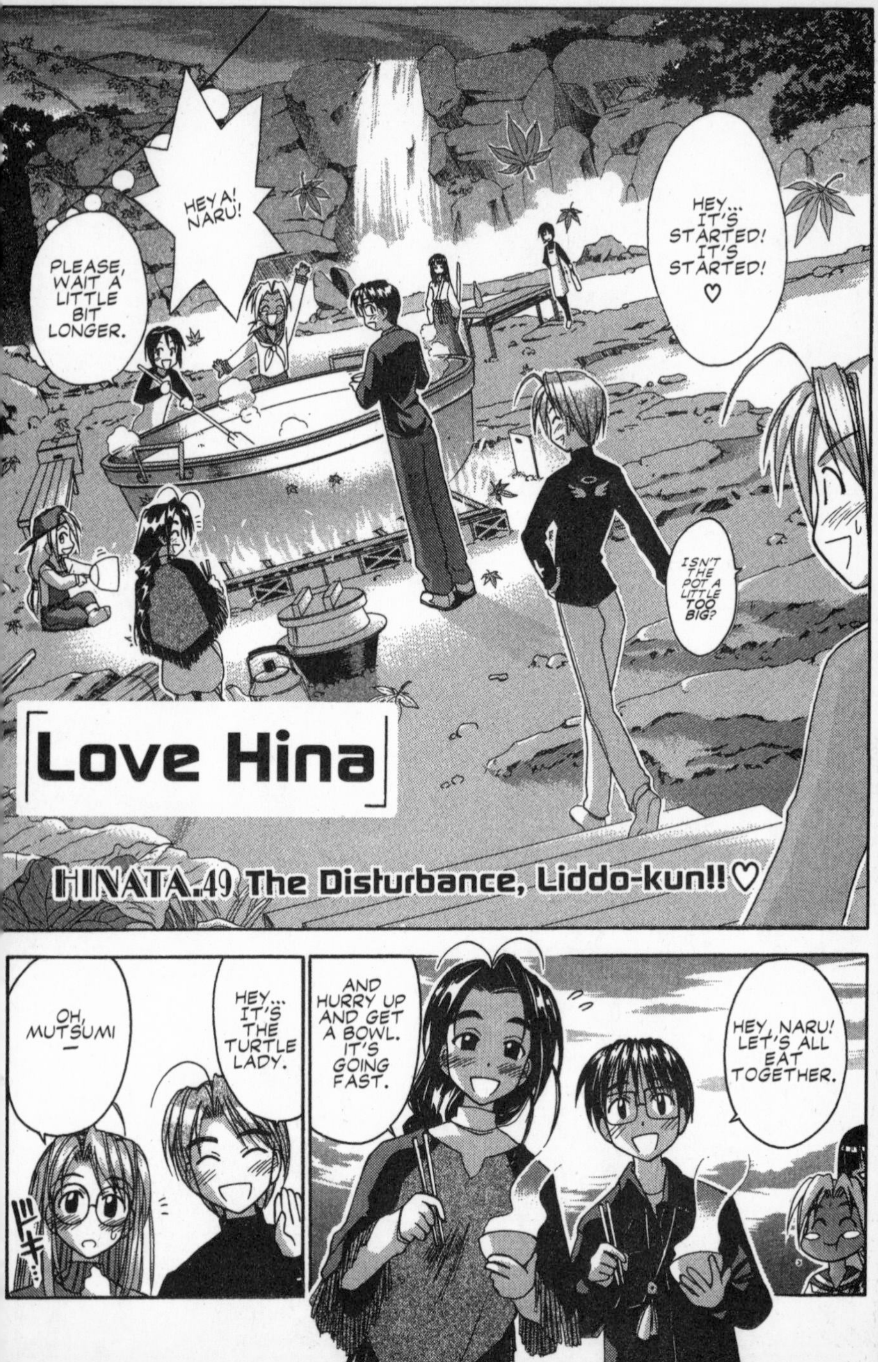
HEY... IT'S STARTED! IT'S STARTED! ♡
ISN'T THE POT A LITTLE TOO BIG?
HEYA! NARU!
PLEASE, WAIT A LITTLE BIT LONGER.
Love Hina
HINATA.49 The Disturbance, Liddo-kun!! ♡
HEY, NARU! LET'S ALL EAT TOGETHER.
AND HURRY UP AND GET A BOWL. IT'S GOING FAST.
HEY... IT'S THE TURTLE LADY.
OH, MUTSUMI —
ドキ...

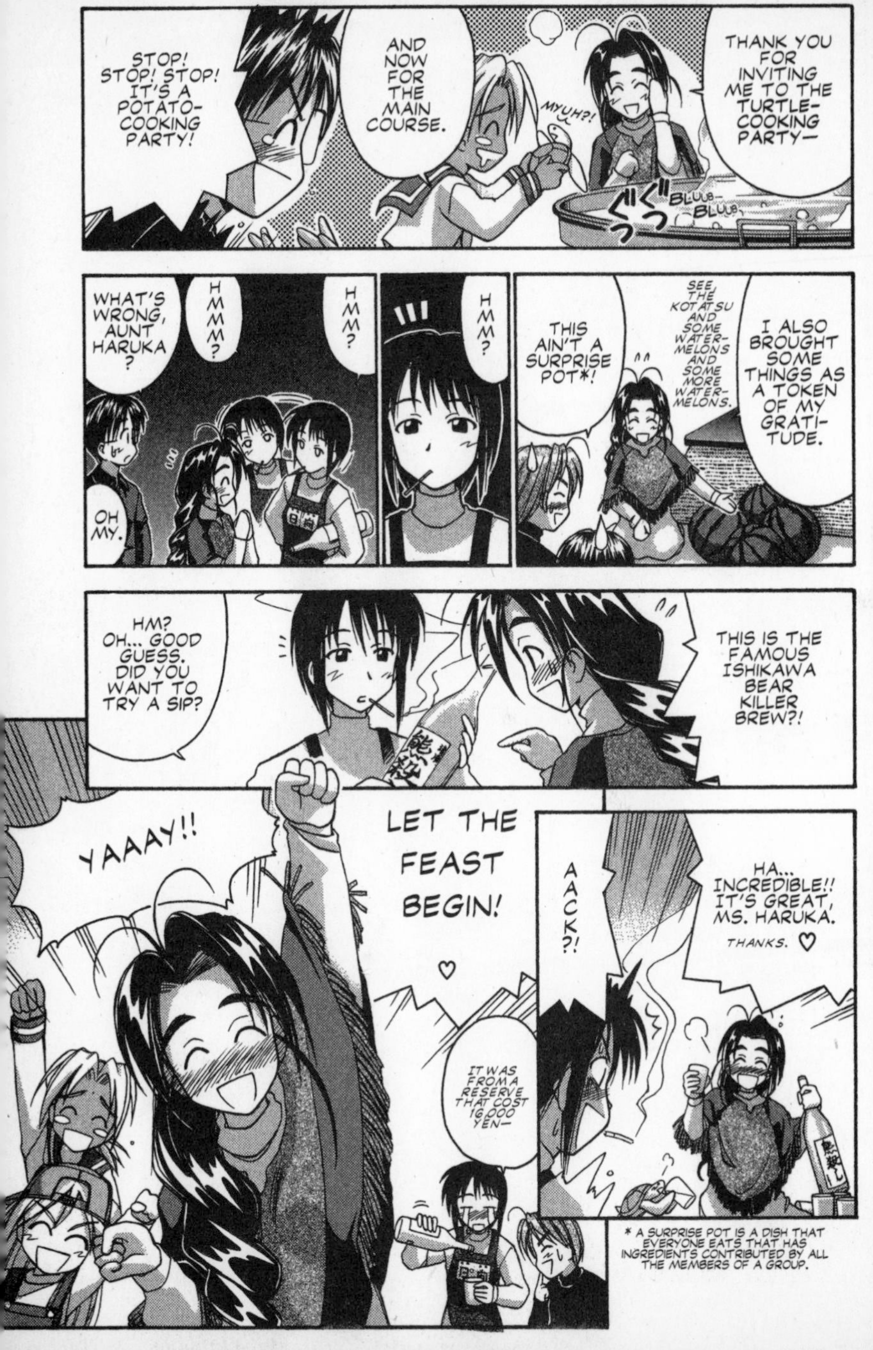
THANK YOU FOR INVITING ME TO THE TURTLE-COOKING PARTY—
MYUH?!
AND NOW FOR THE MAIN COURSE.
STOP! STOP! STOP! IT'S A POTATO-COOKING PARTY!
ぐつぐつ
BLUUB-BLUUB
I ALSO BROUGHT SOME THINGS AS A TOKEN OF MY GRATITUDE.
SEE, THE KOTATSU AND SOME WATER-MELONS AND SOME MORE WATER-MELONS.
THIS AIN'T A SURPRISE POT*!
HMM?
HMM?
HMMM?
WHAT'S WRONG, AUNT HARUKA?
OH MY.
THIS IS THE FAMOUS ISHIKAWA BEAR KILLER BREW?!
HM? OH... GOOD GUESS. DID YOU WANT TO TRY A SIP?
HA... INCREDIBLE!! IT'S GREAT, MS. HARUKA.
THANKS. ♥
AACK?!
LET THE FEAST BEGIN! ♥
YAAAY!!
IT WAS FROM A RESERVE THAT COST 16,000 YEN—

* A SURPRISE POT IS A DISH THAT EVERYONE EATS THAT HAS INGREDIENTS CONTRIBUTED BY ALL THE MEMBERS OF A GROUP.

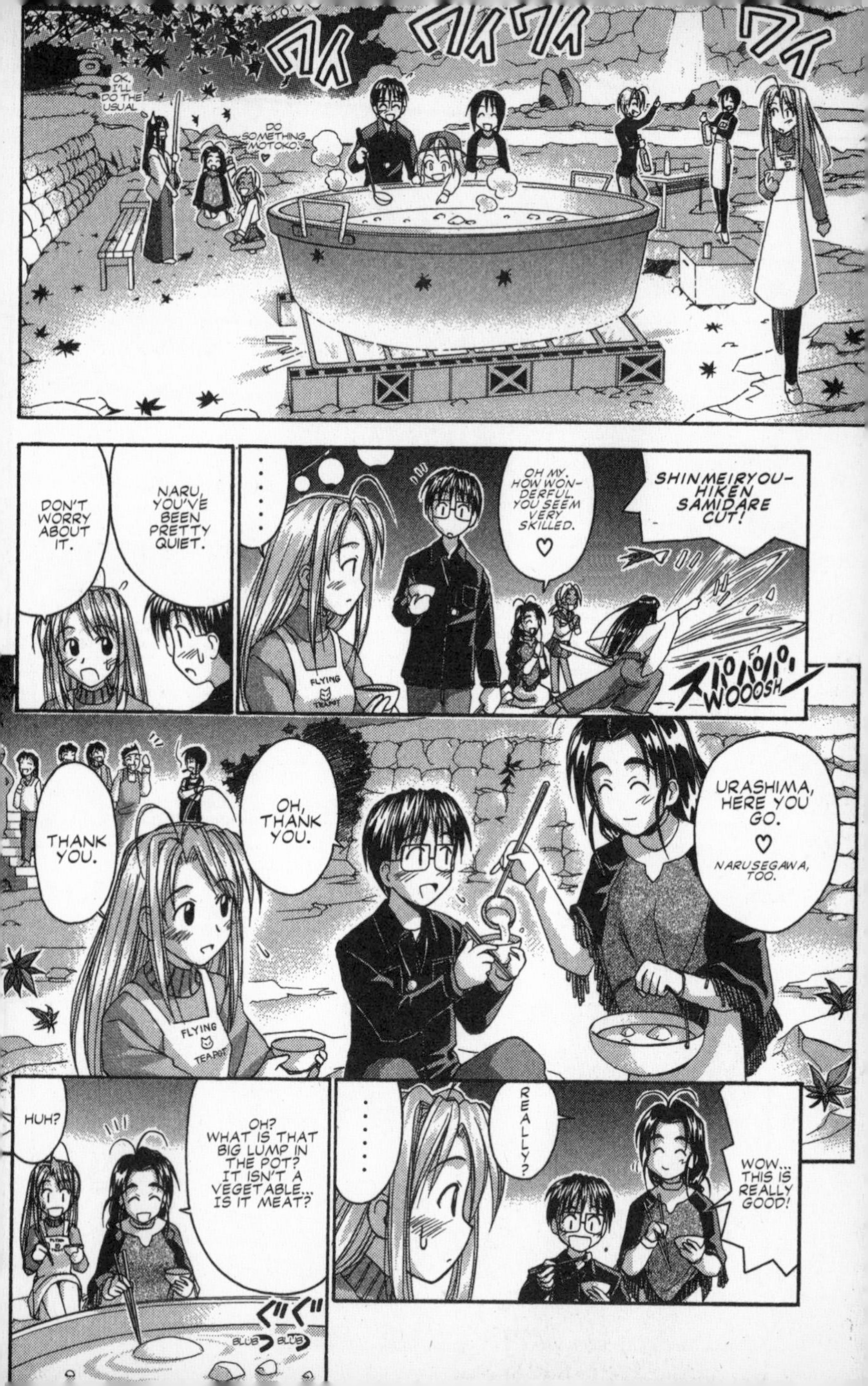
ワイ ワイワイ ワイ
DO SOMETHING, MOTOKO.
OK. I'LL DO THE USUAL
SHINMEIRYOU-HIKEN SAMIDARE CUT!
OH MY. HOW WON-DERFUL. YOU SEEM VERY SKILLED. ♡
スパパパ WOOOSH
......
NARU, YOU'VE BEEN PRETTY QUIET.
DON'T WORRY ABOUT IT.
URASHIMA, HERE YOU GO. ♡
NARUSEGAWA, TOO.
OH, THANK YOU.
THANK YOU.
WOW... THIS IS REALLY GOOD!
REALLY?
......
OH? WHAT IS THAT BIG LUMP IN THE POT? IT ISN'T A VEGETABLE... IS IT MEAT?
HUH?
ぐつぐつ BLUB BLUB

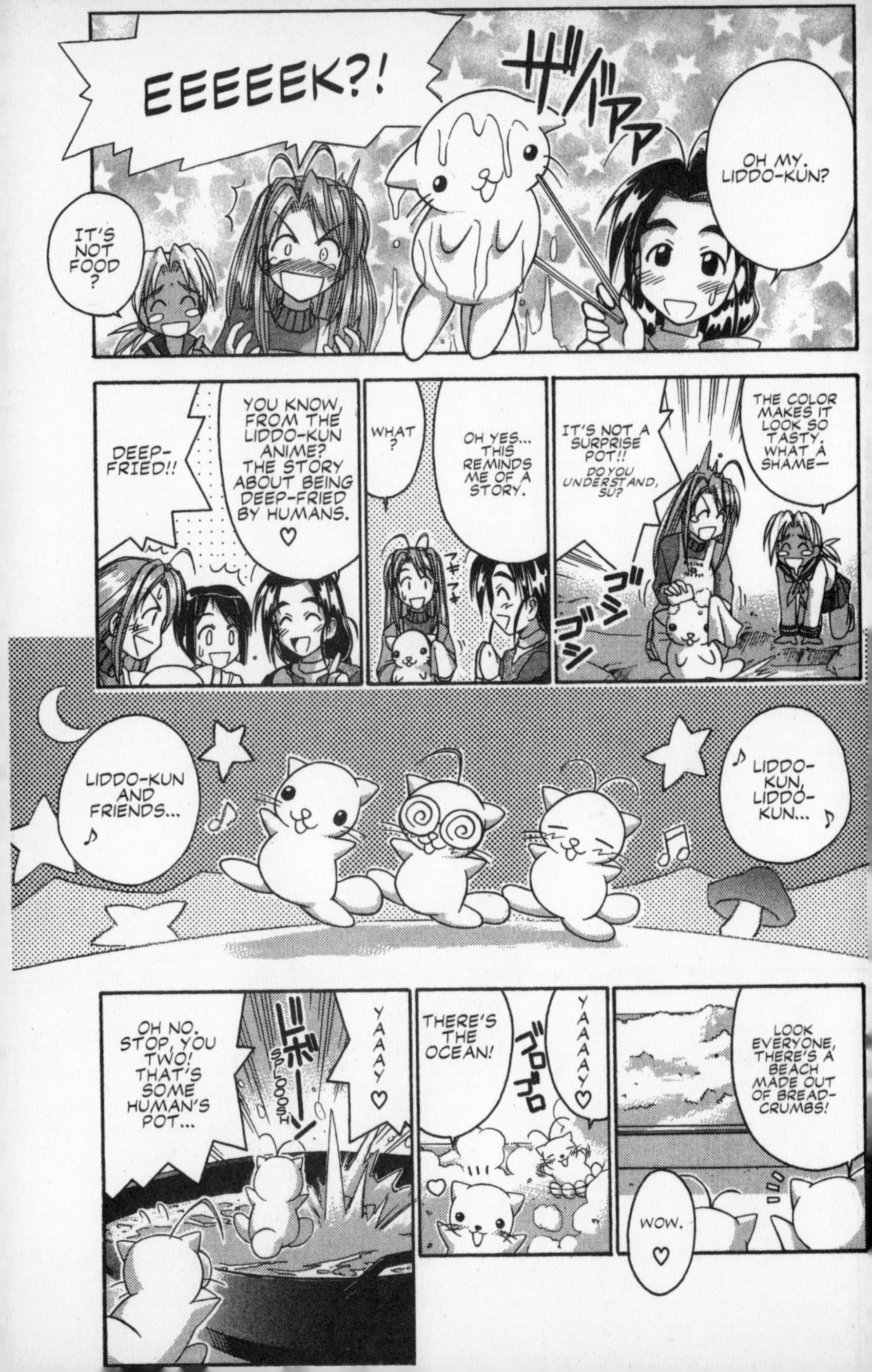
OH MY. LIDDO-KUN?
ザバァァ
EEEEEK?!
IT'S NOT FOOD?
THE COLOR MAKES IT LOOK SO TASTY. WHAT A SHAME—
IT'S NOT A SURPRISE POT!! DO YOU UNDERSTAND, SU?
ゴシゴシ
OH YES... THIS REMINDS ME OF A STORY.
WHAT?
フキフキ
YOU KNOW, FROM THE LIDDO-KUN ANIME? THE STORY ABOUT BEING DEEP-FRIED BY HUMANS. ♡
DEEP-FRIED!!
♪ LIDDO-KUN, LIDDO-KUN... ♪
LIDDO-KUN AND FRIENDS... ♪
LOOK EVERYONE, THERE'S A BEACH MADE OUT OF BREAD-CRUMBS!
WOW. ♡
YAAAAY ♡
ゴロゴロ
THERE'S THE OCEAN!
YAAAY ♡
ドボーン
SPLOOOSH
OH NO. STOP, YOU TWO! THAT'S SOME HUMAN'S POT...

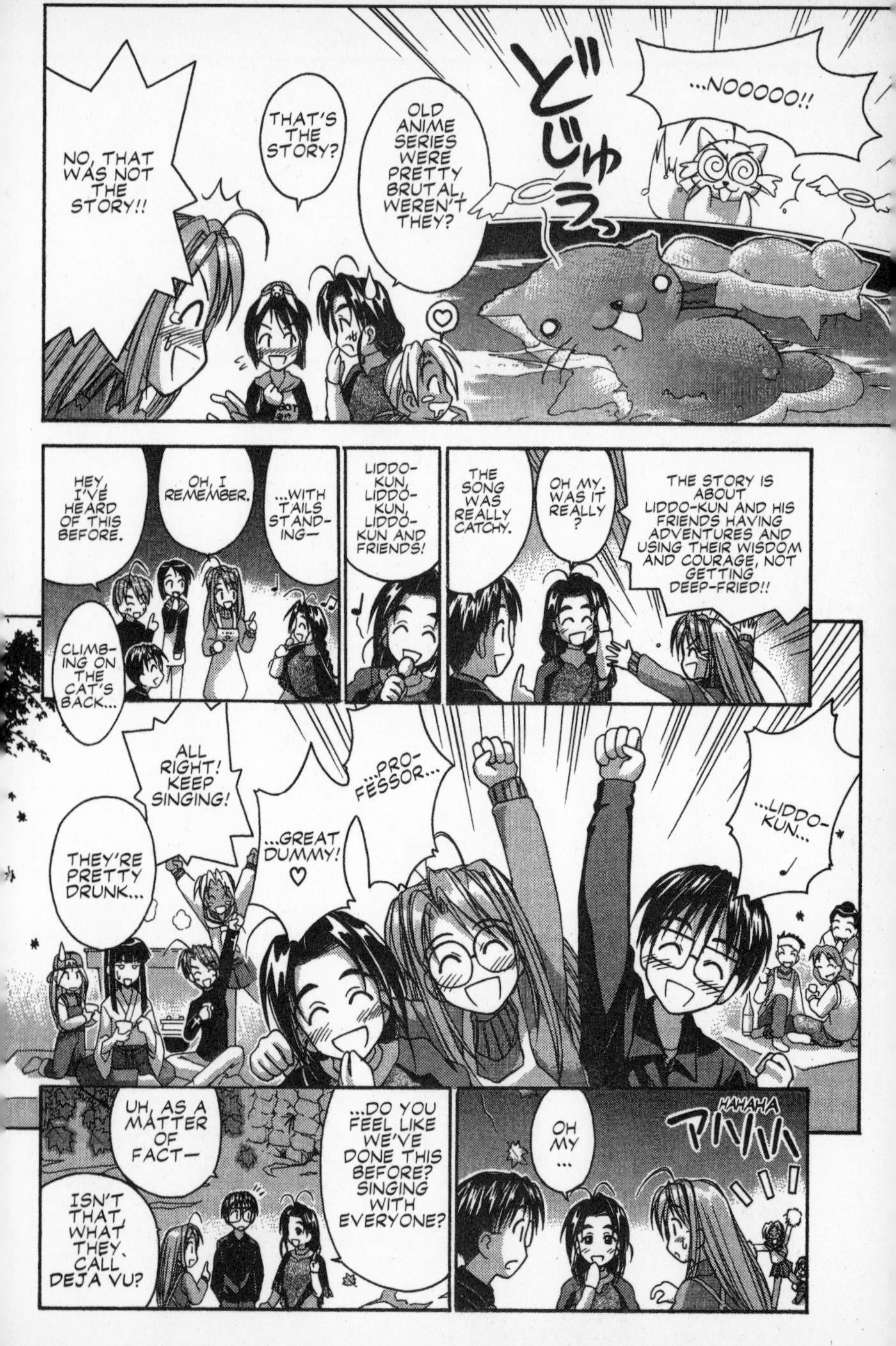
...NOOOOO!!
どじゅうっ
OLD ANIME SERIES WERE PRETTY BRUTAL, WEREN'T THEY?
THAT'S THE STORY?
NO, THAT WAS NOT THE STORY!!
THE STORY IS ABOUT LIDDO-KUN AND HIS FRIENDS HAVING ADVENTURES AND USING THEIR WISDOM AND COURAGE, NOT GETTING DEEP-FRIED!!
OH MY. WAS IT REALLY?
THE SONG WAS REALLY CATCHY.
LIDDO-KUN, LIDDO-KUN, LIDDO-KUN AND FRIENDS!
...WITH TAILS STANDING—
OH, I REMEMBER.
HEY, I'VE HEARD OF THIS BEFORE.
CLIMBING ON THE CAT'S BACK...
...LIDDO-KUN...
...PRO-FESSOR...
...GREAT DUMMY! ♡
ALL RIGHT! KEEP SINGING!
THEY'RE PRETTY DRUNK...
HAHAHA
アハハハ
OH MY ...
...DO YOU FEEL LIKE WE'VE DONE THIS BEFORE? SINGING WITH EVERYONE?
UH, AS A MATTER OF FACT—
ISN'T THAT, WHAT THEY CALL DEJA VU?

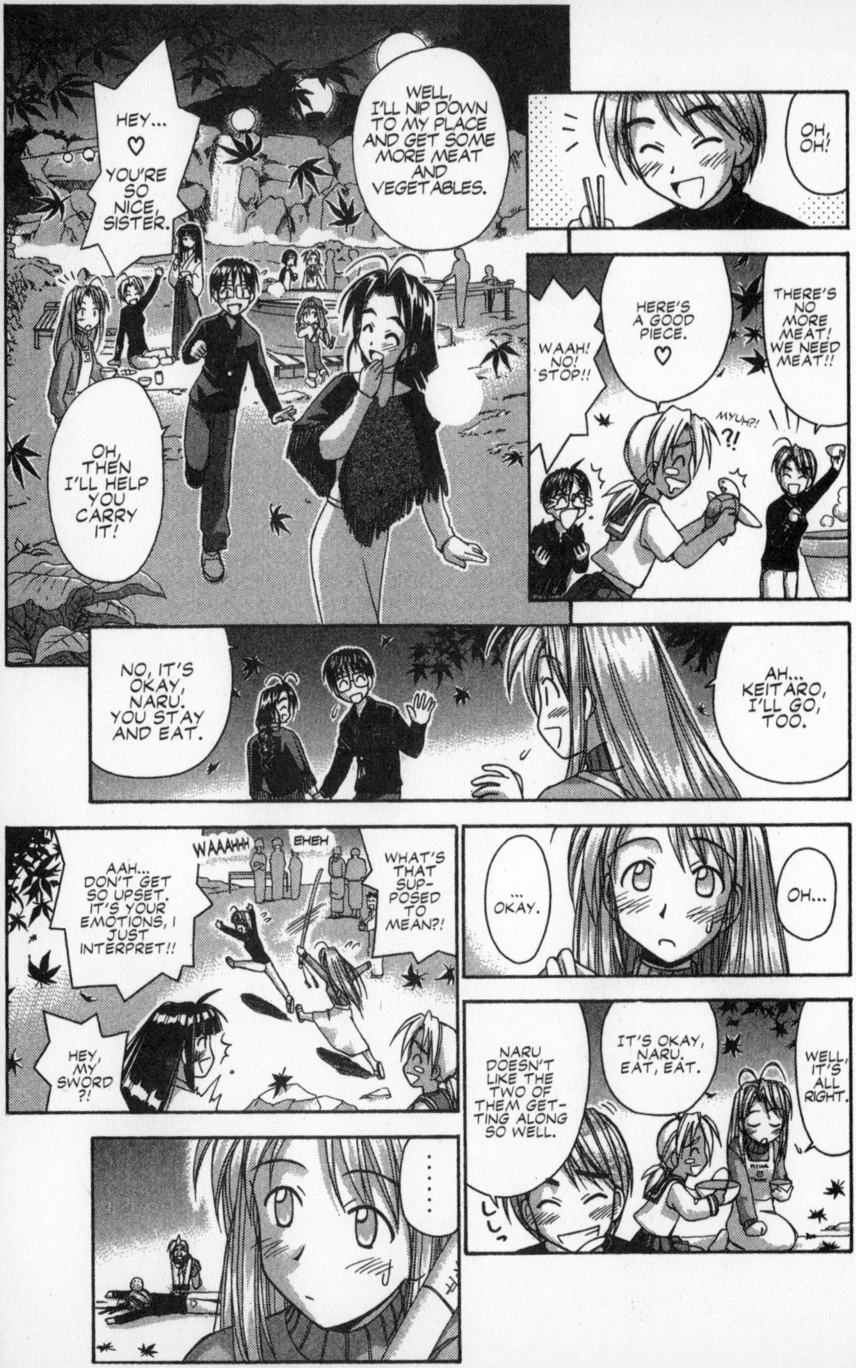
OH, OH!
THERE'S NO MORE MEAT! WE NEED MEAT!!
HERE'S A GOOD PIECE. ♡
WAAH! NO! STOP!!
MYUH?!
?!
WELL, I'LL NIP DOWN TO MY PLACE AND GET SOME MORE MEAT AND VEGETABLES.
HEY... ♡ YOU'RE SO NICE, SISTER.
OH, THEN I'LL HELP YOU CARRY IT!
AH... KEITARO, I'LL GO, TOO.
NO, IT'S OKAY, NARU. YOU STAY AND EAT.
OH...
... OKAY.
WELL, IT'S ALL RIGHT.
IT'S OKAY, NARU. EAT, EAT.
NARU DOESN'T LIKE THE TWO OF THEM GET-TING ALONG SO WELL.
WHAT'S THAT SUP-POSED TO MEAN?!
EHEH
WAAAHHH
AAH... DON'T GET SO UPSET. IT'S YOUR EMOTIONS, I JUST INTERPRET!!
HEY, MY SWORD ?!
......

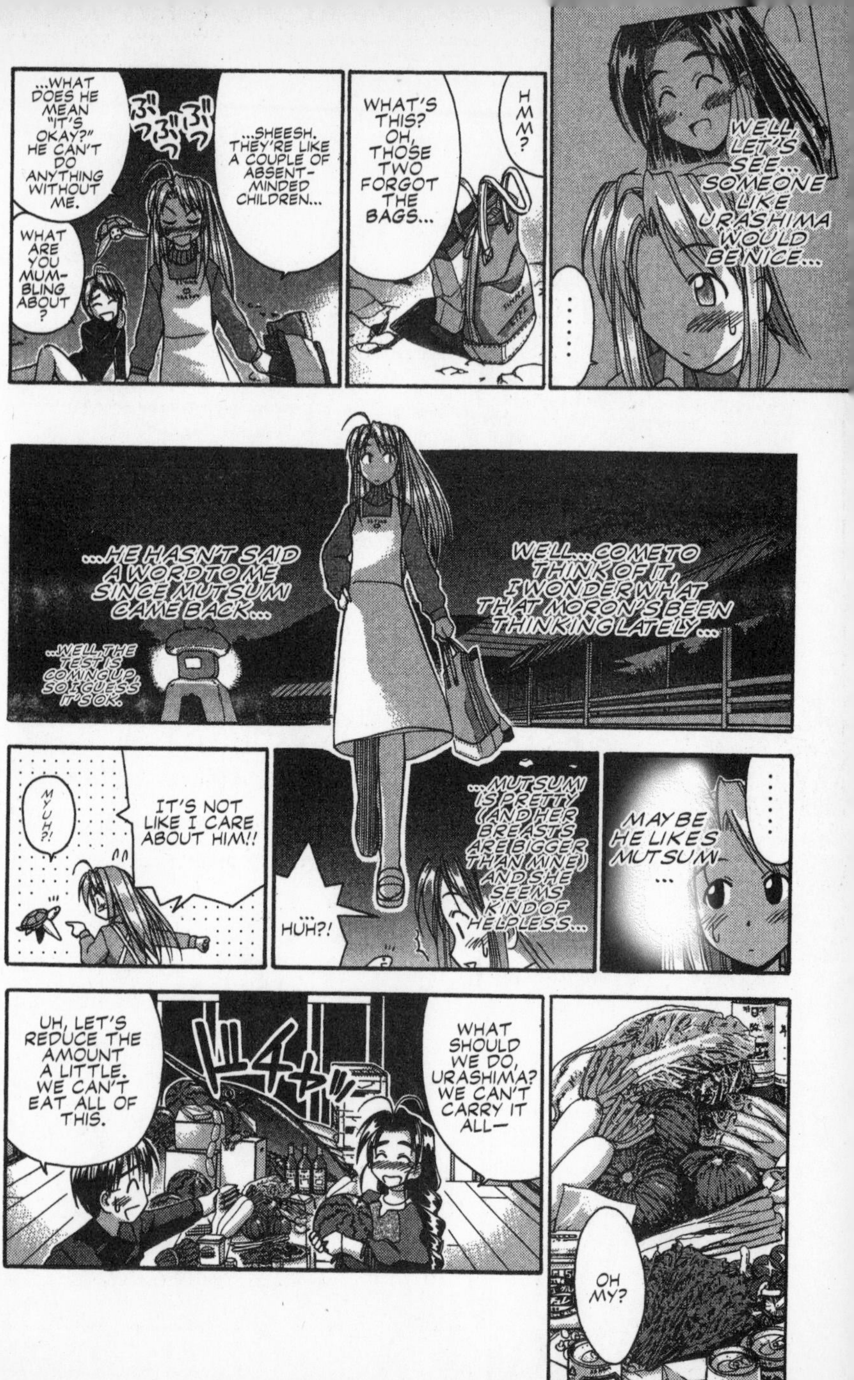
WELL, LET'S SEE... SOMEONE LIKE URASHIMA WOULD BE NICE...
......
HMM?
WHAT'S THIS? OH, THOSE TWO FORGOT THE BAGS...
...SHEESH. THEY'RE LIKE A COUPLE OF ABSENT-MINDED CHILDREN...
ぶつぶつ
...WHAT DOES HE MEAN "IT'S OKAY?" HE CAN'T DO ANYTHING WITHOUT ME.
WHAT ARE YOU MUMBLING ABOUT?
WELL...COME TO THINK OF IT, I WONDER WHAT THAT MORON'S BEEN THINKING LATELY...
...HE HASN'T SAID A WORD TO ME SINCE MUTSUMI CAME BACK...
...WELL THE TEST IS COMING UP, SO I GUESS IT'S OK.
......
MAYBE HE LIKES MUTSUMI...
...MUTSUMI IS PRETTY (AND HER BREASTS ARE BIGGER THAN MINE) AND SHE SEEMS KIND OF HELPLESS...
...HUH?!
IT'S NOT LIKE I CARE ABOUT HIM!!
MYUH?!
OH MY?
WHAT SHOULD WE DO, URASHIMA? WE CAN'T CARRY IT ALL—
UH, LET'S REDUCE THE AMOUNT A LITTLE. WE CAN'T EAT ALL OF THIS.

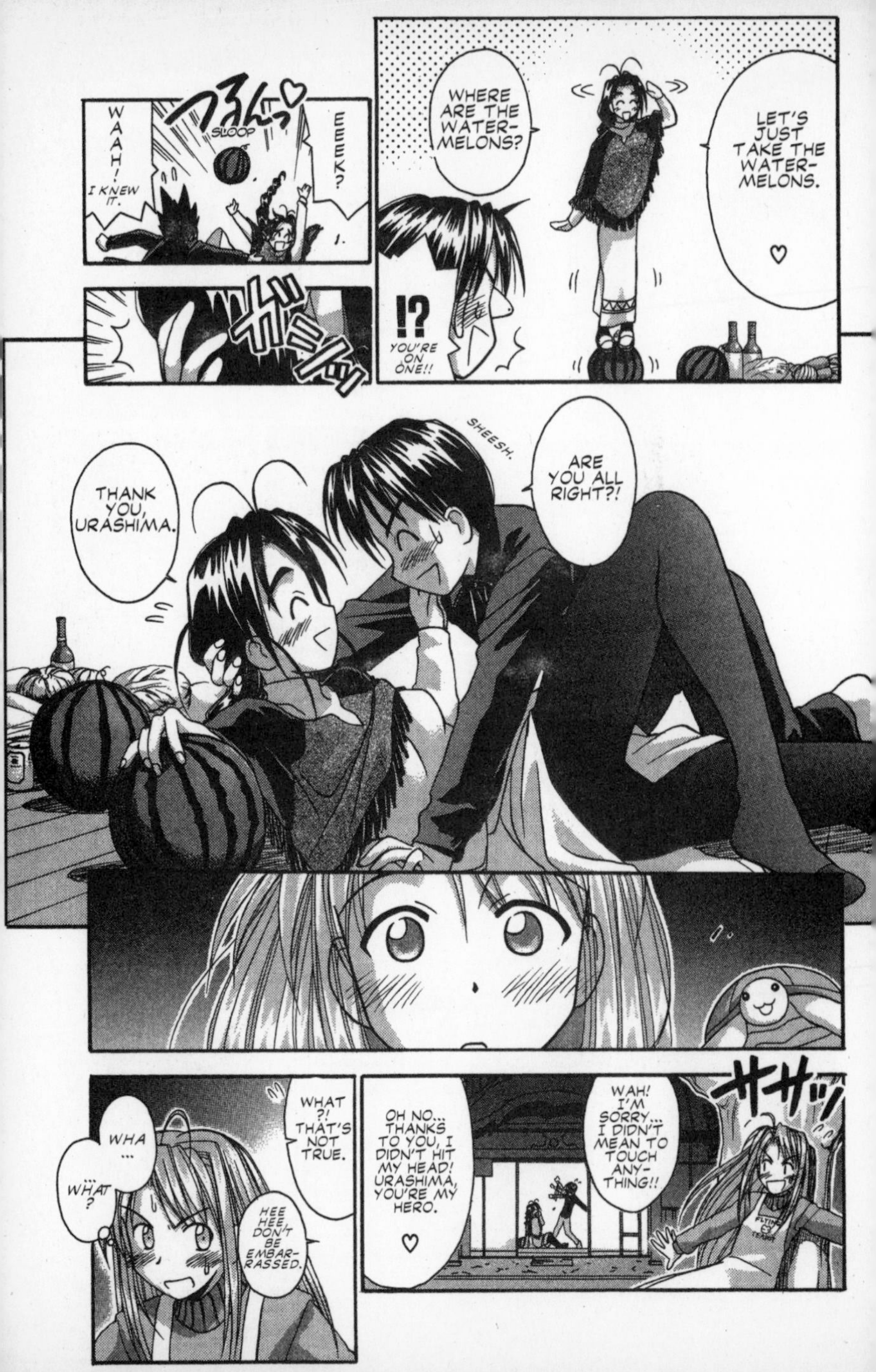
LET'S JUST TAKE THE WATER-MELONS. ♥
WHERE ARE THE WATER-MELONS?
!?
YOU'RE ON ONE!!
EEEK?
つるんっ♡
SLOOP
WAAAH! I KNEW IT.
ガシッ
ARE YOU ALL RIGHT?!
SHEESH.
THANK YOU, URASHIMA.
サザッ
WAH! I'M SORRY... I DIDN'T MEAN TO TOUCH ANY-THING!!
OH NO... THANKS TO YOU, I DIDN'T HIT MY HEAD! URASHIMA, YOU'RE MY HERO. ♥
WHAT?! THAT'S NOT TRUE.
WHA... ...WHAT?
HEE HEE DON'T BE EMBAR-RASSED.

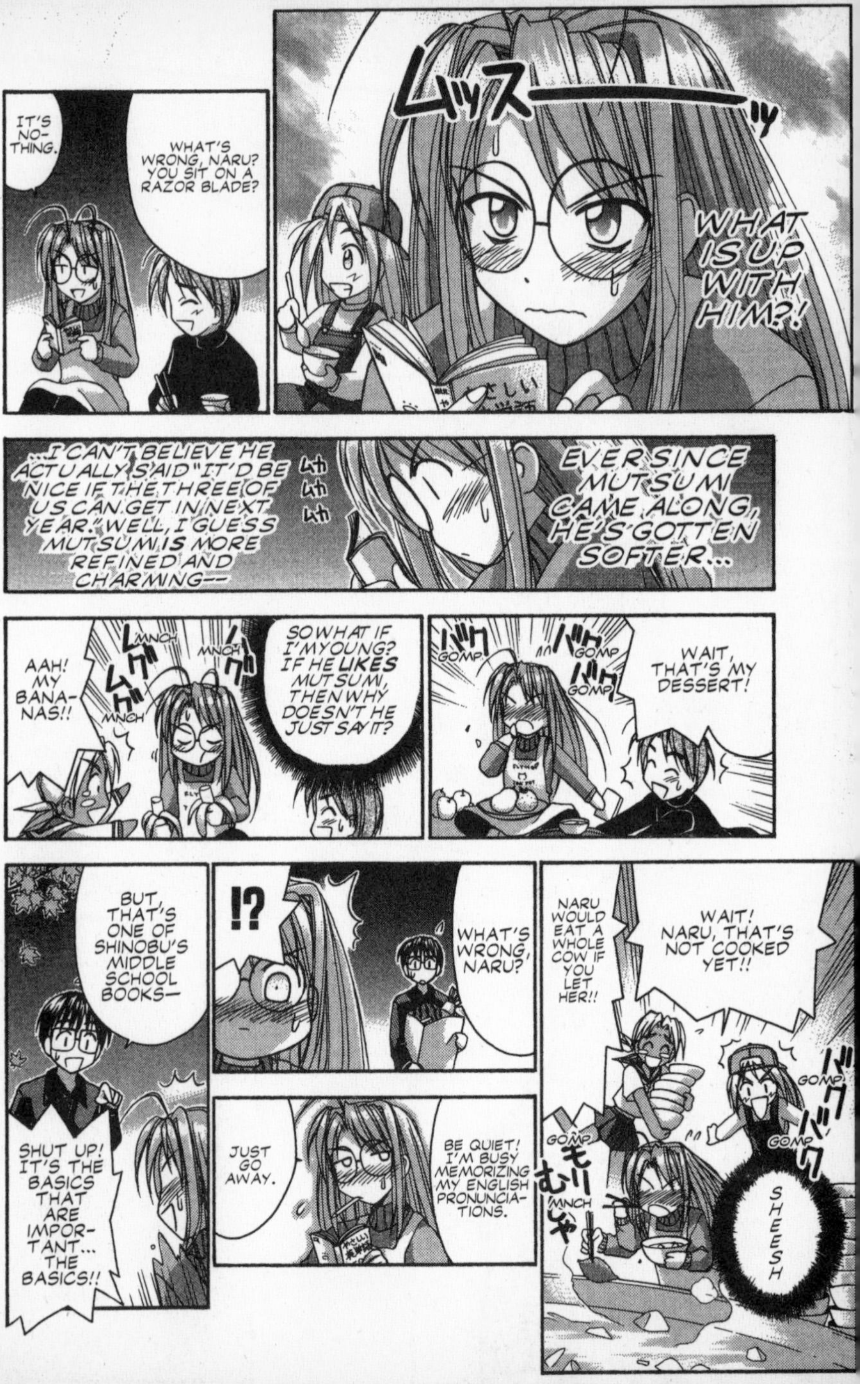
ムッスーーーッ
WHAT IS UP WITH HIM?!
WHAT'S WRONG, NARU? YOU SIT ON A RAZOR BLADE?
IT'S NO-THING.
EVER SINCE MUTSUMI CAME ALONG, HE'S GOTTEN SOFTER...
ムカ ムカ ムカ
...I CAN'T BELIEVE HE ACTUALLY SAID "IT'D BE NICE IF THE THREE OF US CAN GET IN NEXT YEAR." WELL, I GUESS MUTSUMI IS MORE REFINED AND CHARMING--
WAIT, THAT'S MY DESSERT!
バク GOMP
バク GOMP
バク GOMP
SO WHAT IF I'M YOUNG? IF HE LIKES MUTSUMI, THEN WHY DOESN'T HE JUST SAY IT?
ムグ MNCH
ムグ MNCH
ムグ MNCH
AAH! MY BANA-NAS!!
WAIT! NARU, THAT'S NOT COOKED YET!!
NARU WOULD EAT A WHOLE COW IF YOU LET HER!!
バクバク GOMP GOMP
SHEESH
もり GOMP
むしゃ MNCH
WHAT'S WRONG, NARU?
!?
BE QUIET! I'M BUSY MEMORIZING MY ENGLISH PRONUNCIA-TIONS.
JUST GO AWAY.
BUT, THAT'S ONE OF SHINOBU'S MIDDLE SCHOOL BOOKS—
SHUT UP! IT'S THE BASICS THAT ARE IMPOR-TANT... THE BASICS!!

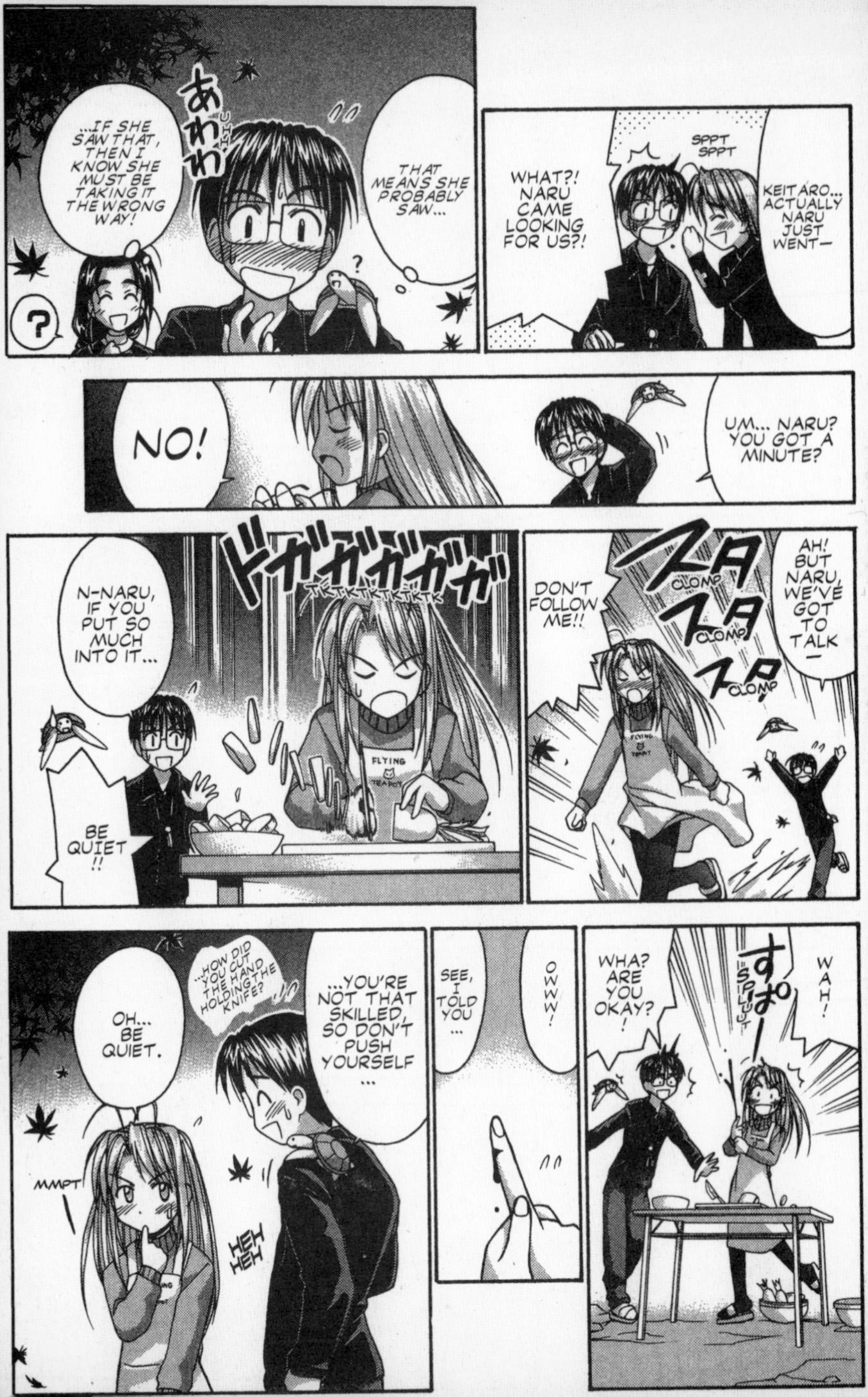
KEITARO... ACTUALLY NARU JUST WENT—
SPPT SPPT
WHAT?! NARU CAME LOOKING FOR US?!
THAT MEANS SHE PROBABLY SAW...
あわわ
UHH
...IF SHE SAW THAT, THEN I KNOW SHE MUST BE TAKING IT THE WRONG WAY!
?
?
UM... NARU? YOU GOT A MINUTE?
NO!
AH! BUT NARU, WE'VE GOT TO TALK—
スタ CLOMP
スタ CLOMP
スタ CLOMP
DON'T FOLLOW ME!!
ドガガガガガ
TKTKTKTKTKTKTK
N-NARU, IF YOU PUT SO MUCH INTO IT...
BE QUIET!!
WAH!
すぱ
SPLUUT
WHA? ARE YOU OKAY?!
OWWW!
SEE, I TOLD YOU...
...YOU'RE NOT THAT SKILLED, SO DON'T PUSH YOURSELF...
...HOW DID YOU CUT THE HAND HOLDING THE KNIFE?
OH... BE QUIET.
MMPT
HEH HEH

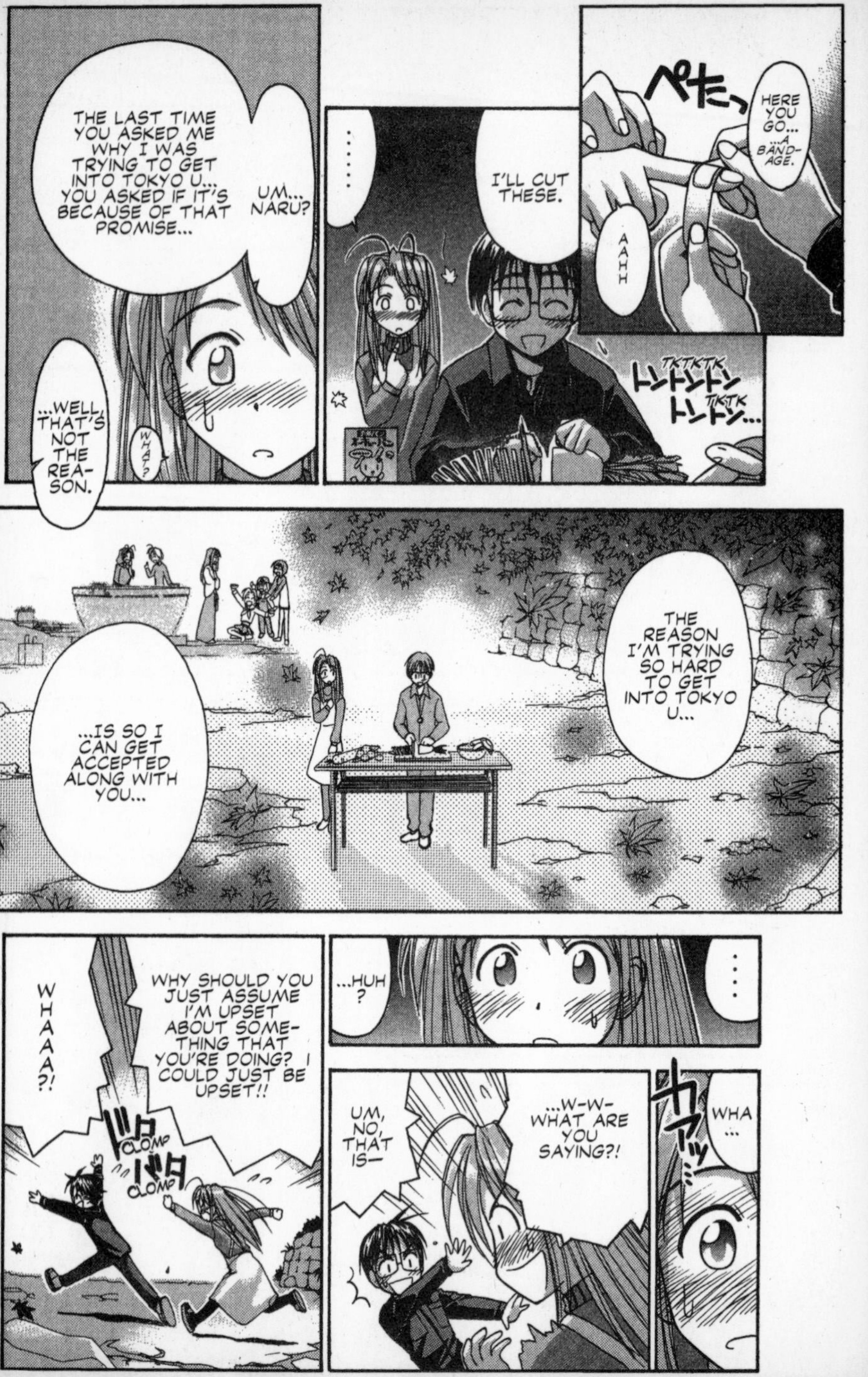

ペたっ
HERE YOU GO... ...A BAND-AGE.
AAHH
I'LL CUT THESE.
......
TKTKTK トントントン
TKTK トントン...
UM... NARU?
THE LAST TIME YOU ASKED ME WHY I WAS TRYING TO GET INTO TOKYO U... YOU ASKED IF IT'S BECAUSE OF THAT PROMISE...
WHAT?
...WELL, THAT'S NOT THE REA-SON.
THE REASON I'M TRYING SO HARD TO GET INTO TOKYO U...
...IS SO I CAN GET ACCEPTED ALONG WITH YOU...
....
...HUH?
WHA...
カアッ
...W-W-WHAT ARE YOU SAYING?!
UM, NO, THAT IS—
WHY SHOULD YOU JUST ASSUME I'M UPSET ABOUT SOME-THING THAT YOU'RE DOING? I COULD JUST BE UPSET!!
WHAAAA?!
ドタ CLOMP
バタ CLOMP

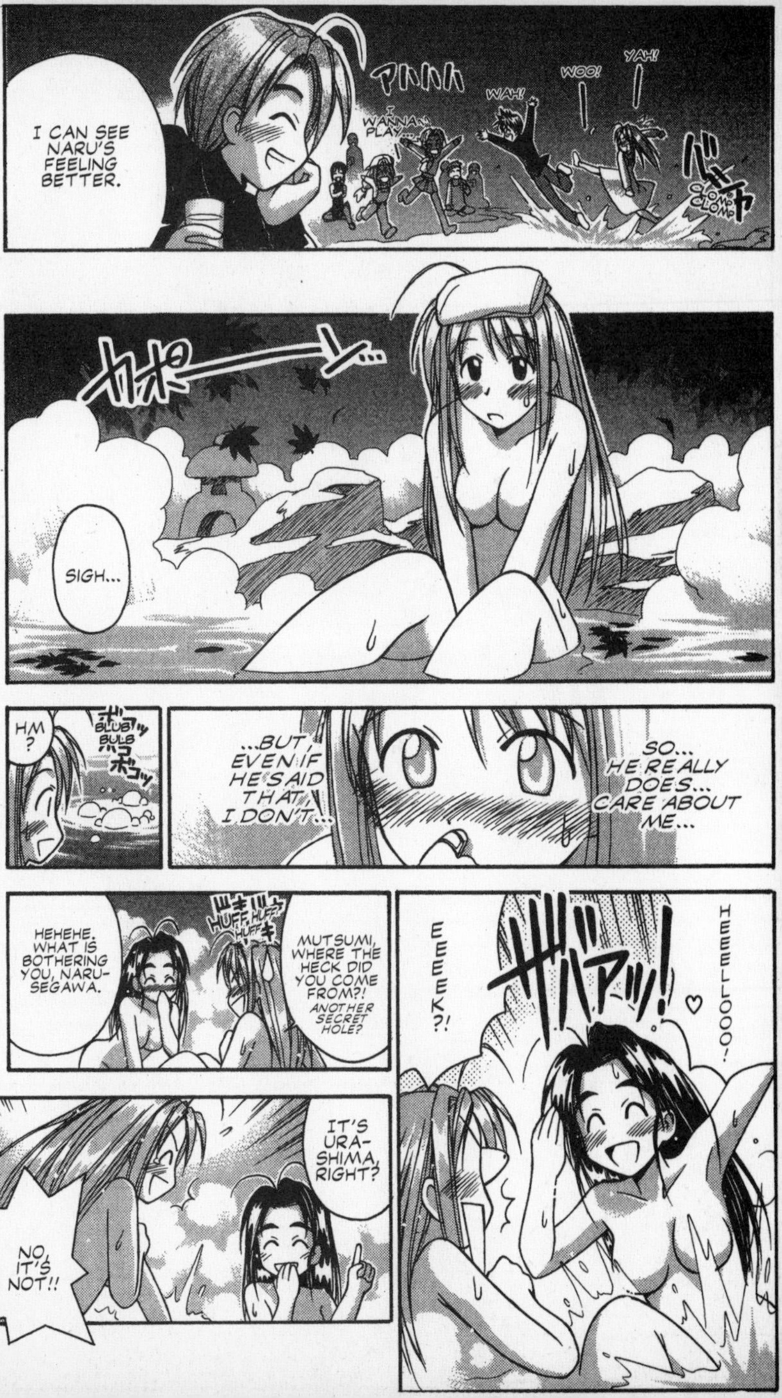

I CAN SEE NARU'S FEELING BETTER.
アハハハ
I WANNA PLAY...
WAH!
WOO!
YAH!
CLOMP CLOMP
カポーン...
SIGH...
SO... HE REALLY DOES... CARE ABOUT ME...
...BUT, EVEN IF HE SAID THAT, I DON'T...
BLUB BLUB
HM?
HEEELLOOO! ♥
ザバァッ!
EEEEK?!
MUTSUMI, WHERE THE HECK DID YOU COME FROM?! ANOTHER SECRET HOLE?
HUFF HUFF HUFF
HEHEHE. WHAT IS BOTHERING YOU, NARU-SEGAWA.
IT'S URA-SHIMA, RIGHT?
NO, IT'S NOT!!

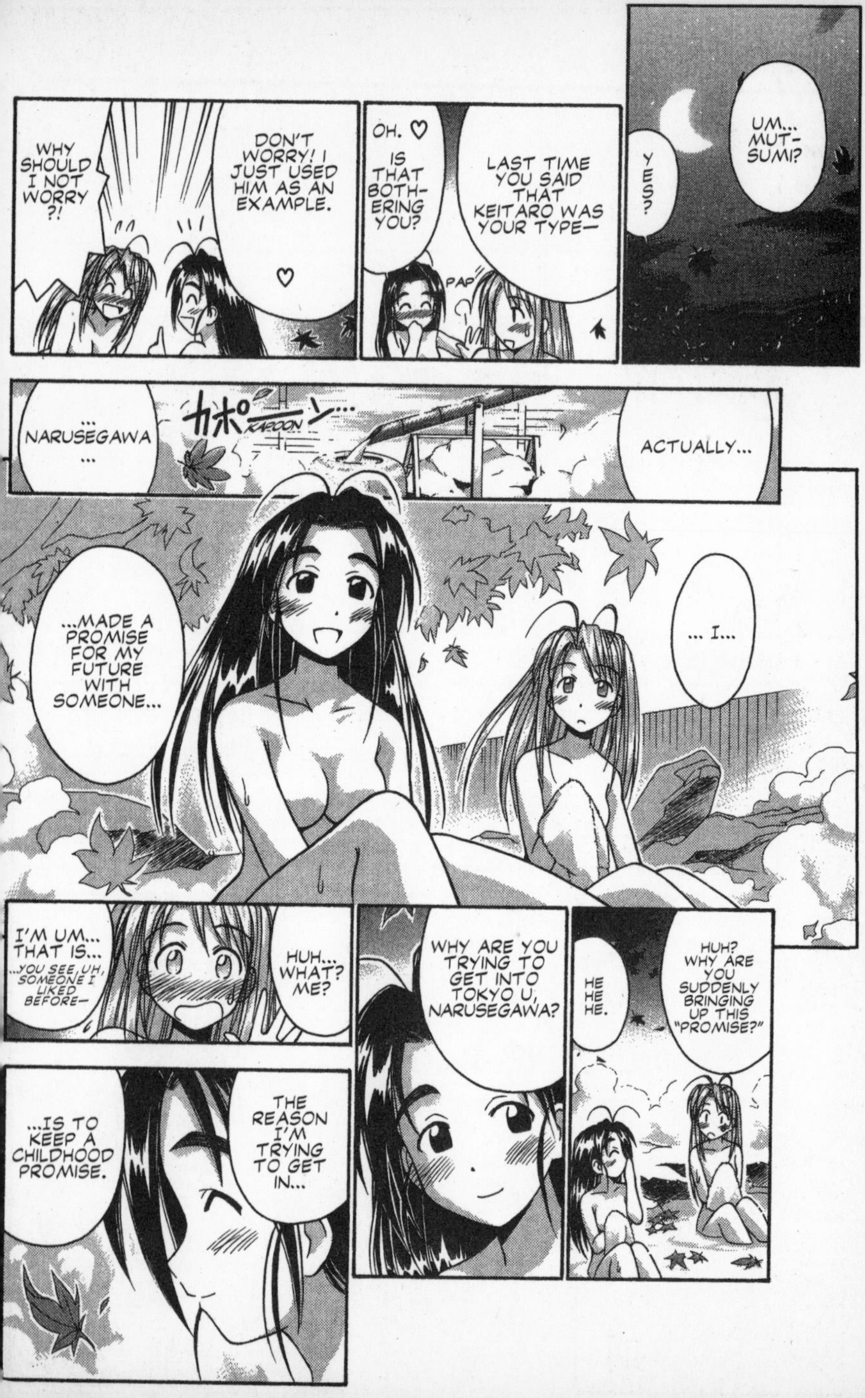
UM... MUT-SUMI?
YES?
LAST TIME YOU SAID THAT KEITARO WAS YOUR TYPE—
OH. ♡ IS THAT BOTHERING YOU?
PAP
DON'T WORRY! I JUST USED HIM AS AN EXAMPLE. ♡
WHY SHOULD I NOT WORRY?!
ACTUALLY...
カポーン... KAPOON
... NARUSEGAWA ...
... I...
...MADE A PROMISE FOR MY FUTURE WITH SOMEONE...
HUH? WHY ARE YOU SUDDENLY BRINGING UP THIS "PROMISE?"
HE HE HE.
WHY ARE YOU TRYING TO GET INTO TOKYO U, NARUSEGAWA?
HUH... WHAT? ME?
I'M UM... THAT IS... ...YOU SEE, UH, SOMEONE I LIKED BEFORE—
THE REASON I'M TRYING TO GET IN...
...IS TO KEEP A CHILDHOOD PROMISE.

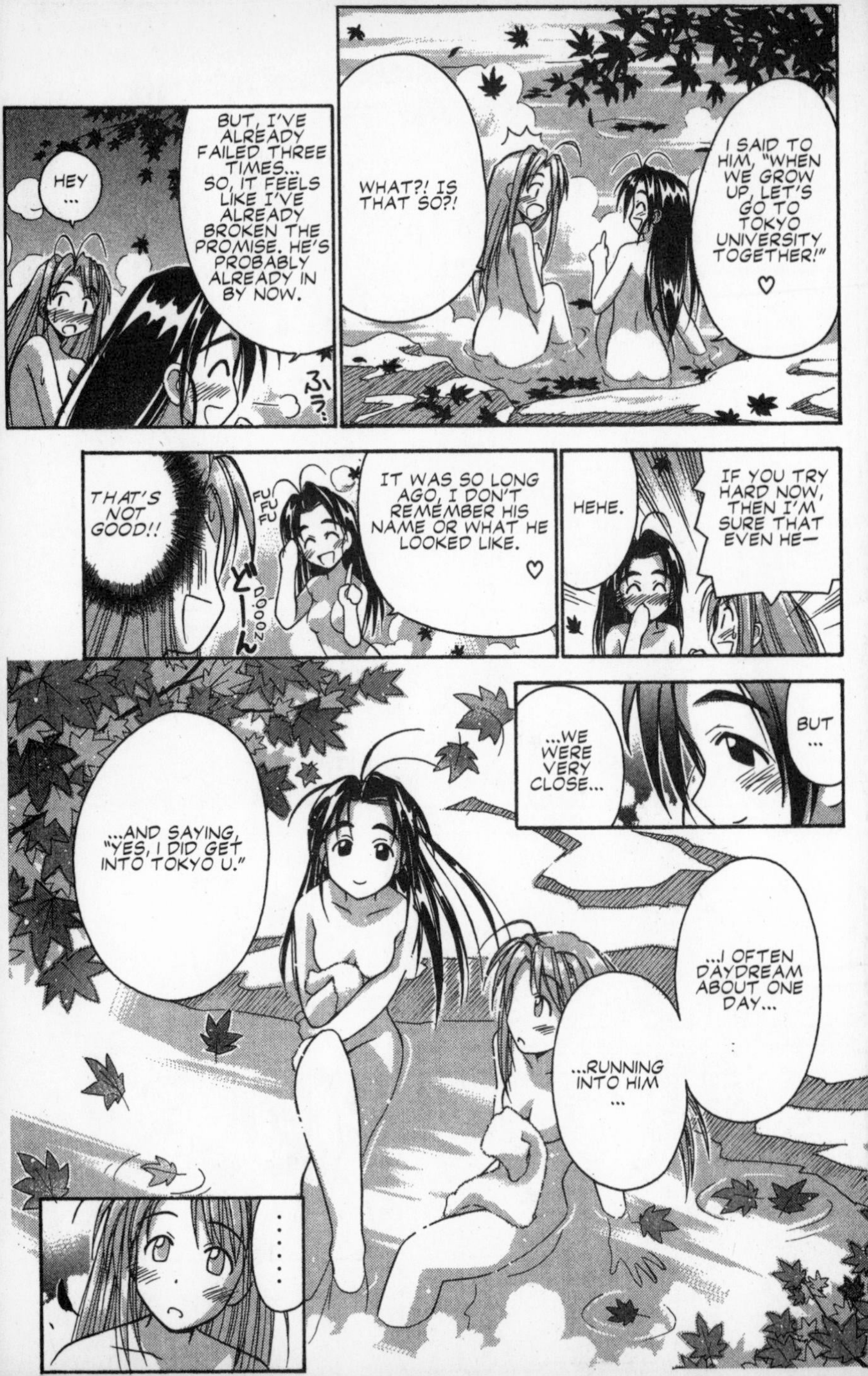

I SAID TO HIM, "WHEN WE GROW UP, LET'S GO TO TOKYO UNIVERSITY TOGETHER!" ♡
WHAT?! IS THAT SO?!
BUT, I'VE ALREADY FAILED THREE TIMES... SO, IT FEELS LIKE I'VE ALREADY BROKEN THE PROMISE. HE'S PROBABLY ALREADY IN BY NOW.
HEY ...
IF YOU TRY HARD NOW, THEN I'M SURE THAT EVEN HE—
HEHE.
IT WAS SO LONG AGO, I DON'T REMEMBER HIS NAME OR WHAT HE LOOKED LIKE. ♡
FU FU FU
THAT'S NOT GOOD!!
どーん
D-O-O-O-N
BUT ...
...WE WERE VERY CLOSE...
...I OFTEN DAYDREAM ABOUT ONE DAY...
...RUNNING INTO HIM ...
...AND SAYING, "YES, I DID GET INTO TOKYO U."
......

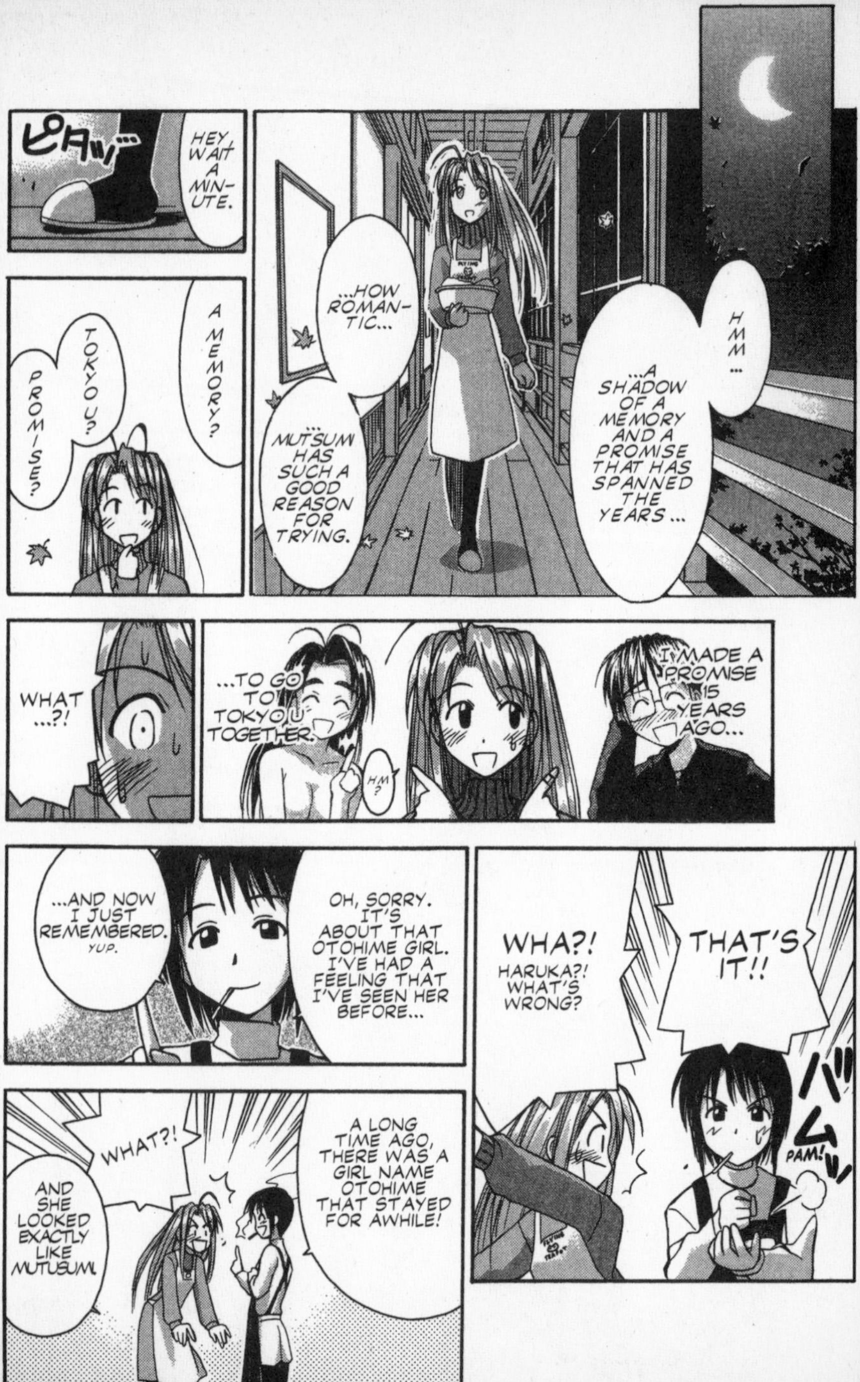
HMM...
...A SHADOW OF A MEMORY AND A PROMISE THAT HAS SPANNED THE YEARS...
...HOW ROMANTIC...
...MUTSUMI HAS SUCH A GOOD REASON FOR TRYING.
ピタッ
HEY, WAIT A MINUTE.
A MEMORY?
TOKYO U? PROMISE?
I MADE A PROMISE 15 YEARS AGO...
...TO GO TO TOKYO U TOGETHER.
HM?
WHAT ...?!
THAT'S IT!!
WHA?! HARUKA?! WHAT'S WRONG?
バム
PAM!
OH, SORRY. IT'S ABOUT THAT OTOHIME GIRL. I'VE HAD A FEELING THAT I'VE SEEN HER BEFORE...
...AND NOW I JUST REMEMBERED.
YUP.
A LONG TIME AGO, THERE WAS A GIRL NAME OTOHIME THAT STAYED FOR AWHILE!
WHAT?!
AND SHE LOOKED EXACTLY LIKE MUTUSUMI.

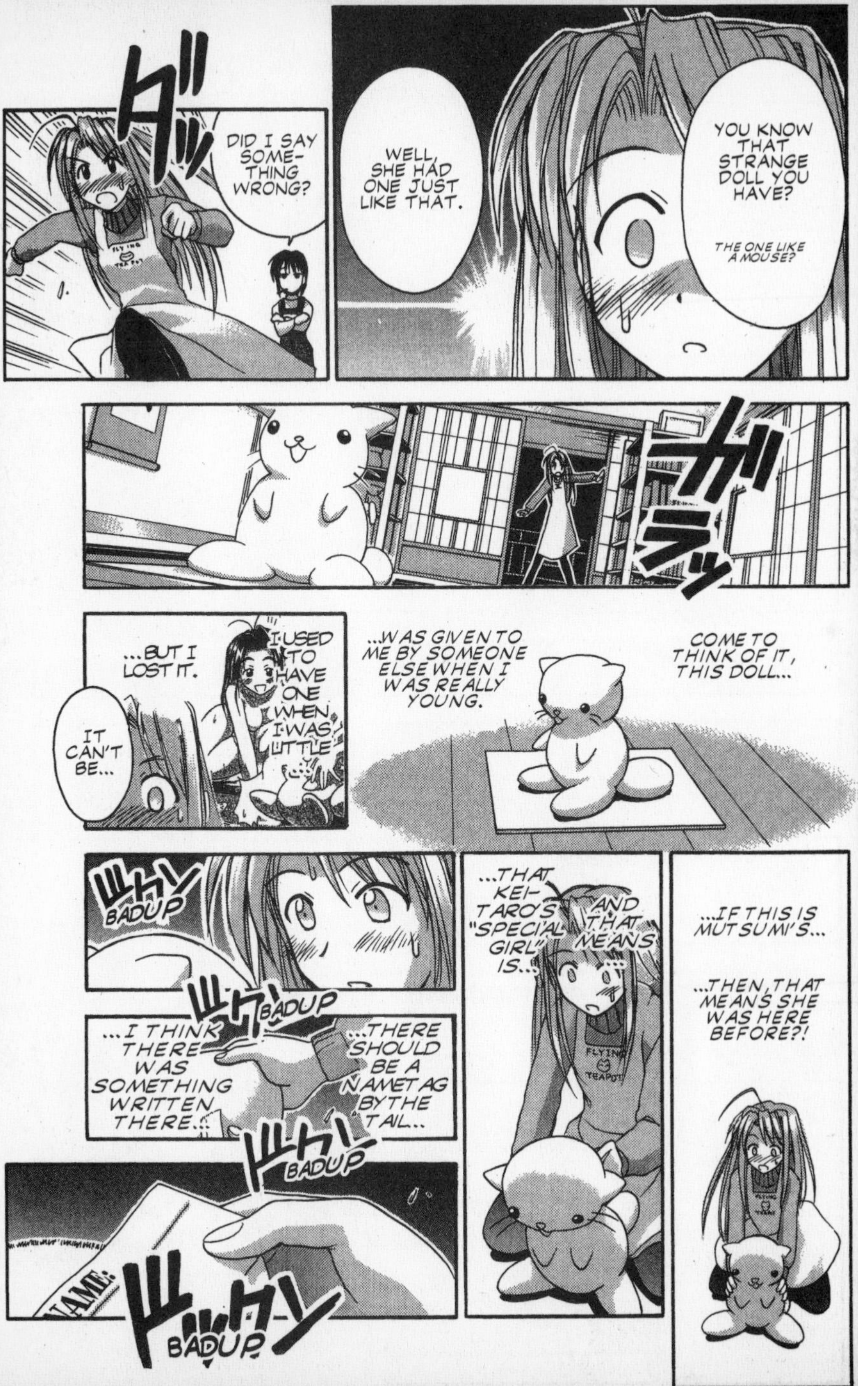
YOU KNOW THAT STRANGE DOLL YOU HAVE?
THE ONE LIKE A MOUSE?
WELL, SHE HAD ONE JUST LIKE THAT.
DID I SAY SOME-THING WRONG?
COME TO THINK OF IT, THIS DOLL...
...WAS GIVEN TO ME BY SOMEONE ELSE WHEN I WAS REALLY YOUNG.
I USED TO HAVE ONE WHEN I WAS LITTLE
...BUT I LOST IT.
IT CAN'T BE...
...IF THIS IS MUTSUMI'S...
...THEN, THAT MEANS SHE WAS HERE BEFORE?!
AND THAT MEANS
...THAT KEI-TARO'S "SPECIAL GIRL" IS...
BADUP
BADUP
...THERE SHOULD BE A NAMETAG BY THE TAIL...
...I THINK THERE WAS SOMETHING WRITTEN THERE...
BADUP
NAME:
BADUP

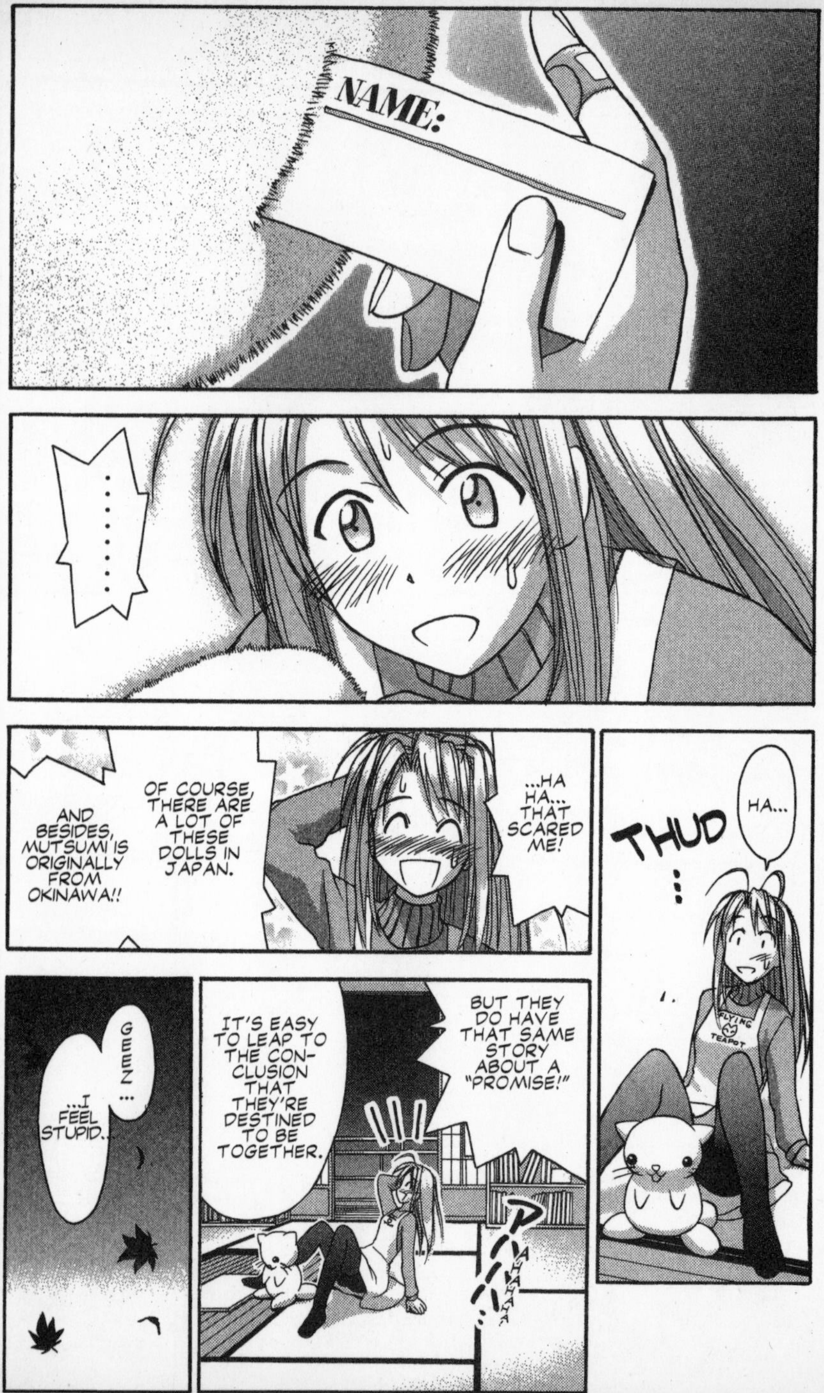
NAME:
......
HA...
THUD
...
...HA HA... THAT SCARED ME!
OF COURSE, THERE ARE A LOT OF THESE DOLLS IN JAPAN.
AND BESIDES, MUTSUMI IS ORIGINALLY FROM OKINAWA!!
BUT THEY DO HAVE THAT SAME STORY ABOUT A "PROMISE!"
IT'S EASY TO LEAP TO THE CONCLUSION THAT THEY'RE DESTINED TO BE TOGETHER.
GEEZ...
...I FEEL STUPID..

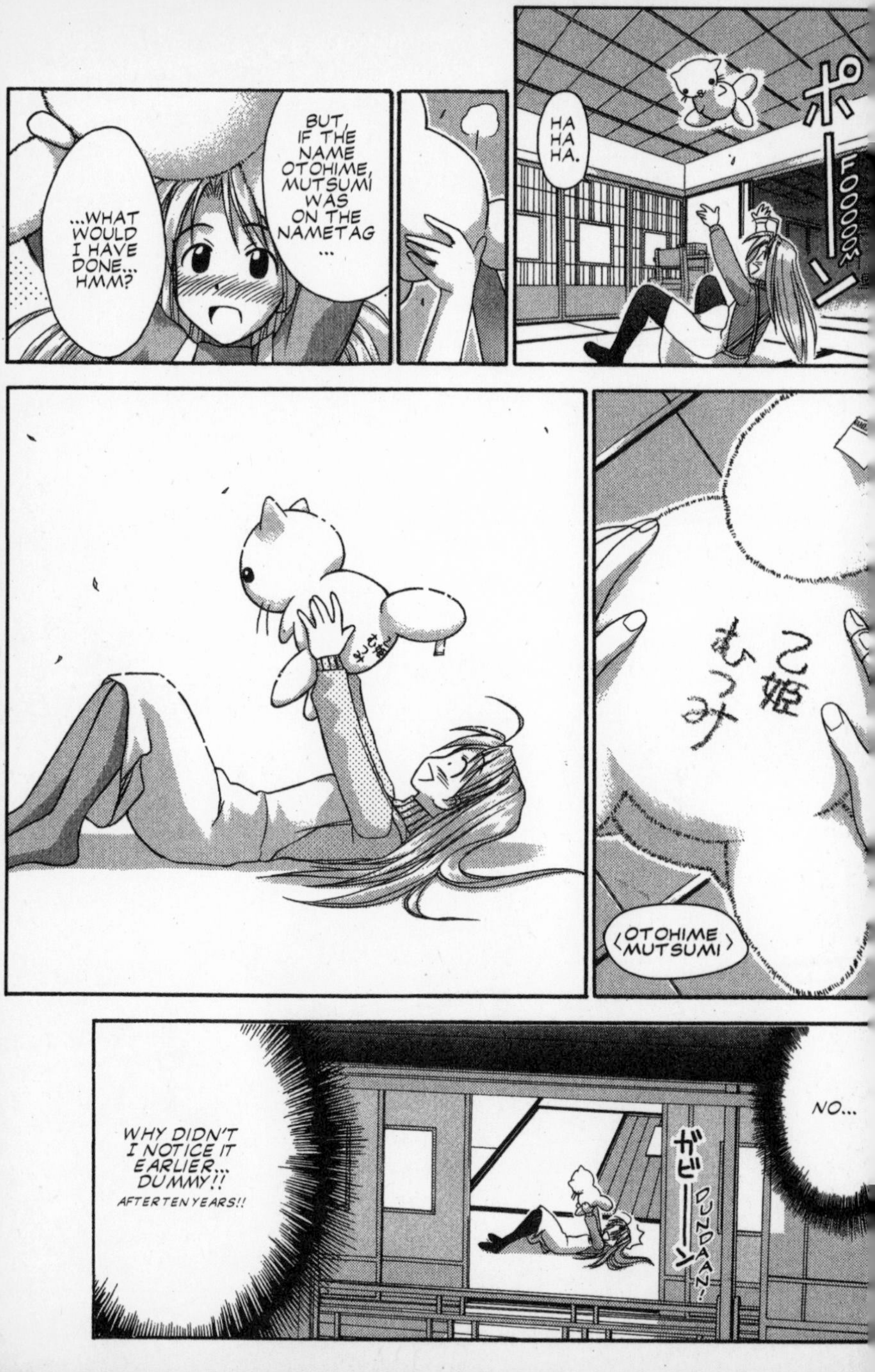
ポーン
FOOOOON
HA HA HA HA.
BUT, IF THE NAME OTOHIME, MUTSUMI WAS ON THE NAMETAG ...
...WHAT WOULD I HAVE DONE... HMM?
乙姫むつみ
OTOHIME MUTSUMI
NO...
ガビーン
DUNDAAN!
WHY DIDN'T I NOTICE IT EARLIER... DUMMY!!
AFTER TEN YEARS!!

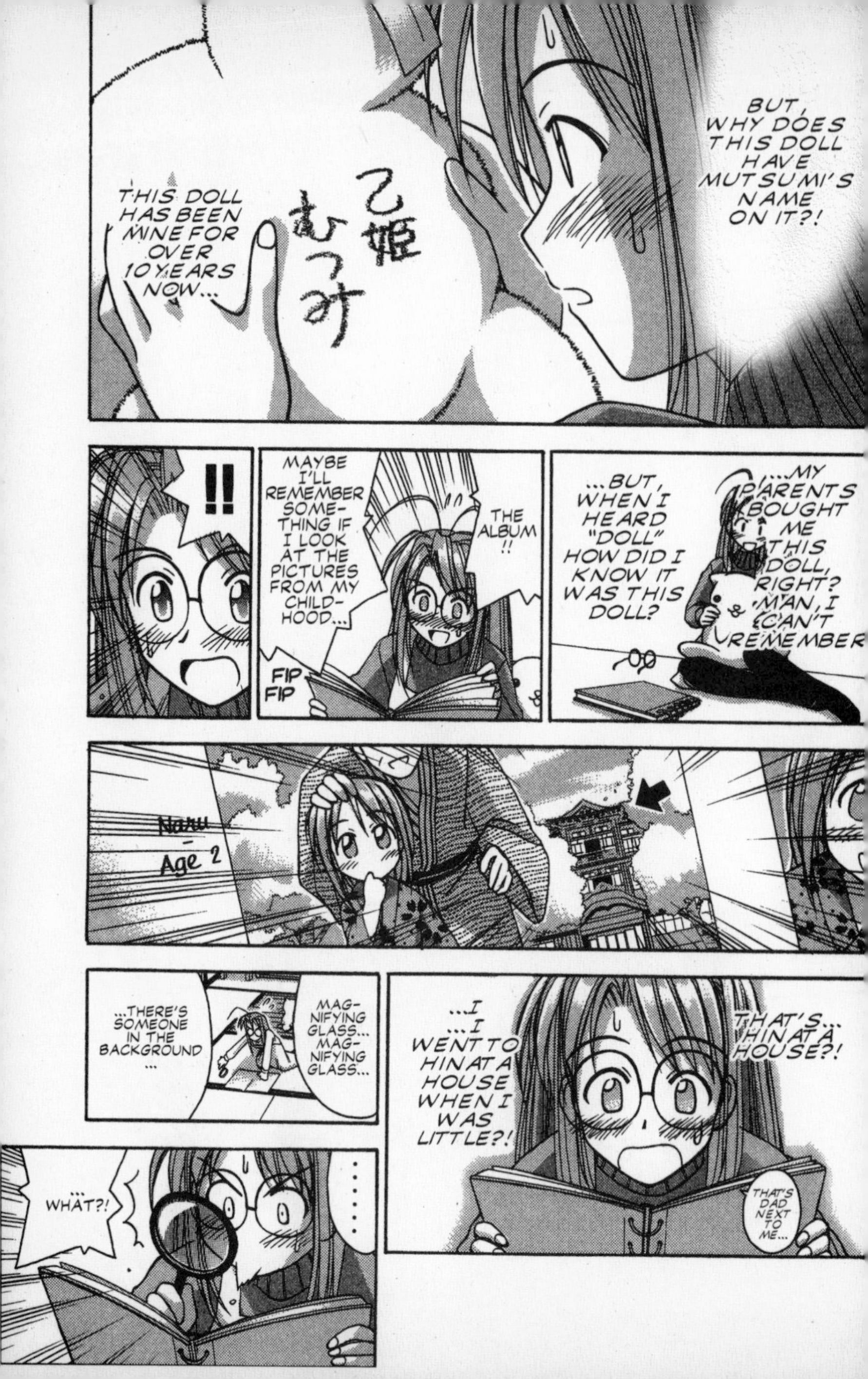
BUT, WHY DOES THIS DOLL HAVE MUTSUMI'S NAME ON IT?!
乙姫 むつみ
THIS DOLL HAS BEEN MINE FOR OVER 10 YEARS NOW...
...MY PARENTS BOUGHT ME THIS DOLL, RIGHT? MAN, I CAN'T REMEMBER
...BUT, WHEN I HEARD "DOLL" HOW DID I KNOW IT WAS THIS DOLL?
THE ALBUM!!
MAYBE I'LL REMEMBER SOME-THING IF I LOOK AT THE PICTURES FROM MY CHILD-HOOD...
FIP FIP
!!
Naru - Age 2
THAT'S... HINATA HOUSE?!
...I ...I WENT TO HINATA HOUSE WHEN I WAS LITTLE?!
THAT'S DAD NEXT TO ME...
MAG-NIFYING GLASS... MAG-NIFYING GLASS...
...THERE'S SOMEONE IN THE BACKGROUND ...
......
...WHAT?!

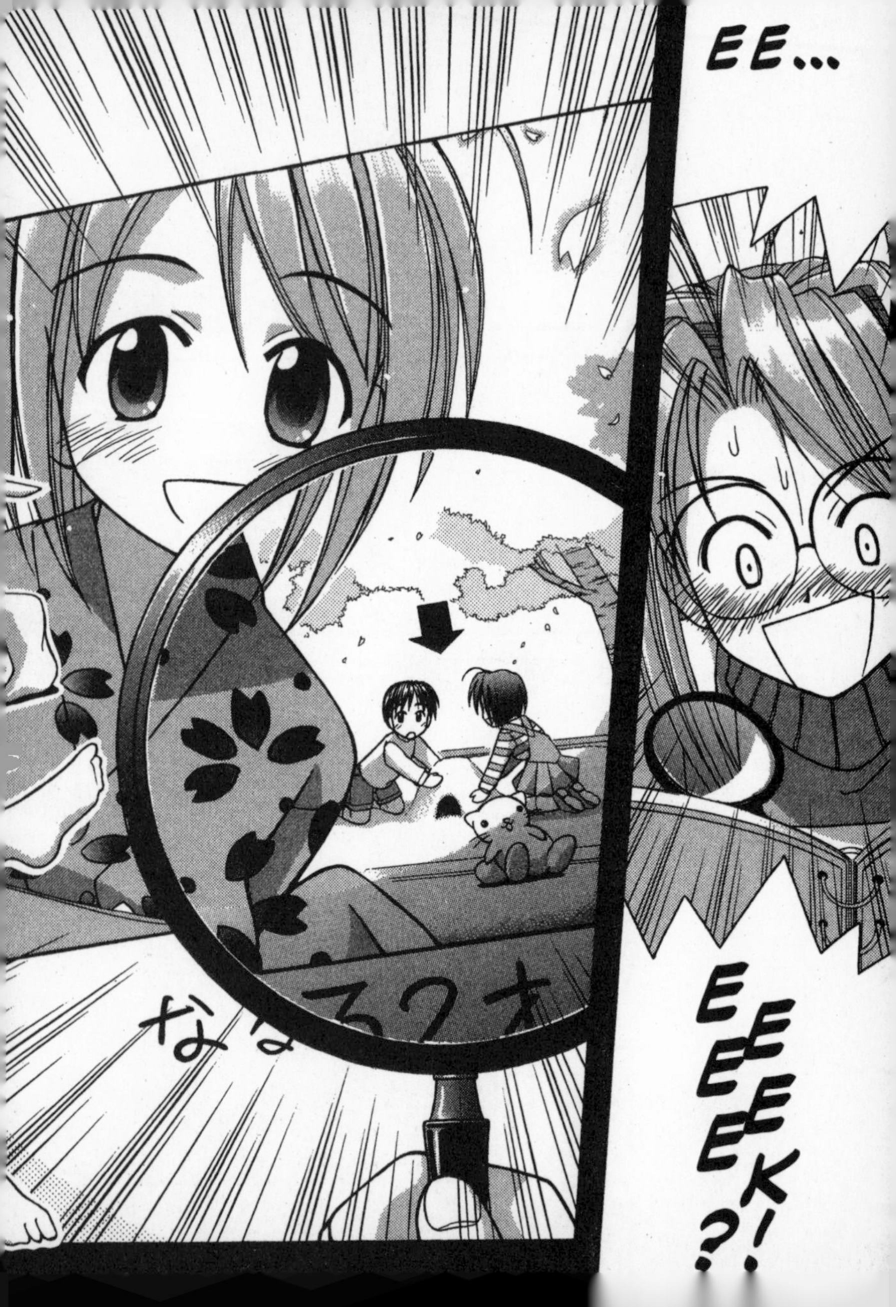
EE...
EEEEEEK?!

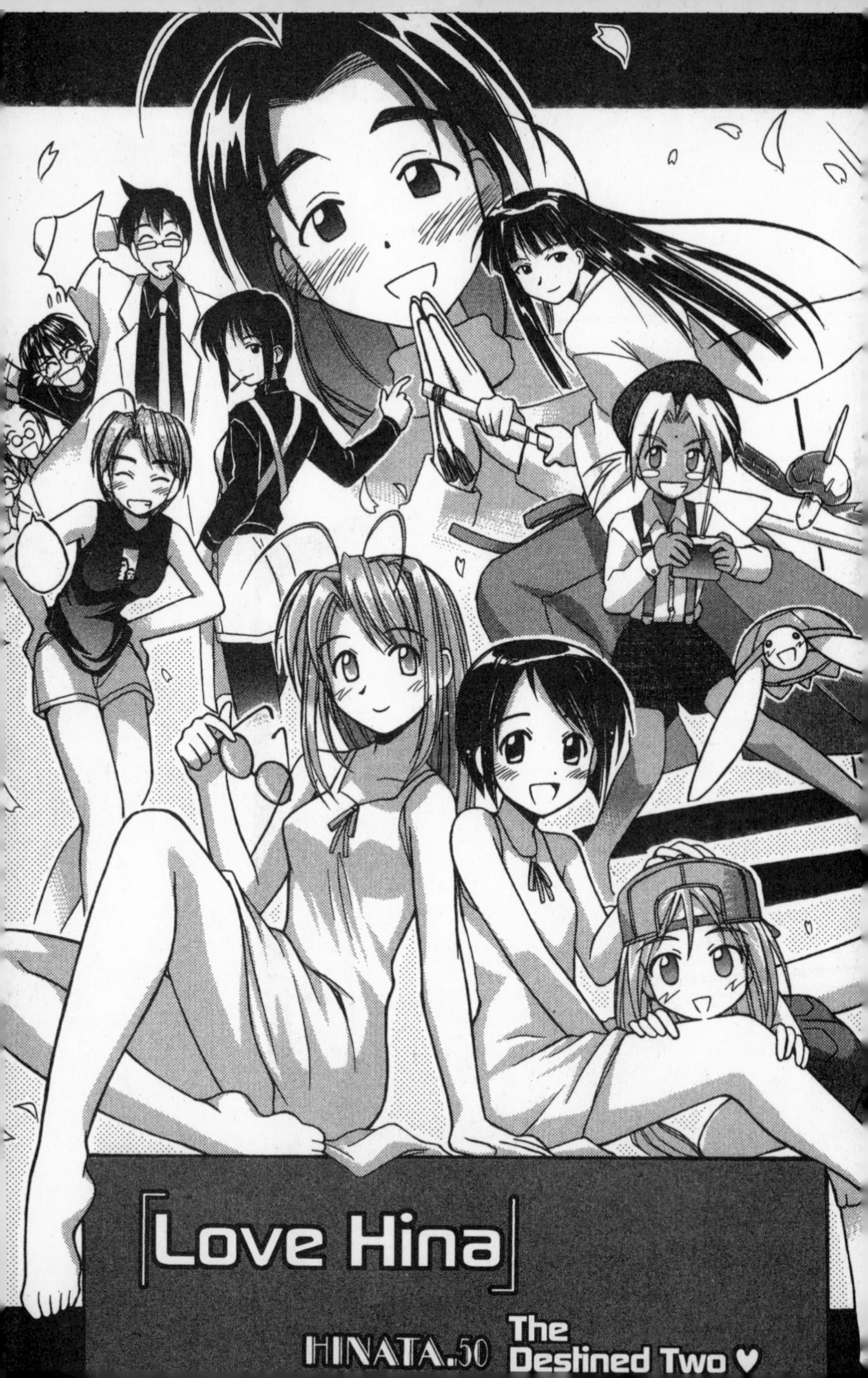
Love Hina
HINATA.50
The Destined Two ♥

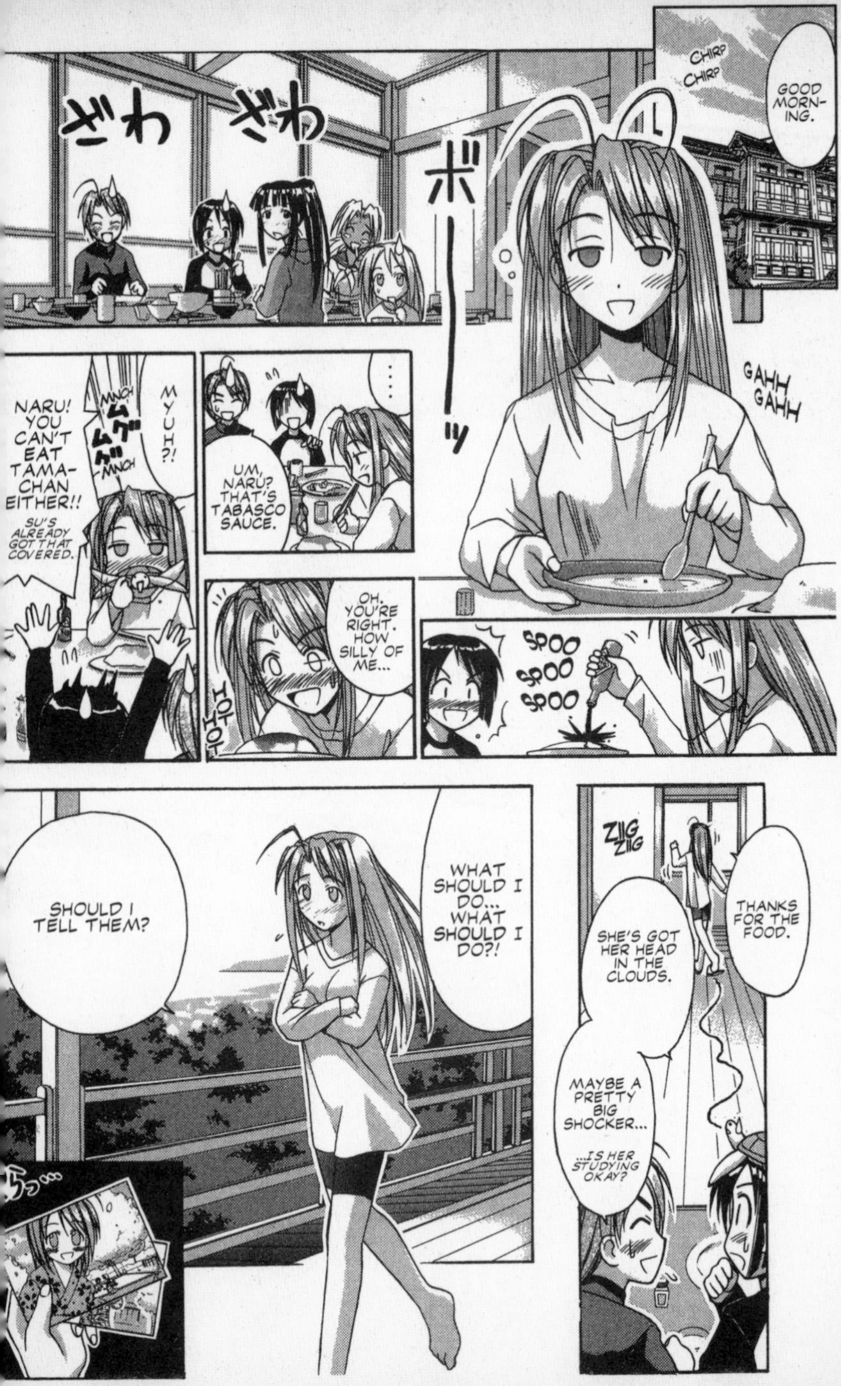
CHIRP
CHIRP
GOOD MORNING.
ボーーッ
GAHH GAHH
ざわ ざわ
. . . .
UM, NARU? THAT'S TABASCO SAUCE.
SPOO SPOO SPOO
OH. YOU'RE RIGHT. HOW SILLY OF ME...
HOT HOT
MYUH?!
MNCH ムグムグ MNCH
NARU! YOU CAN'T EAT TAMA-CHAN EITHER!!
SU'S ALREADY GOT THAT COVERED.
ZIIG ZIIG
THANKS FOR THE FOOD.
SHE'S GOT HER HEAD IN THE CLOUDS.
MAYBE A PRETTY BIG SHOCKER...
...IS HER STUDYING OKAY?
WHAT SHOULD I DO... WHAT SHOULD I DO?!
SHOULD I TELL THEM?

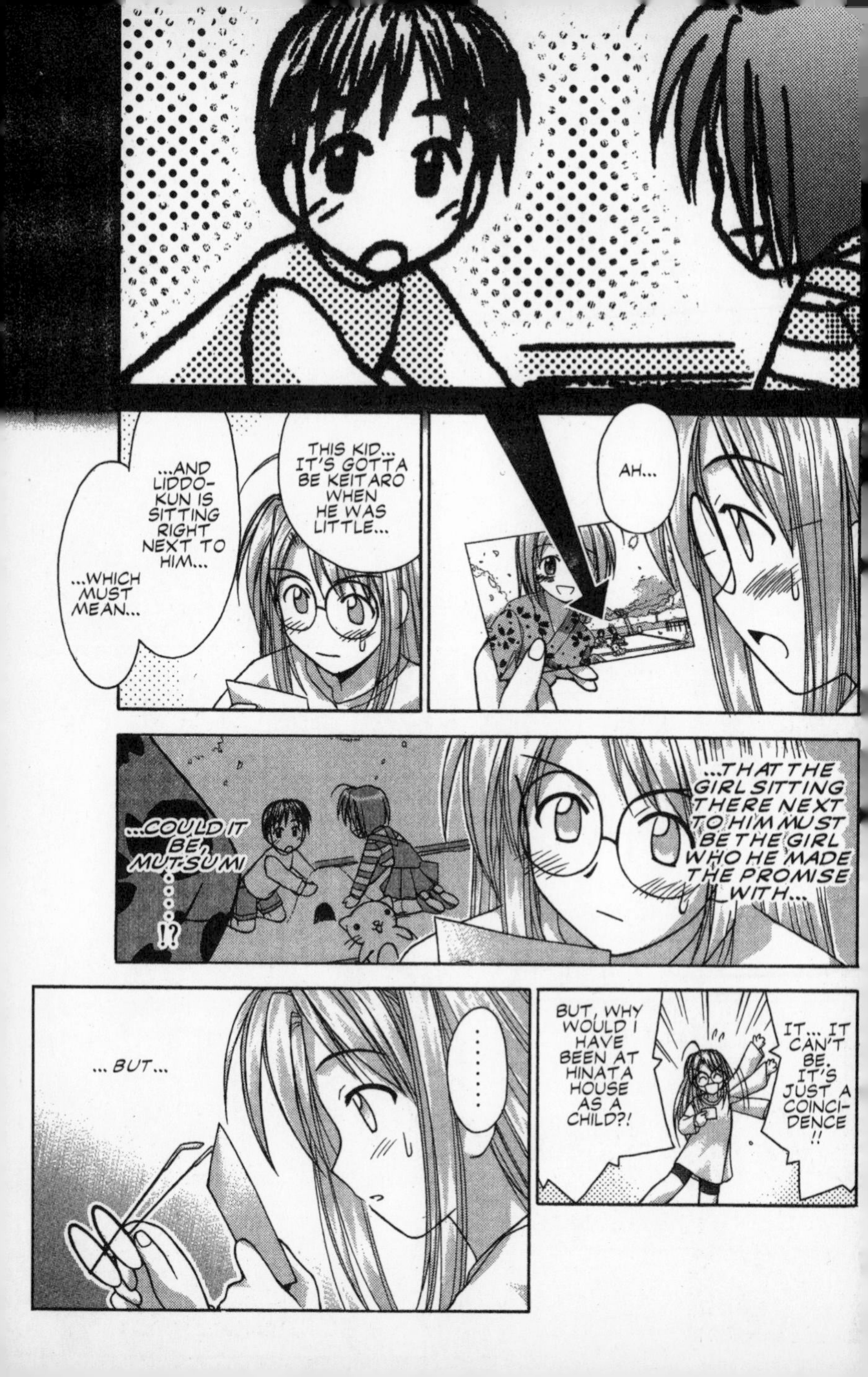
AH...
THIS KID... IT'S GOTTA BE KEITARO WHEN HE WAS LITTLE...
...AND LIDDO-KUN IS SITTING RIGHT NEXT TO HIM...
...WHICH MUST MEAN...
...THAT THE GIRL SITTING THERE NEXT TO HIM MUST BE THE GIRL WHO HE MADE THE PROMISE WITH...
...COULD IT BE, MUTSUMI......!?
IT... IT CAN'T BE. IT'S JUST A COINCIDENCE!!
BUT, WHY WOULD I HAVE BEEN AT HINATA HOUSE AS A CHILD?!
......
... BUT...

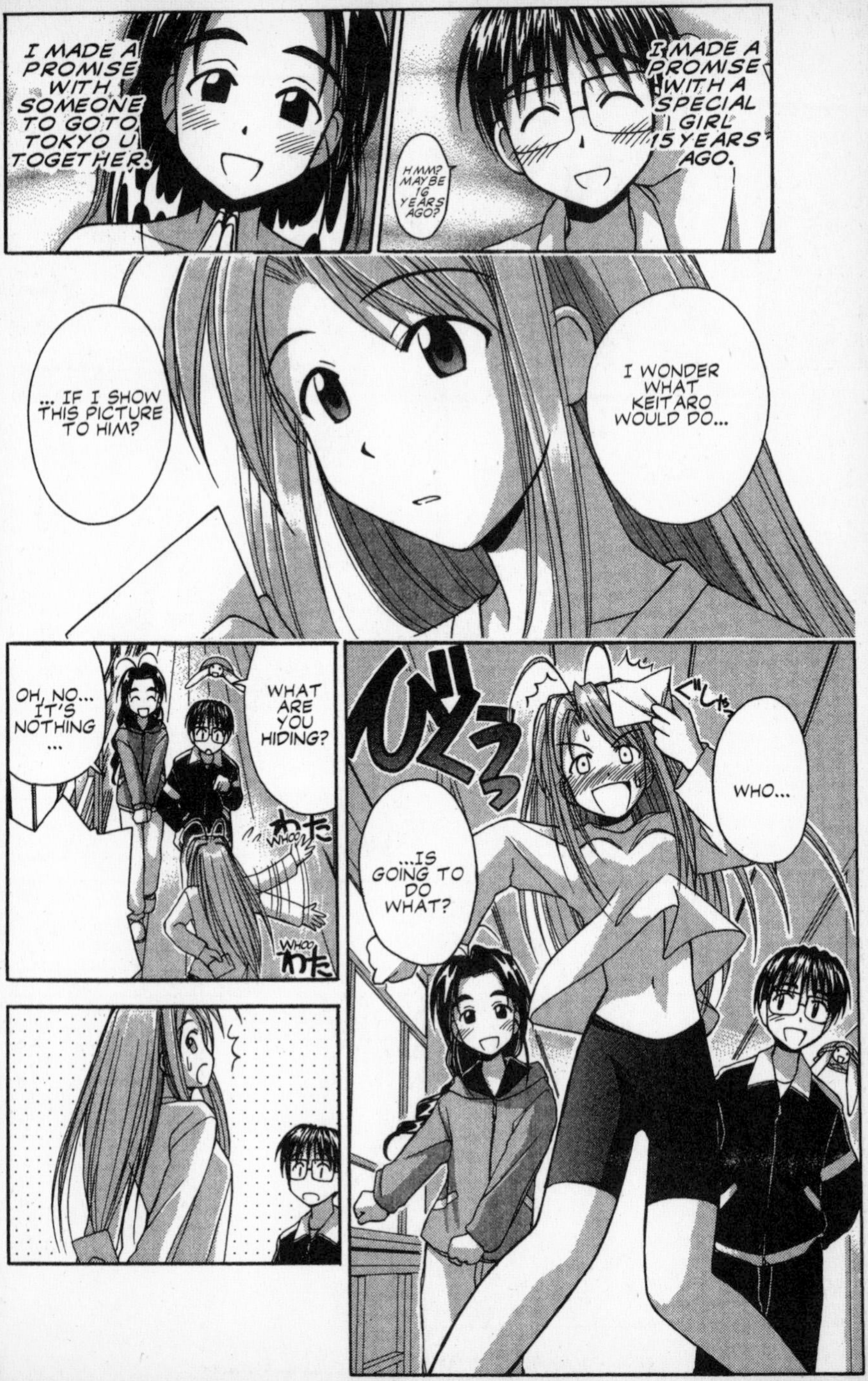
I MADE A PROMISE WITH A SPECIAL GIRL 15 YEARS AGO.
HMM? MAYBE 16 YEARS AGO?
I MADE A PROMISE WITH SOMEONE TO GO TO TOKYO U TOGETHER.
I WONDER WHAT KEITARO WOULD DO...
... IF I SHOW THIS PICTURE TO HIM?
WHO...
...IS GOING TO DO WHAT?
WHAT ARE YOU HIDING?
OH, NO... IT'S NOTHING ...
WHOO わた
WHOO わた

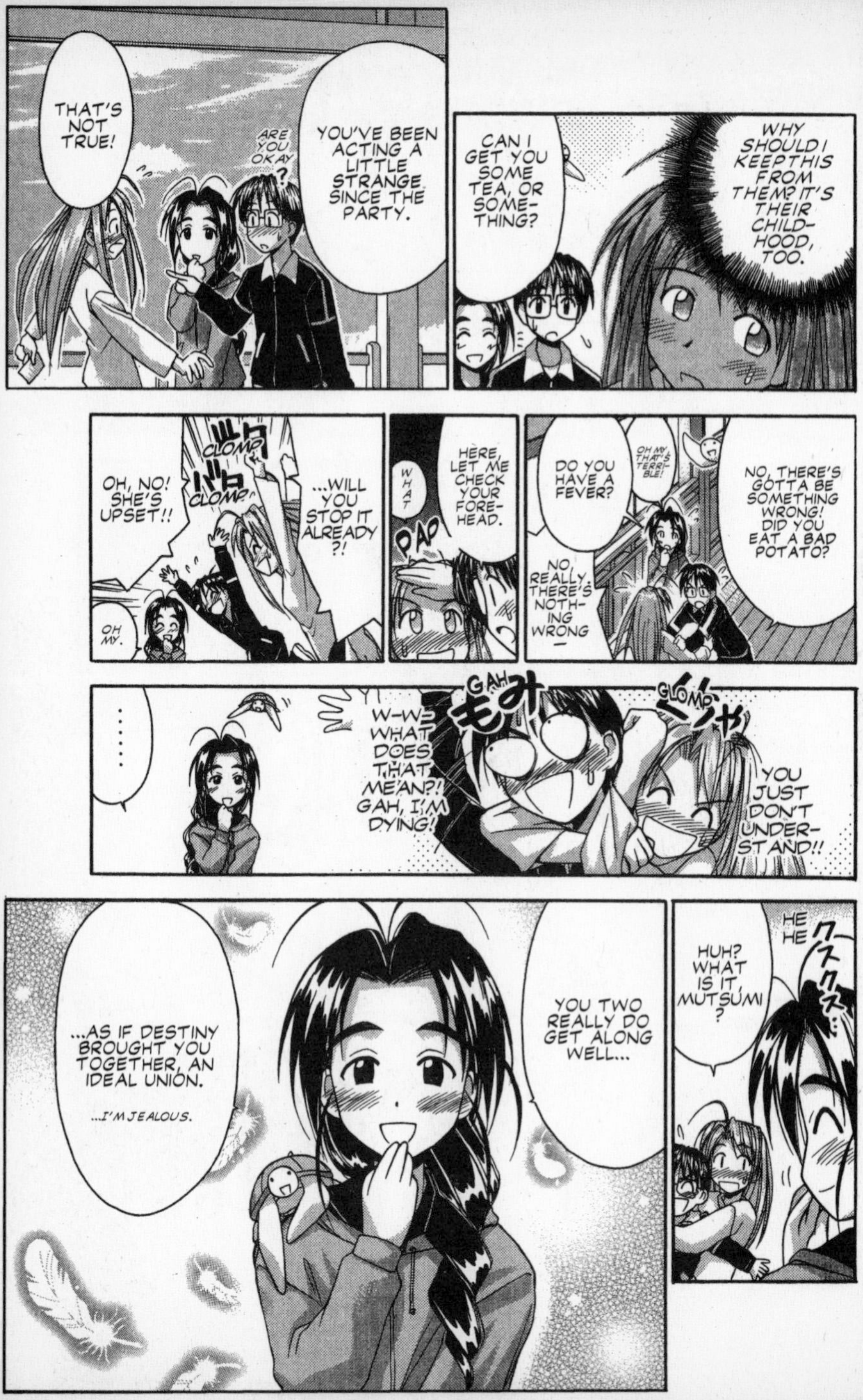
WHY SHOULD I KEEP THIS FROM THEM? IT'S THEIR CHILDHOOD, TOO.
CAN I GET YOU SOME TEA, OR SOMETHING?
YOU'VE BEEN ACTING A LITTLE STRANGE SINCE THE PARTY.
ARE YOU OKAY?
THAT'S NOT TRUE!
NO, THERE'S GOTTA BE SOMETHING WRONG! DID YOU EAT A BAD POTATO?
OH MY, THAT'S TERRIBLE!
DO YOU HAVE A FEVER?
NO, REALLY. THERE'S NOTHING WRONG—
HERE, LET ME CHECK YOUR FOREHEAD.
WHAT
PAP
...WILL YOU STOP IT ALREADY?!
CLOMP
CLOMP
OH, NO! SHE'S UPSET!!
OH MY.
YOU JUST DON'T UNDERSTAND!!
GLOMP
GAH
W-W-WHAT DOES THAT MEAN?! GAH, I'M DYING!
......
HE HE
HUH? WHAT IS IT, MUTSUMI?
YOU TWO REALLY DO GET ALONG WELL...
...AS IF DESTINY BROUGHT YOU TOGETHER, AN IDEAL UNION.
...I'M JEALOUS.

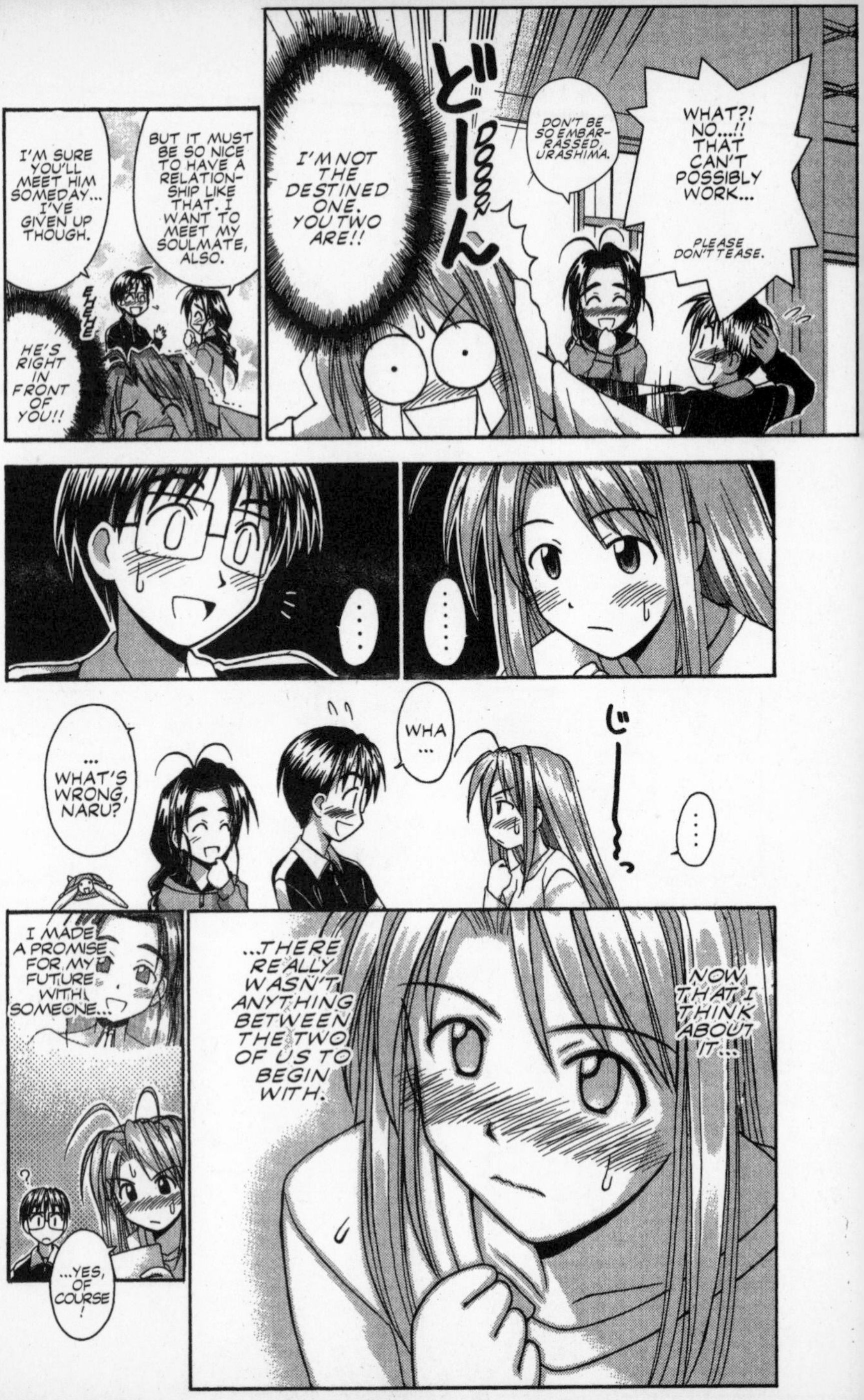
WHAT?! NO...!! THAT CAN'T POSSIBLY WORK...
PLEASE DON'T TEASE.
DON'T BE SO EMBARRASSED, URASHIMA.
どーん
DOOOON
I'M NOT THE DESTINED ONE. YOU TWO ARE!!
BUT IT MUST BE SO NICE TO HAVE A RELATIONSHIP LIKE THAT. I WANT TO MEET MY SOULMATE, ALSO.
I'M SURE YOU'LL MEET HIM SOMEDAY... I'VE GIVEN UP THOUGH.
EHEHE
HE'S RIGHT IN FRONT OF YOU!!
......
.....
じー
....
WHA ...
... WHAT'S WRONG, NARU?
NOW THAT I THINK ABOUT IT...
...THERE REALLY WASN'T ANYTHING BETWEEN THE TWO OF US TO BEGIN WITH.
I MADE A PROMISE FOR MY FUTURE WITH SOMEONE..!
...YES, OF COURSE!

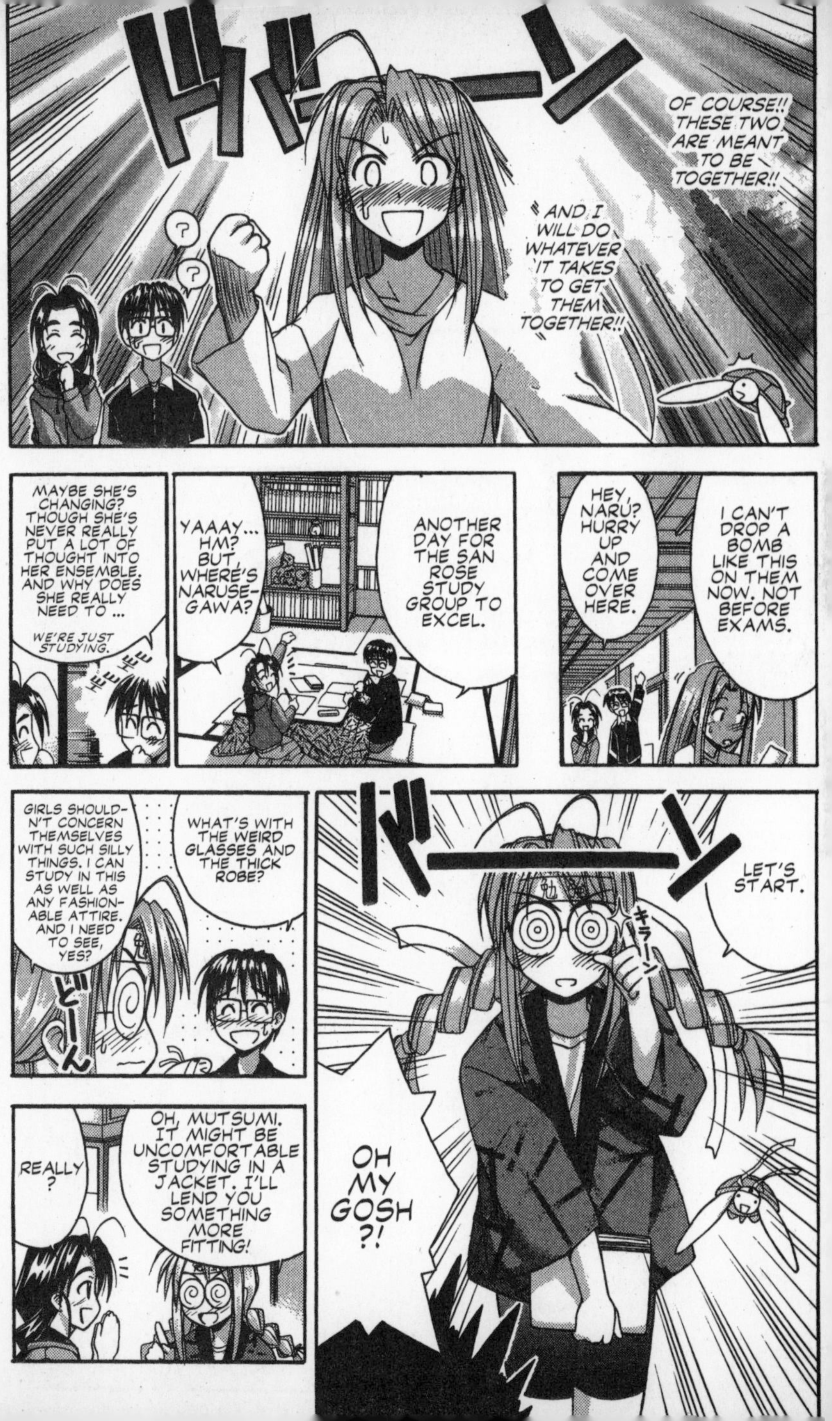
ドバーーン
OF COURSE!! THESE TWO ARE MEANT TO BE TOGETHER!!
AND I WILL DO WHATEVER IT TAKES TO GET THEM TOGETHER!!
?
?
I CAN'T DROP A BOMB LIKE THIS ON THEM NOW. NOT BEFORE EXAMS.
HEY, NARU? HURRY UP AND COME OVER HERE.
ANOTHER DAY FOR THE SAN ROSE STUDY GROUP TO EXCEL.
YAAAY... HM? BUT, WHERE'S NARUSE-GAWA?
MAYBE SHE'S CHANGING? THOUGH SHE'S NEVER REALLY PUT A LOT OF THOUGHT INTO HER ENSEMBLE. AND WHY DOES SHE REALLY NEED TO ...
WE'RE JUST STUDYING.
HEE HEE
ドーーン
LET'S START.
キラーン
OH MY GOSH?!
WHAT'S WITH THE WEIRD GLASSES AND THE THICK ROBE?
GIRLS SHOULDN'T CONCERN THEMSELVES WITH SUCH SILLY THINGS. I CAN STUDY IN THIS AS WELL AS ANY FASHIONABLE ATTIRE. AND I NEED TO SEE, YES?
どーん
OH, MUTSUMI. IT MIGHT BE UNCOMFORTABLE STUDYING IN A JACKET. I'LL LEND YOU SOMETHING MORE FITTING!
REALLY?

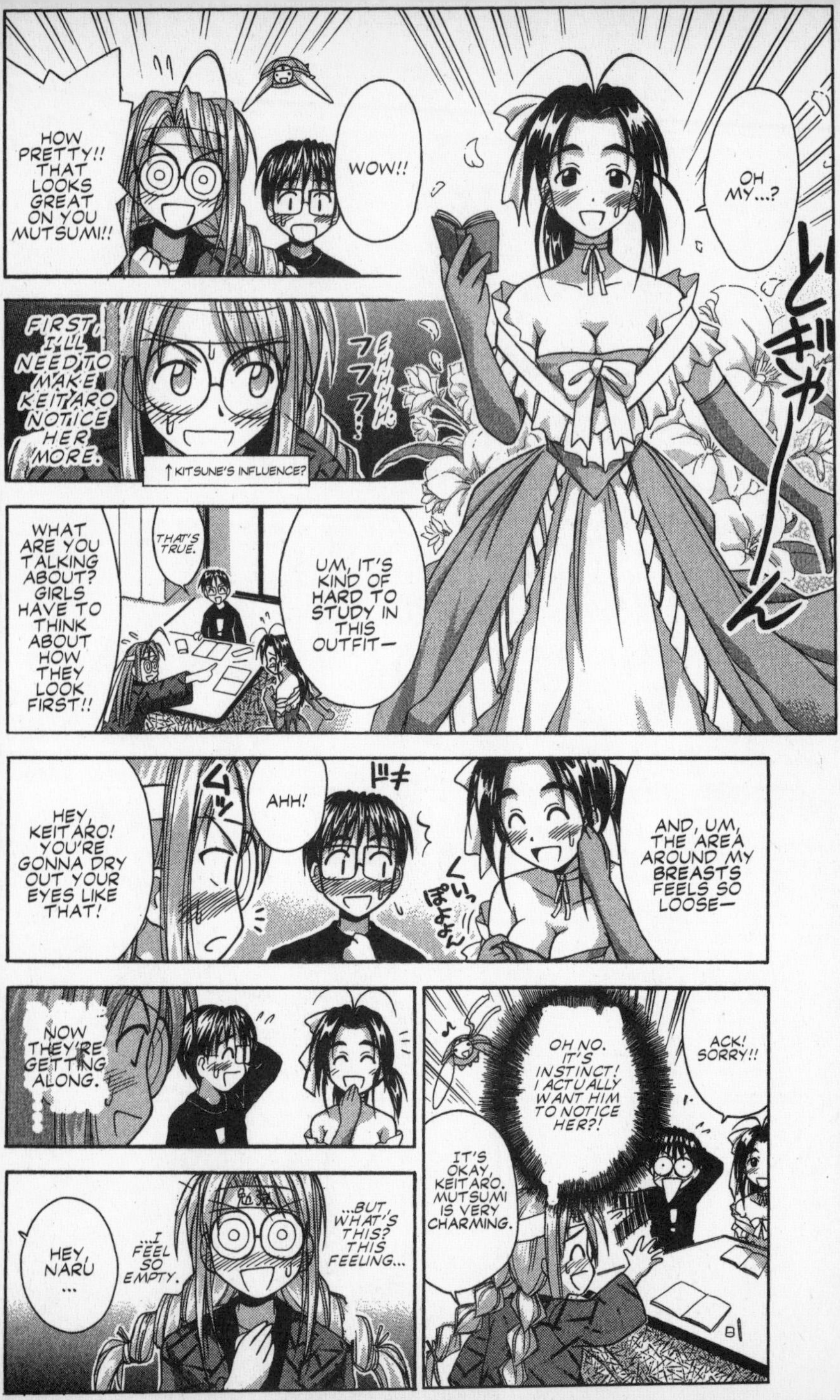
OH MY...?
どぎゃーん
WOW!!
HOW PRETTY!! THAT LOOKS GREAT ON YOU MUTSUMI!!
フフフ...
FIRST, I'LL NEED TO MAKE KEITARO NOTICE HER MORE.
↑KITSUNE'S INFLUENCE?
UM, IT'S KIND OF HARD TO STUDY IN THIS OUTFIT—
THAT'S TRUE.
WHAT ARE YOU TALKING ABOUT? GIRLS HAVE TO THINK ABOUT HOW THEY LOOK FIRST!!
AND, UM, THE AREA AROUND MY BREASTS FEELS SO LOOSE—
くいっ
ぽよよん
ドキ
AHH!
ムッ
HEY, KEITARO! YOU'RE GONNA DRY OUT YOUR EYES LIKE THAT!
ACK! SORRY!!
OH NO. IT'S INSTINCT! I ACTUALLY WANT HIM TO NOTICE HER?!
IT'S OKAY, KEITARO. MUTSUMI IS VERY CHARMING.
NOW THEY'RE GETTING ALONG.
...BUT, WHAT'S THIS? THIS FEELING...
...I FEEL SO EMPTY.
HEY, NARU ...

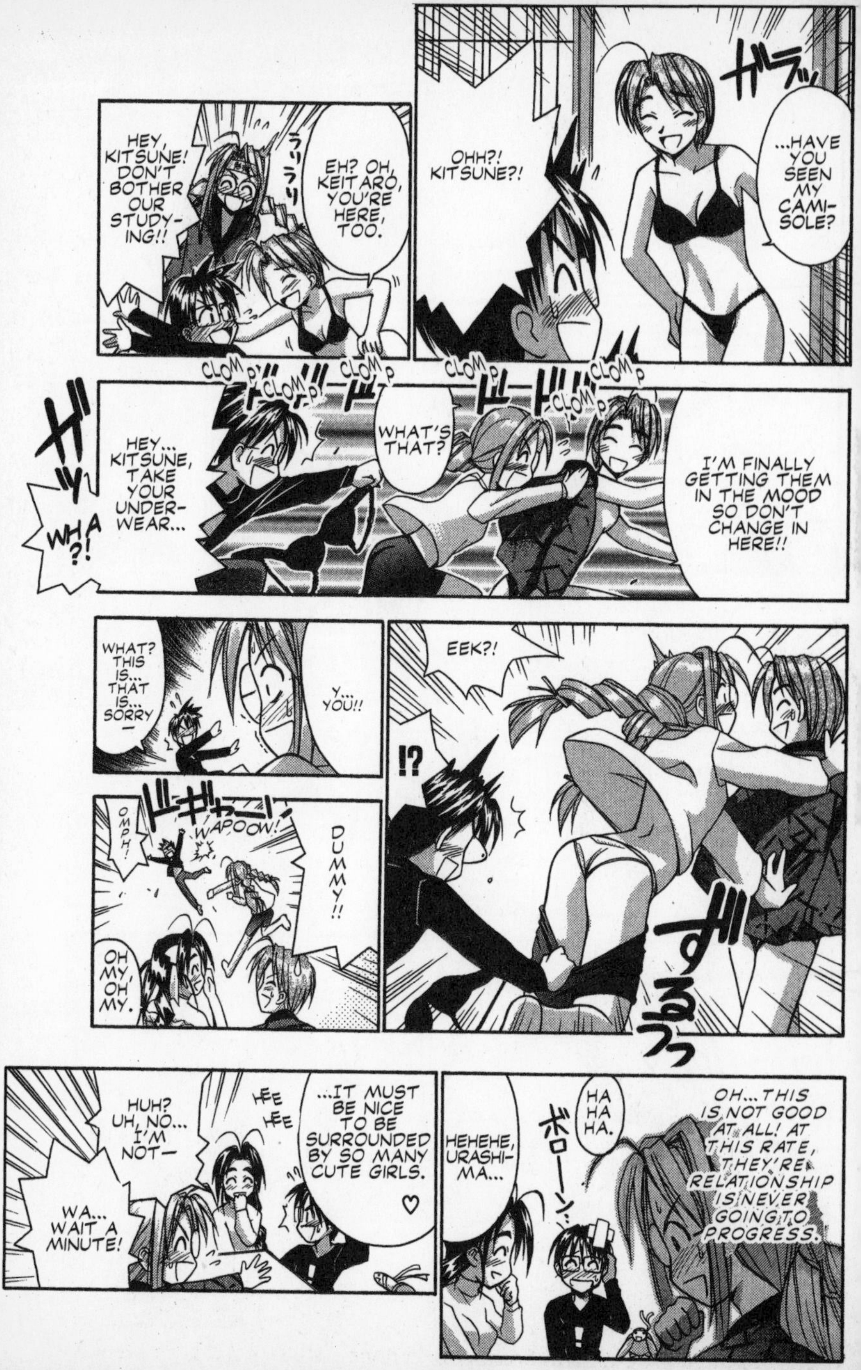
...HAVE YOU SEEN MY CAMISOLE?
OHH?! KITSUNE?!
EH? OH, KEITARO, YOU'RE HERE, TOO.
HEY, KITSUNE! DON'T BOTHER OUR STUDYING!!
CLOMP CLOMP CLOMP CLOMP CLOMP CLOMP
I'M FINALLY GETTING THEM IN THE MOOD SO DON'T CHANGE IN HERE!!
WHAT'S THAT?
HEY... KITSUNE, TAKE YOUR UNDERWEAR...
WHA?!
EEK?!
!?
Y... YOU!!
WHAT? THIS IS... THAT IS... SORRY—
DUMMY!!
WAPOOW!
OMPH!
OH MY, OH MY.
OH...THIS IS NOT GOOD AT ALL! AT THIS RATE, THEY'RE RELATIONSHIP IS NEVER GOING TO PROGRESS.
HA HA HA.
HEHEHE, URASHIMA...
...IT MUST BE NICE TO BE SURROUNDED BY SO MANY CUTE GIRLS. ♥
HEE HEE
HUH? UH, NO... I'M NOT—
WA... WAIT A MINUTE!

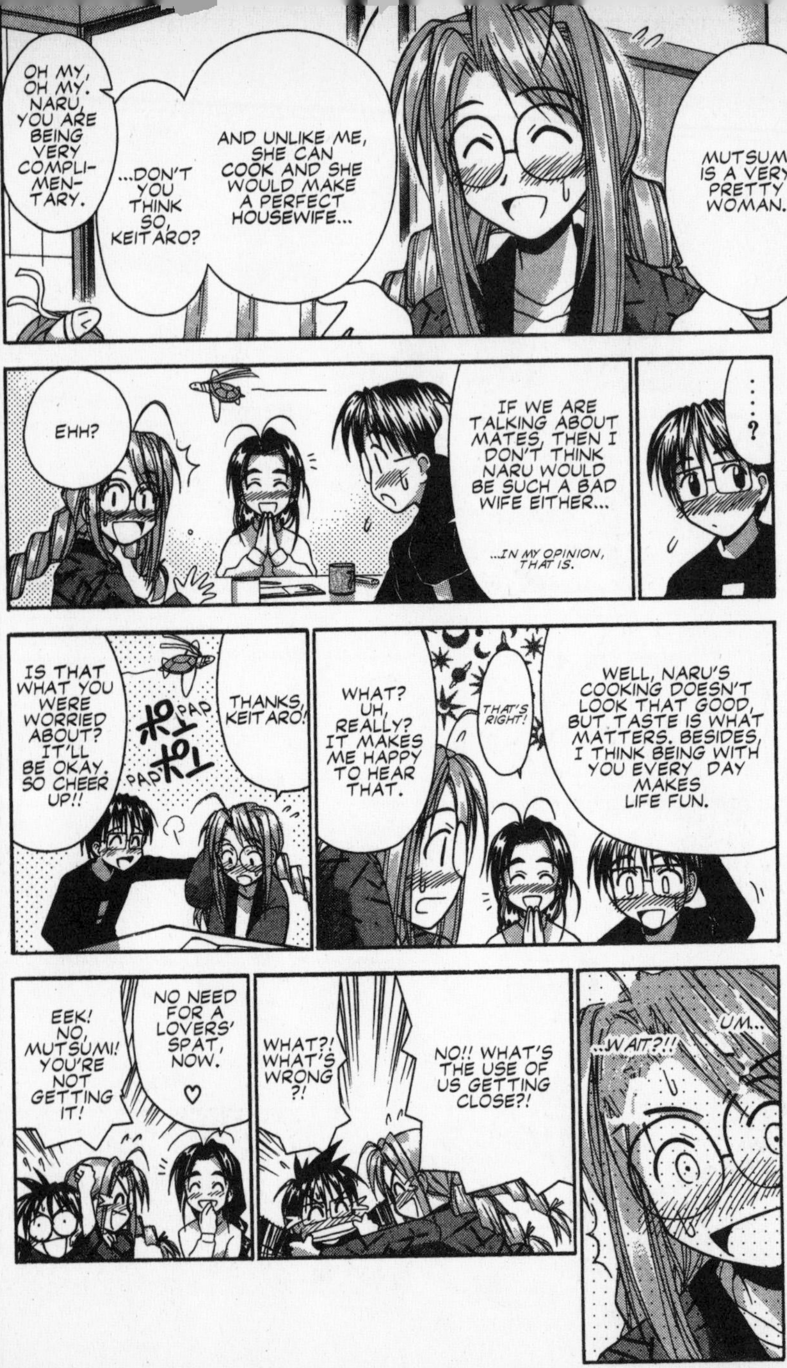
MUTSUMI IS A VERY PRETTY WOMAN.
AND UNLIKE ME, SHE CAN COOK AND SHE WOULD MAKE A PERFECT HOUSEWIFE...
...DON'T YOU THINK SO, KEITARO?
OH MY, OH MY. NARU, YOU ARE BEING VERY COMPLI-MENTARY.
...?
IF WE ARE TALKING ABOUT MATES, THEN I DON'T THINK NARU WOULD BE SUCH A BAD WIFE EITHER...
...IN MY OPINION, THAT IS.
EHH?
WELL, NARU'S COOKING DOESN'T LOOK THAT GOOD, BUT TASTE IS WHAT MATTERS. BESIDES, I THINK BEING WITH YOU EVERY DAY MAKES LIFE FUN.
THAT'S RIGHT!
WHAT? UH, REALLY? IT MAKES ME HAPPY TO HEAR THAT.
THANKS, KEITARO!
PAP
PAP
IS THAT WHAT YOU WERE WORRIED ABOUT? IT'LL BE OKAY. SO CHEER UP!!
UM...
...WAIT?!!
NO!! WHAT'S THE USE OF US GETTING CLOSE?!
WHAT?! WHAT'S WRONG ?!
NO NEED FOR A LOVERS' SPAT, NOW. ♥
EEK! NO, MUTSUMI! YOU'RE NOT GETTING IT!

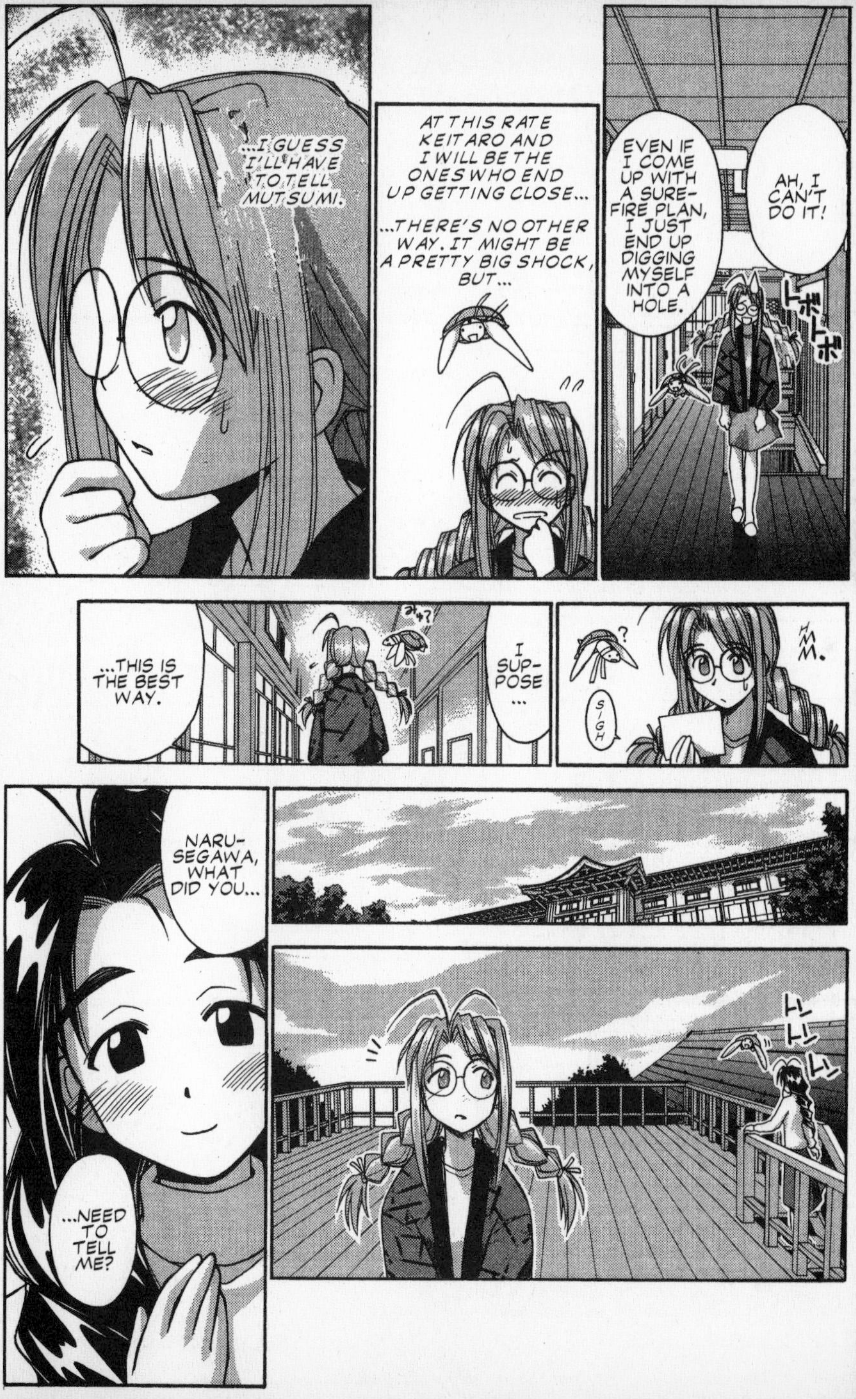
AH, I CAN'T DO IT!
EVEN IF I COME UP WITH A SURE-FIRE PLAN, I JUST END UP DIGGING MYSELF INTO A HOLE.
トボトボ
AT THIS RATE KEITARO AND I WILL BE THE ONES WHO END UP GETTING CLOSE...
...THERE'S NO OTHER WAY. IT MIGHT BE A PRETTY BIG SHOCK, BUT...
...I GUESS I'LL HAVE TO TELL MUTSUMI.
HMM.
?
SIGH
I SUPPOSE...
...THIS IS THE BEST WAY.
NARU-SEGAWA, WHAT DID YOU...
...NEED TO TELL ME?

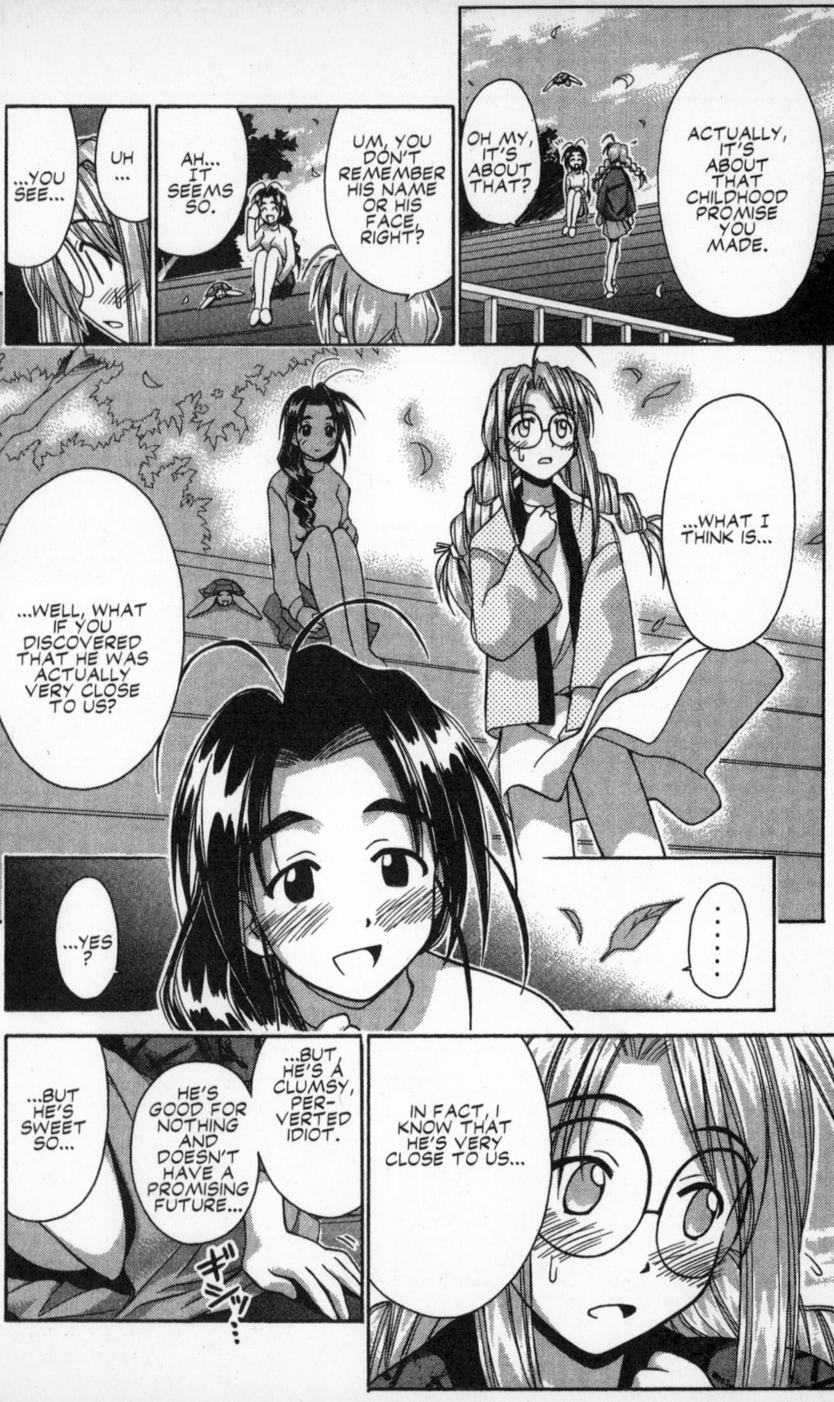
ACTUALLY, IT'S ABOUT THAT CHILDHOOD PROMISE YOU MADE.
OH MY, IT'S ABOUT THAT?
UM, YOU DON'T REMEMBER HIS NAME OR HIS FACE, RIGHT?
AH... IT SEEMS SO.
UH ...
...YOU SEE...
...WHAT I THINK IS...
...WELL, WHAT IF YOU DISCOVERED THAT HE WAS ACTUALLY VERY CLOSE TO US?
......
...YES ?
IN FACT, I KNOW THAT HE'S VERY CLOSE TO US...
...BUT, HE'S A CLUMSY, PER-VERTED IDIOT.
HE'S GOOD FOR NOTHING AND DOESN'T HAVE A PROMISING FUTURE...
...BUT HE'S SWEET SO...
ギシッ…

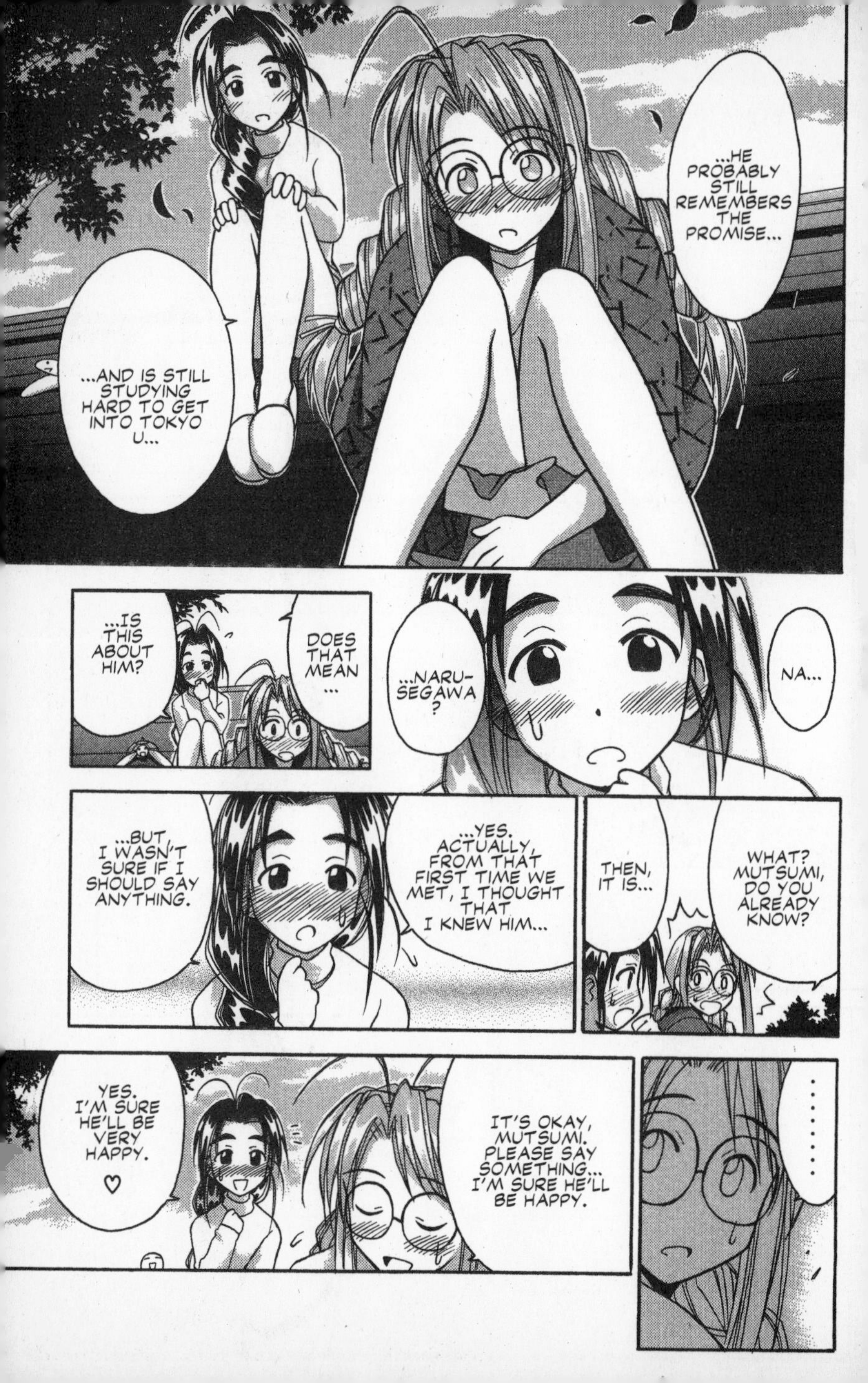
...HE PROBABLY STILL REMEMBERS THE PROMISE...
...AND IS STILL STUDYING HARD TO GET INTO TOKYO U...
NA...
...NARU-SEGAWA?
DOES THAT MEAN...
...IS THIS ABOUT HIM?
WHAT? MUTSUMI, DO YOU ALREADY KNOW?
THEN, IT IS...
...YES. ACTUALLY, FROM THAT FIRST TIME WE MET, I THOUGHT THAT I KNEW HIM...
...BUT, I WASN'T SURE IF I SHOULD SAY ANYTHING.
......
IT'S OKAY, MUTSUMI. PLEASE SAY SOMETHING... I'M SURE HE'LL BE HAPPY.
YES. I'M SURE HE'LL BE VERY HAPPY. ♡

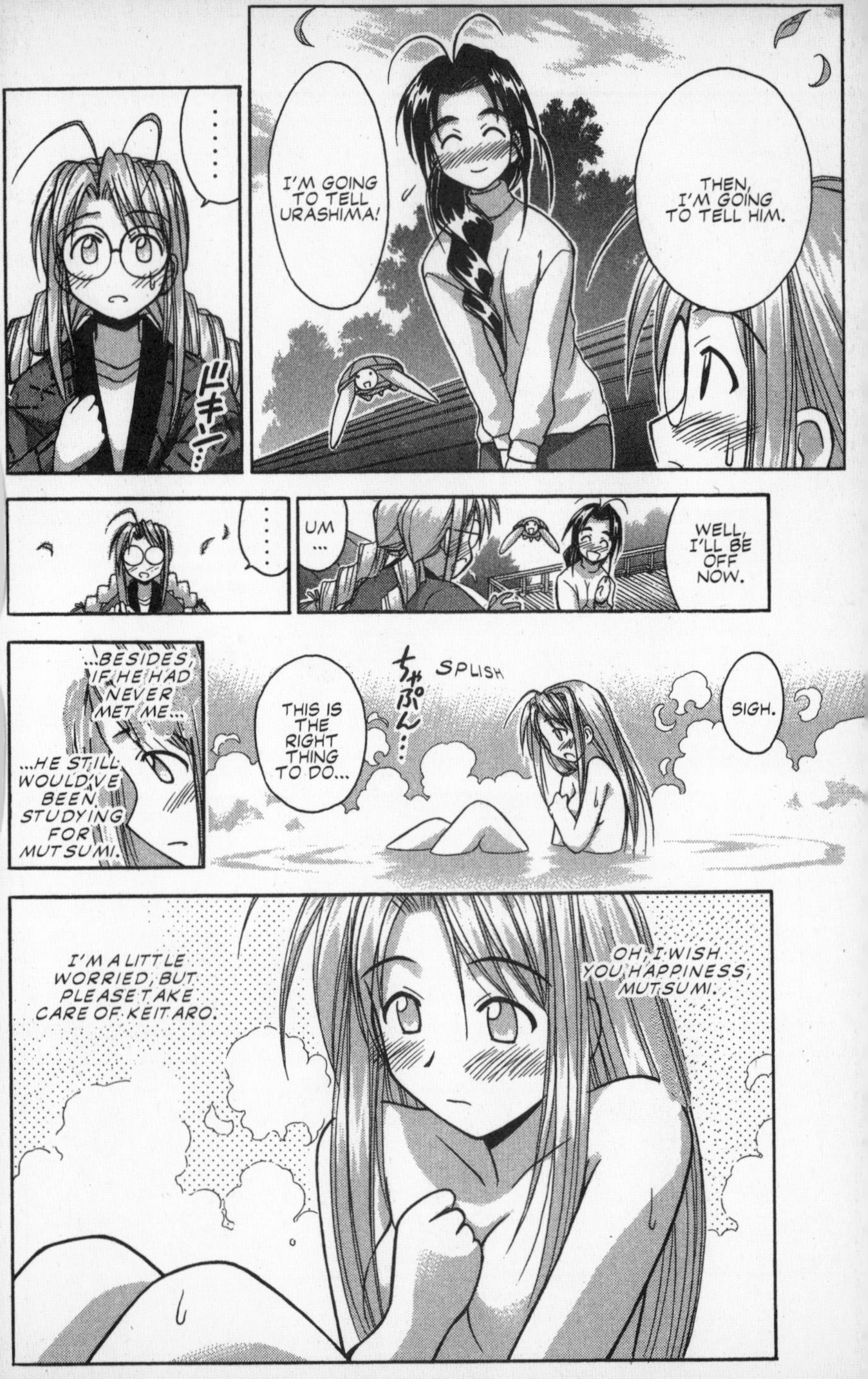
THEN, I'M GOING TO TELL HIM.
I'M GOING TO TELL URASHIMA!
......
ドキュー…
WELL, I'LL BE OFF NOW.
UM ...
......
SIGH.
ちゃぷん…
SPLISH
THIS IS THE RIGHT THING TO DO...
...BESIDES, IF HE HAD NEVER MET ME...
...HE STILL WOULD'VE BEEN STUDYING FOR MUTSUMI.
OH, I WISH YOU HAPPINESS, MUTSUMI.
I'M A LITTLE WORRIED, BUT PLEASE TAKE CARE OF KEITARO.

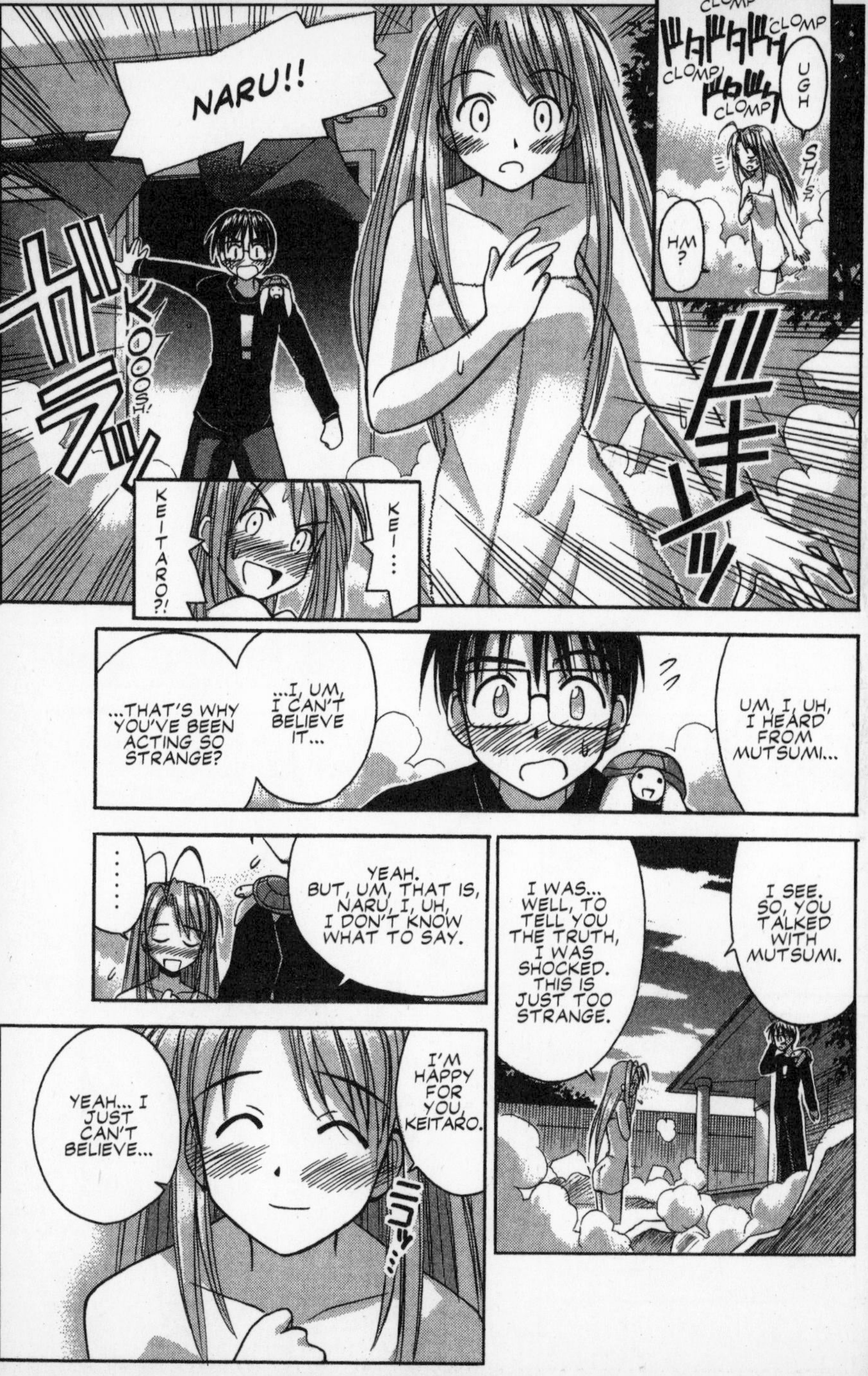
CLOMP
CLOMP
CLOMP
CLOMP
UGH
SHISH
HM?
NARU!!
KOOOOSH!
KEI...
KEITARO?!
UM, I, UH, I HEARD FROM MUTSUMI...
...I, UM, I CAN'T BELIEVE IT...
...THAT'S WHY YOU'VE BEEN ACTING SO STRANGE?
I SEE. SO, YOU TALKED WITH MUTSUMI.
I WAS... WELL, TO TELL YOU THE TRUTH, I WAS SHOCKED. THIS IS JUST TOO STRANGE.
YEAH. BUT, UM, THAT IS, NARU, I, UH, I DON'T KNOW WHAT TO SAY.
......
I'M HAPPY FOR YOU, KEITARO.
YEAH... I JUST CAN'T BELIEVE...

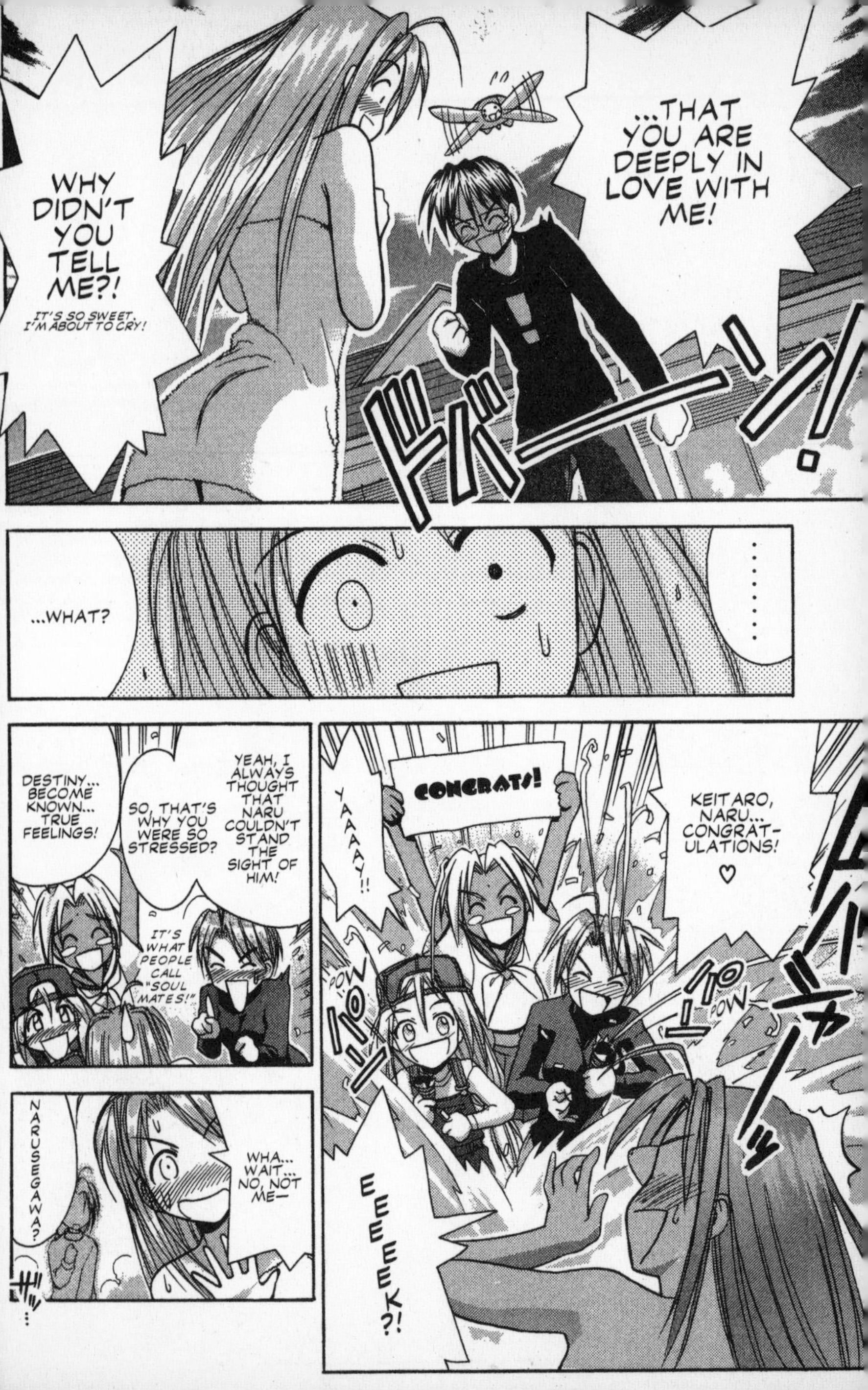
...THAT YOU ARE DEEPLY IN LOVE WITH ME!
WHY DIDN'T YOU TELL ME?!
IT'S SO SWEET. I'M ABOUT TO CRY!
....
...WHAT?
KEITARO, NARU... CONGRAT-ULATIONS! ♡
CONGRATS!
YAAAAY!!
POW
POW
EEEEEK?!
YEAH, I ALWAYS THOUGHT THAT NARU COULDN'T STAND THE SIGHT OF HIM!
SO, THAT'S WHY YOU WERE SO STRESSED?
DESTINY... BECOME KNOWN... TRUE FEELINGS!
IT'S WHAT PEOPLE CALL "SOUL MATES!"
WHA... WAIT... NO, NOT ME—
NARUSEGAWA?

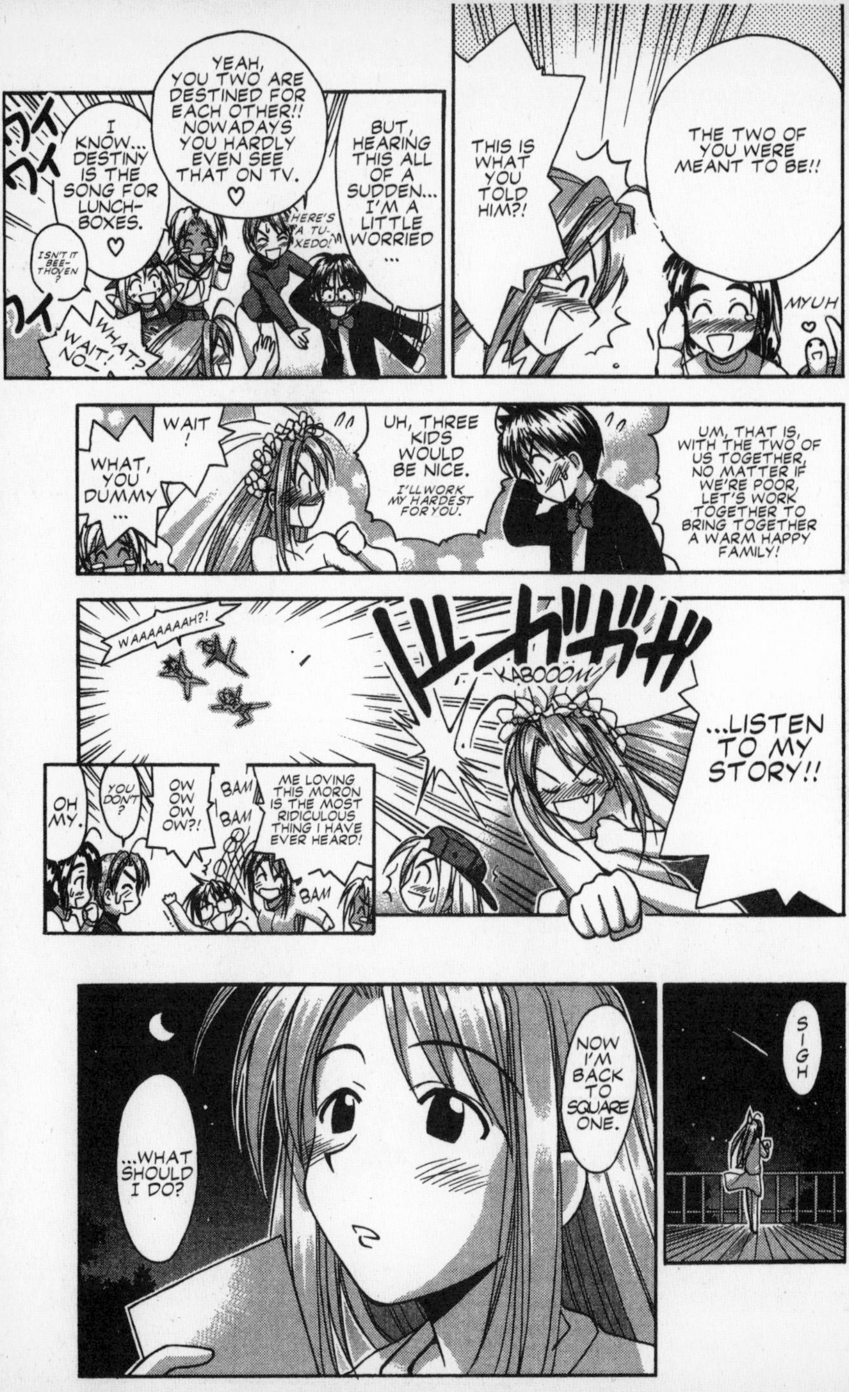
THE TWO OF YOU WERE MEANT TO BE!!
MYUH
THIS IS WHAT YOU TOLD HIM?!
BUT, HEARING THIS ALL OF A SUDDEN... I'M A LITTLE WORRIED ...
HERE'S A TU-XEDO!
YEAH, YOU TWO ARE DESTINED FOR EACH OTHER!! NOWADAYS YOU HARDLY EVEN SEE THAT ON TV. ♡
I KNOW... DESTINY IS THE SONG FOR LUNCH-BOXES. ♡
ISN'T IT BEE-THOVEN?
WHAT? WAIT! NO—
UM, THAT IS, WITH THE TWO OF US TOGETHER, NO MATTER IF WE'RE POOR, LET'S WORK TOGETHER TO BRING TOGETHER A WARM HAPPY FAMILY!
UH, THREE KIDS WOULD BE NICE.
I'LL WORK MY HARDEST FOR YOU.
WAIT!
WHAT, YOU DUMMY ...
KABOOOM
WAAAAAAAH?!
...LISTEN TO MY STORY!!
ME LOVING THIS MORON IS THE MOST RIDICULOUS THING I HAVE EVER HEARD!
BAM BAM
BAM
OW OW OW OW?!
YOU DON'T?
OH MY.
SIGH
NOW I'M BACK TO SQUARE ONE.
...WHAT SHOULD I DO?

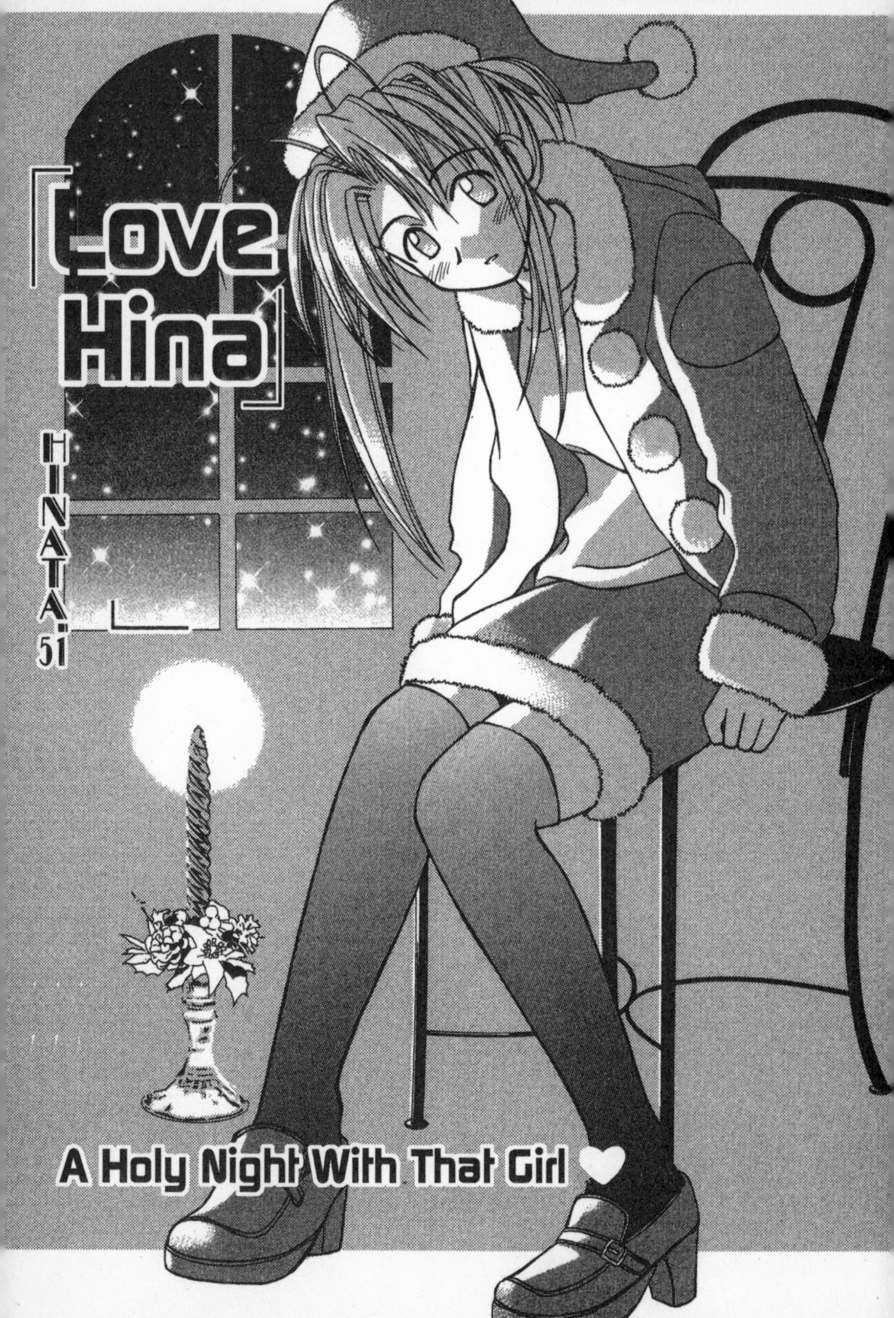
「Love Hina」
HINATA.51
A Holy Night With That Girl ♥

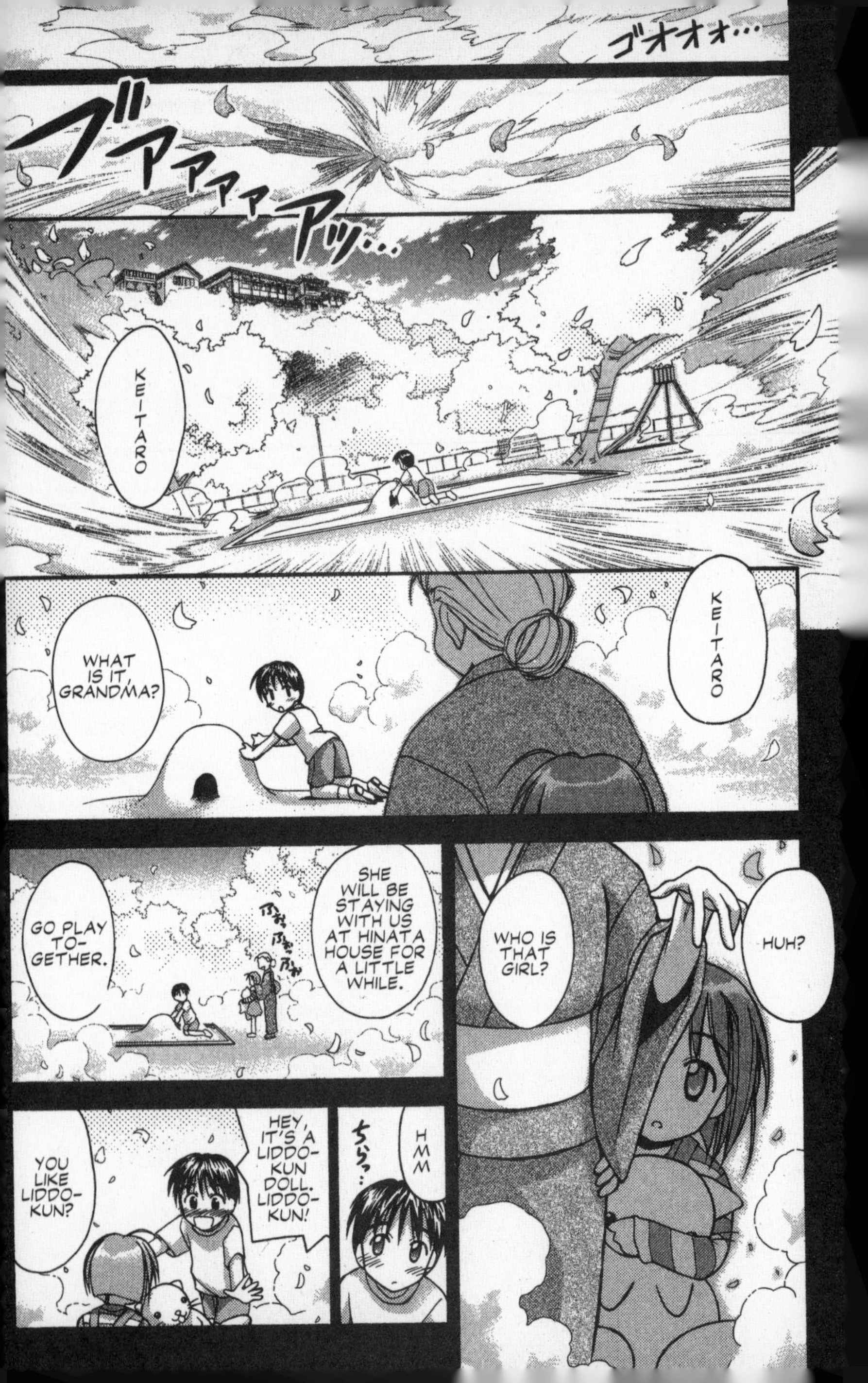
ゴオオォ…
ブアアァアアッ…
KEITARO
KEITARO
WHAT IS IT, GRANDMA?
HUH?
WHO IS THAT GIRL?
SHE WILL BE STAYING WITH US AT HINATA HOUSE FOR A LITTLE WHILE.
GO PLAY TO-GETHER.
HMM
ちらっ…
HEY, IT'S A LIDDO-KUN DOLL. LIDDO-KUN!
YOU LIKE LIDDO-KUN?

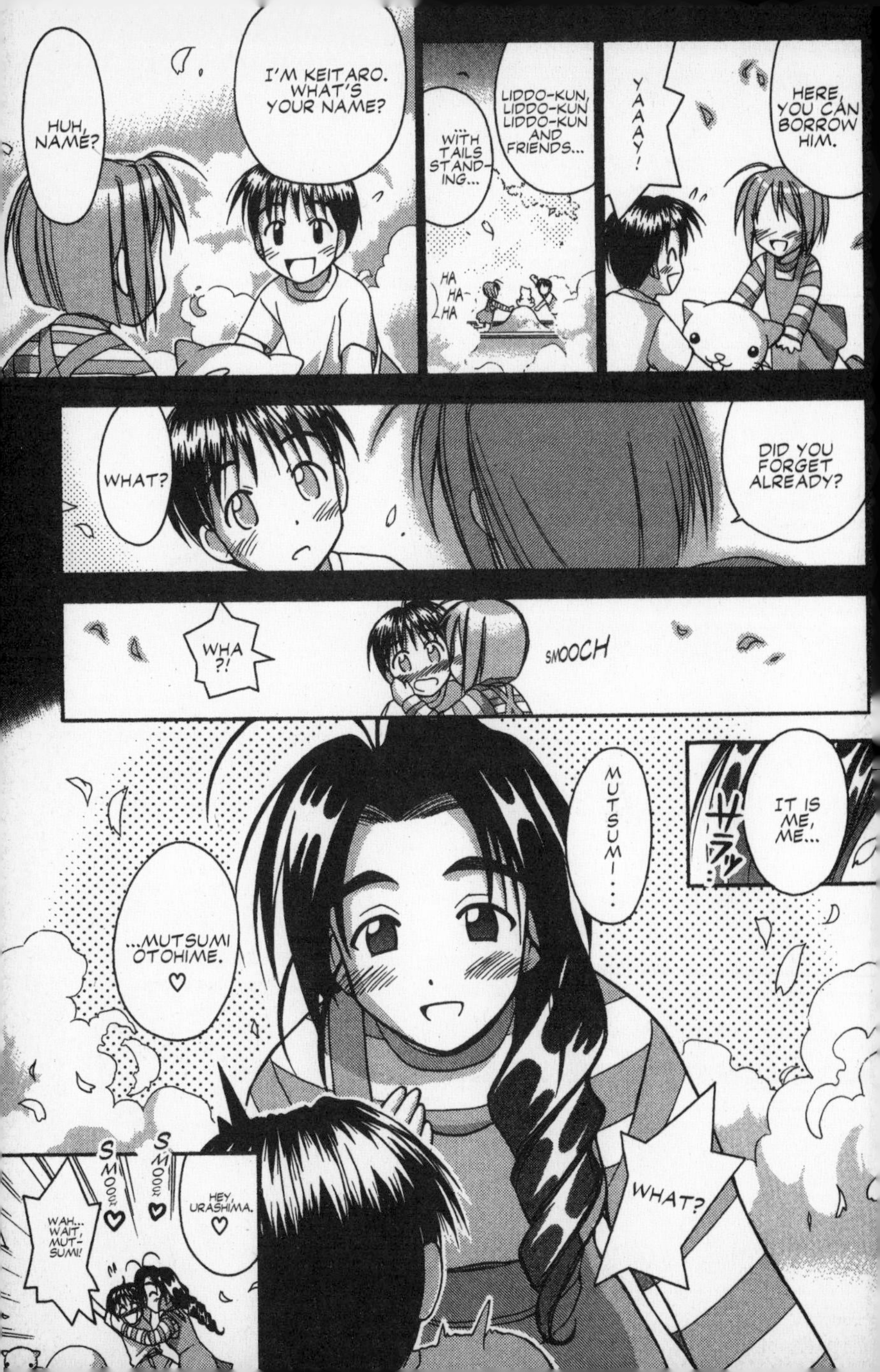

HERE, YOU CAN BORROW HIM.
YAAAAY!
LIDDO-KUN, LIDDO-KUN LIDDO-KUN AND FRIENDS...
...WITH TAILS STANDING...
HA HA HA
I'M KEITARO. WHAT'S YOUR NAME?
HUH, NAME?
DID YOU FORGET ALREADY?
WHAT?
SMOOCH
WHA?!
IT IS ME, ME...
サラッ
MUTSUMI...
...MUTSUMI OTOHIME. ♡
WHAT?
HEY, URASHIMA. ♡
SMOOOCH ♡
SMOOOCH ♡
WAH... WAIT, MUT-SUMI!

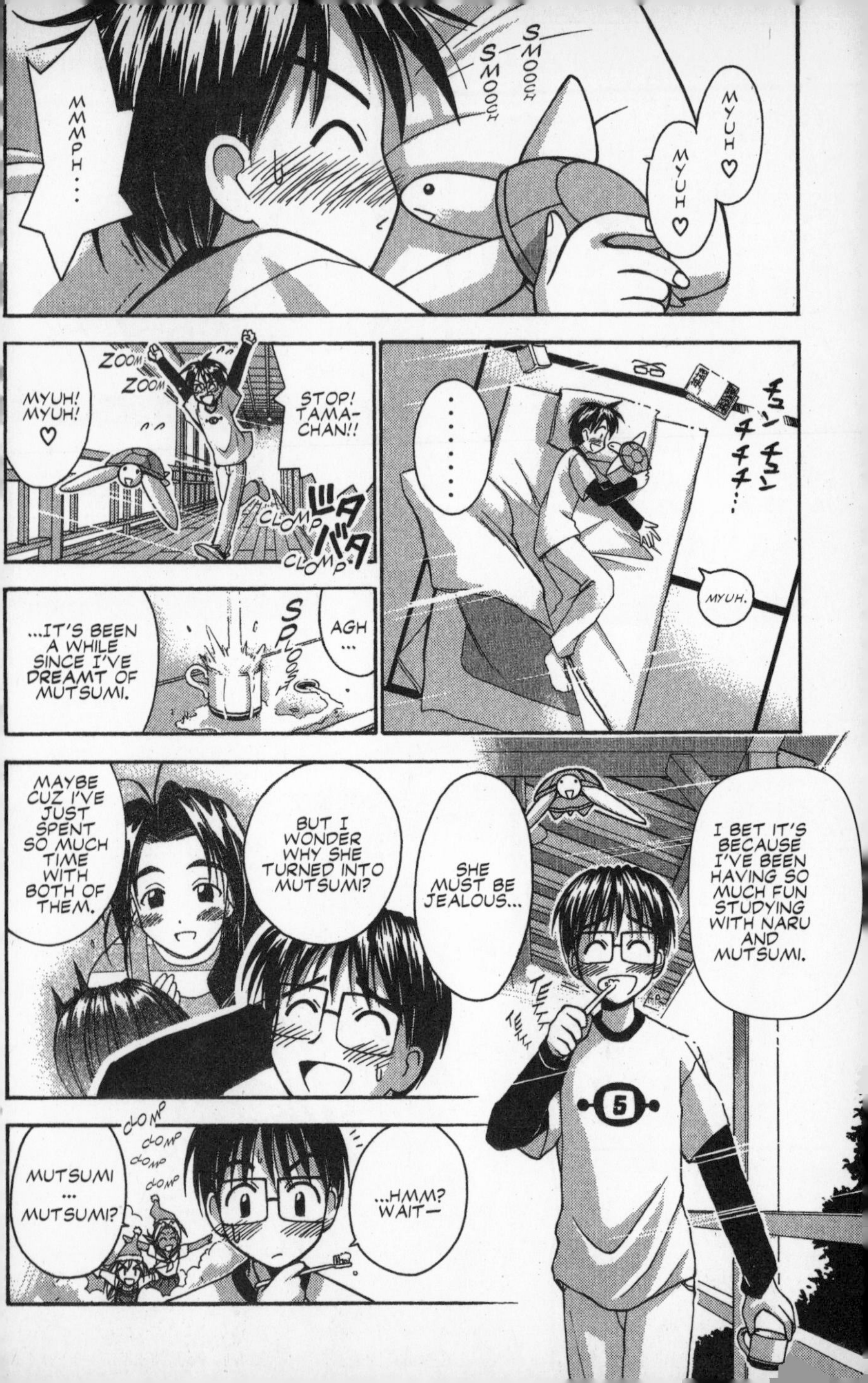
MYUH ♡
MYUH ♡
SMOOCH
SMOOCH
MMMPH...
チュン チュン
チチチ…
......
MYUH.
STOP! TAMA-CHAN!!
MYUH! MYUH! ♡
ZOOM
ZOOM
ジタバタ
CLOMP
CLOMP
AGH...
SPLOOSH
...IT'S BEEN A WHILE SINCE I'VE DREAMT OF MUTSUMI.
I BET IT'S BECAUSE I'VE BEEN HAVING SO MUCH FUN STUDYING WITH NARU AND MUTSUMI.
SHE MUST BE JEALOUS...
BUT I WONDER WHY SHE TURNED INTO MUTSUMI?
MAYBE CUZ I'VE JUST SPENT SO MUCH TIME WITH BOTH OF THEM.
...HMM? WAIT—
CLOMP
CLOMP
CLOMP
CLOMP
MUTSUMI... MUTSUMI?

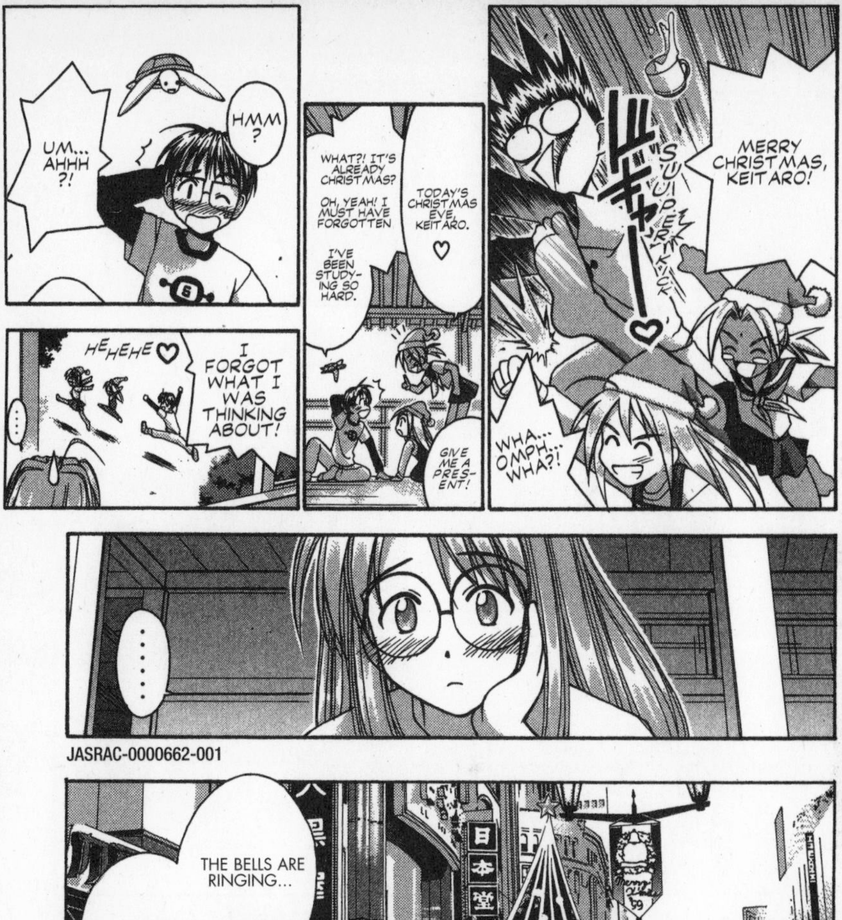
MERRY CHRISTMAS, KEITARO!
SUPER KICK
WHA... OMPH... WHA?!
TODAY'S CHRISTMAS EVE, KEITARO. ♡
WHAT?! IT'S ALREADY CHRISTMAS?
OH, YEAH! I MUST HAVE FORGOTTEN
I'VE BEEN STUDYING SO HARD.
GIVE ME A PRESENT!
HMM?
UM... AHHH?!
I FORGOT WHAT I WAS THINKING ABOUT!
HEHEHE ♡
...
......

JASRAC-0000662-001

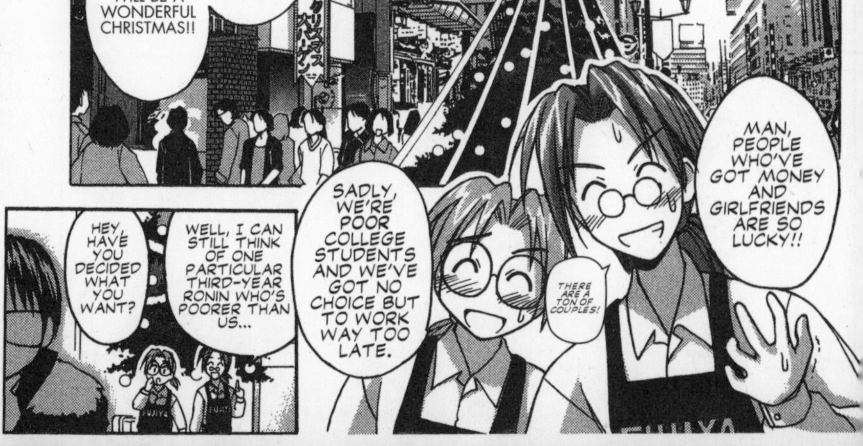
THE BELLS ARE RINGING...
...TODAY WILL BE A WONDERFUL CHRISTMAS!!
MAN, PEOPLE WHO'VE GOT MONEY AND GIRLFRIENDS ARE SO LUCKY!!
THERE ARE A TON OF COUPLES!
SADLY, WE'RE POOR COLLEGE STUDENTS AND WE'VE GOT NO CHOICE BUT TO WORK WAY TOO LATE.
WELL, I CAN STILL THINK OF ONE PARTICULAR THIRD-YEAR RONIN WHO'S POORER THAN US...
HEY, HAVE YOU DECIDED WHAT YOU WANT?

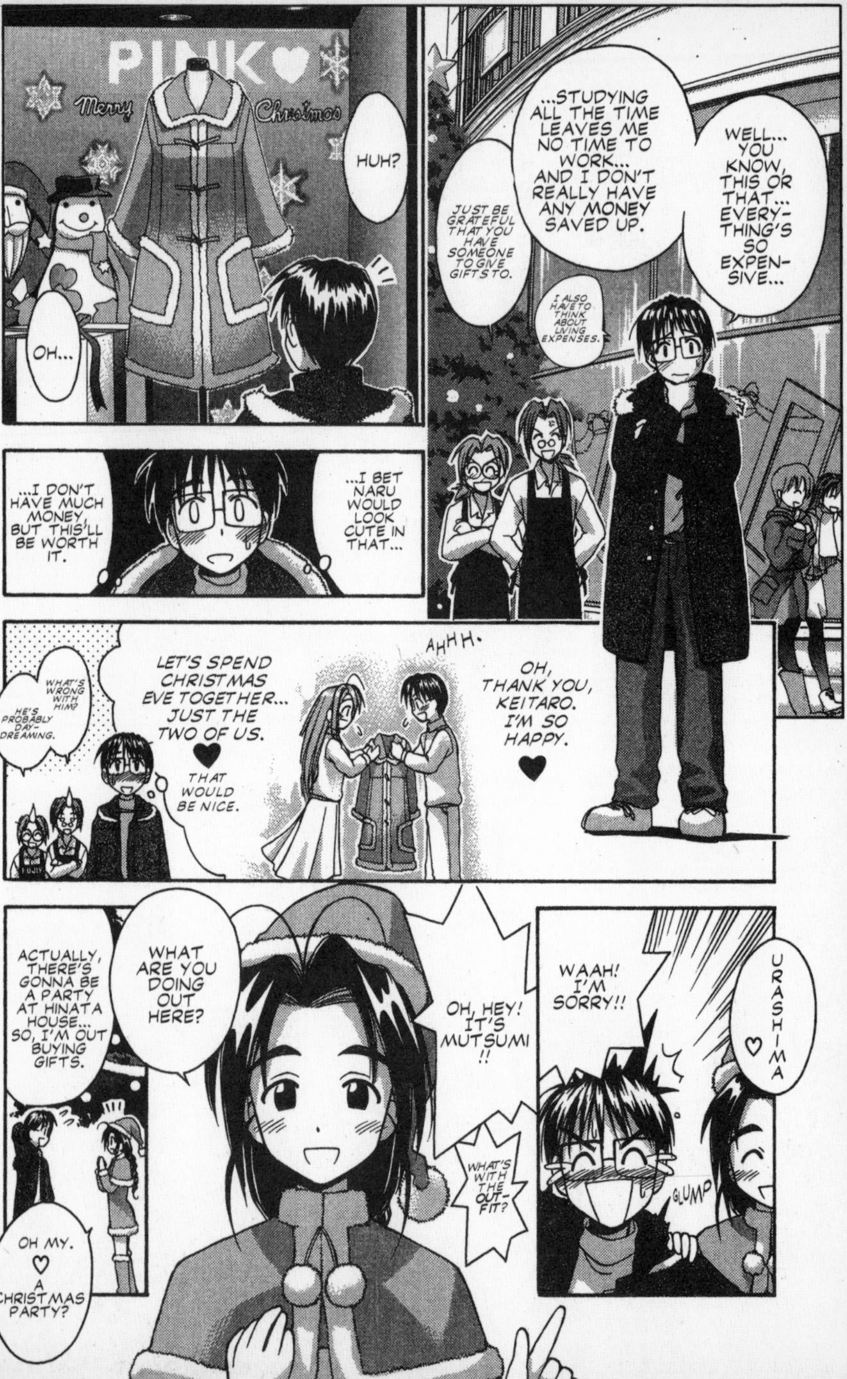
WELL... YOU KNOW, THIS OR THAT... EVERYTHING'S SO EXPENSIVE...
...STUDYING ALL THE TIME LEAVES ME NO TIME TO WORK... AND I DON'T REALLY HAVE ANY MONEY SAVED UP.
I ALSO HAVE TO THINK ABOUT LIVING EXPENSES.
JUST BE GRATEFUL THAT YOU HAVE SOMEONE TO GIVE GIFTS TO.
PINK
Merry Christmas
HUH?
OH...
...I BET NARU WOULD LOOK CUTE IN THAT...
...I DON'T HAVE MUCH MONEY, BUT THIS'LL BE WORTH IT.
AHHH.
OH, THANK YOU, KEITARO. I'M SO HAPPY.
LET'S SPEND CHRISTMAS EVE TOGETHER... JUST THE TWO OF US.
THAT WOULD BE NICE.
WHAT'S WRONG WITH HIM?
HE'S PROBABLY DAY-DREAMING.
URASHIMA
WAAH! I'M SORRY!!
GLUMP
OH, HEY! IT'S MUTSUMI!!
WHAT'S WITH THE OUT-FIT?
WHAT ARE YOU DOING OUT HERE?
ACTUALLY, THERE'S GONNA BE A PARTY AT HINATA HOUSE... SO, I'M OUT BUYING GIFTS.
OH MY. A CHRISTMAS PARTY?

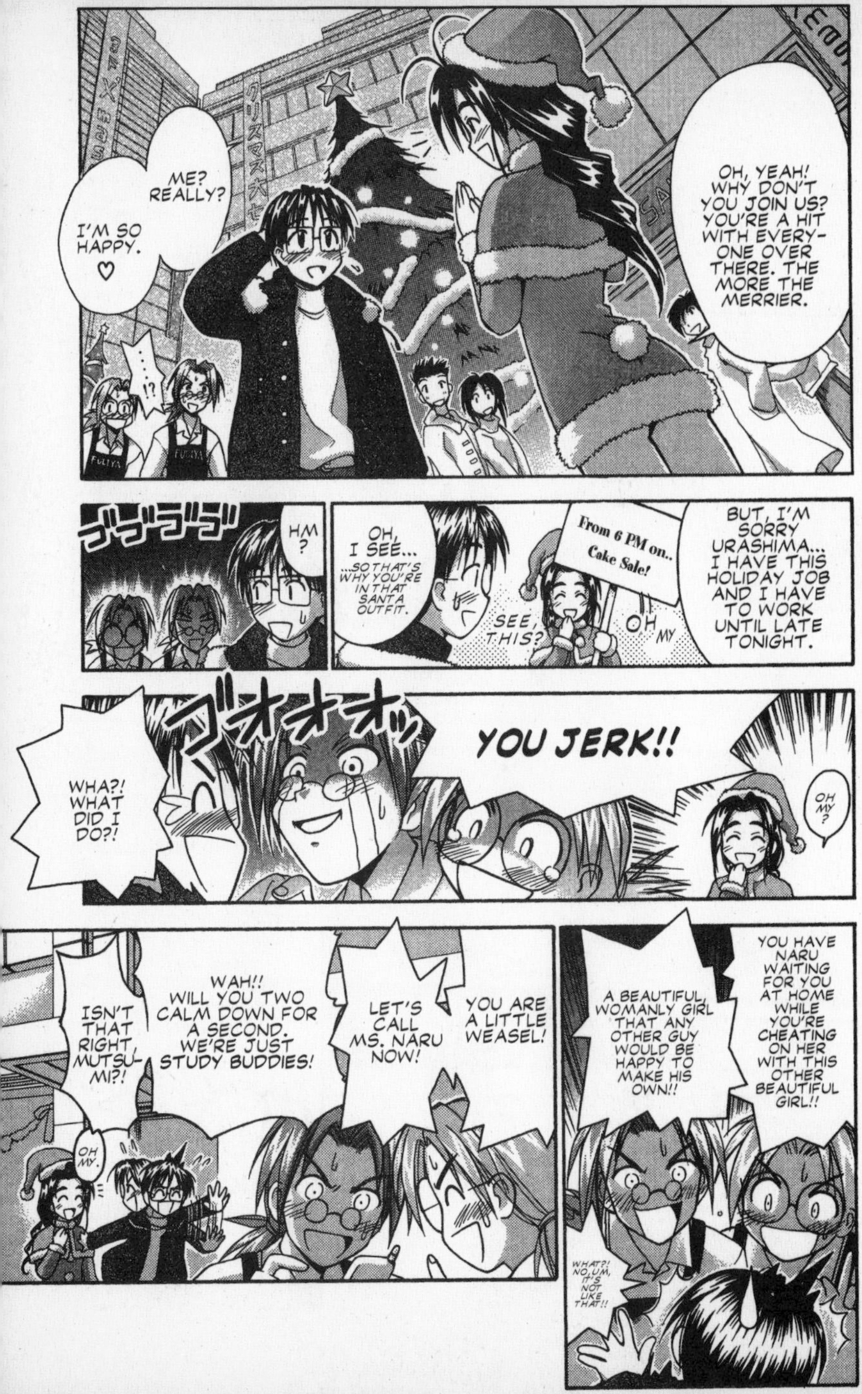
OH, YEAH! WHY DON'T YOU JOIN US? YOU'RE A HIT WITH EVERY-ONE OVER THERE. THE MORE THE MERRIER.
ME? REALLY?
I'M SO HAPPY. ♡
...!?
BUT, I'M SORRY URASHIMA... I HAVE THIS HOLIDAY JOB AND I HAVE TO WORK UNTIL LATE TONIGHT.
From 6 PM on.. Cake Sale!
OH MY
SEE, THIS?
OH, I SEE... ...SO THAT'S WHY YOU'RE IN THAT SANTA OUTFIT.
HM?
ゴゴゴゴ
OH MY?
YOU JERK!!
ゴオオオッ
WHA?! WHAT DID I DO?!
YOU HAVE NARU WAITING FOR YOU AT HOME WHILE YOU'RE CHEATING ON HER WITH THIS OTHER BEAUTIFUL GIRL!!
A BEAUTIFUL, WOMANLY GIRL THAT ANY OTHER GUY WOULD BE HAPPY TO MAKE HIS OWN!!
WHAT?! NO, UM, IT'S NOT LIKE THAT!!
YOU ARE A LITTLE WEASEL!
LET'S CALL MS. NARU NOW!
WAH!! WILL YOU TWO CALM DOWN FOR A SECOND. WE'RE JUST STUDY BUDDIES!
ISN'T THAT RIGHT, MUTSU-MI?!
OH MY.

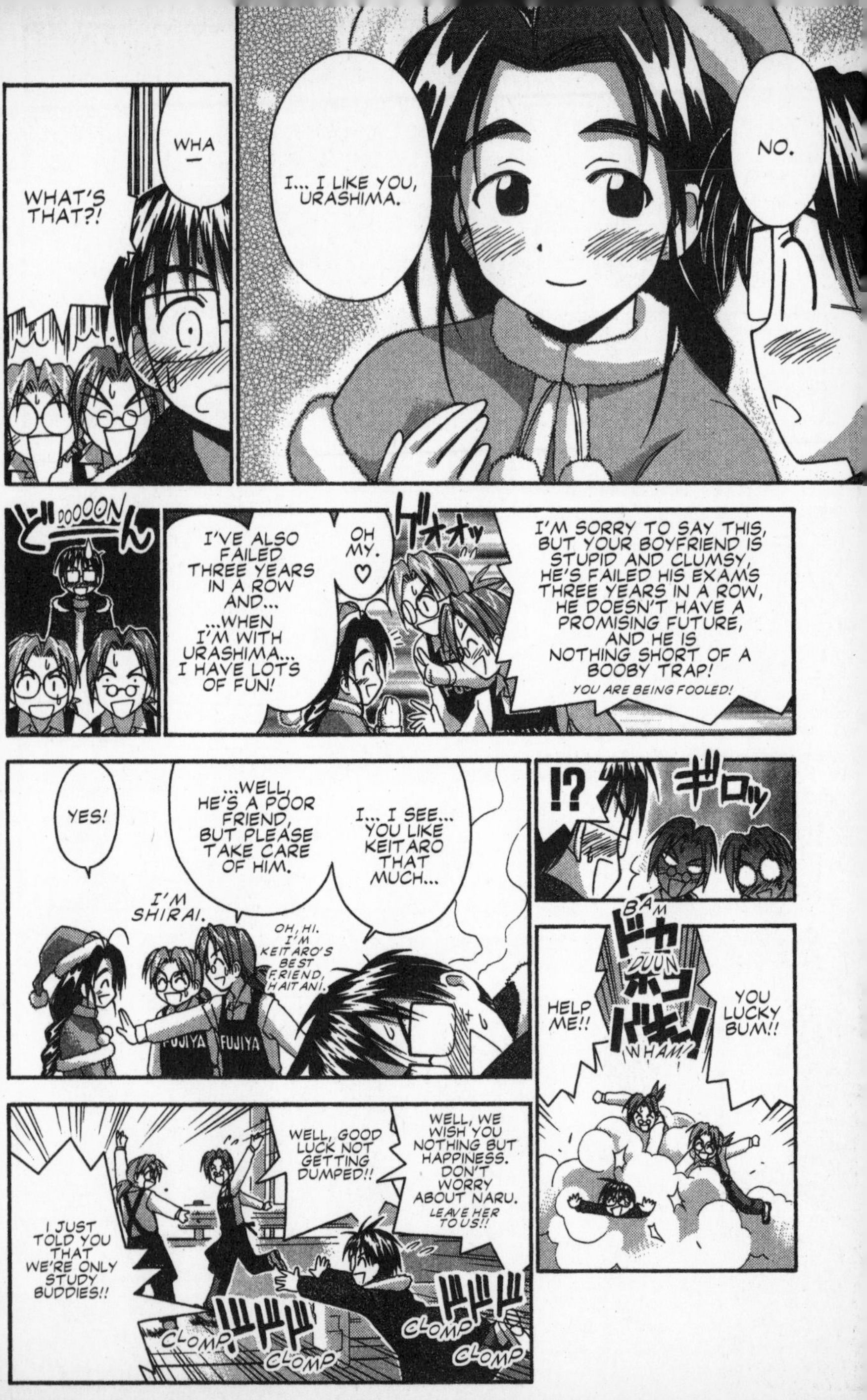
NO.
I... I LIKE YOU, URASHIMA.
WHA— WHAT'S THAT?!
I'M SORRY TO SAY THIS, BUT YOUR BOYFRIEND IS STUPID AND CLUMSY, HE'S FAILED HIS EXAMS THREE YEARS IN A ROW, HE DOESN'T HAVE A PROMISING FUTURE, AND HE IS NOTHING SHORT OF A BOOBY TRAP!
YOU ARE BEING FOOLED!
OH MY. ♡
I'VE ALSO FAILED THREE YEARS IN A ROW AND... ...WHEN I'M WITH URASHIMA... I HAVE LOTS OF FUN!
DOOOON
!?
I... I SEE... YOU LIKE KEITARO THAT MUCH...
...WELL, HE'S A POOR FRIEND, BUT PLEASE TAKE CARE OF HIM.
YES!
OH, HI. I'M KEITARO'S BEST FRIEND, HAITANI.
I'M SHIRAI.
FUJIYA
FUJIYA
BAM
DUUN
WHAM!
YOU LUCKY BUM!!
HELP ME!!
WELL, WE WISH YOU NOTHING BUT HAPPINESS. DON'T WORRY ABOUT NARU.
LEAVE HER TO US!!
WELL, GOOD LUCK NOT GETTING DUMPED!!
I JUST TOLD YOU THAT WE'RE ONLY STUDY BUDDIES!!
CLOMP
CLOMP
CLOMP
CLOMP

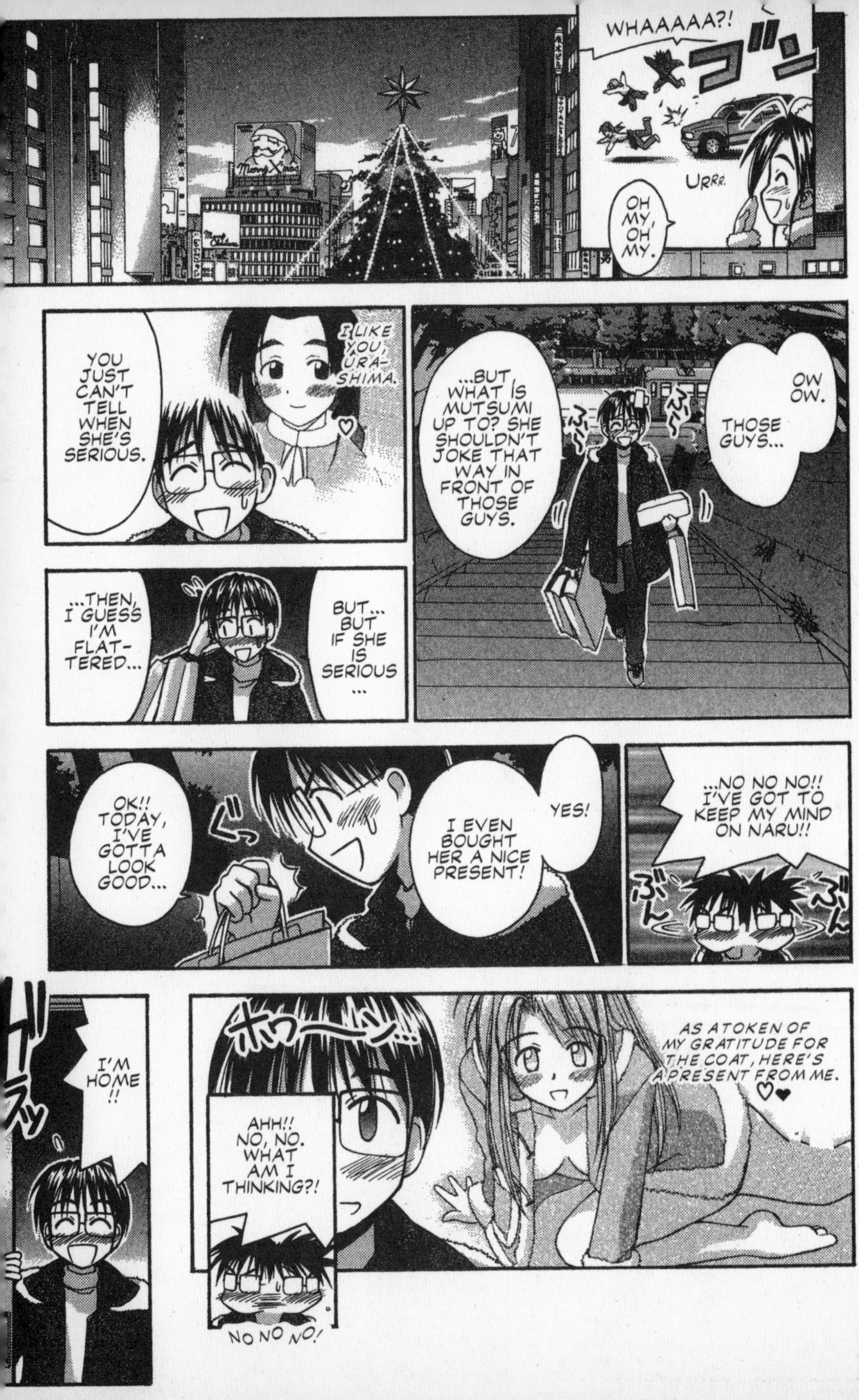
WHAAAAA?!
URrr.
OH MY, OH MY.
OW OW.
THOSE GUYS...
...BUT WHAT IS MUTSUMI UP TO? SHE SHOULDN'T JOKE THAT WAY IN FRONT OF THOSE GUYS.
I LIKE YOU, URASHIMA.
YOU JUST CAN'T TELL WHEN SHE'S SERIOUS.
BUT... BUT IF SHE IS SERIOUS...
...THEN, I GUESS I'M FLATTERED...
...NO NO NO!! I'VE GOT TO KEEP MY MIND ON NARU!!
YES!
I EVEN BOUGHT HER A NICE PRESENT!
OK!! TODAY, I'VE GOTTA LOOK GOOD...
AS A TOKEN OF MY GRATITUDE FOR THE COAT, HERE'S A PRESENT FROM ME. ♡♥
AHH!! NO, NO. WHAT AM I THINKING?!
NO NO NO!
I'M HOME!!

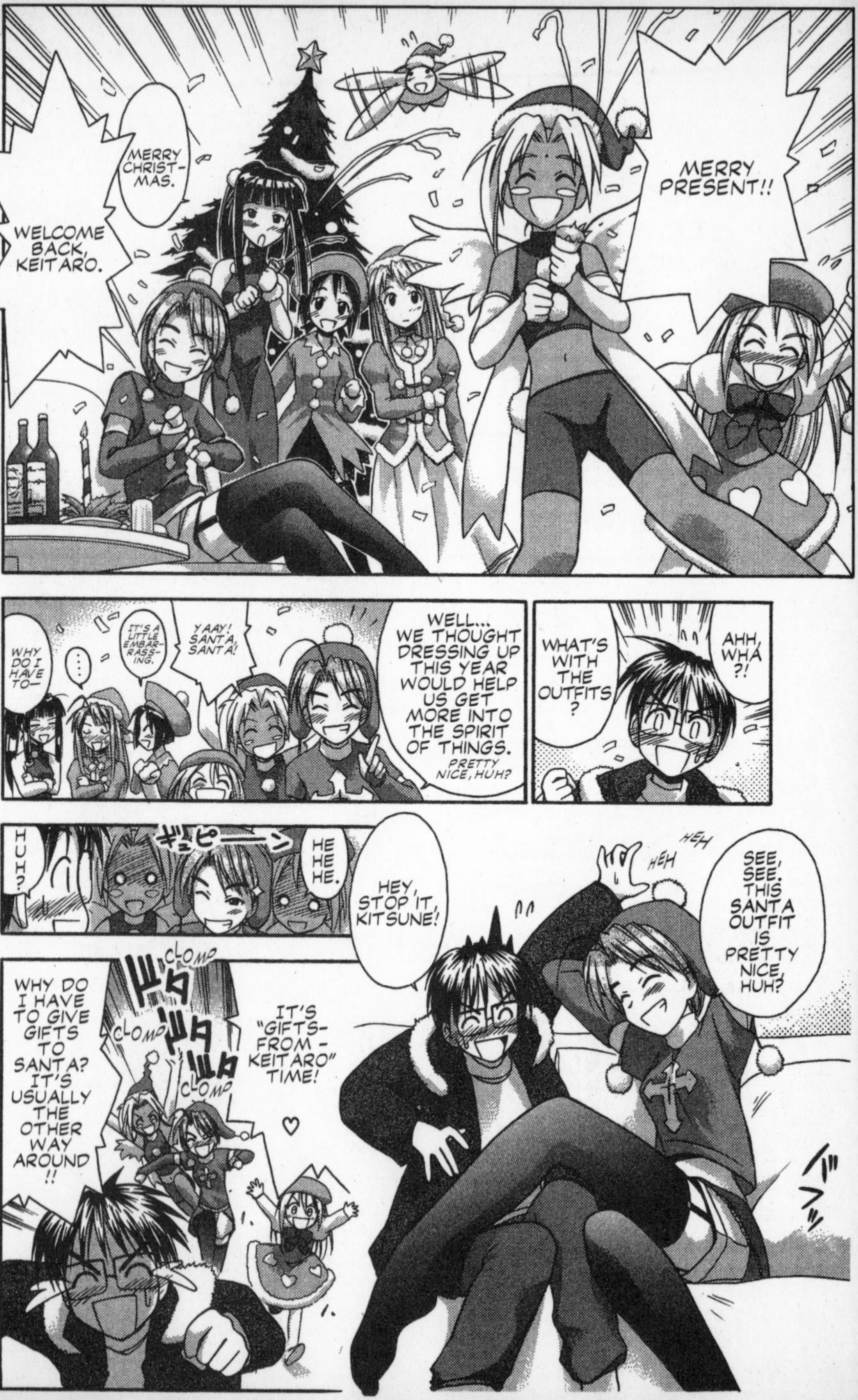
MERRY PRESENT!!
MERRY CHRIST-MAS.
WELCOME BACK, KEITARO.
AHH, WHA?!
WHAT'S WITH THE OUTFITS?
WELL... WE THOUGHT DRESSING UP THIS YEAR WOULD HELP US GET MORE INTO THE SPIRIT OF THINGS.
PRETTY NICE, HUH?
YAAY! SANTA, SANTA!
IT'S A LITTLE EMBARRASSING.
...
WHY DO I HAVE TO—
SEE, SEE. THIS SANTA OUTFIT IS PRETTY NICE, HUH?
HEH HEH
HEY, STOP IT, KITSUNE!
HE HE HE.
ギュピーン
HUH?
IT'S "GIFTS-FROM-KEITARO" TIME!
CLOMP
CLOMP
CLOMP
WHY DO I HAVE TO GIVE GIFTS TO SANTA? IT'S USUALLY THE OTHER WAY AROUND!!

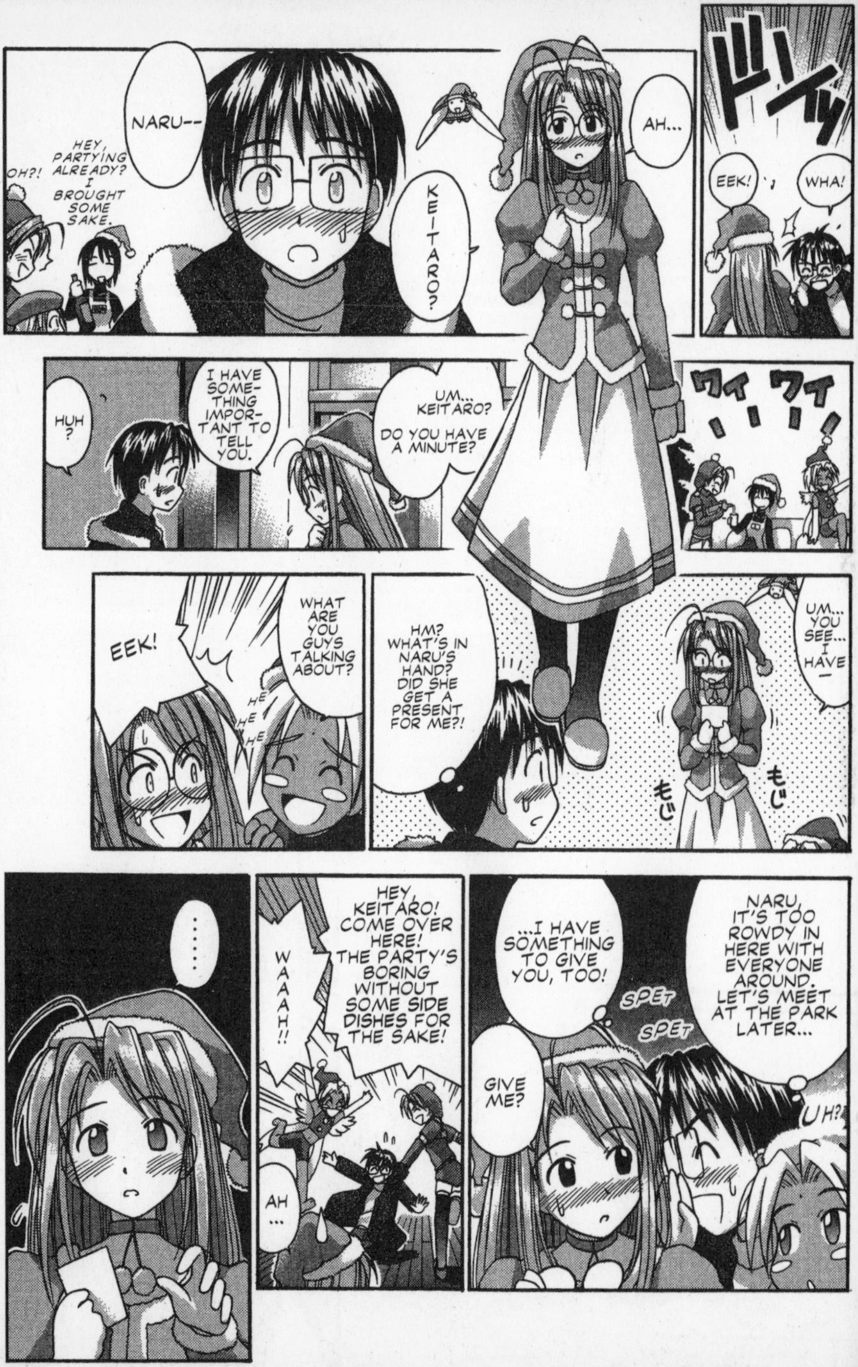

ドンイッ
EEK!
WHA!
AH...
KEITARO?
NARU--
OH?!
HEY, PARTYING ALREADY? I BROUGHT SOME SAKE.
ワイ ワイ
UM... KEITARO?
DO YOU HAVE A MINUTE?
I HAVE SOMETHING IMPORTANT TO TELL YOU.
HUH?
UM... YOU SEE... I HAVE—
もじ もじ
HM? WHAT'S IN NARU'S HAND? DID SHE GET A PRESENT FOR ME?!
WHAT ARE YOU GUYS TALKING ABOUT?
EEK!
HE HE HE
NARU, IT'S TOO ROWDY IN HERE WITH EVERYONE AROUND. LET'S MEET AT THE PARK LATER...
...I HAVE SOMETHING TO GIVE YOU, TOO!
SPET SPET
GIVE ME?
UH?
HEY, KEITARO! COME OVER HERE! THE PARTY'S BORING WITHOUT SOME SIDE DISHES FOR THE SAKE!
WAAAAH!!
AH...
......

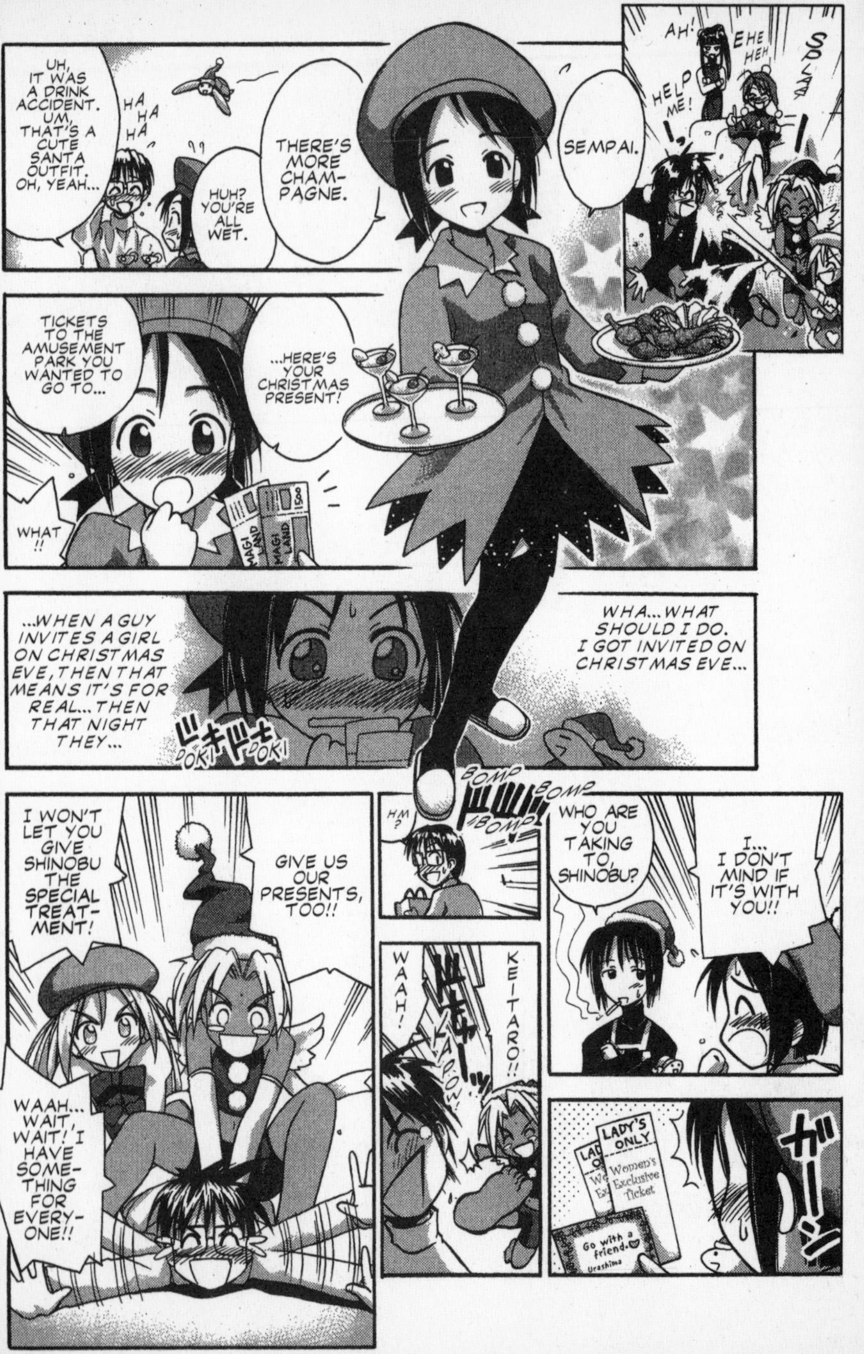
AH!
EHE HEH
HELP ME!
SPLASH
SEMPAI.
THERE'S MORE CHAMPAGNE.
HUH? YOU'RE ALL WET.
UH, IT WAS A DRINK ACCIDENT. UM, THAT'S A CUTE SANTA OUTFIT. OH, YEAH...
HA HA HA
...HERE'S YOUR CHRISTMAS PRESENT!
TICKETS TO THE AMUSEMENT PARK YOU WANTED TO GO TO...
MAGI LAND
1500
MAGI LAND
WHAT!!
WHA...WHAT SHOULD I DO. I GOT INVITED ON CHRISTMAS EVE...
...WHEN A GUY INVITES A GIRL ON CHRISTMAS EVE, THEN THAT MEANS IT'S FOR REAL...THEN THAT NIGHT THEY...
DOKI DOKI
I... I DON'T MIND IF IT'S WITH YOU!!
WHO ARE YOU TAKING TO, SHINOBU?
BOMP BOMP BOMP
HM?
LADY'S ONLY
Women's Exclusive Ticket
Go with a friend.
Urashima
KEITARO!!
WAAH!
KAPOW!
GIVE US OUR PRESENTS, TOO!!
I WON'T LET YOU GIVE SHINOBU THE SPECIAL TREATMENT!
WAAH... WAIT, WAIT! I HAVE SOMETHING FOR EVERYONE!!

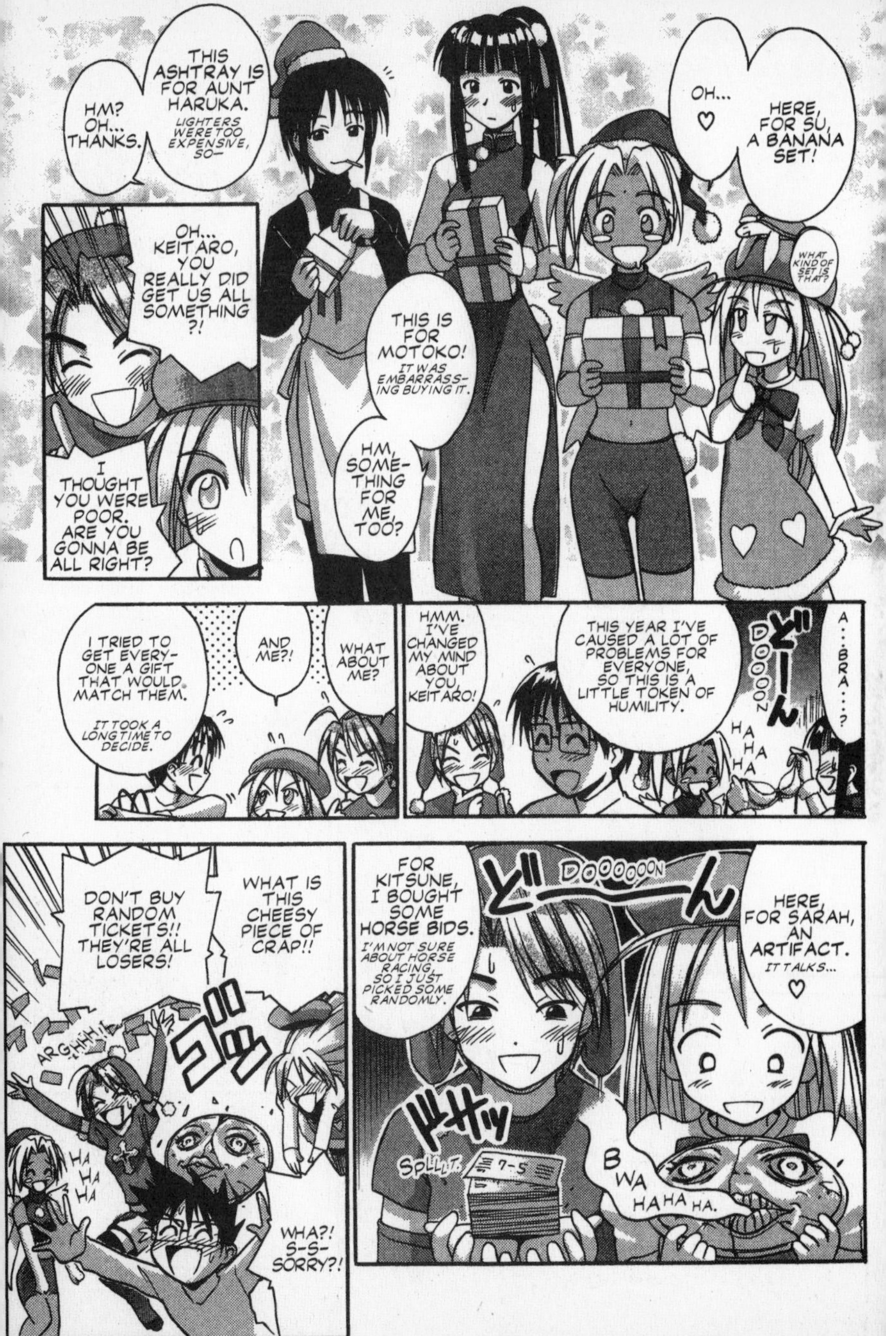
OH... ♡
HERE, FOR SU, A BANANA SET!
WHAT KIND OF SET IS THAT?
THIS IS FOR MOTOKO! IT WAS EMBARRASSING BUYING IT.
HM, SOMETHING FOR ME, TOO?
THIS ASHTRAY IS FOR AUNT HARUKA. LIGHTERS WERE TOO EXPENSIVE, SO—
HM? OH... THANKS.
OH... KEITARO, YOU REALLY DID GET US ALL SOMETHING?!
I THOUGHT YOU WERE POOR. ARE YOU GONNA BE ALL RIGHT?
A...BRA...?
どーん DOOOOON
THIS YEAR I'VE CAUSED A LOT OF PROBLEMS FOR EVERYONE, SO THIS IS A LITTLE TOKEN OF HUMILITY.
HA HA HA
HMM. I'VE CHANGED MY MIND ABOUT YOU, KEITARO!
WHAT ABOUT ME?
AND ME?!
I TRIED TO GET EVERYONE A GIFT THAT WOULD MATCH THEM. IT TOOK A LONG TIME TO DECIDE.
HERE, FOR SARAH, AN ARTIFACT. IT TALKS... ♡
どーん DOOOOOON
FOR KITSUNE, I BOUGHT SOME HORSE BIDS. I'M NOT SURE ABOUT HORSE RACING, SO I JUST PICKED SOME RANDOMLY.
ドサッ SPLLLT.
7-5
BWA HA HA HA.
WHAT IS THIS CHEESY PIECE OF CRAP!!
DON'T BUY RANDOM TICKETS!! THEY'RE ALL LOSERS!
ゴッ
ARGHHH!!
HA HA HA
WHA?! S-S-SORRY?!

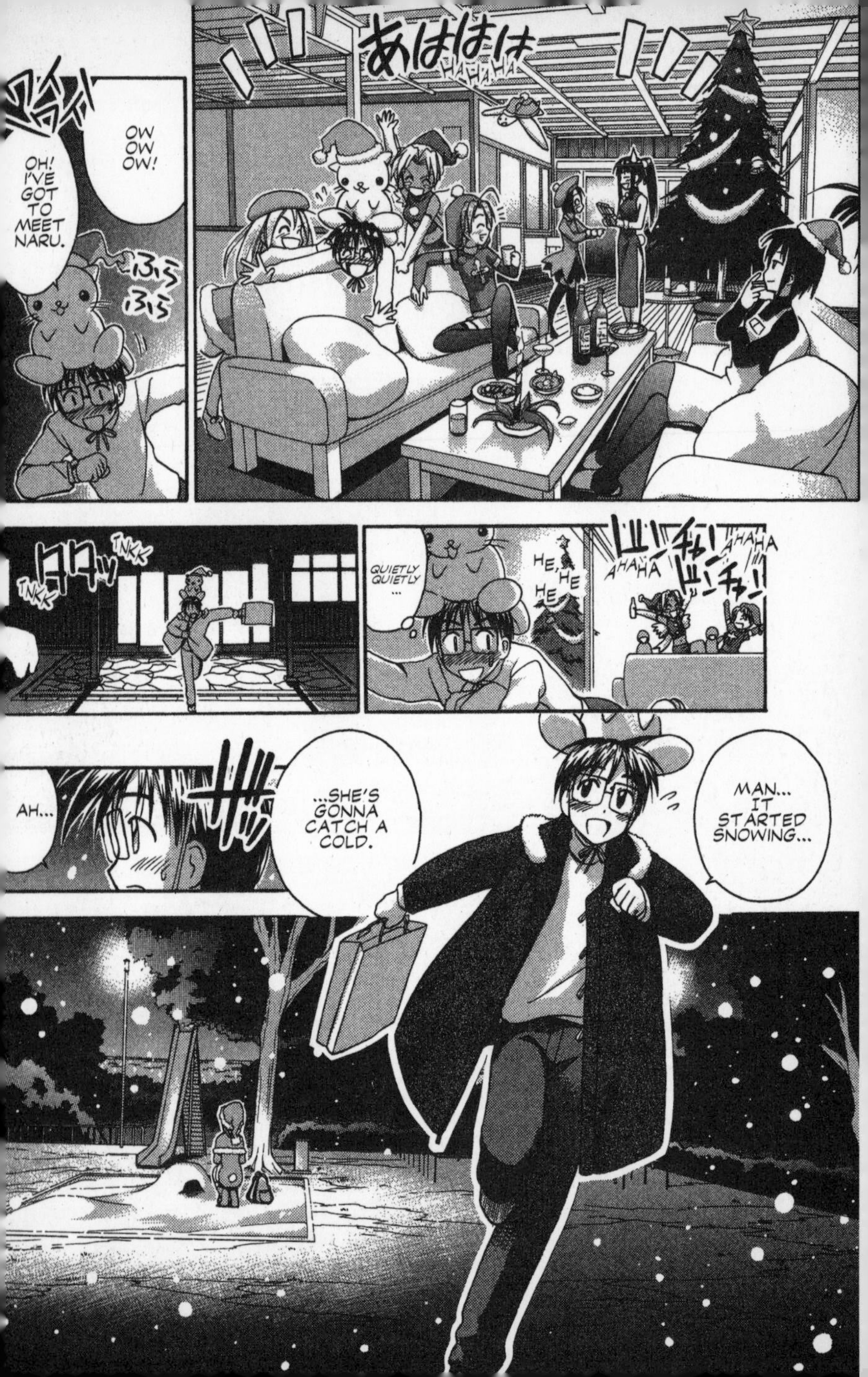
あははは
HAHAHA
OW OW OW!
OH! I'VE GOT TO MEET NARU.
ふらふら
AHAHA
AHAHA
HE, HE HE
QUIETLY QUIETLY ...
タタッ
TNKK
TNKK
MAN... IT STARTED SNOWING...
...SHE'S GONNA CATCH A COLD.
AH...

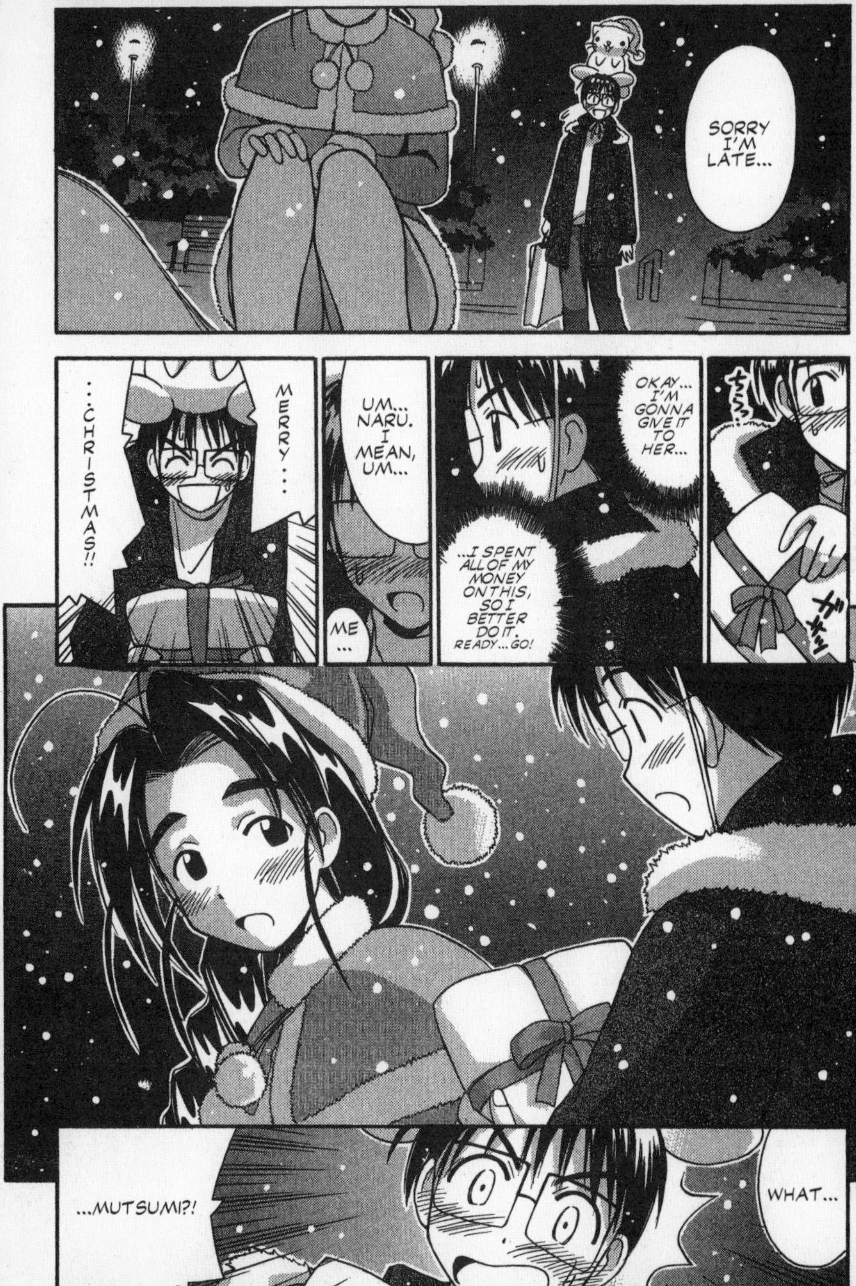
SORRY I'M LATE...
OKAY... I'M GONNA GIVE IT TO HER...
...I SPENT ALL OF MY MONEY ON THIS, SO I BETTER DO IT. READY...GO!
UM... NARU. I MEAN, UM...
ME...
MERRY...
...CHRISTMAS!!
WHAT...
...MUTSUMI?!

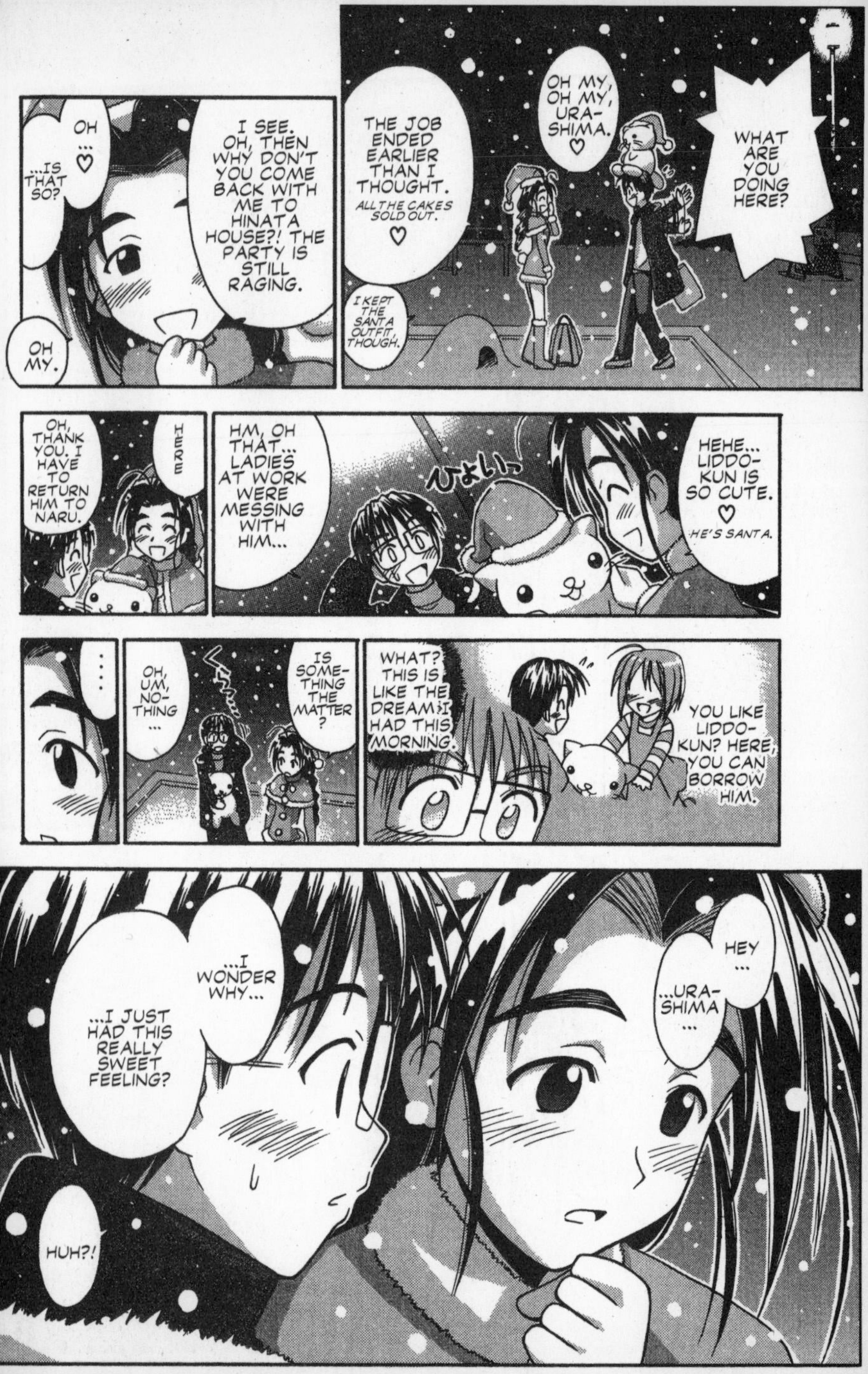
WHAT ARE YOU DOING HERE?
OH MY, OH MY, URA-SHIMA. ♡
THE JOB ENDED EARLIER THAN I THOUGHT.
ALL THE CAKES SOLD OUT. ♡
I KEPT THE SANTA OUTFIT, THOUGH.
I SEE. OH, THEN WHY DON'T YOU COME BACK WITH ME TO HINATA HOUSE?! THE PARTY IS STILL RAGING.
OH ... ♡
...IS THAT SO?
OH MY.
HEHE... LIDDO-KUN IS SO CUTE. ♡
HE'S SANTA.
ひょい
HM, OH THAT... LADIES AT WORK WERE MESSING WITH HIM...
HERE
OH, THANK YOU. I HAVE TO RETURN HIM TO NARU.
YOU LIKE LIDDO-KUN? HERE, YOU CAN BORROW HIM.
WHAT? THIS IS LIKE THE DREAM I HAD THIS MORNING.
IS SOMETHING THE MATTER?
OH, UM, NOTHING ...
....
HEY ...
...URA-SHIMA ...
...I WONDER WHY...
...I JUST HAD THIS REALLY SWEET FEELING?
HUH?!

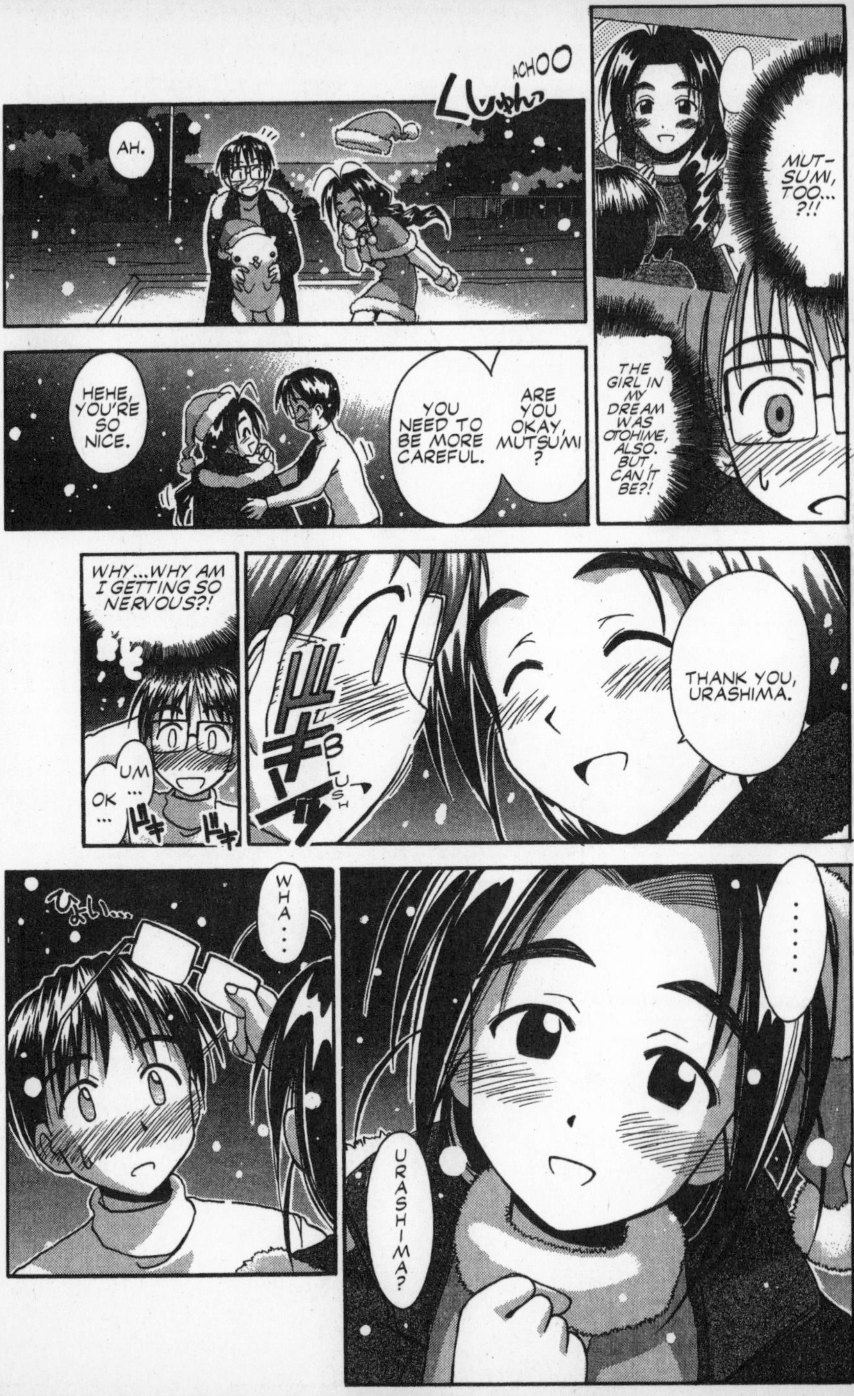
MUT-SUMI, TOO...?!!
THE GIRL IN MY DREAM WAS OTOHIME, ALSO. BUT, CAN IT BE?!
ACHOO
AH.
ARE YOU OKAY, MUTSUMI?
YOU NEED TO BE MORE CAREFUL.
HEHE, YOU'RE SO NICE.
THANK YOU, URASHIMA.
BLUSH
WHY...WHY AM I GETTING SO NERVOUS?!
UM ... OK ...
......
URASHIMA?
WHA....

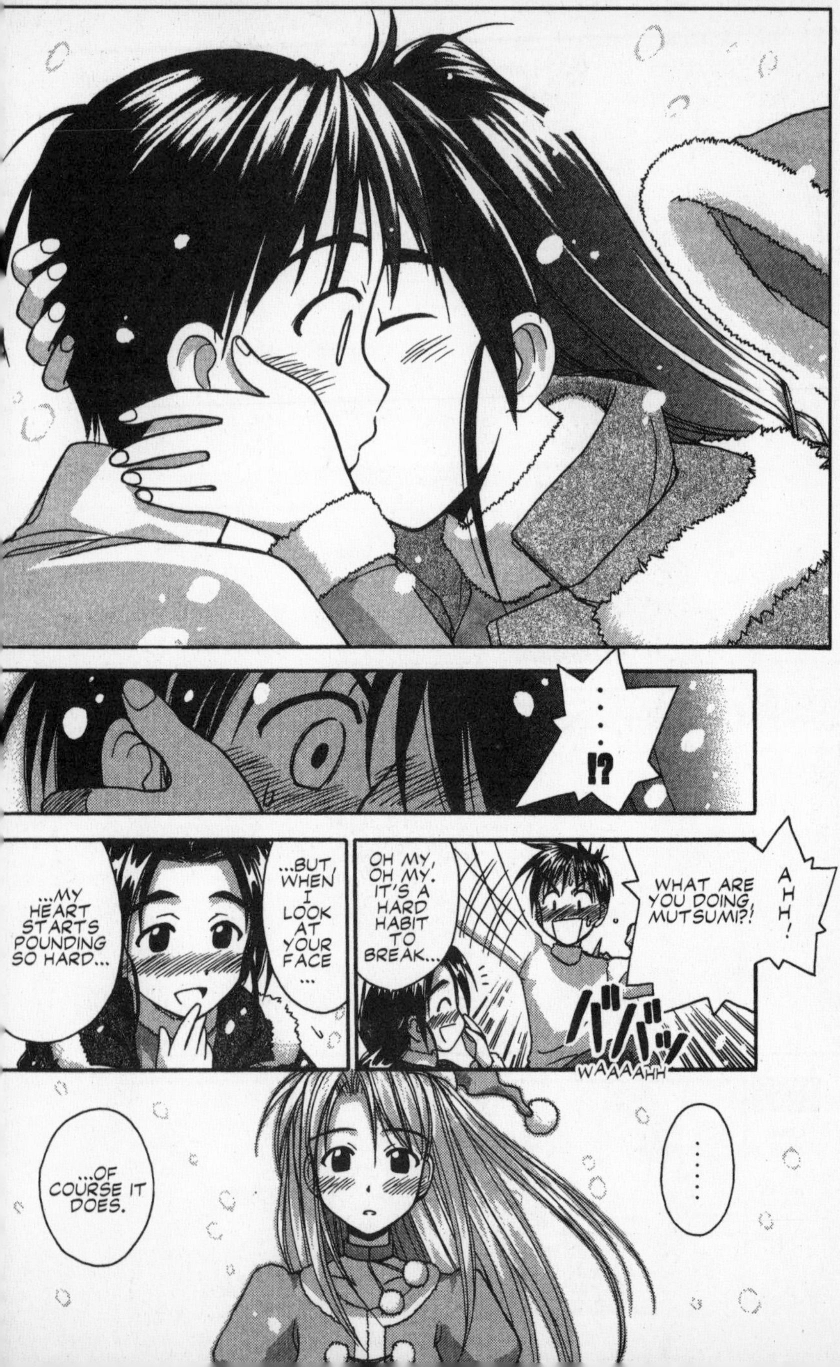
......!?
AHH!
WHAT ARE YOU DOING, MUTSUMI?!
OH MY, OH MY. IT'S A HARD HABIT TO BREAK...
WAAAAHH
...BUT WHEN I LOOK AT YOUR FACE...
...MY HEART STARTS POUNDING SO HARD...
......
...OF COURSE IT DOES.

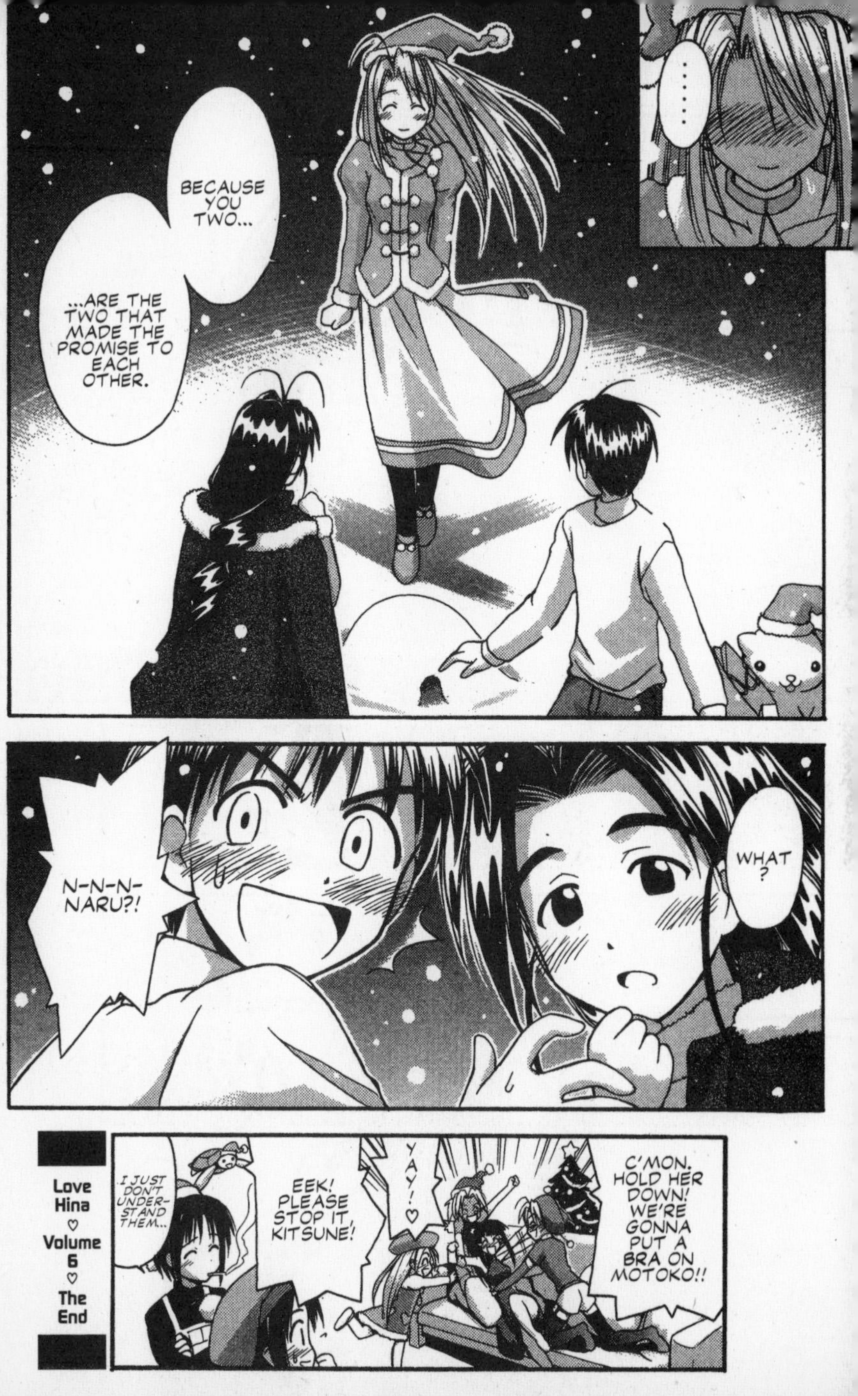
......
BECAUSE YOU TWO...
...ARE THE TWO THAT MADE THE PROMISE TO EACH OTHER.
WHAT?
N-N-N-NARU?!
C'MON. HOLD HER DOWN! WE'RE GONNA PUT A BRA ON MOTOKO!!
YAY!♡
EEK! PLEASE STOP IT, KITSUNE!
I JUST DON'T UNDER-STAND THEM...
Love Hina ♡ Volume 6 ♡ The End

STAFF

Ken Akamatsu
Takashi Takemoto
Kenichi Nakamura
Takaaki Miyahara
Masaki Ohyama
Yumiko Shinohara

EDITOR

Noboru Ohno
Tomoyuki Shiratsuchi
Yasushi Yamanaka

KC Editor

Mitsuei Ishii

Love Hina

Preview for Volume Seven

The secret is out

Keitaro's secret past comes to light - the girl of his distant memories is Mutsumi, or at least that's where Naru's deduction has led her. So, now Keitaro has to start making some decisions, and what better way to make a decision between two absolutely beautiful, dynamic women than to go on a date with both of them... at the same time. Things get stickier when Mutsumi makes herself homeless by burning her house down, landing her in temporary residence at Hinata House... staying in Naru's room... right above Keitaro's room. Ooo, la la.

The New Year is right around the corner and the gang goes out for a celebration at a local shrine, where Keitaro, Naru and Mutsumi all ask for good luck on the upcoming test. But with a packed house and Valentine's day right around the corner, how much time will they spend actually studying?

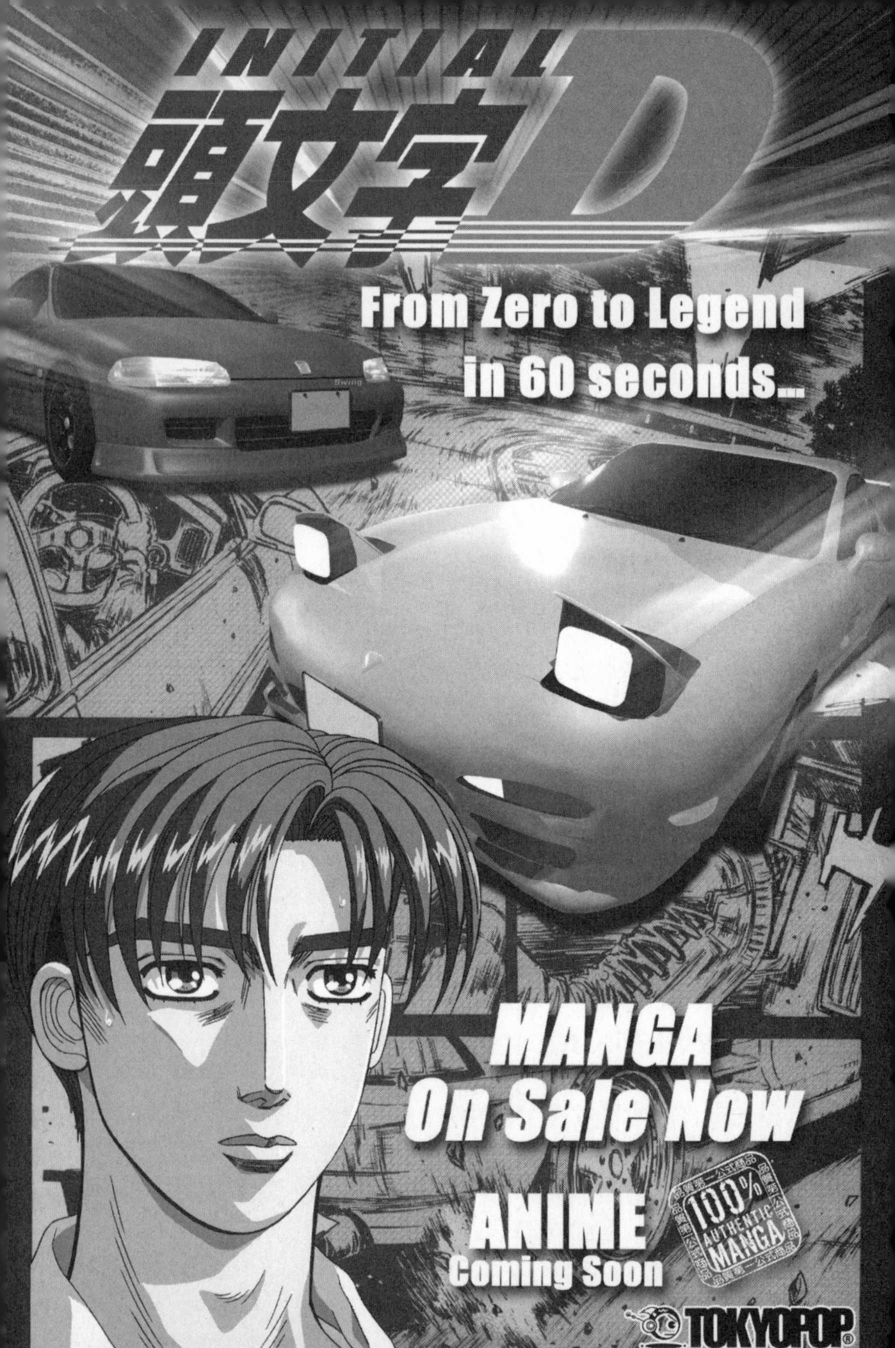
INITIAL 頭文字 D
From Zero to Legend
in 60 seconds...
MANGA
On Sale Now
ANIME
Coming Soon
100% AUTHENTIC MANGA
TOKYOPOP

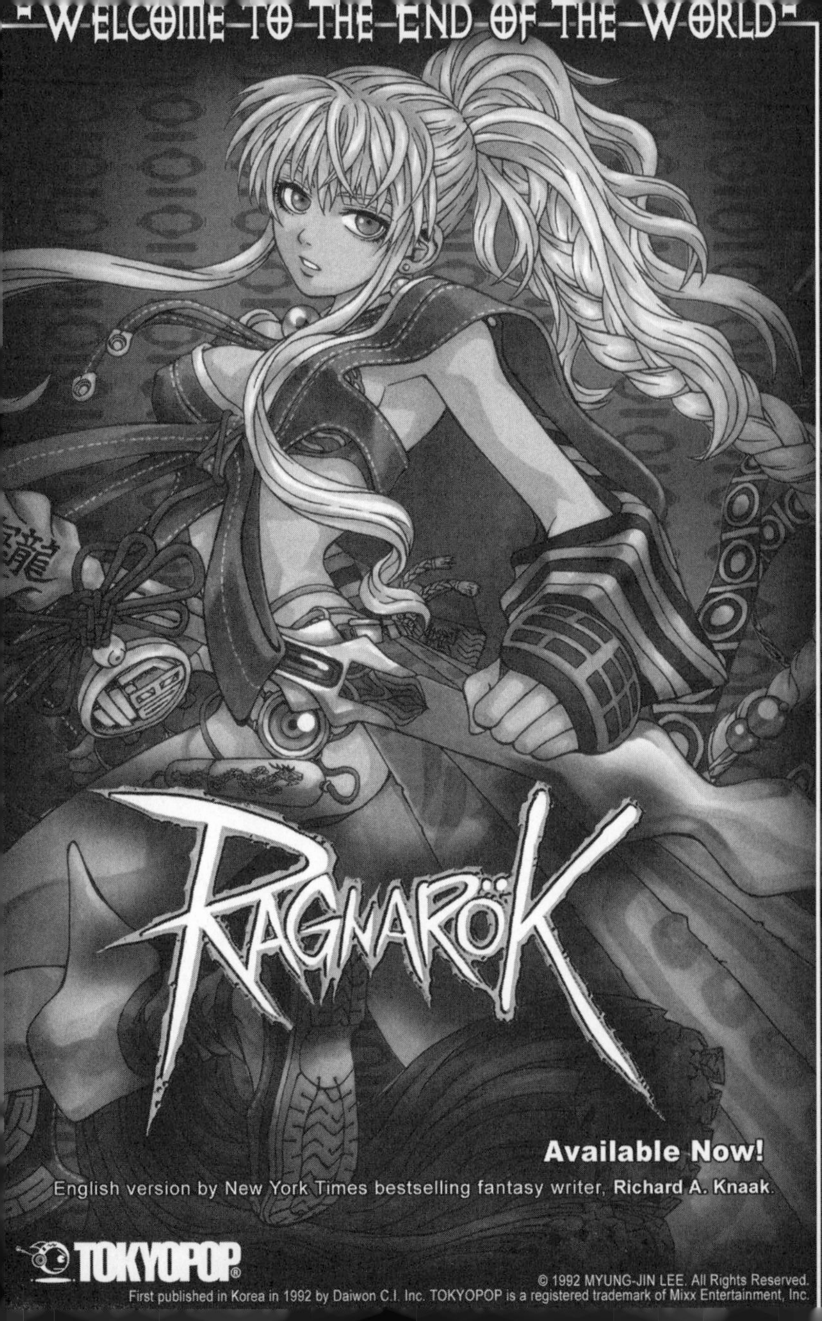

-WELCOME TO THE END OF THE WORLD-
RAGNARÖK
Available Now!
English version by New York Times bestselling fantasy writer, Richard A. Knaak.
TOKYOPOP®
© 1992 MYUNG-JIN LEE. All Rights Reserved.
First published in Korea in 1992 by Daiwon C.I. Inc. TOKYOPOP is a registered trademark of Mixx Entertainment, Inc.

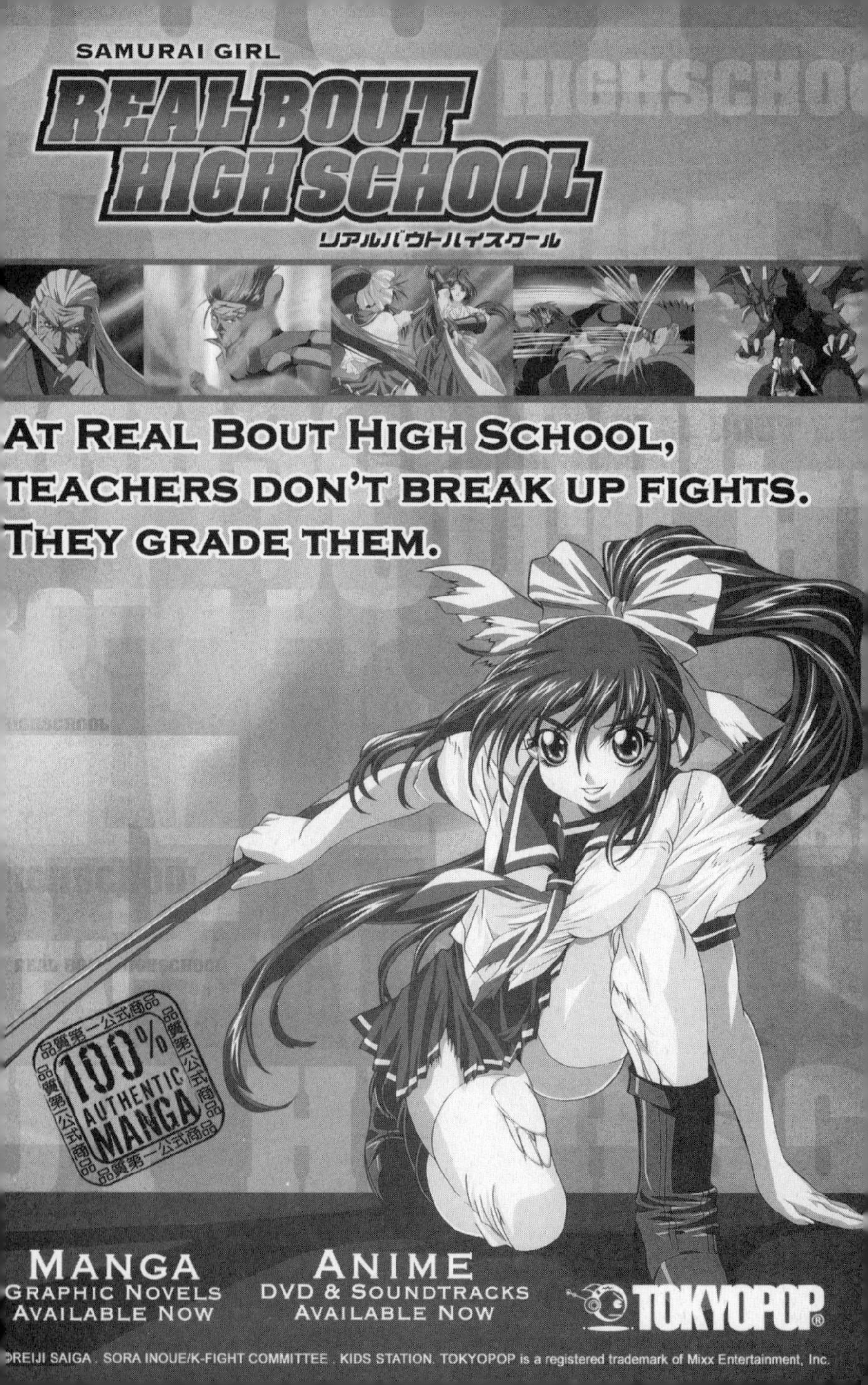
SAMURAI GIRL
REAL BOUT HIGH SCHOOL
リアルバウトハイスクール
AT REAL BOUT HIGH SCHOOL, TEACHERS DON'T BREAK UP FIGHTS. THEY GRADE THEM.
100% AUTHENTIC MANGA
品質第一公式商品
MANGA
GRAPHIC NOVELS
AVAILABLE NOW
ANIME
DVD & SOUNDTRACKS
AVAILABLE NOW
TOKYOPOP®
©REIJI SAIGA . SORA INOUE/K-FIGHT COMMITTEE . KIDS STATION. TOKYOPOP is a registered trademark of Mixx Entertainment, Inc.

Superhero, Rebel, Teacher...He's

GTO

JAPAN'S RUNAWAY HIT HAS HIT AMERICA

100% AUTHENTIC MANGA

GTO

GREAT TEACHER ONIZUKA

FILE UNDER: ACTION/COMEDY

MANGA-ANIME-SOUNDTRACK
ALL AVAILABLE FROM TOKYOPOP

STOP!

This is the back of the book.
You wouldn't want to spoil a great ending!

This book is printed "manga-style," in the authentic Japanese right-to-left format. Since none of the artwork has been flipped or altered, readers get to experience the story just as the creator intended. You've been asking for it, so TOKYOPOP® delivered: authentic, hot-off-the-press, and far more fun!

DIRECTIONS

If this is your first time reading manga-style, here's a quick guide to help you understand how it works.

It's easy... just start in the top right panel and follow the numbers. Have fun, and look for more 100% authentic manga from TOKYOPOP®!